A BAROQUE VISION

100 verse selections from 50 volumes

First published by Liberalis Books, 2024
Liberalis Books is an imprint of Collective Ink Ltd.

Unit 11, Shepperton House
89 Shepperton Road
London N1 3DF
office@collectiveinkbooks.com
www.collectiveinkbooks.com
www.liberalisbooks.com

For distributor details and how to order please visit
the 'Ordering' section on our website.

ISBN: 978 1 78904 585 7
ebook: 978 1 78904 586 4
Library of Congress Control Number: 2023912871

A CIP catalogue record for this book is available from the British Library.

Typeset by Lapiz Digital Services
UK: Printed and bound by CPI Group (UK) Ltd, Croydon, CR0 4YY
Printed in North America by CPI GPS partners

We operate a distinctive and ethical publishing philosophy
in all areas of our business, from our global network of authors
to production and worldwide distribution.

A BAROQUE VISION

100 verse selections from 50 volumes

NICHOLAS HAGGER

For Christopher Ricks

"If you can see it, then you've already done it. Seeing it's half the battle."
EZRA POUND in conversation with
NICHOLAS HAGGER on 16 July 1970

———

T HE FRONT COVER shows James I being drawn upwards to Heaven by angels in Rubens' Baroque painting *The Apotheosis of James I*, which was installed on the ceiling of the Banqueting House, London in 1636. It shows James I as having a potentially divine soul and has the Baroque combination of the sensual and the spiritual. Charles I stopped and looked up at this picture of his father on the ceiling as he walked to his execution in 1649.

ACKNOWLEDGMENT

I am grateful to my PA Ingrid Kirk, who helped me assemble the text just before lockdown.

NOTE TO READER

T HE 100 SELECTIONS that follow are arranged in chronological order, and their titles are not in italics. They have been selected from 50 poetic volumes, whose numbered titles are in italics. For the published works where the selected poems, verse plays and masques can be found, see pp.403–408.

Poems selected from the 30 volumes of *Collected Poems* and the 4 volumes of *Life Cycle and Other New Poems* (see pp.xvii–xviii) appear under their volume titles. Those taken from *Classical Odes*, *Overlord* and *Armageddon* appear under these published titles. All the verse plays are in *Collected Verse Plays*. *The Warlords* and *The Tragedy of Prince Tudor* had already been published separately, whereas *Ovid Banished* and *The Rise of Oliver Cromwell* were first published in *Collected Verse Plays*. *Fools' Paradise* and the three masques were published separately.

As regards volume titles and poem titles, when a volume only contains one long poem, play or masque the poem title repeats its volume title.

Selections from a volume are indicated by the word 'from'. When a poem, play or masque is represented by extracts, 'from' appears before its poem, play or masque title as well as its volume title.

Line numbers are followed by descriptions. Descriptions are intended to be helpful summaries and are not titles.

The poems and extracts in *Collected Poems* and *Classical Odes* are accompanied by notes. These are not reproduced here.

The original volumes have dates where known at the end of their poems, plays or masques, including revision dates. These have been left as they are without being abridged as they reflect entries in my Diaries (for every year since 1963), which will eventually be lodged in my Archive in the Albert Sloman Library at the University of Essex.

⌐ Symbol
A corner-mark (⌐) at the beginning of the line denotes that there is a break or gap before that line which has been obscured because it falls at the bottom of a page.

CONTENTS

CONTENTS

CONTENTS

INDEXES

ABOUT THIS BOOK

N ICHOLAS HAGGER'S 50 volumes of poetry, verse plays and masques from which this selection was made, under their published works (and publication dates):

POETRY VOLUMES

Collected Poems 1958–2005   (2006)
    A Well of Truth, 1958–1963
    A Stone Torch-Basket, 1963–1965
    The Early Education and Making of a Mystic, 1965–1966
    The Silence, 1965–1966
    The Wings and the Sword, 1966–1969
    Old Man in a Circle, 1967
    The Gates of Hell, 1969–1972
    The Flight, 1970
    A Bulb in Winter, 1972–1974
    The Pilgrim in the Garden, 1973–1974
    The Night-Sea Crossing, 1974
    Visions Near the Gates of Paradise, 1974–1975
    The Four Seasons, 1975
    Lighthouse, 1975
    The Weed-Garden, 1975
    The Labyrinth, 1976
    Whispers from the West, 1976–1979
    Lady of the Lamp, 1979
    The Fire-Flower, 1980
    Beauty and Angelhood, 1981
    The Wind and the Earth, 1981
    A Rainbow in the Spray, 1981–1985
    Question Mark over the West, 1986–1988
    A Sneeze in the Universe, 1989–1992
    A Flirtation with the Muse, 1992–1993
    Sojourns, 1993
    Angel of Vertical Vision, 1993
    A Dandelion Clock, 1994–2004
    Summoned by Truth, 2000–2005
    Sighs of the Muses, 2005

Life Cycle and Other New Poems 2006–2016 (2016)
    Life Cycle, 2014
    In Harmony with the Universe, 2009–2016
    An Unsung Laureate, 2009–2016
    Adventures in Paradise, 2010–2015
Fools' Paradise: The Voyage of a Ship of Fools from Europe,
A Mock-Heroic Poem on Brexit (2020)
Earlier volumes:
    Selected Poems: A Metaphysical's Way of Fire (1991)
    Collected Poems: A White Radiance 1958–1993 (1994)
Later volumes:
    Selected Poems: Quest for the One (2015)
    Visions of England: Poems Selected by The Earl of Burford (2019)

ODES

Classical Odes 1994–2005 (2006)
    Book One, A Tudor Knot
    Book Two, In Europe's Ruins
    Book Three, A Global Sway
    Book Four, The Western Universe

EPIC POEMS

Overlord, one-volume edition. *First published in four separate volumes,*
1995–1997, *as Overlord: The Triumph of Light* 1944–1945 (2006)
    Overlord, books 1–2 (1995)
    Overlord, books 3–6 (1996)
    Overlord, books 7–9 (1997)
    Overlord, books 10–12 (1997)
Armageddon: The Triumph of Universal Order
An Epic Poem on the War on Terror and of Holy-War Crusaders (2010)

VERSE PLAYS

Collected Verse Plays (2007)
    The Warlords, Parts 1 and 2 (first published in 1995,
        abridged version 2000)
    The Tragedy of Prince Tudor (first published in 1999)
    Ovid Banished (1999)
    The Rise of Oliver Cromwell (2000)

MASQUES

The Dream of Europa: The Triumph of Peace (2015)
King Charles the Wise: The Triumph of Universal Peace (2018)
The Coronation of King Charles: The Triumph of Universal Harmony (2020)

The Baroque Vision behind Universalism, and the Tradition of Wordsworth and Tennyson

Ricks urges me to select 30 poems in 1979 and 1982, and my poetic identity

A S CAN BE READ in my *Selected Letters* (p.50), when I met him on 20 February 1979 the eminent English literary critic Christopher Ricks asked me to select 30 poems that represented my range and the best of my work.

At the time I was struggling to see what sort of poet I was. I had had some remarkable, indeed extraordinary, inner experiences while writing my poem 'The Silence' from 1965 to 1966 when I was a 26-year-old Professor in Japan, and I was still trying to understand them. I had grappled with them on my own, trying to evaluate vivid images that flooded in seemingly from the beyond but perhaps from my imagination (or Muse), and an experience of the mysterious Light ("a round white light"), and I wrote of my future self, which I called my "Shadow" (my shadow being ever beside me as I walked to and fro under the hot Japanese sun): "My Shadow sees/With a metaphysical eye." (Now that, in my 81st year, I have become my Shadow, to reach which required a subjugation of my "Reflection" or social ego, looking back I can say this was remarkably prescient.)

I sent some of my poems to Christopher Ricks, and wrote him three letters between 1979 and 1982, attempting to pinpoint my poetic identity and the tradition in which these new experiences placed me. These three letters are in *Selected Letters*.

The first letter (dated 18 February 1979) saw me as a Metaphysical poet. On 20 February I visited Ricks at Christ's College, Cambridge. He gave me a brilliant tutorial in the Buttery and, following notes he had made, dwelt on the technical differences between my ruminative approach and the approach of the Metaphysical poets. He said I should make a selection of 30 poems. We then lunched together in the Senior Common Room.

The second letter (dated 1 May 1982) saw me as a Romantic poet. Ricks more or less went along with this. The Romantic poets Wordsworth and Shelley had dwelt on the One – Wordsworth's "A motion and a spirit, that impels/All thinking things, all objects of all thought" and Shelley's "The One remains, the many change and pass" – and my ruminative approach was akin to Wordsworth's "emotion recollected in tranquillity". On this view I could be seen as continuing the tradition of Wordsworth and Shelley.

The third letter (dated 17 October 1982) took account of a development since late 1979 and early 1980 when I reconciled my vision with social and historical events. This letter saw me as a Classical poet, as blending the Classical and Romantic in what I called the Baroque after writing in my poem 'The Silence' "A new Baroque age is born" (see p.387). Ricks went along with this.

I visited Ricks at Christ's College, Cambridge (room B6), on 29 October 1982, after my third letter, and he said I had sharpened my ideas. He said: "I believe in the Baroque, but though everything that is Baroque is Classical and Romantic, not everything that is Classical and Romantic is Baroque." I replied that the mysterious Light is central to the new Baroque. He said: "I think your work is Baroque. You got there, even though your itinerary surprised you. You must anthologise 30 poems, each no longer than a page. Make your entry and then expand."

On 31 October 1982 I wrote to Ricks, "To be Baroque a work must have the Light, a sense of transformation, an awareness of the dynamic nature of the material world, and a mixture of sense and spirit, so yes, although Baroque is Classicism and Romanticism, Classicism-and-Romanticism is only Baroque if it has these elements." See 'The Genesis and Shaping of the New Baroque Vision' in the Appendix of *Collected Poems* ('Vision and Technique in the Collected Poems'), section 3; which is also in Appendix 1 of *Collected Prefaces*.

My non-delivery

By then I had written *The Fire-Flower* (1980), a volume of my most Metaphysical poems that included 'A Metaphysical in Marvell's Garden'. Even then my poetic output was bulky, and it was hard to come up with 30 pre-1979 poems that caught my poetic identity clearly. I was also a busy Head of English with 'A'-level marking to keep abreast of, and new poems kept coming.

Immersed in my ever-increasing output during the 1980s and 1990s I found it impossible to whittle either my pre-1979 or my life's work down to 30 poems, the challenge Ricks had set me in 1979 and 1982. Every time I wrote down a poem that might be included in a draft selection of 30 poems a dozen other poems clamoured to replace it like unruly children, and I could not be sure that in relation to my true poetic identity they did not have a better claim. I was also aware that I had works ahead of me, including the work I discussed with Ezra Pound in 1970 (*Overlord*), and I felt that if I delayed I would be able to include passages from what was still to come. So I bided my time.

Ever since then my poetic output has increased each year. My *Collected Poems 1958–2005* contains 1,478 poems in 30 volumes, and *Life Cycle*

(2006–2016) contains a further 210 poems in four more volumes.* *Classical Odes* (1994–2005) contains 317 classical odes in four books, and I have also written two poetic epics: *Overlord* about the Second World War from D-Day to the Fall of Berlin (1994–1996 in four volumes, collected edition in 2006, 41,000 lines of blank verse) and *Armageddon* about the War on Terror from 9/11, which includes the American invasions of Iraq and Afghanistan (2008–2009, 25,000 lines of blank verse). I have also written five verse plays, having revived the verse play in 1994 with *The Warlords*, and these are in *Collected Verse Plays* (2007); and I have written three masques and *Fools' Paradise*, a poem on Brexit, and am working on a sequel, *Fools' Gold*, and on a volume of new poems.

My three Selected Poems had different perspectives. My first selection, *Selected Poems: A Metaphysical's Way of Fire*, was a selection of key poems written before 1991 that reflected my Mystic Way, which transformed my consciousness into an instinctive unitive vision. (On 21 August 1984 I had written in my diary that my "Ricks collection", then titled *A Way of Fire*, should reflect my Mystic Way.) My *Selected Poems: Quest for the One* (2015, 423 pages) demonstrated that my poetic work reflects the fundamental theme of world literature: a perennial dialectic and tussle between a quest for the One and satirical condemnation of follies and vices, one of which has always predominated for over 4,000 years during any generation or time. *Visions of England*, poems selected by the Earl of Burford (2019), presented 100 poems about places in England written before 1999. None of these presented the 30 poems (and by implication, the poetic identity) Ricks had requested in 1979 and again in 1982.

A new perspective and this selection

In 2019, after my 80th birthday, I completed *Selected Letters*, letters I had written about all my works including my poetic works, and then *Collected Prefaces*. In 1991 I had revived the Preface, a form Wordsworth used so effectively in his Preface to the second edition of *Lyrical Ballads* in 1801 and, greatly expanded, in the third edition in 1802, and in *Collected Prefaces* I present my 56 Prefaces (including this Preface).

Rereading my letters relating to Ricks' urging of 30 poems (see pp.50 and 60 of *Selected Letters*), and all my Prefaces, gave me a new perspective, and I suddenly saw how I could choose 30 poems written before 1979 (the year Ricks first mentioned 30 poems) as Part One of a two-part selection that would end in 2019. I jotted down titles, and later drew up a spreadsheet with decades across the top, from the 1960s to 2010s, and all the key subjects, genres, forms, techniques and verse lines I had used down on the left. I posted the titles of key poems into the spreadsheet so I could check that my selection covered every decade, key subject, genre, form, technique and verse line that I had used in 61 years of writing poetry.

My initial task was to choose 30 poems written before 1979, so I have devoted Part One to delivering 30 Baroque poems from the 17 volumes written before then, an average of 15 poems per decade. Part Two presents another 70 Baroque – Classical and Romantic – poems (an average of 17.5 poems per decade for another even more prolific four decades) from another 33 volumes written between 1979 and 2019. My life's poetic output at present is in 50 volumes – 34 volumes of poems written over the years that can be found in *Collected Poems* and *Life Cycle and Other New Poems*, two epic poems, four books of classical odes, five verse plays, three masques and two poetic volumes to be published in 2020/2021, *Fools' Paradise* and *The Oak Tree and the Branch* – and I have drawn on all 50 of these 50 volumes in this selection, which now reflects my life's poetic work.

I arrived at 100 numbered poems by counting each titled poem as one poem. My two epic poems therefore count as two of the 100 numbered poems (even though *Overlord* was published in four separate volumes before being published in one volume). Each is represented by excerpts which are all under one title and together count as one poem. I have regarded these two epic poems as special cases as (at 41,000 and 25,000 lines of blank verse) together they comprise over 66,000 lines, and my excerpts total around 3,440 lines, around 5% – the minimum amount needed to give a feel for their narratives, root them in the epic tradition (via invocations to Homer, Virgil, Dante, Milton, Tennyson and other forerunners) and bring out their Baroque features (including visits to Heaven and Hell and focus on the Light).

The Baroque vision

This selection tells an underlying story within my 61 years of writing poetry, a kind of subliminal narrative that invites connections between poems. The selected poems show why I saw myself in my three letters to Ricks in 1979 and 1982 as a Metaphysical poet writing of the Mystic Way and came to see myself as being in the Romantic, and later the Classical tradition, and as blending the Classical and Romantic in what I called the Baroque vision after two lines in 'The Silence' (1965–1966): "While naked on the petalled lawn,/A new Baroque age is born." The second line came straight from the beyond, and for some years I did not fully understand it.

I see from consulting my archive, which is held in the Albert Sloman Library at the University of Essex, that it did not find its way into the poem until April 1973, when it was handwritten in the margin of a version of the poem corrected in blue ink, and that it later appeared in a typed version in April/May 1973. (See p.387.) (Looking at the many papers connected with

'The Silence' in my archive in the University of Essex, I was stunned by how many vivid lines I cut out of the final version. There must be a hundred or two which would grace any of my poems.)

I also described 'The Silence' in the poem's dedication as "This string of baroque pearls". This was written in Japan some time after the writer Frank Tuohy took my wife and me to the office of a pearl dealer called Meiras, so he could buy two necklaces of irregular baroque pearls in Tokyo on 20 October 1965. I returned to Meiras with my wife on 16 December 1965 and bought her a necklace of baroque pearls. The dedication "To Mr F.T." was to Frank Tuohy, who, having read the poem and suggested I should add marginal glosses in the manner of Coleridge's 'The Ancient Mariner' to present a clear narrative, would understand how my irregular chunks of verse in 'The Silence' could be described as misshapen baroque pearls. (See my diary entries for these two days in *Awakening to the Light*, pp.202 and 222.)

The full dedication at the beginning of 'The Silence' was: "To Mr F.T./ This string of baroque pearls,/To be told like a rosary." The last line of this dedication brings out the poem's religious associations – each irregular chunk of my verse was like a bead in a rosary to be meditated over as if in prayer – and evokes the religious associations of the historical Baroque.

I believe it was in 1967 that I found in a bookshop in Tokyo's Kanda district Germain Bazin's description of the Baroque in *A Concise History of Art*. (It is first mentioned in my diary entry in *Awakening to the Light* for 7 February 1967.) Bazin sets out a life cycle of artistic styles first suggested by Déonna in Geneva in 1913 and developed by Faure (in 1927) and Focillon (in 1934): a primitive, archaic pre-classical stage or Age; a classical stage or Age; an academic or post-classical stage or Age (Neoclassicism); and then a pre-baroque Mannerist stage or Age. The end of Mannerism – its cure – is the baroque stage or Age in which "the spirit is again in contact with the world, the imagination drinks deeply of its forms, and at the very source, with an eagerness born of long deprivation. The cosmos itself seems to be throbbing in the soul, filling it with inspiring emotion" (Bazin, p.528). I now began to understand how my work might be regarded as Baroque.

The historical Baroque period which produced the artistic baroque style began around 1600 and ended around 1750. It influenced all the arts, and in literature it inspired the Metaphysical poets, Milton's *Paradise Lost*, and the Augustans. The Baroque consciousness is open to, and combines, both the spiritual and the sensual: the Romantic infinite and the Classical social outlooks, the soaring grandeur of Heaven and the sensuous, emotional exuberance and movement in the everyday. Bach, Handel, Bernini and Rubens – in all the arts the Baroque soars to Heaven, as in Rubens' painting *The Apotheosis of James I* (see front cover), which was installed in the Banqueting House, London in 1636. James I was the father of Charles I, who commissioned the painting, and in his 'apotheosis' (elevation to divine status, deification) he is shown being drawn upwards to Heaven on the Banqueting-House ceiling, which I first saw when I visited the Banqueting House on 8 July 1966. (See my Preface to *The Coronation of King Charles*.)

In literature the Baroque includes the profound poems of Donne (including 'Aire and Angels'), the Metaphysical poets and Milton that confront death, and the social satire of Dryden and Pope. And, because they blend the spiritual and the sensual, the poems of Tennyson which succeeded the poems of the Romantic Wordsworth can be seen as blending the Classical and Romantic as neo-Baroque. I have sought to achieve a similar blend between the Classical and Romantic in my neo-Baroque poems.

Baroque poetic inspiration can be seen as images bursting into the poet's mind from the beyond like windfalls bursting through the leaves of a tree, like my image of a new Baroque age being born on a petalled lawn. In 'The Tree of Imagination', first written on 31 December 1979 and ruminating on my visit to Ricks on 20 February 1979 (not included in this selection), I wrote: "So images burst round a poet's head,/Windfalls from a leafy beyond that heal/A sick society...."

My inspiration derives from the 17th century, the time of the Metaphysical poets, masques and Milton's epic poem (as I had realised by 1963, when I wrote 'The 17th-Century Pilgrim'); but also from the 18th century, the time of social satire, and the 19th century, the time of the Romantic poets, of Wordsworth's 'Preface to *Lyrical Ballads*' and of Tennyson's blend of Romanticism and Classicism in his '*In Memoriam*', his "Nor winks the gold fin in the porphyry font", his long narrative works and his poems on national events such as 'The Charge of the Light Brigade' about an event in the Crimean War.

My poem 'The Silence' (1965–1966) derives from Modernism, but after an evening with Ezra Pound in 1970 I decided that abbreviated narrative in an emotionally-linked sequence of images was not for the epic and narrative poems I wanted to write, and I consciously headed back into the 19th century and the 17th-century Baroque for my inspiration, where it already was subconsciously.

My range

My questing poems led me to look into disciplines outside poetry, and these were reflected in my poetry and extended its range. I now regard my poetic works as drawing on seven disciplines: literature, of course; mysticism; philosophy; history; religion; international politics and statecraft; and world culture.

In this selection can be found poems on aspects of my literature ('Authorship Question in a Dumbed-Down Time', 'On the Death of Mr Nicholas Hagger'); on my mysticism ('The Power by the Lake', 'The Silence', 'Visions: Golden

Flower, Celestial Curtain', poems from *The Fire-Flower*); on my philosophy of the universe ('Night Visions in Charlestown'); on history (an excerpt from 'Old Man in a Circle', 'At Otley: Timber-Framed Tradition'); on religion (excerpts from *Beauty and Angelhood*); on international politics and statecraft (excerpts from 'Archangel', *Ovid Banished* and *The Tragedy of Prince Tudor*); and world culture (my classical ode 'At Virgil's Tomb', *Overlord*, *Classical Odes*).

A stag with seven-branched antlers

I see myself as an Epping-Forest stag with seven-branched antlers. One antler's seven branches symbolise the above seven disciplines. The other antler's seven branches symbolise the branches within literature I have pursued as a man of letters: poems and poetic epics; verse plays and masques; short stories and novellas; diaries; autobiographies; letters (*Selected Letters*); and my statement of the fundamental theme of world literature (*A New Philosophy of Literature*).

My Universalism

As can be tracked in my *Selected Letters* and *Collected Prefaces*, my writings show a developing Universalism in the above seven disciplines and in all branches of literature. At both finite and infinite levels, Universalism deals with every known idea and so can focus on: transformation by the Light; seeing from the perspective of the Whole and therefore seeing things as a whole; the blend of sense and spirit in (for example) Rubens' *The Apotheosis of James I* (which shows a king becoming a god and reinforces the Divine Right of Kings, but also shows a man with a divine soul); the transcending of death; the possibility of Angelhood (which can be found in 'Archangel' and *Beauty and Angelhood*); and the prospect of Heaven.

At both finite and infinite levels (Classical and Romantic) Universalism sees the universe as a unity and sees humankind and all disciplines as a whole. So philosophical Universalism studies the whole universe in its finite and infinite aspects (hence *The New Philosophy of Universalism*); historical Universalism studies all history, including the rise and fall of civilisations (hence *The Rise and Fall of Civilizations*); political Universalism sees one political union of all humankind (hence *World State* and *World Constitution*); and literary Universalism sees the whole of literature, the fundamental theme of world literature: hence *A New Philosophy of Literature*, which sets out the fundamental theme as a generational dialectic between a quest for the One and satirical condemnation of follies and vices, between the Metaphysical-Romantic and the Classical – Universalism synthesising or reconciling both. See *The Essentials of Universalism* (coming shortly) for the key passages about Universalism in my prose.

Looking back on my works and on my experiences of the Light and the way I received crucial ideas and understanding in my sleep (recorded in *My Double Life 2: A Rainbow over the Hills*), I sometimes wonder if I was sent down to the earth and took human form in the year the Second World War began to confront the world's problems, reconcile all the disciplines and promote peace. I resonate with the feeling in Donne's 'Aire and Angels' that "Angells affect us oft" and are sent down to earth to complete a mission and tasks, and that at the very least we have divine souls, as Rubens showed in his painting of James I.

My Baroque development, forms, genres and verse

The poems and verse excerpts in this selection catch my development over the decades, my Universalism, my early mysticism, my Metaphysical approach ('The Silence', *The Gates of Hell*, 'A Metaphysical in Marvell's Garden' and other poems in *The Fire-Flower*), my Romantic outlook (*The Gates of Hell*, 'The Four Seasons'), my later Classicism (*Classical Odes*), my war poetry (*Overlord*, *Armageddon*, 'Shock and Awe'), and my awareness of the One ('The Silence', *The Gates of Hell*, *The Fire-Flower*, God of the One in *The Coronation of King Charles*). Elements of Classicism and Romanticism can be found in all my works, which I therefore regard as neo-Baroque.

In this selection can be found examples of the forms and genres I have written within: my sonnets; my lyrics; my odes; my social satire; my verse plays; and my masques.

My verse has become more Classical as the decades progressed. I began by exploring stress metre (four or five stresses in a line) but soon opted for iambic pentameters and blank verse, and on occasion heroic couplets. The turning-point was the evening I spent with Ezra Pound in Rapallo on 16 July 1970. I discussed the best line for writing an epic and became convinced that his Modernist approach in *The Cantos* of abbreviated narrative in emotionally-linked sequences of images (which I had defended in an essay in a book to mark Eliot's death, *T.S. Eliot: A Tribute from Japan*) was not the way I should pursue narrative verse, and when we walked round Oxford on 21 June 1993 Ricks confirmed my feeling that I should write an epic poem in blank verse. My classical odes on the culture of Europe are in rhymed or alternately-rhymed lines, and I use rhyme in most of my lyrics, odes and of course my many sonnets.

In this selection can also be found narrative, lyrical, reflective and dramatic verse; my early stress metre; lines of 2, 3, 4, 5, 6, 7 and 8 feet either rhymed or alternately rhymed; my standard iambic pentameters, blank verse and heroic couplets; and stanzas of 4, 8, 9 and 10 lines.

Alternative views of my poetry

In poems in this selection can be found the alternative views and perspectives of my poetry I identified in my Preface to *Visions of England*: my journeying along the Mystic Way (*The Gates of Hell*, 'Journey's End', 'Pear-Ripening House', *The Fire-Flower*); my developing Universalism ('Crab-Fishing on a Boundless Deep'); my social, satirical poetry ('Zeus's Ass'); my reflecting of Western culture ('On the Waterfront', 'Question Mark over the West'); my Nature poetry ('The Flight', *The Four Seasons*, *The Weed-Garden*, 'Sea Force'); my war poetry (*Overlord*, *Armageddon*, 'Shock and Awe'); my carrying forward of the tradition of the Metaphysical poets ('A Metaphysical in Marvell's Garden', *The Fire-Flower*); and my Classical and Romantic neo-Baroque poetry.

Also can be found poems on my local Epping Forest ('An Inner Home'); on my home town and childhood memories ('Among Loughton's Sacred Houses'); on my old school, which I later acquired ('Oaklands: Oak Tree'); on my Cornish sea ('Sea Force', 'Crab-Fishing on a Boundless Deep'); and on life and death ('A Crocus in the Churchyard').

In the tradition of Wordsworth and Tennyson

I have pictures of both Wordsworth and Tennyson within the vicinity of my study desk.

I see myself as being within Wordsworth's tradition of *The Prelude* and his 'Preface to *Lyrical Ballads*' (1801/1802), and the picture on the cover of *Visions of England* shows me sitting with the Wanderer's cottage in the background.

Ricks, arguably the leading world authority on Tennyson after his standard *Tennyson*, urged me to model myself on Tennyson, who had a vast range that included lyrical and narrative verse and events of international history such as 'The Charge of the Light Brigade' (set in the Crimean War, 1854), and who lived at Beech Hill House, High Beach, from 1837 to 1840 (very near where I live in Epping Forest), and heard the "wild bells" ring out from Waltham Abbey.

He urged me to correct my past poems as Tennyson did to improve lines, and I have always done this, as in my reworking of 'Strawberry Hill' (1974) into 'Clouded-Ground Pond' (1980, not included), and 'In Marvell's Garden, at Nun Appleton' (1973, not included) into 'A Metaphysical in Marvell's Garden' (1980). He said to me as we walked round Oxford on 21 June 1993 and I settled on blank verse for *Overlord* (the subject behind my discussion with Ezra Pound in 1970): "Nothing's changed since Tennyson technically. Go back to him."

I describe in a letter to Ricks in *Selected Letters* (dated 29 July 2008) how I was aware of Tennyson's presence when I spent several days staying at Farringford House, his home on the Isle of Wight from 1853 until his death in 1892, both while I wrote in his study and slept in the bedroom he used.

Since then I have sensed that Tennyson has often been with me as a Muse, and frequently acts as an editor and draws my attention to where I could improve a word (see *Fools' Paradise*, p.145). Tennyson wrote after the Romantic Age and blended Romanticism and Classicism in his own way that was neo-Baroque. It may be significant that I took the world anthem for *World Constitution* from six lines in Tennyson's 'Locksley Hall', and in *World State* named my World State 'The United Federation of the World' after Tennyson's lines in that poem. I also quoted at length from Tennyson's 'Ulysses' in my speech in Moscow's Civic Chamber on 22 April 2019 (see my website for video). Besides deriving from Wordsworth I also derive from Tennyson, as I hope this selection will demonstrate.

Having had an early interest in Modernism and having taught the poems of T.S. Eliot in great detail to Japanese students between 1963 and 1967 when I was a Professor of English Literature in Tokyo (part of the time in a room where William Empson taught between 1931 and 1934), and having turned back to the 19th century after my evening with Ezra Pound, I returned to the 600-year-old tradition of the iambic pentameter that dominated English verse from 1380 to 1980 and was followed by both Wordsworth and Tennyson. My essay 'A Defence of Traditional Poetic Method or: Poking the Hornets' Nest' (1999, revised in 2005) can be found at the end of my *Collected Poems* and of *A New Philosophy of Literature*.

My "mission" and project: to develop my Baroque vision into Universalism

Ricks, with whom I have corresponded for 40 years as *Selected Letters* shows, spoke with me at Worcester College, Oxford, on 1 July 2019, before giving a lecture about the iambic pentameter as "the music of the English heroic line" (Dr Johnson, 'Life of Milton' in *Lives of the Poets*, 1779). Over drinks before his lecture we discussed my recent visit to Russia and my call there for better relations with the West, and he said to me (two octogenarians together who had known each other a long time), "You have been on a mission since you left University." And I wondered if I had indeed worked on one lifelong project ever since I left Oxford in 1961, 58 years previously, even longer than the 57 years that Pound had been writing *The Cantos* when I visited him in 1970. (See my letter to Ricks in *Selected Letters* dated 3 July 2019, which also mentions that he told me I had used the heroic line in *Overlord*.)

I thought he meant that during all my travelling of the world and my writing I had been on a mission to arrive at Universalism and to set out my Universalist vision in literature and extend it to six other disciplines. (He had once said to me that art comes out of a quarrel with oneself, not with the world, and he knew that I had sought to understand the universe so I could elevate my poetry – while preserving the approach of Keats' "negative capability", responding to life fully in the moment.) But, having completed the selection of the poems in Part One of *A Baroque Vision*, I awoke on Christmas Day 2019 with the realisation (which had come to me in my sleep) that he had remembered my three letters to him in 1979 and 1982 and meant that my Universalism was rooted in and grew out of my Baroque vision in my poems, that my "mission" and project was to develop my Baroque vision into Universalism. Whether he meant this I do not know – and it may already be obvious to diligent readers of my *Collected Prefaces*; but I had woken with what was for me a new perspective, and I was stunned.

Evidence for the connection between my Baroque vision and my Universalism

I got up and looked in my Prefaces for evidence of the connection between my Baroque vision of 1982 and my Universalism of 1991.

I saw I first stated my Baroque vision in my Preface to my *Selected Poems: A Metaphysical's Way of Fire*, 'On the New Baroque Consciousness and the Redefinition of Poetry', which, though published in 1991, was first written in September–October 1982 (and revised in August and October 1989 with the addition of "as Classical Baroque" at the end of the title). I saw I first stated my Universalism in a Preface written in April 1989 and also published in 1991 (Preface to *The Fire and the Stones* titled 'Introduction to the New Universalism').

I looked in my *Collected Poems*, and I now saw that the turning-point which shows my Baroque vision giving birth to my Universalism was in my poem 'Night Visions in Charlestown', first written in 1983 and revised in 1990 ("So hail the Universal Age of Light!.../New rising of Baroque in its own right...").

I looked in my diaries. I saw that on 21 August 1984 I wrote that a selection of my poems for Ricks should be called *A Way of Fire* (which became *Selected Poems: A Metaphysical's Way of Fire*, published in 1991, on my Mystic Way). I saw that in early April 1985 I had a number of intense experiences inspired by Charlestown in Cornwall, and in my diary entries for 7 April (which are in *My Double Life 2: A Rainbow over the Hills*, pp.185–187) I wrote:

> Soul and body together – the very essence of Baroque.... Artists create the next age, which will be a Baroque one, uniting Classicism and Romanticism. A new word for it?... A new flowering of the Romantic age amalgamated to Classicism.... So what is the Age?... Think. It is a new ism, after Romanticism and Classicism, in artistic terms Baroque.... I still need a word for the next age.

On 9 April, inspired by the night view of the stars over the sea from Charlestown, in my diary I pondered the next age, a Universal Age, and came to the brink of declaring a Universalist Age:

> I see so clearly from a Cornish cliff, and that is why I must buy a cliff-top house in Cornwall, e.g. Charlestown.... My 'trade mark' is man in the universe, against the stars, not the social man.... I see a man against the stars, a frightening vision that permeates my '[The] Silence' and which should still permeate my work.... I am a Universalist – a word that has the idea of Holism, the whole, i.e. all universes, and all that is universal; while going for the Light which permeates the universe. Universalism.... That is the new philosophy, which has characteristics of the Baroque. Especially if Universalism includes soul and spirit, 4 levels of man's being.... A Universal Age. After Realism and Nominalism came Humanism, the human scale (mind and body, not soul). Now Universalism, the scale of the universe, which includes the soul, for entry into the soul takes us out into the universe. The Universal Age.... There are as many stars as sparkles, and they fade and form like the jumping lights on a sunlit sea – one perception I have had which takes me to the truth about the universe – "bunches of grapes of 5,000 galaxies each". An age that raised its eyes from the street and social concerns to its place in the universe.

I saw that in April 1985 I had described Universalism as "the" new philosophy with "characteristics of the Baroque". I added in *My Double Life 2: A Rainbow over the Hills* (p.188):

> After a few days of intense thought I now regarded myself as a Universalist announcing and heralding in a Universal Age, in which Universalism would succeed Humanism. I wrote [in a later diary entry on 9 April 1985] that any selection of my poems "must go with the Universal Age" and that I should write "an essay on our Universal Age which has Baroque features: on communications, the global view, but also on man's role in relation to the universe, which the new Renaissance is making possible.... The new science has opened up the stars and enlarged the soul, and my work must respond to this."

This passage written in my diary on 9 April 1985 caught the turning-point from "a new Baroque age" to a coming Universal or Universalist Age "which has Baroque features", and I was now clear that my Baroque vision had given rise to my Universalism, which opened to the universe and the perspective of Heaven as in Rubens' *The Apotheosis of James I* and took Heaven's view of the whole universe, all civilisations and a united humankind in a World State – God of the One's view in *The Coronation of King Charles*. I had dealt with this in *My Double Life 2: A Rainbow over the Hills* and had somehow forgotten, and Ricks had reminded me in his throw-away mention of my "mission".

I saw in my 1987 diary that on 10 October 1987 I was at the Frankfurt Book Fair and spoke with a German representative of the publishers Fischers, Reiner Stach. I told him about my coming work *The Fire and the Stones* and explained that just as Einstein had a hunch about varying speeds of travel, which led to his Relativity theory, lying in a meadow and mentally travelling back up a sun-ray, so I had a hunch about the cause of civilisations, which grow out of a mystic vision similar to the Baroque vision into a religion. He said, "You have developed a universalist theory of world civilisations," and his use of the word 'universalist' chimed with my own earlier use of the word on 9 April 1985 ("I am a Universalist").

A new Baroque Age behind a new Age of Universalism

I saw that I recorded in my diary on 29 April 1989 that I "woke with the beginning of my 'Introduction to the New Universalism' [the Preface to *The Fire and the Stones*] in mind and wrote it in vest and pants". I had received it in sleep, just as I received the meaning of what Ricks meant by my "mission" in sleep, and I was in such haste to write it down before the words I had seen evaporated that I did not wait until I had finished dressing. In the Preface I wrote, "A new baroque Age, an Age of Universalism, is ahead." In my diary entry for 29 April 1989 I added, "I believe I have devised a new discipline.... I have devised Universalism."

The Baroque vision behind Universalism has unified all my literary and Universalist works

I was now sure that my Baroque vision was behind my Universalism, that I had developed my Baroque vision into Universalism, that Ricks had known this on 1 July 2019, and that I had been on a "mission" and had followed one project throughout my life.

I could now see that all my books came out of the third part of 'The Silence', and that it was the origin of both my Baroque vision ("A new Baroque age is born") and of my early Universalism. In Part III of 'The Silence' (excerpts included) can be found all the features of the Baroque – the Mystic Way, a centre-shift and transformation, the Light, the sensual and the spiritual, the unitive vision, the One, the Romantic infinite and Classical order – and, in the cross-disciplinary context of Freeman's experience, all the disciplines

Universalism (which sees the universe as a unity, embodies the unitive vision) unites: mysticism and religion (the irregular chunks of verse as beads on a rosary, "In the meditation hall", the "round white light"); philosophy (the universe seen from a beach in lines 896–913, and lines 1438–1442); history (vision of the ruin of European civilisation in lines 1414–1426); international politics ("all men are a part of One", at one with all humankind); and world culture (the meeting of East and West in the poem).

Also written in 1966, the year I finished 'The Silence', were other poems with Baroque/Universalist features: 'Archangel' (history, international politics and closing vision of a World State); 'Old Man in a Circle' (history and international politics, the decline of the British Empire and the rise of Europe); and 'Two Moral Letters after Horace' (not included), the first being 'An Epistle to an Admirer of Oliver Cromwell' (history), and the second, addressed to His Imperial Highness Prince Hitachi, Emperor Hirohito's second son whose tutor I then was ("Imperial Highness on your birth-day,/Spare a thought for the poor of the world./Use your influence like your father…").

All this came as a staggering revelation that Christmas morning for it thrillingly unified my literary and Universalist works. I now saw the jigsaw pieces of my 52 interlocking books as one picture, a whole. Once again my mentor Ricks had been breathtakingly discerning, and, in a seemingly-casual remark, with a true mentor's skill had guided me into seeing that my Baroque vision grew into and was behind my Universalism.** I had put a new gloss on my Baroque vision: Universalism. I saw that my Baroque vision passed seamlessly into Universalism, which is fundamentally Baroque.

I now saw that the poems I wrote between the mid-1960s and early 1980s embodied a truth that I had not fully understood at first and had not fully grasped rationally until then. I was reminded of Yeats writing in the year I was born, "A man can embody truth but cannot know it" (letter to Lady Elizabeth Pelham, 4 January 1939). With age sometimes comes wisdom. Now I am 80 I would amend what Yeats wrote to: "A man can embody a vision of Truth and he can come to understand it."

Having waited 40 years to present a selection of 30 poems I wrote between 1961 and 1979, I am very pleased to be presenting this selection of 30 poems (40 years late) in Part One of *A Baroque Vision*. And, having now understood that the Baroque poems I wrote between 1982 and 1991 were the seed-bed of my Universalism, I am very pleased to be presenting a selection of 70 poems I wrote between 1979 and 2019 in Part Two. These Baroque poems in this selection represent my life's poetic work over six decades, and the realisation that their Baroque vision is behind and has grown into my Universalism and the coming Universalist Age has satisfyingly unified all my Prefaces and all my 52 literary and Universalist works within one lifelong "mission" and purposeful project which, if political Universalism is fully implemented in a World State, can only be to the eventual benefit of all humankind.

17–21, 23–25, 27–28, 30–31 December 2019; 2, 8–13, 21–22 January, 15 February 2020

---

*Since this was written *The Oak Tree and the Branch* (2024), containing seven more volumes, is set to appear.
**See pp.389–399 for five letters written by Nicholas Hagger to Christopher Ricks on *A Baroque Vision*, the last two in reply to an image he received from Ricks on 2 March 2021 (see p.395).

A view of the oval painting by Rubens, *The Apotheosis of James I*, which was installed on the Banqueting House ceiling in 1636. It shows James I being taken to Heaven by angels, and was commissioned by his son Charles I, who looked up at it as he walked to his execution in 1649.

Nicholas Hagger with Christopher Ricks (above) after his last lecture as
Oxford Professor-of-Poetry on 11 May 2009 and (below) at Worcester
College, Oxford on 1 July 2019

PART ONE
1961–1979

30 POEMS

from *A Well of Truth* (1958–1963)
Ode to a Prospect from a Window Frame

I sat in wonder at the window edge
And breathless watched the peace of day recline
Over the still green hill. The soft grass sedge
Waved to the fleeing evening beneath the pine,
And oh what glory in that dying light!
My heart leapt clear to streaks of russet cloud,
My mind fell free and walked with unscaled eyes
Down flimsy-paper streets at triple height
And peered through panes. My body was a shroud;
The wilting world wept at my spirit's size.

But then the cooling window froze to night;
There was no noise to disturb the sleeping grass,
No chirp of bird or insect. I had no sight
To glimpse a moonlit movement, for – alas –
Too soon my tingling nerves grew calm and sour;
I saw my hands caress a picture-frame,
A wilderness of art in nature's paint.
My heart was heavy in that shrouded hour,
An artifice that left the feeling lame,
And left the well of knowledge to the saint.

O for a well of Truth that all might see,
A well of clean and lasting Light to soothe
The souls of all who dip their hands, to be
A cure for hearts that are like a soundproof booth.
That picture will soon be in winter's sprawl
And slow Decay will sing the frost of time
And the slow dance that sighs the grave's embrace
For years to come, for aeons past my fall
To a lich bed, beneath the hoar-frost's rime,
Beyond the eternal smile of Beauty's face.

To capture beauty now should be our aim,
Undarkened by the shadow thrown by death
Across the water-lilies breezes tame
And whip to fury with their dying breath.

Who has not stood and looked into the lake,
And seen the dancing pictures flow and fade
Deep in the grey pool's heart? And soon each one
Will dance again. Now sleeping souls awake.
The fleetest shadow might be Beauty's shade.
Behind each shadow reigns a glorious sun.

1961; revised 10 October 2012

2

from *A Stone Torch-Basket* (1963–1965)
The Seventeenth-Century Pilgrim

"Wyrd oft nereth unfaegne eorl ponne his ellen deah."
("Fate often preserves the undoomed warrior when his courage is strong")

Beowulf

Once I complained of many bitter facts,
Of ruins and epitaphs on empty hopes,
That I was born to die despite my acts
Or the futile benedictions of the Popes.
Yet as I watched the seasons ebb and flow
I saw the tides that swirled across my brain
In fickle flood and moon-fall – παντα ῥει;
No self of mine felt constant agony.
And I resolved to evolve from pointless pain
(My Hell) and grow a Paradise that I could know.

Since then I have journeyed through rocks and pines,
Have sat by rivers in the summer sun,
Watched timeless dawns flush golden Eastern shrines,
And knelt to my shadow when the day is done.
Now I am still a sequence of moments;
But my abiding eye of strict assent
Nakedly loves the underlying Power
That pulses through existing's every hour.
Don't ask me where I'm bound. It brings dissent
To analyse perfection's senseless sense.

And yet I know from the wild wind's sound
I too will rot to nothing underground.

5 December 1963; revised 2012

3

from *The Early Education and Making of a Mystic* (1965–1966)
The Power by the Lake

No missing breakfast that week. I was down
Early, searched the pigeon-holes daily, until
My father's envelope came. I left the Lodge,
Walked past the Cottages to the College gardens,
Meandered to the lake, sadly detached
From my doom, the entire future pressing,
And I observed my feelings, free
Yet foreordained. Could I abandon Law
For Literature? Under the stone arch, alone,
I opened it, swallowed the broken surrender,
"I consent", and some great shadow of authority
Shattered into fragments. Sun-flecked, lawless,
Free, I wept.
        The early morning blazed,
Trees of every green linked earth and blue-white sky
In the lake. Adazzled, a great power filled me.
Purified, I grew, head sun-scorched, feet earth-rooted,
Stomach pulsing water-trees; I towered
Giddy, vast as God, I had always existed,
Earth-trees-sky would die, not I, the life-beat
And order, the permanent sole meaning.
I knew without understanding, as now
Without thinking, I know my own surname.
All creation was me, a pounding power,
And infinitely good.
        Breakfastless in my room,
I pondered the impure sleep of my lake-like mind
Which, when woken with such purified force,
Could be transformed by such a mystic power.

4

from *The Silence* (1965–1966)
from The Silence
(A Meditation on a Quest for Meaning and Self-discovery)

To Mr F.T.
This string of baroque pearls,
To be told like a rosary

[from I. Dying: Shadow, lines 249–273, Freeman encounters
his Shadow]

Freeman rebels against society and glimpses the form which he believes can bring meaning to his life: a future state of himself as a higher consciousness which perceives meaning.

Said Freeman, "I have rebelled," and arrogantly stood alone,
Opposed to the drifting High Road, parting shoppers like
   a stone.
But what dream hung over the church, what surpassing
   image
Like the dream of a fallen seed in a dying season,
What dream like a twilit moon?

                    In a broken life-line
Is a sunset in a library, when, laughter in veins,
What could prevent if one had the belief, what save one's
   own will?
     To a violin's scales
     I made a renunciation;
     Weeping arpeggios
     I unchose my self for a Law routine.
But now in the electric light each man's shadow spread
   years before him;
And can they not see, looking through the Hobbies,
   the motor magazines,
Can they not see that each is awaiting creation,
Awaiting the features of a giant or dwarf?
Do they not know they are sculpting themselves,
This one his drooping jowls, that his sparkling eyes,
Can they not see that every second carves the future idea?
O Shadow, can I not ascend to you? Who are you,

Out there in the future like an inscrutable sage?
    The vision faded like a dream
    Into foggy air;
    An artist's quest began again,
    A Tammuz resumed his despair.

[from II. In the Underworld: Moon on the Northern Dead,
lines 800–840, death of father]

His father
has another
stroke, and his
suffering and
death seem
meaningless.

What is that scream from the summer roses
Like an unbearably beautiful pain?
And what disturbance in the condemned men's ward
As madness raged in a provincial's bleeding brain,
As with terrible logic he proved his tormentors wrong,
What triumphant shriek like a discordant chord
And then silence and the patter of rain?
In a lucid moment, lying in the bottom of a bed,
He groaned, "What have I done, what is the reason?"
And seeing him fall apart into a collage of bones,
I could not shake my head and say, "It is all in vain."

In the lush serenity of a sultry hollow
A distant rumble closed a prayer, and echoed
When will all this suffering reach an end and serenity follow?

In the angry autumn a storm came,
Breaking summer defiance,
Licking down from heaven with a white-hot tongue,
Leaving behind
A blasted bole in the after-calm,
And a charred inside.
Weary, he resigned his pride,
Surrendered a slurred confession to his inquisitors
And heard the twitter of migrating birds
In evening skies.
At nightfall in the unfriendly room,
Baffled by the indifferent lights of a lifetime lost,
He sighed at the yawning nothing round the flimsy moon
"This is the end," and shivered at the early frost.

And looking at the moon, he understood:
On a blind and slumbering retina, one flicker of light

And a universe; was no more:
Man, nothing and all.
He saw through, saw through.
An endless night.

He cried out – panting, labouring, groaning, he cried out –
    groping for my hand, grasping, clutching,
        clutching the living, gripping, gripping
           under the lamp
And I was all and helpless; while downstairs
The TV picture shrank into a
           postage stamp.

      Night.

[from III. Rising: Reflection on the Clouded Ground, lines 865–913,
challenged by the silence in the universe]

    Temples on the pine slopes, red carp in a shoal....

Freeman is now a Professor in Japan.

Withdrawn from a Professor's role,
Behind the outer smile,
Is as present a silence
As round a microphone;
Centuries of contemplation
The Western sneer derides
Have fertilized this valley
And peep through a worker's eyes;
Here let Eastern silence feed your soul.

His feeling of being different from other people is more pronounced, and he begins to live behind his social 'I'.

Walking past noteless bars of telegraph wires
And the rattling of metal balls in *pachinko* dens
I passed under the twilit metal web
Whose cruel threads had trapped an exhausted tram
And on the trembling bridge I inhaled the smell
Of the drifting layers of scum on the green canal,
I connected the tang with oyster shells, and rejoiced in
    the banal.
But watching him while he acted out his expected role,
I knew he was a stranger who did not belong,
I heard them whisper, "With what disarming charm
He walls himself within the language barrier,"

Or, "See how loosely he wears his position
Yet see how he pulls it round him when alarmed,"
I knew what they respected with their questions,
I knew their code.
                              In the train,
I did not have to hide my dislocations
Or alienate to an awesome distance;
Openly strange, I felt an expatriate's peace.
And when I came out of the station I couldn't get a taxi
And the great sweep of the Milky Way was frozen and crisp
And my heart welled out and flooded the universe.

On a beach at night he realises that the stars are meaningless without man.

The sea sighed like a lover,
Explored the face of the shore with webbed fingers,
Blind in the dark phase. And in a glittering sweep
Some of the hundred thousand million suns
In one of a hundred thousand million galaxies
Whirled on in a fiery band, shot out rays
To traverse the silence for a hundred thousand years
And beam on the man who crouched by a whelk-shell.
On a Japanese beach, my terrestrial illusions shattered,
I fell headlong into a deep, dark silence
And floating like an astronaut, I shuddered – for
     I was nothing.
Suddenly a great flood of being surged in me,
Streamed out into the stars, brightened their fires
And released affirming voices in my blood:
"Without your creating eye would they exist, those cinders,
Without your moist cheeks would they have meaning?
Beside one creator, what are space or number or time?"
While the sea reached and tenderly smoothed away
     my footprints.

[lines 1027–1066, quest for meaning]

A dozen attendants bowed and gestured me forward;
And turning the corner, I checked myself in the middle of
     a step
For the figure I saw in the mirror was unreal.
In the limousine I averted my eyes from the chauffeur's
     mirror
And we purred past choirs of silent angels until we saw

The moated majesty of the bouldered Palace walls,
Obsessing like the centre of a *mandala*.
Turning the corner, what happened, for weren't you
    anti-Establishment?
In the centre,
Arranged in a rich hierarchy of meaning,
I glimpsed myself as a meditating Buddha.
Withdrawn from dark suits, why shouldn't he sit in a
    dark suit?.
And the form I saw in the mirror had become unreal....

He cannot
reconcile his
contradictions.
By the sea
he falls into
despair.

And is this the end of the quest, is this all,
Is there only this uncontainable complex whole,
This pattern of Becoming, and nothing more?
                        This carpet on this floor?

I shall sink to the floor so, and tear out tufts of hair.

Poet of the Self,
You who gave your youth to questioning despair,
Stare in the mirror, and question each greying hair.

In the early spring,
Observing a sea-slug spinning a yellow thread
I transcended my yearning:
XYZ,
It exists; there is no why; it might be dead.

Sunlight on a wrinkled sea.
The jumping of exploding diamonds and the sparkle
    of crystal,
I flashed jubilation like a white hot mirror:
Might be dead.

Turning in the seasons of my sunlight
I shall continue to seek,
Transcending the indifference of will-less fatalists:
A luminous sapphire-cell expiring on the beach.

[lines 1110–1144, choosing a dynamic view of the self]

Reflection and Shadow
Man can repeat *and* grow
An upward striving stem
Splitting a resisting shell.

Walking among shop-windows he is confronted by his Reflection, the normally taken-for-granted embodiment of the repetitions whose dictatorial rule has impeded his growth. He rejects this Freudian devil's static and repetitive view of himself for the Shadow's dynamic view of himself, and affirms the importance of the artist's role in society.

I met my tempter in a wilderness of windows,
A gaunt Reflection like a repetitious bourgeois,
Evasive like *Ambroise Vollard.* "You know
The outer real reflects your dream here,"
He said, "your self-important fantasy;...
You poor, neurotic exile from reality."...
                                        I countered:
"I reject you. With absurd belief I hung
A lamppost at the end of my future self
Like a moon at the end of a deserted street;
I have my purpose and so I progress.
Do not expect me to live like those consumptive men,
Coughing their fatalistic disbelief
And infecting such as you with their 'normal' breath;
Undiagnosed in an unreal world, they need
My solitary journey, to know their lack of health.
My place is apart from their consuming ease.
I will pour my being into this outer dream....
        I cannot live by Freud:
        There in his mirror
        I cannot create
        A towering image of man against a void."

[lines 1157–1312, centre-shift and transformation]

In a Zen temple Freeman is confronted with the spiritual world and with the irrational basis of his existence, the metaphysical ground of his being.

In the meditation hall
Each breath is unreal;
There on the silence
As the dawn shadows fall
The empty seekers feel
Empty and full existence;
As when the ruffled surface calmed –
Beyond your reflection
You saw the clouded ground

And the towering depths around your
rational question.

And when I emptied myself and looked beneath
I was speechless, speechless –
There were no foundations in that darkness,
I understood nothing, confronting that silent ground.

He feels divided.

It was all round me, like a cloud of exhaled smoke
And later in the twilit air I knew it would enfold me again,
Rising like a haze from a subterranean furnace, and choke
Me with questions, I knew I must live with it, and live
    in pain.
Under a scaffolding of rusty girders,
I heard a whisper, as if from a lunch-time stroller,
"Now you will always be two unless you refuse;"
And, queuing for damnation in a mirage of heat and fumes,
And switching off the engine, have you never inquired
"Who is this 'I', intruding on silence?"
And seen your two profiles split in a mirror of cubes?…

                       Through the cracked glass

On a railway platform he accepts the irrational depths of himself. Like a reclaimed Tammuz who understands and accepts Inanna's role, he is about to escape his Underworld,

They were like husband and wife waiting for a train
In a grey and bleeding dawn,
Hands clutched by the androgynous central child,
Divider and reconciler of their scarred disdain.
Watching the white orb boil in a platform puddle
While, adjusting darks, she said, "Isn't it like a moon?"
I knew why, I knew why she completed me, what
    I had projected…
As when, turning the wheel and lowering sunlight,
I drew a shattered reflection from the moon-dark well.
And I knew I must live between, in the child's place,
And, turning to a stranger by the wall,
As to a Reflection who would not abdicate,
I said, "I accept my inner being, I accept it all,"
And saw him slope away, disconsolate.

                    I perceive, falsely,
                    A Reflection that is *me*;
                    To smash it is to be.

and it seems to
him that the
power of his
Reflection is
finally broken.

⌐ Leaving the station, I groped down empty streets
Until, near the stadium, I went down a yawning stair
And lost my way into a hall of Buddhas.
I saw them, my thousand selves in tiers
Like a football crowd at prayer;
Lost in a labyrinth of plaster whores
I panicked, but there,
Beneath the central image, confirming a brawl
I had no fears.
                              The lift went down a well
Into a mine of gleaming diamonds
And golden gods with Egyptian heads were drawn past my
        closed eyelids.
Through falling masonry I rushed up into the shaking street –
And seeing the city crumbled into a thousand ruins,
And the dancing dead, I did not cry out or weep,
Wandering in the girdered rubble of an old personality.

He undergoes
a personality
shift from his
Reflection to
the irrational
depths of
his inner
being. He
experiences
illumination,

And when i awoke, i was a floor below my thoughts,
Looking out at the dawn as from a tiled bungalow –
And suddenly, nourished by silence
My seed-case burst into a thousand I's
And a central stem broke through the tiled crown of
        my head.
Hallelujah! in a dazzling universe i had no defence,
round that round white light, life and night were one
and i was afraid, for i did not know
                              if the sun reflected
my reflecting sun

and perceives
the unity of
the universe
and is face to
face with the
divine world
and with
metaphysical
Reality.

and in that four-sided garden
rock and sea and sand
mountain and cloud and earth
mirrored in an empty mind
reveal a refutable truth
between stone and stone
in an arbitrary frame
there is no difference, all is one
still or moving, all existence is the same

⌐ An Eastern sage tempts:
"(+A) + (−A) = Nothing,
The Absolute is where there is no difference."
The Being behind Existence

Rationally
he resists
the prospect
of personal
immortality,
first in terms
of death,

the stone garden reflects
what you want to see
a mirror of
subjectivity
and on this hill
bristling with monuments to synthesis
gape, earth, and reveal
a thousand insights into the abyss
and, backslider, do you now deny
between system and finality there is no difference?

and secondly
in terms of his
fellow men.

A blossom of white light
illuminates the cosmic night,
my heart welled out −
a volley, and three men bowed low like acrobats
and under this ghastly sky, the condemned of all nations
are limping and crawling and groaning up the scorched hill,
writhing, screaming, feel their chopped bleeding, be faithful −
Freeman, be faithful to your fellow men;
see − some are ignorant of such matters
but that spurting flesh is yours, you're one of them
and whoever they are, would you abandon one?
between man and man there is no difference.

And when a headlight lit his stump of an arm

In a graveyard
he retreats
from the
metaphysical,
and for the
time being
rejects
immortality
as a privilege
he has yet to
come to terms
with, and
immediately
stakes all
on existence,

In a graveyard of uniform stones, I looked for the stars,
No matter what escaped old bones, I stood by my fellow men.
I thought: 'If just one is damned or dealt extinction,
I will be too, and if all men are a part of One
And all shall be eternal, without exception,
Then without effort all are guaranteed,
And I reject a truth that ends all striving.'
And when I had shaken my head, my mind was calm,
In a long rhythm of shadows, of days and nights
Like the scudding clouds on the unruffled
    moon-centred pool,

which he now perceives with meaning. He sees things as they are, objectively, without interference from his sense of 'I'. He perceives Being as opposed to Becoming.

I mirrored the glory,
I was all existence in the silence of that stone garden.

> Darkness within
> Throws a chaotic waste on the empty screen;
> A disc of white-hot will
> Throws an orderly meaning on the sunlit screen;
> And the centre of the universe is in the self
> When only what one is is seen.

> A red-winged ladybird
> > in sunlight,
A meaning of gullwings by the turning tide.
To be
Is to perceive the world
As a stone-like unity.
Therefore, '*percipere est esse*',
To perceive truly is to be.

I was all 'I', Becoming,
Before the Journey;
Now I share the sky
i perceive truly
> and feel all Being flow like a surging tide.

I saw them at the break of day,
All my exorcised ghosts, sullenly skulking away.
And from the baked land joyously burst a prepuced palm.

And I was weary, weary – I prayed for rest, knowing
$(+A) + (-A) =$ nothing;
Between red and black, the blaze of azaleas
And the dignified weeping of a dying piano,
In a disintegrating summer I became nothing,
I surpassed myself, on my way to becoming nothing.

And I was at peace.
> And I had liberated
A great tide of will I did not want to cease.

[lines 1313–1354, inner unity, vision of new Baroque form]

As a result
he is united
with his
Shadow and
he glimpses
his future
task: he must
communicate
his vision to
his inauthentic
Age.

I turned the corpse with my toe, then climbed on up the
    iron tree
Until our stony land spread out in the Western evening;
Then my Shadow obscured the sun at my feet
And spoke retrospectively from a future dawn:
"Now that you have overcome and nothing but time
    divides us,
And know you are real, that your soul is eternal,
I can reveal what is in store for your generation.
Through your rejection of social ego, which history has taken,
And static Freud, already discredited,
And of reduction of all existence to partial, rational terms,
And of the will-less image of man which destroyed
    your fathers,
Who, lacking the forward vision, accepted defeat
Or reacted in historical transition,
You will escape. And what you will rebuild,
The 'new' form your age needs for ancient energy –
History will take that too, but you will have lived.
Your growth, not an enduring form, will be your goal.
Therefore turn the wheel."

    To outgrow all ideas
    Save the important one,
    The upward thrust of the sap
    To a form of pagan height
    And the quiet, stout-timbered shrine,
    Or in the fading light,
    At one with his fellow man,
    The giant Buddha's calm;

    to begin in inner silence
    behind the outer smile
    as empty as the stone garden
    between central stem and Shadow
    in the mosaic
    between child and irrational woman
    like the four-faced striking clock
    that woke me as a child
    and measures an exile.

⌐ I heard a cry from the old Professor's darkened room,
"The Age of Analysis is dead!"
Books lined with dust, a buzzing fly....

                    While, naked on the petalled lawn,
A new Baroque age is born.
                    Member, fingers,
Hands, lips, mouth, hair, eyes, nostrils, crown,
    face – WHOLE.

[lines 1355–1413, Freeman as a metaphysical artist seeing meaning
and knowing what is real]

"O fool, fool," said Freeman, "I have been a fool
For I, a metaphysical, have clung to reason.
I gaze and show my Age, and the way to live.
I have been tempted away from my true work, my art.
I am a maker, not a changer in a school;
I show man, and all the dreams and contradictions in
    his heart.
I have two lives. I grieve, but I am apart.
I am a detached artist; I do not preach....
I am not a leader of movements, I am an artist with
    a frown....
I bear truths from the spirit, and images
I will fix into a pattern on a well-glazed jar
So action and contemplation are held in balance."...

Freeman now sees himself first and foremost as a metaphysical artist.

On Edogawa Bridge

In the noon glare I saw my shadow lengthen
Into a self completed; a vast illusion,
Like a glimpse from ten years' solitude in mountains
Or in Nitria, hearing more certainly the living word.
I am my consciousness: always in the now,
Inextricable from a situation,
I was a succession of states of mind.
Wandering at dusk in a forum of broken statues, I shuddered,
I was severed from my past, I had no meaning,
Like a Caesar severed from his plot, I had no meaning,
And at night, woken by silence from confused dreams,
I felt like a stranger in a vast museum.
Freedom breaks history, but does not give us knowledge.
Now I have taken possession of myself, have occupied my life,

Freeman no longer perceives with meaningless immediacy. He now takes stock. His self-discovery and the knowledge he has won will carry him forward.

I have strung moments like beads on a Catholic's necklace,
I have ordered images in the Louvre of my soul.
And so wandering at dusk in a forum of statues – hurrah!
      hurrah!
I felt a wind blowing my past into future.
That old man waiting on the village bench, he sees the now
Like petals dropping on water, like petals rising
From the stream of a quietly flowing Year.
Or as wave succeeds wave against the Trenarren peninsula.

Freeman, I said, there has been a real development
Between withdrawal endured and withdrawal chosen;
Vowing and defying, you seized your own,
Knowing only a rebel can create himself,
For vitality is only won from opposition.
Now you are mature and know what is real,
Now your soul is an eternal, silent glow,
And to know your inner Being is to know your possibilities;
You have found peace and a real way of looking,
But like an improvising actor with a knowledge of Act
      One only,
Remember, the forces which control your present
Are forces which determine but are not unbreakable,
Just as a free act only enslaves until its revocation,
Creates a system that only limits freedom
If, by absence of denial, it is daily rechosen:
That yard of heads and torsos behind the exhibition.

[lines 1414–1449, the ruin of European civilisation, and Reality]

Despite a vision of the ruin which is eventually in store for European civilisation, "No crumbling forces are unbreakable," Freeman had said.
Grass sprouted from these rotting roofs and walls
But, dictating progress reports, nobody noticed;
And from this Monumental height men are crawling like
      ants

Hither and thither in a pile of rubble and iron,
Hither and thither without a unifying idea
In a heap of crumbled machinery and falling spires
And, exhausted by aimlessness, drag weaker, falter,
Watch from now smouldering compost in the hard,
    clear dusk,
As with slow, regular flight,
A steel bird soars towards the crimson sun,
And fall, now burning; and, in a crimson conflagration,

                                                    expire.

Freeman glimpses Reality near Trenarren and is able to affirm.

The angry years, an age like wind and foam.
Let us leave this inner kingdom, let us awaken to that blur.
A skylark twittering above the wheat,
Cows on green fields, primroses in the hedgerow.
Let us dip back into the mind and fly to Trenarren.
Rejoice from this headland, my Shadow, let us rejoice
At this sea pounding these rocks, at these sparkling waves,
    this tide.
Now let our eyes open to this sparkling, dancing sea,
This watery stone garden, lapping round still rocks.
It images: the starry universe, whose waves
Of cosmic radiation fill the blue sky,
And all Existence enveloped in Being;
The one ocean of manifesting Being;
The Void of unmanifest Non-Being
Behind it; and the One which contains both
For $(+A) + (-A) = $ zero,
Great nothing, the Infinite.
                Let us be

The blue meaning of the foaming round the rocks.
Let us be the fourfold sea!

My Shadow sees
With a metaphysical eye.

Let us be the sea!

January 1965 – June 1966; revised August 1970; 25–26 July 1974 and later

5

from *The Wings and the Sword* (1966–1969)
from Archangel

[lines 1–32, Cathedral of the Archangel, Moscow, and divided Europe and world]

Like domes of a cavernous mind
These groined and frescoed vaults
Over pictured pillars and walls
Dream out a recurrent theme
In this Kremlin mausoleum:
Grand Dukes and palaced Tsars
As haloed, Orthodox Saints
Pursue a spiritual quest
In an unequal Christendom
While apart from the rich man's feast
Are rebellions of the starving,
Bread-fisted Leaders and skirmish,
And, as in the nearby palace,
The future tyrants of well-fed Peoples' States.

Like a collage of propaganda in a self-divided brain;
Leave these bare-footed porters and gaping bars,
The tapewormed squatters under the blackened Hong Kong church
And, shaking your head at this exhausted, yellow earth,
Cross over the guarded bridge between decaying rails,
And then, to triumphal singing, sweep past laughing girls
Who wade in green-brown water, or till fertile fields,
Pass whitewashed walls to a blue-clad, virginal city
And the dark, censored silence round puritan Kwangtung;
Or, well before midnight, in a dim-lit nightmare,
Pass pocked and terraced, ruined Berlin turrets,
And, after the dark waste and the row of search-lights,
The final river, approach the "protective" wall
Until, near the floodlit gate and the outstretched angel,
The blaze of jumping neon thinks unrepressed words.
Behind those squinting eyes is a schizophrenic's mind;
How but by containing both sides, can we heal
This split down the mind of Europe and the world?

[lines 249–302, People's Square, and vision of a united Europe and world, a World State]

The old men huddled, the woman slunk away;
And, standing at dusk on the crowded People's Square
As on the grey cortex of a great remoulded brain
While, like happy slogans, obedient faces
Wandered painlessly round and round against sterilized museums,
I knew, only in such nightmare cities of ordered streets
And thoughts like lighted windows in Ministry hotels,
Could that cross be a centre, like the Forbidden City –
Like the Archangel Cathedral within the Kremlin wall
The Church must be denied to contain Christ's vision.
Otherwise, established ally of that Welfare board,
In a dwindling parish of tired, habitual aims
And loudmouth individuals whose only quest
Is for a group of skirts near the broken kiosk,
The vicar raffles liquor in the crumbling porch,
And the visionary walks apart in deep forests;
And where, oh where, is that spiritual way of life
That takes for granted icons and sad-eyed Saints,
And could drive all those howling slogans in Trafalgar Square
And shame to shallowness the Red inquisitors
Who, in agonised compassion, wade in blood,
And then, to save the many from their own tormented brains,
Degrade them beneath the values of compulsorily happy States?

                    Indifferent Tsars and tyrants,
                    Compassionate inquisitors;
                    Can nothing bring together
                    Enslaving Leader and Saint?
                    As I stared at the murals' centre
                    In this Cathedral-tomb,
                    The Archangel became a Shadow
                    With a sword and wings outstretched,
                    And I saw in the second icon
                    The future of the West,
                    From the Atlantic to the Urals:
                    Into the People's Square,
                    From the Cathedral gates,
                    File in the morning rush-hour
                    An *élite* of self-made Saints
                    Each still on the last hour's quest.

They reach the central banner
In the forum of statues and graves,
The great mazed *mandala*
Under which the supplicants wait;
Decades of contemplation
Show in their white-haired peace
As, trusting to perfect feelings,
They value each equal they greet;
Until, whispering on silence,
They glide to the Leaders' Hall,
Their hearts, with a World-Lord's wholeness,
At the centre of life, of all,
Their hearts where all past and future meet.

An outstretched angel of Paradisal vision,
And a dream of an escapist dreamer in an impossible heat.

11, 20 June – 23 July 1966; revised in 1968

An Inner Home

"The forest which surrounds them is their godhead."

(From a review by MR. GEOFFREY GORER of *Wayward Servants*,
a book on the Mbuti pygmies in the Ituri rain forest, N.E. Congo.)

I have followed the Waltham stream:
Winding through sunny meadows,
Stilled by lilies and reeds
It seems a long way from
King Harold's rough-hewn bridge
And Edward's two arches,
Till under the Abbey's tower
On either side of stone
Under two modern humped bridges
With a sudden tugging of weed
The stillness overflows
To plunge in a cascade down
And froth into gentle channels
And trickle underground
And I turned away in a panic,
There was weed in my hair and toes.

That child, who, sick from fleeing a baying form,
Lay on the humming Stubbles near the Witches' Copse
Like a sacrificial victim near Stonehenge,
And, seeing a six-spot burnet, suddenly felt secure,
Walled round and alone in a forest enclosure;
That child seemed a long way from that adolescent
Who, sick at having seen the universe
In a string of bubbles blown through a child's wire-ring,
Stood in Loughton Camp among writhing pollards
Like nerve tracts rising to a memory rooted in
The skulls of Boadicea's unconscious dead,
And, under the dark grey cortex, distinctly heard
The silence beneath the distant hum of cars
And knew himself under the patter of falling leaves;
And that young man, who, retching at one last sigh,
Stood where he fished as a child with sewn flour-bags
And skidded to the island on an icy slide
And stared past his reflection in the gravel pit
As if seeking an image in an unconscious mind,
Until his darkness split, and in the autumn sun
The pond blazed in an unknowable revelation,
He said Yes, and, looking back through the blinding leaves,
He longed to be a statue between the two ponds
And gaze for ever on the thrusting of those trees;
Or that poet, who, sick with impending exile,
Having driven round Lippitt's Hill to Tennyson's estate,
Crunched broken glass in the littered Witches' Copse
Alone in the centre of a living *mandala*,
And knew, although before him was approaching stone,
Like a hermit enfolded in a godhead he projects
He would always be enfolded in this Forest,
In this unchangeable image of an inner home.

Like the tree-enfolded face a still stream reflects
Below humped bridges where waving weed is pressed
Before it plunges down and is lost in foam.

13–16 October 1966; revised in 1968 (?)

6

from *Old Man in a Circle* (1967)
from Old Man in a Circle

"The year is the prototype of all cyclic processes (the day, the span of human life, the rise and fall of a culture, the cosmic cycle, etc.)... The year (or the wheel of the Zodiac) is usually represented by the figure of an old man in a circle."

J.E. CIRLOT, *A Dictionary of Symbols*

[lines 1–22, the cyclic year shown in a medieval miniature as a bandy-legged old man in a circle (God) surrounded by signs of the Zodiac, and the birth of a new age]

The spring has gone, and the hot sun
Has grown a crop of glass and iron
Among the Gothic spires of Europe.
Steamboats have carried steel harvests
To ore-rich jungles, capitalists
Have driven loin-clothed gangs to chop
And wound the earth with mines and railways,
And guarded their investments: the flag flies.
But in the centre of this Wheel of Life, a plump
Old man with ape legs weighs
Sun and moon like a juggler with bent knees,
And now, with an earth-shaking bump
Like a balance-pan weighed down, the Year
Turns towards Aquarius. And see, under
A rising moon lie the ruins of ten
Western empires like palaces
After an earthquake. The spires are in pieces,
All is multiple, mirrors and stone. Then
Pale and sickly abstract faces. In the middle
Hands clutch round a courtyard fire. All huddle
For the long dark night of the Year's return
At Pisces' end and a new age's dawn.

[lines 23–149, 183–205, the British Empire's decay and follies of national decline]

From the heels of Europe, a low black cloud of dust
Hung like a shroud across a blood-red Greenwich sun,
And in a New York noon men counted bags of gold

While a white-flagged convoy steamed over a crimson ocean;
And now, under planes that hang like flies in a billowing smoke,
In a ghastly, red-brown light, the scorched horizon glows,
The Prince of Wales sinks, the Midway victors cheer,
And now, in smouldering ruins, while Red tanks crawl,
The protector of Europe waits like a butler on the American elbow,
Waives his indemnities under a boiling mushroom cloud;
Shivering in snow, in a power-cut early dark
A threadbare rationed people queues for coal –
I see lorries leaving Greece, and GIs trundling in,
I see flurries of dollar bills, like autumn leaves, in eighteen cities,
And flights of Allied planes heading for Berlin,
I see lights going on in Hindu and Moslem India, in Ceylon and Burma,
I see lights going on in Palestine and Iraq, and the sun setting over Africa,
I see a servant saying "Careful" in Korea, and piqued at his master
For befriending the plaintiff who lost him his fortune,
I see twilight in Malaya, in Cyprus, in Suez,
And a dolled-up Cnut stopping the night with a policeman's palm
And his master saying "Fool, can an old man stop the earth?
Wind up the clocks, for your dark is our morning."
I see a black cloud advancing from the East, and eyes turning West,
I see a giant and a shrivelled dwarf under a Bahaman sun.
I see deserted streets and skeletons shuddering at a car backfire,
Trapped far from Cuba between orange and white night,
I see a black cloud racing up from the South
And thirteen lights going on in Africa, as in a block of council flats,
In Gold Coast and Nigeria, Tanganyika, Sierra Leone,
In Uganda and Kenya, Zanzibar and Nyasaland,
In Zambia and Gambia, Bechuana- and Basuto- and Swazi-land,
I see lights going on in Algeria, the Congo, Libya,
I see a thundercloud over the western horizon,
Over Jamaica and Trinidad, over British Guiana,
I see twilight in Aden, in Rhodesia, and frowns in a conference chamber,
I see Hindu and Moslem embrace under a hammer and sickle,
I see Common Wealth leaders flinging dollars to their poor,
I see Marlborough House a museum, and, outside the wall of Europe,
A suffering servant in motley, rejected of men
Talking to himself, saying "Careful in Hanoi," as, with one last shaft,
On the Falklands and Fiji, Hong Kong, Mauritius, and the Rock,
The curved orb slid into the sea, and the land grew suddenly dark.
Northern Ireland, Mozambique…. Panama, Iraq….

⌐ The golden sun set and a moon tinted all silver.
I heard a voice cry, "Watchman, what of the night?"
"Rise and fall," the watchman said, "rise and fall:
The morning cometh, and also the night –
The Habsburgs rose and sank into the night,
The British rose and shone against the night."

O Churchill.
There is silence in Whitehall
Save for the muffled drums;
The flag-draped gun-carriage crawls;
Sailors with reversed guns;
The launch moans up the river,
The cranes dip in homage
Under a fly-past to Rule Britannia
And the passing of an Age.

Put another nickel in
In poor old Winnie's treacle tin
Screeched "a Jutland veteran" with a black peg leg
And all down Piccadilly, the indomitable Grand Fleet steamed,
71 battleships and battlecruisers, 118 cruisers,
147 destroyers and 76 submarines;
And on the dreadnoughts our guardian angels sang
"Rule Britannia, Britannia rules the seas."
O 15 St James's Square, O Edward the Seventh,
Clyde, Scott and Franklin, Burgoyne and Lord Lawrence,
Like a gallery of summer ghosts in the winter dark.
Ah Palmerston! Leaving the HQ of de Gaulle's Free French,
Sauntering down the Waterloo steps
And meandering along the Mall to the Admiralty Arch –

skyyyyboltbluewaterstreaktsrtwoooo,
A pair of F-111s skimmed like swallows underneath
Where Vulcan and Victor, coupling blue steel wings,
Droned towards the warning web at Fylingdales,
And, near Holy Loch and closed-down shipping yards,
Disregarded the fish with the independent fins,
The Polaris sub with the interdependent scales.

Aegospotami and Midway. Ah the maritime:
One blink and a whole armada is knocked to bits

Or sold abroad, or stored, as "obsolete",
And shipless Admirals' voices float from aerials
To 4 aircraft carriers, 2 commando ships,
2 cruisers and a few destroyers and frigates –
O Senior Service.
As I left Downing Street during the Seamen's Strike,
Big Ben peered over the trees and pulled a face
And Nelson raised an arm.

In an angry crowd of cotton and motor workers
As I waited for the "grim-faced" union leaders,
Sighing over the Times front page, while, on a transistor,
A newscaster told of uproars in Parliament –
As I shook my head
An NAB man twitched my sleeve, and said:
"We're much better off now than we were after the war, mate.
Look at them all these days, with their mini-skirts and their records.
We went to Austria again this year, on the cross-channel steamer,
Why, I got a hundred quid tape recorder last week,
And we'll soon have made the last payment on the car,
And now our Jimmy's left school he's bringing in twelve pound a week
And that means Vi can go to the bingo parlour now and again for a
       little flutter,
She couldn't do that just after the war, you know, not bloody likely.
Empire meant nothing to ninety per cent of us, except wars.
I had a brother. Killed in Cyprus, he was, and what good the Empire
       do him?
No, the Empire was a drag, mate, and we was lucky to chuck it,
And you don't wanta worry about what's happening here, this is just
       stop-go.
No, we're all right, mate, we're more prosperous than we've ever been."

But round the corner on the blackened Treasury wall
Alongside RHODESIA WHITE I saw
MENE, MENE TEKEL PERES, and I was appalled.
(Many, many shekels – perlease.)
              "The-Tax-man's-tak-en-all-my-dough
              And-left-me-in-my-state-ly-home,
              La-zing-on-a-sun-ny-afternoon,"
Sang Lord Roberts the landowner with shoulder-length hair.
Beside him, under the equestrian statue in a packed Trafalgar Square,
Slouched Sir Eric Porter, the civil servant's son,

And, yawning with one hand limp on an ND banner,
The Marxist grandson of a Tory Chancellor,
Toby Long, a praefect at Winchester;
"Up the workers," shouted Roberts, "up the Viet Cong,"
And nearby a scowling nobody with a spurned and rejected air
Cocked his *Look Back* with a revolutionary's stare –
"'*Vous vous êtes donné la peine de naître*,'" he sneered,
"Screaming Lord Roberts with your shoulder-length hair."…

          Ring a ring a roses –

O how is this faithful city become a harlot.
As under purple flowers rooted in basement cellars
Your memory still shudders at a siren's whine
And breathes fresh air beneath your festering wounds;
But now you are charcoal and bubonic black, and you are weary, weary,
The skin on your face is peeling, like mildewed yellow parchment,
You are full of sores, and germs scuffle under your crumbling spires,
Foreign bodies clog your veins and choke your aorta,
Fevers throb hot and cold in your indecisive brain,
The whole head is sick, and the whole heart faint,
Your coins show an outline Queen, here are smudged Churchillian crowns,
And you burn to the pealing rooftops with rosy rings;
Ah London, your sins are as crimson, your silver like impure snow,
Your moons rise on feasts of indulgence, all varieties of vanity,
Two decades your ingrown flesh has turned grey and rotted with dirt,
Wash you, make you clean.

O how the Assyrians advance from the East….
I see the peoples of Eastern Europe take to the streets,
I see the Russian empire crumbling into dust,
O the Cold War. You resisted

While you rotted in bitter freedom.

Make you clean.

[lines 353–380, the renewal of European civilisation]

          Because the creative few
          Found an image for the Fire

Our civilisation grew
With the thrust of a Gothic spire;
The descent round the old man's light side
To the ape-feet turn of the Year
Went through a Sistine giant's "pride",
A bull burnt in a square,
Through a root and branch Puritan,
A Copernican measuring-rod
And men made of steam and iron
To a static, fairy-tale God.
Carved images in Chartres
Attract no energy,
The Cathedral has lost its art
To inspire growth in the many,
And with such aimless leaders
And grey-suited diplomats
And doubting philosophers,
What could we do but contract?
We must reject them all
And dredge up for our dying Age
The tight-lipped growth ideal
Of the Fire-gazer's message
To carry it in its ascent
Up the old man's dark left side,
Up the backbone ligament,
Back to the bearded, Byzantine pride.

[lines 415–440, the crash of an old European age and the birth of a new European age]

In this Wheel two Ages hang in the balance,
And in between is an anguish, like the Black Death
And war and schism between manor and court;
O the dust as the nations crash like falling walls,
O the wailing as a settled system crumbles
Like a bombed-out Archduke's palace or Cathedral,
O the rage as tormented, questioning men
Shake fists at crown and flag and tradition
Like "barbarians" jeering at "Gothic".
Dynasties have crashed, empires have crashed,
And over the rubble of nations, near the Ministry
With the seventh-floor lights in the Brussels snow,
Towers a skyscraper with a giant beam,

The Cathedral-Hall, the Lighthouse of Europe
Whose new system mirrors a reborn soul,
A Counter-Renaissance; we are the rebuilders.
After the Mannerist sickness, our images
Throb with Baroque, with the whole of Being,
We are the new mystics.
I heard a cry
From the old Professor's darkened room,
"The Age of Reason is dead";
But the deaf stared on, intent on measuring the moon.
Compasses, dividers, and rules to measure yawns;
We have flown over mountains like chopped, veined cubes,
We have seen angular deserts under green Siberian dawns.

[lines 465–516, the new Europe's Shadow over Mount Brocken]

From the mountainside I saw a giant Europe burst into light;
Descending, I walked in the neon-streets of its automated cities:
London, Brussels, Paris, Amsterdam, Berlin,
Rome, Vienna, Prague, Warsaw, Budapest, Bucharest;
They throbbed with a dull pounding, as if from an iron lung,
And, as from a plastic heart, conveyor belts carried things
That were fed into glass tissues by arms and shoots and slides:
The people were calm and gentle, and there was a peace in the air.
Then I came to a City of Images, and I stood in the station
And stopped a passer-by who looked like myself.
"Our time?" he said, recognising me, "Things aren't all that
Much better than in other uniform times, I shouldn't imagine.
Oh yes, there has been progress in the macrocosm – these machines
    and amenities;
There has been amelioration, and everyone is cared for now;
But nothing lasts. Buildings decay, machinery crumbles; money gets short,
    squalor sets in.
Cities sink into the earth. Rise and fall, rise and fall."
I closed my eyes in Whitehall and sighed:
O the Treasury wall, O the broken spires,
Black black black is the skin of this dying city;
O the agony in the body, the sores, the sores
As old John Bull dies away from his greatness like a sick ego,

And, mid dreams of dreadnoughts and distant fires,
Hears remote voices like leaves shaken in the wind;
O the torture as the factories run down for lack of oil,
O the anguish of blasted out city-windows –
O Israel, O Portugal.
O the torment in this dying, before it is understood!
Did not Harold weep when he prayed before the Waltham stone?
O this giant Europe, these nations as federal states.

    Time has gone beyond
    Winged Kairos with the scales;
    On the golden zodiac clock
    On Anne Boleyn's rose-web gate;
    The black hand with the sun
    Has crept up the dark Year,
    Like a blood clot that will stun
    An old man's unpurified stare.
    But, at the first glimmer of dawn,
    While the winter sun is low,
    Above the wind-beaten watchman
    On the rocky mountain brow,
    High over the East-West border,
    On the cloudy skies of Europe, newly born,
    Raising his arms like a Conductor
    With a cleansed Archangel's scorn,
    A lone huntsman hails the future:
    The giant Brocken Shadow sounds his horn!

O the giddy hopes as a civilisation gathers its spirit together,
O the grandeur of the new God it throws across the heavens!
O the sadness of the far-seeing huntsman, as undeceived,
He blows the last post for the eventual extinguishing of the
    Lighthouse beacon!

20 December 1966 – 13 March 1967; revised in 1968

7

from *The Gates of Hell* (1969–1972)
Orpheus Across the Frontier

At five, hens squawked, dogs barked. I was woken by shots.
There were more shots at six, at nine the Tripoli street
Was deserted, the police had gone. Idle knots
Of people on the corners held radios, a discreet
Armoured car dropped soldiers who aimed at
The sky. Then someone said, "There's been a *coup*."
And the shooting.... For a day we crouched in our flat
While the bullets whined, then we were allowed out to
Shop. Army men fired shots in the air every hundred yards,
In the supermarket, soldiers shouted, "No beer."
They wore plimsolls, they crept in, our "freedom's guards".
The skull-capped greengrocer muttered, "King good man here."
So history changes by stealth, and lacking the power or
Will to crush it, the West's frontier contracts a little more.

Ghadames Spring
(Poems like Bubbles)

I drive through the desert, two days of sand
And Czech lorries, till I reach the necropolis
Of Ghadames – a hill of tombs, palms and
Tuareg who live underground in this oasis,
In a Hell of chambered tunnels. Near the Hotel,
Glory! I sit by the spring, on polished stone
Steps: clear water, and green weed; a square well
And bubbles wobbling up in the sun. A lone
Tuareg peeps through his head-scarf's slit, and I know
That at last my hopelessness is over. As old
As the Great Pyramid, this overflow
Fills Roman baths where toga-ed citizens still hold
Court. I have found the forgiving spring in my heart
Whose Divine bubbles pour up into art.

On the Waterfront

I walk on the waterfront, after the Libyan *coup*.
Arabs sit in the cafés, the sea splashes.
I walk tensely to this latest rendezvous.
I am a target. If I am shot now, my ashes
Will be "the remains of a Westerner who was rushed,
Who represented a decolonising power
That has been liberal when it would once have crushed".
I am its response. At a dark, secretive hour
I wait for the car, the hand that will give me a wad
So I can go to the supermarket and drop the bright
Notes among tins; enough to buy a squad
Of men for a civilisation that has lost the will to fight.
I am a lost mystic, who should be kneeling in a church,
Not loitering here on the waterfront, on the Devil's research.

Journey's End

So as always I, wounded, seek out Essex,
This green-gated house with its pear tree on the lawn
Under whose eaves I slept, heard tappings that vex,
Strange creaks, cowered from shadows before dawn
As a boy. Now all is October gloom and scorn.
Dusk darkens this dining-room, I sit by the piano
Alone, deaf as this Beethoven to your "No".
I wander out to the garden. And suddenly there
I see myself: a spider hanging in the pear.

Like a spider exuding thread, I wove a web
And wrapped you in a beautiful silk cocoon,
I rolled you into a ball and held you, till the ebb
Of autumn blew you free, my mayfly. Too soon
You turned bitter, bitter, and headed for the moon.
I stand on the darkening lawn, and wish that I
Could leave this wretched flesh, and quietly die
Into those roots and twigs and leaves, so that my tears
Could drop each anniversary autumn as ripened pears.

Here I must make up my mind, within this fence,
Among these Michaelmas daisies, under these

Rosy apples, by this wet bark; I must make sense
Of choosing against my will what I dread, to please
You. I feel my trunk and next year's blossom slowly freeze
In the chill night. You were not true – true to yourself
In that – yet I loved you. Like pears on the cellar shelf,
My tears…. But no, these stars the night weeps – for you
My branches shake them down, like drops of morning dew.

Flow: Moon and Sea

I loved you like the tortoise-shell
You loved up on the Downs with me.
The light leaps off your Worthing sea
Like shoals of leaping mackerel.

The sea flows like a bent hawthorn.
Now, up the night, the harvest moon
Floats and sails like a child's balloon
Over this darkly rippled corn.

This glow behind the moon and sea
Affects my way of seeing.
What, oh what is happening to my being?
I thrill to a pebble's flow, and a bumble-bee.

3–4 September 1971; revised 7 December 1972

Visions: Golden Flower, Celestial Curtain

That weekend I lay down and breathed at twilight,
Looked into my closed eyes, saw white light flowing
Upwards…, a tree of white fire, flickering.
Then a spring opened in me, for an hour bright
Visions wobbled up like bubbles: from a great height
A centre of light, a gold-white flower, shining
Like a dahlia, the centre and source of my being;
A chrysanthemum; a sun; a fountain of white
Light; strange patterns; old masters I was not certain
I had seen before; old gods. I was refreshed, after this
I fell on my knees in the dark, and breathed "I surrender"
To the white point. It changed into a celestial curtain

Blown in the wind, like the *aurora borealis*.
I feel limp, an afterglow in each moist finger.

10 September 1971

More Visions: The Judge

I buried my eyes in the crook of my arm and saw
A dome of light like a spider's web, an old
Yellow and purple tomb; later a gold
Death-mask, the face of God. I felt shaky, more
Like a child that has taken tottering steps, before
I walked to the Brompton Oratory to hold
A candle lit from the eternal basket, and fold
My hands. Later I saw an egg; a mirror;
Christ on a cross; a flaming devil who trod
Down a haloed saint. Visions poured up: a globe;
A yellow rose; black thorns against a sundial;
A foetal child, and a crowned Eastern god.
Now – o frontal Christ in thorns and a red-brown robe
Gathered with a pin at the chin, help me through this trial!

11 September 1971

Visions: The Pit and the Moon

Frostleaves on glass. Hints of a white flower
And suns and shafts of light. My arms must free
These eyes, black out the dark. A starless, revea-
-ling night, an outline of a rim, a tower
As if I look up from a dungeon-pit, in the power
Of Hell. A point of white light breaks, I see
A long white-hot line, like the trunk of a tree
Down the centre of my being. "I surrender," cower-
-ing, I gasp, and the light swells into a city
Moon. Squatting, I feel a refreshing stimulation,
I feel wobbly at the knees, but now I know
That time is the cutting up of Eternity
Which can be known through this silence. My imagination
Relieves this prison stretch with this mystic glow.

11 September 1971

February Budding, Half-Term

The buds are flecks, hawthorn and beech,
A great tit see-saws near its nest,
A squirrel listens from a branch,
Like my daughter, too quiet for speech.

On Strawberry Hill, a sky like smoke
Threatens the suffering, tearless twigs
And looking at this mossy knoll
I know the endurance of a much-gnarled oak.

I feel the rising rhythm thud,
As I scuffle through last year's leaves
The scales unfold around my grief
And burst into joyful bud.

11 November 1972

Visions: Raid on the Gold Mine

I have been seized by God. I felt the Divine
Presence steal up from the shaft below and fill
My soul, slow my breathing, locking me still
As a fakir. I lay and descended down my spine,
Surrendered the deepest crevices of my gold mine
Of visions – golden furniture, temples with thrill-
-ing columns, a brown head, the celestial curtain – till
I saw a diamond in luminous blue light shine,
The first time I have seen the colour blue
In my secret excavations. Then the Golden Flower,
And an hour of flashing down my inner night
Like a dawn. Slowly the raiding Presence withdrew,
And now I record it in this "newspaper
Of the Eternal"; lifted to a great height.

8 April 1972

The Furnace

Again I have been rapt. Aglow with Fire
I sat and looked at the lights of Chelsea,
At dusky windows, and felt God enfold me,
I sat rigid, then lay down full of desire.
I murmured, "I have surrendered entirely.
Enter me." I was breathing heavily,
Possessed, in union, till in a sighing glee,
Slipping away, a voice said, "Your loss will inspire
A dark generation, I will give you greatness."
I do not want self-glory. On these fired pots
I paint the mystic truths, as they are revealed
In my vision. Now I know I will have less
Going out. From my window I look down. Among lots
Of plane trees, a white magnolia. I am healed.

17 April 1972

Vision: Snatched by God, a Blue Light

I have been snatched by God. Idly looking
Over Chelsea, I felt peace rise, attack
And enfold me. I put down my spoon, pushed slack-
-ly at my chair, sat cross-legged, hands clasped, gazing.
Soon I was breathing deeply and sinking
Into a trance, locked rigid – glory! From that black
Night of closed eyes, a pale blue light shone back,
And became a dazzling white like a diamond shining
In the sun. I sighed out in ecstasy
As if I were throbbing in a pleasure-dance,
Stiffly I rose and lay on my bed an hour
And the Light came and went, only more faintly
This time. Then I came slowly out of my trance,
And the rest of the day have felt full of inner power.

22 April 1972

8

from *The Flight* (1970)
from The Flight

"Yaren soran soran soran soran soran;
Oki no kamone ni shiodoki kikeba,
Watasha tatsu tori, nami ni kike."

"When asked about the tide, the seagull replied,
'I'm flying away, please ask the waves.'"
(Japanese fishermen's song)

[lines 1–98, childhood memories of Epping Forest]

I A Green Country

Apples are green under a fluttering flag,
Green are my daughter's eyes, green is her breath.
Green are the children among brambles and ferns,
"Oi-olly-ocky," they yodel, "I see Liz,"
Stealing on tiptoe like scrumping thieves.
And let us run together now, across the road, down the hill to the Forest,
To where the stream trickles from the long arched tunnel,
And, legs astride it, hands on the curved walls, walk bow-legged
And stand under the grating overflow, as if in a Hellish dungeon.
I took you there, and found a Victorian penny.
O this Blackweir pool, where I fished up green frogs in flour-bag nets!
We scuffled up through leaves, leaving the water boatmen and dragonflies,
And at a meeting of green paths plunged right, into beeches,
I held your hand and said, "Look, the banks,"
And we ran on back into blackbirds and sticklebacks and newts,
And there, still under water-lilies, was the pond I had not found for two
    decades,*
The Lost Pond!

        Apples, pears, wasps.
I came from the Essex flats, green fields round beech thickets.
When the daisies were humming with bees, I lay under summer skies.
I see a clearing where I kicked a ball, where my father swung his lame leg

And scored with a toe-punt. There I picnicked with two boys from the
    first form.
I ran through the Forest in the summers.
I caught caddice in the ponds, I had a glass aquarium that cracked at
    the top,
And green slime slopped down the sides. Near a fallen apple tree
I grew tall to the trembling of leaves. Upstairs, under green eaves,
I sniffed my death. I said to my brother
"I will live to be a hundred," clicking and reshutting the small black
    cupboard door
Until a voice from downstairs called "Go to sleep."

Brown is the earth of this Clay Country, and hard under frost,
Hard are the fields around Chigwell where we were sent on walks,
Stepping over iced hoof-marks in the frozen mud,
O those glistening stiles and brown dark thorns!
Crisp are the leaves of the heart in winter
When the bonfires smoulder no more. Bright is the air,
Remote the golden suns smashed across the icy pool of the sky.
Fingers are numb, cheeks pink, breath misty, clear.

I and my grandfather walked for tobacco in fog,
He fell and blood streamed from his white hair.
He had a stub of a finger he lost in a Canadian saw-mill.
Later my father took me for a walk. As we left the gate
The siren wailed. We wheeled to a white white flash,
The whole street shook, the windows clattering out.
Five bombs had fallen. Two houses up the road were annihilated
And the cricket field had a hole in it. The war –
I lay in a Morrison shelter and read books, swapped foreign notes,
While in the blue air puffs of smoke ended pilots.
When I moved home, I carried my battleship.

Red bricks and lilacs droop over the wooden shed.
On our rockeries, young hearts have wept and bled.
Ivy, and a garden hose.
A home is a rattling front door,
A broken flowerpot under a scarlet rose.

Green are the clumps of Warren Hill, green and scummy pond,
Green are the Oaklands fields, green round buttercups,
Green are those fields where children squat in camps,

Green is the ride down Nursery Road, purple the thistles,
Green are the Stubbles and the open heath,
Green is Robin Hood Lane, green past Strawberry Hill,
Green and brown are the two gravel pit ponds,
Green is High Beach, green around Turpin's Cave where beechburrs cling
    to hair,
Green round Lippett's Hill and the Owl, green the fields beyond,
Green back through Boadicea's camp, where you climbed the brown mud walls,
Brown are the leaves round the hollow tree we climbed,
Green along Staples Hill, where we shuffled through leaves to the
    brown stream,
Green past the Wheatsheaf, green up to Baldwin's Hill
Where we ran down to Monk Wood, and you were remote from me;
Green holly, green beech leaves, green oaks, and only the trunks and banks
    are brown.
Green to the Wake Arms, green to the Epping Bell,
Green down Ivy Chimneys, green up Flux's Lane
Between the poplars and the farmers' fields
Green are the trees round distant Coopersale Hall,
Green are the fields of Abridge and Chigwell,
Green is Roding Valley before hilly Debden,
Green fields, wide open, back into cratered Loughton,
A green country with hosannah-ing pollards, arms raised in jubilation.
And green is that gate, green the lime trees that hide the green porch door,
Green is that house of echoes. O how you despised my cradle!
You found the buildings false, the people mean and ugly,
But couldn't you feel the kiss in the swishing wind?

O the medieval churches of rural Essex:
Magdalen Laver, Abbess Roding, Great Canfield
With its 1250 fresco of Mary offering her breast;
A flat country of fields of wheat and rape
And Elizabethan barns and sleepy hamlets,
3 Lavers, 8 Rodings and 2 Easters.
O Essex, I love your green and drowsy haunts!
All this we have known in the green time, and more.
These are the places I return to now, in my heart-sorrow,
These Essex flats. Here I stood, waiting to meet you,
Here I knew you, in a green glade among beechnuts.
Here the city is a boot among yellow lilies, an iron roof that blocks the sun.
All this I left for the city, with a young man's impatience;
All this I left, seeking to meet a loyal woman.

I have starlings under my sunflowers.
I love the trunks of these pear-trees, whose ant-bands are sticky.
O these images that haunt me, that I fly to, to which I cling!

August–September 1970

9

from *A Bulb in Winter* (1972–1974)
The Sun
(Remembrance Day)

This morning's winter sun put out his head
Over the trees of Hereford Square
Like an overalled painter asking the time
Near his dazzling handiwork.
I was out for the Sunday papers, and
All around Gloucester Road Station
People stumbled southwards, their hands in front
Of their eyes like desert look-outs
And wandered smiling northwards, silhouettes
Of twos in a yellow brilliance.
I could not look. I crossed the road to the shade.
But then I had to walk back, stand
Outside the International and watch
The bare trees, the buildings, children,
The men fixing the burglar alarm in
The Post Office – angels splashed in
Golden paint. While the sun shook down his hair
And greeted me with a blinding wink.

11 November 1973

Ode: Spring

Horace, I have been reading about your spring.
What great themes you and Catullus found, what sense,
What skill in hexameters and hendecasyllabics,
What banality occupies today's audience.

Your Bandusian spring I saw one spring afternoon.

41

I drank its cold water sixteen years ago,
In your Sabine hills. I am limpid, pure, I gush
With refreshing liquor for others to know.

Maecenas gave you your farm. How nice if the wind,
Rearranging, stirring these winter leaves,
Handed me a country spring to make famous.
I have only the gushing of this spring between my sleeves.

20 December 1973

IO

from *The Pilgrim in the Garden* (1973–1974)
(23 Elegies for England)

Strawberry Hill
14th Elegy

At the top of the drizzling hill, a break in the trees.
We park on mud and cross the road in the breeze
To bulrushes, a brown pond, yellow lilies. It is cool.
We could stay here all morning at the Horseman's Pool,
But it is too near the road. We take the Forest track
Past the log. There are stones in the clay. We turn
Into bracken, hawthorn and beech. And now, beyond the holly
A pond within gorse and birch, under a fallen tree.

This pond has seen the agonies of the seasons:
How Essex fathers died in autumn; the reasons
Young men chose to marry, be exiled, live alone,
And their returns – all these the pond has known.
The stealings-up through sawing grasshoppers,
The secret comings far from eavesdroppers.
It has heard small girls crouching in these gnarled roots.
And dreamt of searches, and the netting of speckled newts.

Now there are sounds of autumnal raindrops,
Children's voices. Ducks clack. Dogs splash, a robin hops.
Two horses take their drink. Now a rustle rolls
Through the silver birch, where in spring, tadpoles

Cluster like thorns round a submerged stick. One afternoon
The shimmering mirror, teeming with the leaves of June,
Blazed into flames. My heart gave a bound
Behind the flickering face drowning in clouds, resting on ground.

Today a touch of sadness in the summer tint:
My daughter is going abroad tomorrow. A hint
Of absence only as she skips round this gravel pit.
It reflects the Eternal. Across its stillness flit
The changing moods and shadows of our time,
Newt and lily months. Sticklebacks stirring slime.
My heart is in this Forest, its gravel is like honey;
And the heather beyond the gorse smells of strawberry.

All is dark, but I teem with life. The hidden sun
Can join the heights and the depths, fuse into one
The clouded ground. Here in its higher spirit
I can be still, and join with the blue sunlit
Muse and inspiration that blows through all.
The one lily, raised above the water, is a call
To Essex men to leave their cars, and say Yes
To this divine image of well-bordered stillness!

4 August 1974

I I

from *The Night-Sea Crossing* (1974)
from The Night-Sea Crossing

[lines 1–39, 118–148, the night voyage of a man crossing to the Underworld]

Night. Sea and stars, a trail of foaming wake,
The dark shape of the ship, engines throbbing.
I lean over the rail, the dark troughs pass,
I perch on this rail like a hook-billed gull
Resting from the exertions of a long flight.
I am tired, tired. My heart thumps and pounds
To the pistons of the engines. Is this how it will end,
Out on the dark sea, under star-dripping night,
Apart from loved ones, alone? Among strangers

Who will not care? Is this my destination?
I have learned to fear the thickening in my blood.
If this artery should widen and release the clot
So that it floats up and blocks the heart, then what?
Where will the sea be, where this dark night then?
Eternal nothingness, blackness for always –
Will I be that before the dawn steals up,
Just a darkness? I am ready to let go,
Will not seek help – much good that would do me here –
But I wonder. Waves lapping at the sides,
Sunlight on sea-hills, pines bent by the wind,
Gulls wheeling round the harbour fish-market,
Her smile as she lay down – are all these things
Mere sunshafts before nightfall? No more than that?
What does my life amount to? What meaning
Have these images? Out on this heaving water
I remember life and make my peace with death.

And yet I have known a calm
Where all is purpose, where the days and years
Are steps of a celestial staircase up to heaven
From suffering to joy. The ascent of history!
The meaning of prayer! Fold hands and breathe,
And breathe and breathe. And… sink into a silence.
Heart beats in unison with the universe,
Accepts it and is filled with ecstasy.
Breathe and breathe. Heart burns to a tree of fire.
White light. The vine. Does this make any difference?

I ask too many questions.
                    I look beyond the sunset….

What is death? Not knowing dragonfly wings
Or wind bending pines or the crimson rose.
I will let my soul unfold like a rose. What are
These fallen petals? My heart grows my spirit,
And round it this satin lushness of Unknowing.
And lo! outside the veil, such a sun! The light
Of holiness! I will be sinless to unfold my soul.
Let me breathe in rapture, like a summer sea
Washing the shingle, lapping at landing stage,

Tugging bladderwrack on a breakwater!
Let me breathe stones, let me drag back across my age.

Death is in the corner, hooded like a monk.
Death is creeping up on me. I feel the chill
Round my feet. Wash-wash at my port-window
This night-sea, foaming and flooding under me,
I cross it and pass over to the other side,
All must cross with me to that sinister slip of land.
Death, I will look at you, look at your face.
You hide round my bunk, you cling to the shadows,
But I will see you! I will see you.
Death the skeleton, skull in a monk's cowl,
Waiting to reap me, this growth from a jellied seed.

Crops of summer. Fields of wheat, orchards
Bending with fruit. Windfalls, wasps and ripeness.
The hot long grass of summer. The gnat-stream,
Dry mud like bone. Growth, all is growth, and I
Was a long day's dying.

The sea of minutes, hours, days, weeks and months
I am crossing. Heroes of old England
Were carried out on a barge at night. May I
Achieve an understanding in this dying heart.

1 2

from *Visions Near the Gates of Paradise* (1974–1975)
A Vision Near the Gates of Paradise

Hell is a dungeon like Wandsworth prison,
With a portcullis and gate clock. How many know
Paradise is a Cathedral a sun shines on?
We are admitted through studded doors, below
Statues of saints, to the sunshaft under a rose-
Window, where God sits in the centre. Bright
Planets surround Him, great saints. The blue that glows
In the petals of that Kingdom of azure light
Is Eternity's air. Here stand, Heaven streaming

Down on the bare floor. Paradise is a fire in the eyes.
Peep in this afternoon quiet, see the guarding
Angels dance and cavort like butterflies
Round the portal, welcoming each peaceful heart, flit-
-ting round new souls' petals, sipping each nectared spirit.

13

from *The Four Seasons* (1975)
from The Four Seasons
(A Sonata for Four Voices)

Each of the four voices explores one theme: a season; the spirit; memory;
and the decline of Western civilisation

[Summer, lines 1–12, 214–218, 261, 263–265]

I

The spring has set, and the first mosquitoes whine
In the West. O these images from summer! They rise
From water like chestnut candles, heavy, swollen,
In brilliant reds and greens. A stream through green fields
Where the swallow dives and skims, gnats dance. Twilight
Creeps under a giant elm. Blue irises
And buttercups, the satin of red roses
Where, on a log, a Red Admiral spreads its wings.
Lime-trees. Violets on the sea-cliff. Stitchwort
Like summer stars under a gold and crimson sun.
Golden windfalls under a harvest moon.
Neptune rises out of the water, wearing a garland of waves....

IV

A sigh for the sunset.
A skylark rises like a stone over these chalk-cliffs.
A pheasant scurries under the hedge as I drive past.
Ploughed fields and one lapwing.
The stars are flecks on the stone-egg of this universe....

A Red Admiral and a dragonfly....
Images spill through my fingers like frog spawn.
Dragonfly wings gleam on the shimmering pond.
I dribble childhood memories like a shuffling old man.

[Autumn, lines 245–258]

A sob for these fragments of civilisation.
After a night of heavy rain, the sun rose
Over Waterloo, burning the sea into ribs
Of copper, at noon shone over the largest
Empire the earth has known. At night I saw
The Union Jack dismembered. The crumbling
Sooty closes of Edinburgh's Royal Mile,
Or, like a bridge under construction,
Belfast's rainbow arch.
Said Mr. Widgeon, cigarette drooping from lips,
Not realising it is what you bring to it,
"I have no time for religion."
I am sad for this ruined civilisation
Which collapsed when its spirit vanished like a rainbow....

[Winter, lines 1–13]

I
Frost sparkles on fences and crisp white grass,
Whitens roofs, glazes windows with swirling leaves.
Feet crunch on frozen furrows, the ridged earth.
Ice in hoof-holes, breath floats into bare trees.
All is ribbed, spare. Twig has shed leaf, structure
Triumphs over tumbling outline. Cheeks are cold,
Nose is cold, fingers numb. This is a lean time,
All luxury and luxuriance pared down
To bark and bone, rib and ridge. From a white sky
Float the first few flecks of snow. December.
A distant carol. A fire flickers through a window,
And a Christmas tree with coloured fairy lights.
Faces shine from the branches of our society....

[Spring, lines 1–15, 377–405]

I

Buds drip from the beech trees. This gorse crackles,
Yellow laburnum flames. What a shower
Has fallen round my head! What a fire spits
With this new teeming, abundant intensity!
The earth is soft again, and sighs up shoots
For love, which flicker and blaze in the leaping joy.
For love, all is lush, tender, heady. The green
Grass is soft and young in this sharp sunlight.
Crocuses and snowdrops bask beside the Abbey,
A robin sings among the stone ruins.
A new, rejoicing time, for shoot and root
A new warmth, a new manifold, one surge.
Hosannah for this rain-fire! Spring fell in a shower today,
I saw buds like raindrops drip down an arched branch.
Eternity is the colour of a young green leaf....

Buds drip from the beech trees. Now blossom is like snow.
Now chestnut candles shine down the avenue.
Eternity is a flowering of blossom and bulb,
And I am now flowering after a long winter.
We are no longer torn, in our new self;
Spring images sprout like buds along the soul.
The water-clock plashes and splashes time,
The girl has apple blossom twined in her hair.
Time is the top of the stream that moves to the overflow,
Eternity is the still water below.
Time is the dying leaf, the crumbling city,
Eternity is the bud and renewing spring,
The spirit that rises out of the ashes.
In the imperial palace, all the clocks are wrong
For gaze at these hills ablaze with furze, these drops
Of dew on a spider's thread! These daises on the lawn!
O tadpole in the shallows, struggling shorewards,
Turn round and swim towards the white-hot sun!
O four wonderful seasons, and four voices
You will come again and again like the figures on this dome.
I am a tree in spring, I put out leaves
And sing in the wind, with the west wind's rhythms.
Eternity is the wind in the leaves of time.

O spring that renews the earth with this brief beauty,
Shine out of time, like the art in this circular frieze,
Shine in the ever-now of the memory,
Shine for the self-renewal of a singing destiny,
Shine like chestnut candles for our Golden Age,
And come again and again after the spring has set!

14

from *Lighthouse* (1975)
from Lighthouse
The Dark Night Easter Temptation of a Somewhat Saintly Man
(A contemplation inspired by the fugal form)

[lines 1–21, a retired diplomat staying in a hotel near a lighthouse is tempted to visit a wedding guest, conflict between spirit and sense]

A dark night. A sea-mist, no stars. As I peer
Out of this hotel window I am enfolded in cloud.
Out there, beyond the garden, waves crash and pound
The rocks, wind foams in trees. Out there, somewhere,
Is a sea-swept light. I cannot see it. Waves thump and roar.
Down the corridor my tired relations sleep
And will wake fresh for tomorrow's wedding feast.
The wind rattles my windows, rain lashes. A snore....
I alone am awake, splashed and blown by a storm from my old
Life, pacing far from the hidden flashing lamp
Of my new.
          And she is awake, in the end room at the back,
She is waiting up for me. O these cold
Desires! O these frothing appetites! I know
That appetites not whipped up are soothed to a breath,
I know the benefits of spiritual soberness
When the tranquil soul gives out a peaceful glow,
I know it mortifies concupiscence, subduing sense
For a spiritual calm, I know that marriage mortifies;
But o her breasts, o how her dark eyes smiled!
Let them spatter my soul with the spray of their turbulence.

[lines 231–239, he overcomes his temptation]

                                  … Can I really knock
On that closed door? She will say, "Who is it?" And can I shout
From here? What if she rings the night porter down-
-stairs, and there is a commotion? Will I say, "The clock –
I could not sleep and I came out to look at the time?"
The shame as doors open…. The humiliating scowls!
But no, the issue is not 'Dare I', or 'Can I last without',
But 'Am I to succumb?' or 'Can I – can I climb
Above this temptation, and resist it?'….

[lines 243–246, 251–262, his Dark Night while waiting on God]

Now I am back in my room. My sea-wanderings
Are over, I am home. A Dark Night, a sea-mist,
I am enfolded in cloud. The light is still hid-
-den out there. O these labyrinthine sufferings!…
In a tempestuous time a little more spray
Would have made no difference. The calm will still
Come. When I am old I will sit in such a window as this
And count recriminations, and I will say,
"That Easter I hesitated in a labyrinth corridor
When I should have acted with a clean white blow
Like the thrust of an ivory knife into an envelope,
And so I am alone." Here I sit and claw
My shilly-shallying soul, switching off the electric light,
Doubting the virtue I have won over vice, and the tri-
-umphant victory I gained over my darker mind,
Waiting on God, like a ship that is lost in the night.

[lines 295–315, the Light shines into his soul]

Night. I lie back and wait, and my warring quietens.
Lo! Through the blackness a round white light breaks, shines out.
O my lighthouse! The mist is lifting! The cloud
Lifts! O my beacon! You are still there! I must cleanse
The windows of my soul to receive this divine infusion
Till it flashes off, and I must climb back down into darkness

Again. I am so unfit. You are the radiant guest
I should visit. Shine on me, bring me to a conclusion.

Dawn is breaking. Sparrows chirp, sea-gulls scream.
The wind has dropped. Calm has returned again.
The sea is at rest. Come, let us go outside, take
The cliff path to the little church by the stream
That trickles on to the sand. Let us sit among the graves
And peacefully watch the fog lift over the placid
Rocks by the tower, whose light is now extinguished,
Like a candle, for the sun to take over. The waves
Are tranquil. Let us hear the wapping in the caves
Of the heart. Let us give thanks, for calm has returned.
We have united ourselves, till Dark falls and flesh burns.
Let our hearts burn in the sunrise with the fire of the waves!
Let us glory in the sunrise at the sparkling beyond the graves!

15

from *The Weed-Garden* (1975)
from The Weed-Garden
(A Heroic Symphony drafted in Cornwall)

This poem is a symphony in four movements: the first contains an exposition, a
development and a recapitulation; the second is in *Aria* form; the third contains
three minuets; and the fourth is in *Rondo* form

1. THE SOUL IN AUTUMN

[lines 1–5, astronaut's view of the earth]

Rinse your eyes with this floating astronaut's view
Of America down there, and Europe to the Urals;
The Western World like yellow cockleshells
Set in a green flower-garden round a blue
Puddle. You can just see Cornwall under cloud....

[lines 185–203, in the autumn of Western culture spring growth of flowers is not possible and gardeners give equal place to weeds]

Is there not a Golden Age outside, where there
Used to be a Hell?
                What matter if, for all
This autumn levelling for 'equal seeds'
And outer landscaping, or because of it,
Gone are the discrimination of the gardener, his
Pruning and training, so he now grows weeds,
And gone are restraint and discipline, which delayed
The growth of 'blooms'? Chickweed, groundsel, bellbind
Are nourished on the dry hard earth, why
Should not flower-seeds be choked? Gone are standards like the spade.
In the culture-garden, roses once unfolded,
But now, no 'élitist' growth; neat, ordered doubt
And nothing. Two thousand years of root and shoot
Disfigured man with a Golden Flower, remoulded
Him through Light. Where there was a 'Paradise'
Is there now a Hell? So what if the seven
Deadly weeds are allowed to grow unchecked
And are called by the names of flowers, which deny their vice?

3. A THOUGHT FOR WINTER

The Fertile Soil of Nature: January to June
[lines 404–487, how Nature can still nourish souls]

O how souls would grow if they used their eyes
And ears on the *flora* and *fauna*, the butterflies,
Birds, animals, flowers, hedgerows, trees and seas
That nourish throughout the year! See hive bees
Swarm in January, the male yew flowers, a mistle
Thrush and – hear – a great tit call near a thistle.
Gorse flames, ash twigs are in bud, and plu-plu-plu
Plu-plu-plu, sings a green woodpecker. Through
Honeysuckle buds, see, woodbine, blackthorn.
Coltsfoot hangs its head now it rains, trout spawn;
See the footprints of the water vole under ivy
Fruit, hear the vixen scream, the dog-fox yelp in the early

Dark. Now a brimstone flutters near elm and alder
Flower, and hazel catkins, and the yellowhammer
Chirps, "A little bit of bread and no cheese."
See footprints of squirrel and stoat. Red toadstools squeeze
Through near the barren strawberry. Jackdaws flap
Round the church tower, blue tits chase, twitter and scrap.
Wrens search for spiders. Now, from winter sleep
In rafters, Red Admirals and peacocks peep,
And small tortoiseshells. Sticky horse-chestnut buds
Unfold in the sunshine, a great white cloud scuds
Over blue. A squirrel and a wood pigeon feed
On fresh green leaves. See, thrushes and blackbirds speed
North. Wheatears and chiffchaffs flit. A chaffinch sings
From telegraph wires, a white bar on its wings.
Violets, sallow, and a hare. Marsh marigold
Blaze near some toad-spawn, a necklace of cold
Eggs. See: a mole, a shrew, and a sleepy hedgehog.
Now it is primrose time. By this Forest log,
Crab apple and guelder rose. Shh! a heron, in that copse.
See ravens on those crags, crossbills in the fir tree tops.
Now all Nature is awake. Cowslips, bluebells.
Oak, beech, walnut put out last leaves, and smells.
Willow catkins are out. Horse-tails. An orange tip,
A small copper, a holly blue, all skip
By a seven-spot ladybird eating greenflies
On a leaf. Newt eggs on pond weed, and in the skies,
Swallows, house-martins return, and the cuckoo.
See willow-warblers, blackcaps, nightingales through
Leaves, see nests of thrush and blackbird, and in high
Thorn, the domed nest of twigs of a magpie.
Now is the month of flowering trees and plants.
All is fresh and bright and green, the beech woods dance.
There are orchids in the meadow, and white hawthorn,
White candles on horse chestnut, bats above the lawn.
See, a blue tit is eating a caterpillar up,
While mayflies gad round a water buttercup.
Dandelions by a wasp's nest, fairy ring
Toadstools. Swifts scream and circle in the fine evening.
The hen-pheasant sits, the water forget-me-not
Blinks yellow eyes. In the birch and bracken a spot-
-ted flycatcher, a nightjar. A wealth of song!
Linnets, goldcrests, tits clamour all day long

For food. Young robins. Now the scent of new-
Cut hay being cocked and carted disturbs two
Rabbits. Weasels, rats, hedgehogs, partridges, stoats,
Owls fly for mice there, voles search near river boats
For young. Here pick woodruff and smell new-mown
Grass in winter. In field and wood, on ston-
-y moor and heath, by mountain and waterside:
Butterflies. White admirals, large blues glide,
Fritillaries, ringlets. Caterpillars teem,
Tortoiseshells' on stinging-nettles, lime-hawks' gleam
On lime trees. Birds have bedraggled feathers,
As they approach the moult. In certain weathers
See swallow skim, see the vermilion hind wing
Of a cinnabar moth near ragwort, fluttering
On the downs, or lacewing near the field rose.
Black slugs. A snail eats leaves near a garden hose,
Gnats and midges dance over the water butt,
The foliage teems with grubs round the summer-hut,
The garden is full of crawling, hopping pests.
Humble-bees in the foxgloves, a honey-bee quests
In the dead nettles. Scarlet poppies in the corn-
-fields, boletus in the woods, the newly born
Bullhead fish – "miller's thumb" – dart in the pond,
Near ferns: moonwort and adder's tongue. Beyond
Yellow water-lilies, red deer and badgers' earths.
The seashore is strewn with starfish and afterbirths:
Jellies, seaweed. Bladderwrack, Irish moss,
Green laver. Sand sedge, sea rocket, hound's tongue toss
In the wind. In the rocks limpets, whelks cling to a slab
Near a strawberry anemone, and a hermit crab.

[lines 488–491, 498–519, how medieval closeness to Nature nourished souls]

O how men decay without being fed by the praise
Of Nature, like seeds on the stone of their cities:
Pavements, walls! Petrol fumes of cars and buses
Smog up the air so the sun is in a haze....
Men drive to forests their fathers used to lop
For firewood, use them as luxuries, to please.
Here their ephemeral heads are measured by

The Eternal, here they see horses crop grass,
Not cars filled with petrol. Here they see cows pass
With swollen udders, not a packeted supply
Of milk in a supermarket. On this farm they
Can speak to their transport, their food. O go
To Canterbury, and before St. Thomas's ho-
-ly shrine, where pilgrims have knelt since Chaucer's day
And polished the floor, examine the mosaic
Pavement with its thirteenth century roundels,
Twelve signs of the zodiac in yellow medals,
Virtues, sins, occupations of the months. Pick
Out the two-headed god, looking forward and back,
Then: warming hands; digging; pruning; hawking;
Mowing; weeding; reaping; and boar-hunting;
Then: treading grapes, and after the too smooth, black
November sign, killing pigs. This was how
Men lived traditionally, close to the land,
Which fed their souls and helped them to expand.
O the folded-up souls of city-men now!

4. LILY FOR A DISTANT SPRING

[lines 815–821, spring renewal foreseen]

A new spring is ahead for the weed-garden.
Europe's cluttered exhaustion is now done,
It belonged to autumn: dry ground before a storm!
Winter is coming! Have faith in spring renewals!
In a growing season art and philosophy
And religion are one. Now one unified mind will
Keep the civilisation alive, with silver bells!

[lines 822–823, 829–842, 855–876, astronaut's view of the declining West]

London,
        Paris, Brussels, Bonn, Rome.
                Washington, Moscow.
It is Golden down there....
                Down there is Cornwall, like
A long lost heart. This hot autumn day the lake
Sparkles. Ragwort and knapweed line the fronts

Of the high hedgerows, old tin-mine chimneys and
Green fields. Tintagel Castle looks over the sea,
Looks down on Merlin's cave and its pebbled beach.
Crocosmia flame over the flat green land,
Fowey water is calm, as the ferry crosses from
Polruan. Little fishing harbours. The road
As we fly runs down past the rocks where the hermit of Roche
Perched like an eagle on his perilous, som-
-bre nest, runs down to Marazion where,
Across the causeway this low spring tide, a pil-
-grim path winds up to the Benedictine chapel....
The soul can bloom again in these open calms
Although fishermen have heard the muffled boom of fathomless
Church bells toll beneath the waves off the Seven Stones Reef
For the darkness that will fall upon the Western sleep,
That once fell on the lands of Tristram's Lyonesse.
Rinse your eyes with this space-suited moonman's view
Of America up there, and Europe to the Urals,
The Western World like cockleshells round a puddle.
"Will this still globe ever turn towards darkness, this blue
Tin spin? Will light ever fall on Arabia, Africa,
Asia? The East? Sons and daughters of Europe,
Must we unfold our souls? Must we sow our minds, must we reap
Our hearts? Must we water our proud wills? Are we sicker
Than we think? Let us drill our oceans! We, unlike the past,
Are immortal!"
       What pride! What folly! We must spin
Away and round again. In the spring we will shine out, seeing
μυεντες with a divine eye, not at all downcast.

There is a curtain in my window. It is certain
To darken this small room as it is drawn.
I have drawn an autumn lily. There are more
Of these spring-like flowers woven on this Western curtain.

16

from *The Labyrinth* (1976)
from The Labyrinth
(Images from a Dying Mind)

[lines 121–159, 188–194, 207–232, a statesman shot during the Cold War reflects on his life as he dies on the edge of Epping Forest]

Now I lie on this bed and search this Labyrinth
For the meaning of it all. I am lost in a maze
Of memories, I wind through prickly illusions
Like a stream through thickets. Yet when I look through the window
At the Forest spread out below me, like a tablecloth
On a Nursery table, it is all so orderly,
What could be more simple than a brook winding through trees?
I lie in this old house, which is more draughty
Than the hospital, and feel its peace, and ponder
How suffering teaches us love, opens new glades
In the woods of the soul, new places of sunlit feeling
Where a heart can flower unseen, and one's self does not matter.
I took risks, I stood up and spoke out – and was cut down by the sea
For my pains. And now I am sinking, waiting for my love
To come and read to me and dandle our son.
It is a violent time we live in, and I stood up to it,
And so I lie here in a peace like a swishing breeze.
I stood for order, and was felled by the forces of chaos,
I stood for Light, and must find meaning in this dark.

It is the whole Forest that has purpose.
What is the fate of one tree beside the Forest?
Does not one tree flower and fruit for the Forest?
I put out my candles and made my contribution
To the flowering and fruiting of a great Forest,
Which will sticky bud and leaf-fall for centuries after my dark.

The months, our seasons bud and shed leaf against
The eternal wood of the deciduous Forest
Which measures our time through now green, now russet leaves.
Eight hundred year-old oaks, five hundred year-old beeches.

Their ponds mirror the changes which time furrows
On my soul's face. Turpin's Cave, the Owl are gone,
But the silver birch round this little church endure.
In this graveyard I will be lowered, I will pass
Into its earth, my heart will feed birch roots,
Will sing up the sap and wave in the new spring leaves.
I will pass into the Forest and be eternal.
My life was a ramble through time, as I ramble now
Through my dying mind, through this wooded Labyrinth.
Streams dry, trees rot, but the Forest abides for ever....

O life. It seemed such a long journey at the time,
But now I have dreamed my way through this Labyrinth
To plunge over the edge like a waterfall, go underground
Like a stream going through a grating under a road,
Now how short it seems. All those evenings – a few breaths.
My soul came alive through pain, and bloomed in the sun,
It dazzled like white magnolia against a blue sky....

Are these rooms or chambers of my mind, that I wander through,
I who thought I was paralysed? What palace is this?
What mosaic floor? What flooding white light around me?
Is that me, or is it my old self, lying on that bed
Below, as I float in this light? Has my body fallen away
From this light, like a thrown-away match that has done its lighting?
Is this a garden, this Labyrinth, or is it Paradise?
Was earth Purgatory without my knowing it?
Am I an Angel, floating in this brilliant light?

From the dark to the dark, alone, alight. It is time
To sleep. It is time for the rabbit to enter its burrow,
Its barrow. It is time for the ditch to be dry.
It is time for me to pass into the wood,
Time to become the sap of Eternity,
This white light that pulses through all things, this current of LIFE!
In my mind there was a stream, a tree, a bird.
There was white light in the stream, the tree, and the bird.
I am the stream and the tree and the bird that flies,
I am all life in the Forest. And I am the sea.

The tide is coming in.

Alone. Alight. Sea foams.
One last hissing, exhaled, exhaled breath.
Sea foaming for Eternity.

Alight!
Dark. Blackness round a bed and flesh that was.

It is dark round the axed horse chestnut tree.

22 February 1976

17

from *Whispers from the West* (1976–1979)
Wistful Time-Travellers
(First version)

Sitting here in our flat, after dinner,
We can turn on the past. One TV knob, and Lord-
-s of Time, we are back eight years at the Marathon.
It could be twelve years ago on a tape-record-

-er. Our voices will speak from that Christmas, at a touch
Of a key. Or if I put up a screen, I could be
Me as I was at a wedding fifteen years back
In a garden of celluloid Eternity.

We Westerners are all time-travellers now.
We glide at the speed of light. For a few pounds
We can put back the clock to yesterday,
Fill the present with yesterday's sights and sounds –

Football, cricket, boxing, thrillers, or songs,
Memories on tape or film or a round disc,
Available in the home, or the waves of the air,
To escape the present for a vicarious risk.

We needed the past when we were doddering.
We looked nostalgically back to the Golden noon
When the West held, baffled that the mightiest,
Most inventive civilisation, whose offshoot reached the moon,

⌐ Should, after D-Day, shrink in senescent ruin,
　Retreat in a world which prefers the tyrant's prime
　To our old system. Whispering disapproval,
　We Westerners wistfully escape the present time.

26–28 April 1976

PART TWO

1979–2019

70 POEMS OR SELECTIONS

18

from *Lady of the Lamp* (1979)
Blindfolds: Lady of the Lamp

I close my eyes and peer into the damp
Of a clouded dark, like a traveller groping and find-
-ing his way in a night fog; one gleam, and not blind
Now, I am lit by the Lady of the Lamp.
I follow a misty reflection like a tramp
Who sees a roadworks lantern tilted, inclined
From a derelict basement. On the walls of my cellar mind
I see a dancing light guide me down a ramp,
And now I turn a corner, and the Lamp burns through
And gathers to a roundness and shines out,
And behind the dark is lit by the greyish blue
That unveils all seaside gloom and ghostly doubt.
But oh if I could see the hand that holds
The Lamp that scorches away my veiled blindfolds.

January 1979

19

from *The Fire-Flower* (1980)
A Metaphysical in Marvell's Garden

The House is hidden down lanes of the mind,
It stands "Strictly Private" amid green fields,
Over the redbrick front, a weathercock.
Behind, sunny lawns. Shaped evergreen shields
A huge cedar. And here a long green pond
Winds past the stone arch of a nun's chapel.
A Roman tomb ponders the October,
The ragged roses remember Marvell.

Here shed body like a sheepskin jacket,
Discard all thought as in a mystery school.
By this nun's grave sit and be the moment,
A oneness gazing on the heart's green pool.
A universe unfolds between two stone columns

And takes a leafy shape on clouded ground.
The sun-lily floats. Question its waters,
It will trickle through your fingers and be drowned.

The South Front sundial says in coloured glass
"*Qui Est Non Hodie*". I am a bowl.
In the North Hall the piano-tuner
Ping ping pings and trembles through my soul.
Who would not live in this delicious quiet,
Walk among columns, lie on the grass and wait?
Who would not teach a Fairfax daughter here,
Escape all bills, be free to contemplate

A flowered soul rooted like a climbing rose,
Metaphysical swoon of gold moments
Whose images curl down through thorns and leaves
(Wit and wordplay), spirit and satin sense;
Petalled layers and folds of whorled meaning
In whose dew-perfumed bowls a divine breeze blows;
Or like the prickly flame of the firethorn
Which crackles where purgation merely glows?

With drowsed eyes glance at solid grass and be
In whirlpools of energy like a sea.
Breaths heave the light, and answering currents pour
Through spongy stones and stars, or seaweed tree.
Now see with eye of mind into swelled form,
Imagine sap wash, oak wave in acorn.
Knowers are one with known, and are soaked by tides
That foam and billow through an ebbing lawn.

Gaze down on galaxies in a stone bowl
Like curved rose petals (small tip, large end),
Bent, cracked to holes. Travel faster than light
Through wisdom to where many curled worlds bend,
See nightmare multiplicity, then go
Where the bud of each universe is found,
The great Rose-tree of light where grown Ideas
Drift into form as petals fall to ground.

The vision has now passed. Condemned to crowds,
Town seers must teach hordes and leave halls' green waters

To lords who never peep for secret flowers
Or climb their souls up walls; and to their daughters,
And now a cloud flits through a fairy ring
And I glimpse for an instant my little "T.C."
And feel a dreadful shudder across my calm,
A "May it not come yet, but wait for me".

Wall-high climbers, whose many blooms reflect
Glimpses of the rose on the great Rose-tree
Which forms all souls in Time from one rose-hip,
Whose past growth glows gold moments they still see,
Are, in the present moment, one essential rose;
Which novices may see as a watery
Dark's shimmer and glimmer of the timeless
Dew-filled bowl of one gold water-lily.

Nymph everywhere, for whom men sacrifice
Paradise for a mortgaged, salaried mask
To keep you where Tennyson longed for Maud
Or where you board, we town climbers only ask
That, eyes closed, you grow a golden lily
And be a bowl for it, and simply start
To wimple in your wanting. May you be
A rose-sun-leaf-ground-cloudy fire-gold heart.

24, 28–29 October 1973; revised 4, 16–17 February 1980

A Crocus in the Churchyard

Hoofs clop clop clop between the silver birch
That hide the arrowed spire and this Forest church.
Come through the lych-gate, down steps by the yew:
Where the bracken tangles, wood-pigeons coo.
On this green carpet, pause: a nightingale
Sings through eternity by a black rail.
A crocus blooms where every heart believes
That unknown faces mean more than autumn leaves.

The aisle is quiet, tiptoe to the chancel.
Altar, pulpit, stained glass, lectern eagle,
Hammerbeam roof, a tiled Victorian floor,

The font and cattle brands, organ by the door.
Here on the wall two marble tablets state
The Ten Commandments, and how to contemplate.
Red and black, a life like scullery tiles;
Where a robin hops, a wife is wreathed in smiles.

"No graven images", "no gods but me",
No murder or covetous adultery.
A time when no host wanted, it would seem,
And manna was not yet a juicy dream.
A city smile is like a warm pillow,
Here girls are like a shower of pussy willow.
A rooted life, like the evergreen yew:
No glass or redbrick spoils each woodland pew.

The church is faithful to its hillocked dead.
Whether poet, agent, or Department Head,
Their deeds, like bluebells on a mound of moss,
Attest a Britain like a marble cross.
They, like bent gardeners in their commonwealth,
Cut bellbind and preserved their belief's health,
Conserved the diamond lead window standards
From the stones of revolutionary vanguards.

Silver birch, bracken and folk who seldom sinned
Now feed the silence under this March wind.
Shh! rest in the eternal; hear a snail
Dragging beneath the warbling nightingale.
Here rustling moments are time's muffled thieves;
Faces under hillocks, unlike old leaves,
Are compost so a crocus can proclaim:
To glimpse a Golden Flower is man's true aim.

Under this hillock, a decaying heart
Feeds the roots of a crocus and takes part
In the lost blowings of time from a windless
Ecstasy's silence and brimming stillness,
And, filled with dews, can, like an art-work, hold
A mirror down to Nature and still gold
Sunshine so posthumous meaning can wave
From fields of silver light beyond the grave.

Under the spire that towers from the slate roof
With arrowhead and vane like rational proof,
Look up at a high tripod which can view
White clouds that scud across the darkening blue,
And startle God at His theodolite,
As, measuring the angles of clouds and night,
He takes a reading of time's speed and flow
And calculates the centuries still to go.

Death has its beauty. A hearse, a squirrel's tail,
And your coffin is lowered by this black rail,
Between laurel and holly. For companions,
Unknown Belshams, Cookes, and rhododendrons.
A crocus under buds, now blink and brim
At dew-dipping finches, a tinkling hymn,
Snug in grass, safe from brambles; and in fine rain,
Gaze at the still arrow on the windless weathervane.

24 March 1974; 17 February 1980

Pear-Ripening House

A gable behind lime trees, a green gate
Which says "Journey's End". In the porch we wait
By the grained door, then go by pebbledash
Garage and shed which have seen small boys bash
Centuries before lunch against Australia,
Past roses (at square leg), a dahlia,
And a splurge of storm-beaten daisies, for
The old pear tree tumbles by the back door.

Now in this room peep – under four black beams,
Sloping ceilings – for the mirror where gleams
The yearning of a reaching out to moons,
Where flit the ghosts of a thousand afternoons.
This, and the black Victorian clock that cowers
Between two prancing horses, measured the hours
Of falling generations, crops of pears,
The sunsets and winters up and down the stairs.

⌐ Here floats a battleship on a lino sea;
The day war ended, this was ARP.
Here slides the ghost of a brooding schoolboy,
A fire-warmed clerk reading in lonely joy.
Here flits a brief affair, a wedding eve,
Here steals a separation. The shadows grieve.
Families, funerals…. A Parthenon,
This house is permanent, we are the gone.

Now thirty years are less than the straggly twines
That were honeysuckle. And still the sun shines!
Dressing for church is the green of last spring's
Lilac; young ambitions and hankerings
Are now the floatings of a dandelion clock.
What meaning had they? Is Time just the block
And blackened stump of a hewn sweet chestnut?
Cascading ivy that drowned a summer-hut?

Young wants and hankerings have a meaning
To the hard-skinned ego's slow mellowing.
The journey through maturing hours and years
Ends in wrinkling pith and pitying tears.
Cores fill with heavy juices from one flow
Whose sap softens to soul the hard ego.
All life ripens to drowse back to the One:
Fruit and old men fall earthward from the sun.

Ripe pears return pips to the ground, and sow
A next life's genes, patterned on this one. Know
That soul inherits genes from its last spring now
To gush a vision of buds upon a bough.
Leafy lives fill with the sap of all that's green
And are God's mind, whose code is in each gene,
And grow centuries of purpose into fruit
And show: soul ripens so new seeds can shoot.

We journey through a house and garden, shore
Up, improve, order and pass on the law
Of growth and fruit. The long way gives ample
If we soften to the universal

Sun. We journey, pick pears and paint old wood,
Teach sons. Seed is the end of parenthood:
The hard, small pear on the tree on the lawn,
And a ripe pip sprouting in a distant dawn.

4 August 1974; revised 23 March, mid–April, 26 May 1980

Two Variations on One Theme

I. TIME AND ETERNITY

I held her hand at this Omega gate,
She wanted to paint the yew,
And now the moment has blown away
Like dandelion fluff on blue.

Now, on the High Beach forest church
The passing clouds and years
Are like pattering footsteps in the porch
Or the silence under bedsit tears.

In the city I am scattered like poplar fluff
Blown on the wind of echo,
But here I breathe, with the quiet of stone,
The white light these dead men know.

Oh bury me behind this grave,
At the low black rail,
That all who have suffered and been brave
May pass the yew and wail
For all whom golden hair enslaves,
Till the past is a squirrel's tail;
Then, like the boom in childhood caves,
Oh hear beneath the breeze
The mystery that flows through stars and seas,
Where the autumn bracken waves.

2. THE BRIDE OF TIME

I

Time held a dandelion that day,
Blew the clock by this yew;
Now the moment has blown away
Like fluff across the blue.

To the porch of this forest church
The passing clouds are years;
Pattering feet feed silver birch
And silence under tears.

In the city men are scattered
Like poplar fluff, and waste;
Moss enfolds all who are shattered:
An embrace that is chaste.

All who are broken and are blown
On the wind of echo
Here breathe in the quiet of stone
The light these dead men know.

Eternity connives at pains
Which mould spirits that sinned,
But trembles when tears ooze from veins,
Consoles like whispering wind.

II

Listen beneath each gentle gust,
Hear the meaning of life;
The silence of the after-dust
Taunts like a flirting wife.

Seek her, she hides yet will be found,
Cooing from leafy den;
This nothingness empty of sound
Pregnantly woos all men.

Nothingness round an empty tree
Is full of rustling love.

A something woos men passionately
Like a cooing ring-dove.

A black-hole womb sucks in dead things
And then thrusts out new grass,
But waves of light and angels' wings
Swirl down where ebbed fins pass.

This black-hole void preserves all souls
Like fish in tides of love.
Expanded souls are like a sea
Sucked out from a foxglove.

Eternity lets all men know
She loves stillness not haste,
Yet preserves tides fish-spirits flow
Before their bodies waste.

III
Eternity blows in the breeze,
Yearning for years and graves.
Hear her soul pant through stars and seas
Where sighing bracken waves.

O carve two verses on a grave
Before this low black rail,
That all who suffer and are brave
May pass the yew and wail

For all whom golden Time enslaves
Till Time's a squirrel's tail;
That, like a pshsh in childhood caves,
Trembling a leafy veil,

The wind may whisper through these trees
With a soothing shsh of "still",
Drop to a hush, reveal and freeze
A hidden Void of will:

"Eternity blows like a bride,
Billowing springs and graves.

Her meaning foams through star and tide,
Teases where each leaf waves.

Seek her secret beneath the breeze,
Leap this three-stone-stepped stile:
Hear silence surge though years and seas,
Know her mystery, then smile!"

14 November 1972; revised 21–22 June 1980

20

from *Beauty and Angelhood* (1981)
from Beauty and Angelhood

Four country retreats focusing on the four centres of human identity:
body, mind (or soul/psyche), spirit and divine spark/Angelhood

I. HIGH LEIGH

[lines 1–8, 33–72, the Light in relation to body]

Drive down the long drive to the ivied tower
Where the grand House stands, walk its maze-like lawn
With low wall, fields and trees, and warbling birds.
Here in the last war, Unesco was born.
But now it knows the bareness in the heart
For it reveals, like an old mystery school,
The "esoteric Christ" of hidden fire.
Will we find what we're shown, in a new Rule?…

Here Beauty can be found, down these green lanes.
By this gate where sheep graze, be a skin-bowl.
As Lovers close eyes to open, here pause.
Get to know Beauty like a hidden soul.
Will there be entry to Beauty tonight?
Not while the thunder growls, winds howl and blow
Till rain hisses and explodes from puddles,
Not while light speaks from the sky to say No.

Morning. Eucharist, or "thank you". A priest
Fumbles at candles, which he cannot light,

Slops wine, shuffles, prepares squares of brown bread,
Prays words without feeling. Now rise and fight
To kneel at the rail, take "Spirit-bearing food",
Feed your spirit with the bread of life, be host.
He who calls fire to Mass has gone, but think:
This rosé is like blood for a tombed ghost.

Now in the library let the body
Be a Grail-bowl for Light through the priest's Lord's Prayer.
All cup hands, quiet, rise as the white fire glows,
Breathe down to throat this Light, breathe out dark air.
Thy will be done – let it come down to the heart,
Let it shape the heart into a Golden Rose.
Say "Come in God, come in" as flesh tingles,
Scalp prickles, hair stands up and tired skin glows.

White power surges through legs and burns darkness,
Volts probe each limb. Breathe in Light, breathe out love.
Draw Light as "daily bread" into the stomach,
Draw cleansing Light down into the groin, above
The red-hot rod which trespasses, cup hands
To the heart, draw power up to lips from earthed spine.
From the forehead raise it up, offer it back,
This circulating Light that makes skin shine.

Here Beauty can be found like a bare heart.
Sneak to her secret place from a hermit's room,
Lie down and love her lowered eyes, white fire,
Be a veined rock in the tides of her womb.
As Mount's Bay fishermen raise a crab-pot
From Tristan's Lyonesse where coral blows
And thrill as drowned spires toll out hermits' prayers,
Beauty, I found you like a desert rose....

May and 31 July 1981

2. HAWKWOOD

[lines 1–8, 16–40, the Light in relation to mind (or soul/psyche)]

Sunshine in the Cotswolds. Drive up hedgerows
To the grey façade of a country hall,

73

Fields, iron railings, cows, horses, daisies.
Unpack above the old monastic wall
Where black monks still surprise old gardeners,
Then stroll among tall trees and quietly pass
Other silent walkers, listen for hawks,
Like a Romantic fed on leaves and grass....

Now sit near a reflected Tree of Life.
The goat-bearded Teacher in sweater finds
Linked branches of triads and *sefirot*,
Grows *neshamah*, then *ruah* in our minds.
"Feel power flow round our enclosing circle."
Churn it on round like wheels of water-mills.
Though we are solid, we are like water
When our psyches convert to power that stills.

"Mirror images from the leafy world."
On watery mosaic, peacock and lyre
With hopscotch maze ascend a Tree of Life
To a large head of Christ and Crown of fire,
A Roman Jesus on a bathhouse floor
Near the sea, under olive trees. An ark
Hangs in a dark cloud while flames burn all round:
Merkava chariot in fiery dark.

"See Angels." They approach with veil-like flames,
Blowing like net curtains, visions that tease,
White brightness nothings where faces should be,
Five heavenly hosts fluttering in a breeze.
Then a large ring of celestial beings
With a dark centre, flame-like folds of veils,
And that black-hooded monk, no face at all –
Can Lucifer stay masked in such wild gales?

June and 1 August 1981

3. KENT HOUSE

[lines 1–8, 25–56, the Light in relation to spirit]

The Canon in retreat. Walk past green fields,
Go past a wooded pond to a tree board,

Then turn off up to where the old ruin
Of an Edwardian House has been restored.
A tree grew through this floor and this ceiling.
But now, in this long room of easy chairs,
Sits a Community, and on the throne
Its Ionan Master of silent prayers....

The woods have bushes that obscure clear sight,
Thickets that snare the pilgrim from the corn,
Hide the deeper life from the noisy Way:
This murky pond whose still reflects each thorn.
As pond in woods is heart found within head.
Sink down to where 'I am' beneath all mind,
The still place of the spirit from past lives
Beneath all words and wants of loud mankind.

Great mystics mined their hearts like Cornish tin –
Engine-house, stack, then long Dark Night of Sense
Emptying rock of earthly images,
Shaft sunk to a deep level of silence
Where lamplit spirit finds veined Truth like ore –
Yet were still one with fiery divine air.
Now West's heart is like ruined East Wheal Rose:
A deep shaft filled with water and despair.

Beneath the slime of this foul pond, 'I am'
More than my body, emotions or thought,
And, poised in stillness like a water-gnat,
Beyond cloud of delusion this life brought,
Mirror a past meaning in detachment,
And wonder if this muck can be pumped dry
So the West lets go everything 'out there'
And lets warm sun shine on shaft mud, not sky.

In Michael's chapel, mystic life in deed!
"Deep in your freest recesses, see Light."
As sunlight probes the depths of Forest pools
A watery Beauty breaks our caddice sight.
Blind as Master brings spirit bread and blood,
Swallow and gulp, Beauty above heart's eye,

Ezekiel's fire. We revere flight in all,
But are these young grubs really dragonfly?

June and 2 August 1981

4. ST PETER'S CONVENT

[lines 1–24, 33–80, the Light in relation to divine spark and Angelhood]

The country showdown. Turn at the gate, go
Through pines to the secluded convent where,
In front of Gothic porch and tower with cross,
A dozen old men sit and take the air.
This is a convalescent home now, run
By twenty-six old nuns and divine grace.
St Peter stands outside the chapel door
And looks in vain for girls to take their place.

Nuns excavate souls like a Mithraeum,
Then flame to Beauty, which sparks each Angel,
Spirits dug out like caves whose lamps hold fire.
Join dark flames for their Office at the bell.
As veiled, wrinkled hermits genuflect, see
Bare legs and buckle clogs from a lost age.
Spirits made flames who see One Fire, they are
Like the flame in sanctuary's blue lamp-cage

Or candles in Smeaton's wave-pounded tower
Whose granite tree turned cross with two-flamed beam.
Saturday *Feria* includes three psalms.
Singing quiet prayers for all near death, they seem
Dark Angels for the dying and blue light.
They file past us, their hands inside black sleeves.
We eat lunch in an enclosed garden, meet
The lady in whose scheme Peter believes....

My dream is of a movement *in the Church*,
Of masses shown the Mystic Flame *in pews*,
Not "New Age" communes outside "old" churches,
A Steiner cult, dying out of the news.
The West is in crisis, the young cry out
For churches to beam out a wave-swept Light,

But, lost in dark, are rocked on Eastern sects.
What other Luther, Wesley, is in sight?

The meeting has begun, I must speak out.
The Eastern menace lowers like a storm cloud
And darkens all Christendom, which unites.
Let Europe blaze against the night, be proud!
The West longs for great mystics' quartz to strike
Steel-ruled spirits to sparks, so, kindling, all
See the world as One Fire, Beauty's blue Flame.
Christendom yearns, oh will you fail her call?

The Light has moved my tongue, I am at peace.
But who can see that far, the Dark Age pour?
The Light has moved me, but they cannot see
Revolutions destroy, reforms restore.
Remysticised Christendom? He replies,
"We must go on from here, not think of goals,
Take our pace and direction from the ground.
We are not ready for great mystics' souls."

And now I stand under the tower outside.
A dream has turned as sour as old men's love.
They wait in their wheelchairs to be taken
By veiled Angels back to their wards above.
Sour, sour as I watch Angels terrify.
Lovers, Teachers, Masters and Angels care
For body, mind, spirit or divine spark.
Angels care for all four while breathing air.

Angels have veiled heart, soul, spirit and flame
In this life or past lives, from earthly damp.
Angelhood is earned like a peerage for
Spirits flamed Grail-gold in Beauty's blue lamp.
God renews Church through Angels veiled outside.
Nuns see One Fire, give flames to souls in dark,
He serves new forms, I the old Mystic Way.
Old Church receives new life, old fire new spark.

Accept. Like nuns he shows 'cripples' the Light –
Invalids in wheelchairs – and does not ask
Why Michael spears the Dragon in Mount's Bay.

77

Farewell, silent Angel, I have my task.
I will build words like Smeaton's Tree-stepped tower
So all can know what lights a hermit's night.
Sadly I leave. A dream caught fire and blazed.
Now blown embers glow blue, Angels' blue light!

21–22 July and 2–3 August 1981

21

from *The Wind and the Earth* (1981)
Crack in the Earth

The room is calm, her breath is still, she knows.
All quiet save for the hissing of oxygen.
Nurse listens with her stethoscope, then goes.
Windows are closed, we whisper on quiet again.
Across her we brothers recall seaside holidays,
Inviting her to listen and share, but not to speak.
And now "Oh dear" she moans and as I gaze
Two nurses sit her up and feel her cheek,
Puff up her pillows, change her water-bag,
Remake her bed, say "Would you like a drink?"
Standing at the end of the bed, my hand like a gag,
As she sips water I can see as I blink
The crack in the earth through which I crawled, to cry.
O why do we live in order to die?

Autumn 1981; revised 23 August 1993

22

from *A Rainbow in the Spray* (1981–1985)
Crab-Fishing on a Boundless Deep

Go out in a boat in early morning mist
As fishermen put up sail, with a hose thaw bait,
Slice slabs of ray whose smear spreads through the fist,
Leave the Mount for six miles out, where gulls wait,
Where the bay is sheltered from the east-west tides,

Where crabs do not bury themselves in sandy spots –
In this autumn equinox each crustacean hides –
And winch up the first string of dripping crab-pots.

In the first pot, put down an arm and throw
Good crabs into a tea-chest; into the sea lots
With soft bellies, or crabs too small – no
Meat: dash and smash diseased shells with black spots,
Bait the trap with fresh ray, pile pots at the back,
When the string is done throw them in; with a knife, and Frank,
Nick each crab between each claw, and hear the crack!
Then drop it, powerless to nip, in the water-tank.

This sea which is so calm can blow up rough
If the wind comes from the south-east and whips
Water to waves, and this calm can be tough
In winter storms that keel and roll big ships:
The waves wash onto deck from the windward side
And fishermen need sea-legs to see-saw
High, stomach above the horizon, then slide
Down into a trough, as the boom becomes an oar.

This sea encompasses each horizon's tide
And we are alone on a dipping, lapping bowl.
This sea, which yields such crabs, on every side
Is an irreducible, inseparable whole,
Ebbing from east to west, pulled by the moon
Till it floods back from the west as the moon goes by.
Its tides make currents from which crabs hide in a dune,
This boundless water is ruled by a ball in the sky.

As so it is on land, that misty cloud.
Trees, earth, stones, rocks, clouds, water, air and fire
Are seen as different as each wave, as proud-
-ly separate, yet all are part of an ocean of mire
As indivisible as the inseparable sea
Whose waves rise, dip, and then return to the One.
I see currents of Existence pulled inexorably,
Till crops flood back again, by the moon and the ripening sun.

⌐ Both sea and land first came from air – from night.
As an unseen sun made Being's atmosphere
To unfold a world of currents pulled by Light
So our sun whirled a collapsed cloud to air –
The dust and gas which cooled into planets –
Whose cold froze molten rock, then melted seas
From ice whose water clouds raise as droplets
To fall as rain on hills, so that rivers please.

And now I see this vast expanse of sea
Is like the unconscious mind on which 'I' stand,
Which came from Being's air and sun – psyche.
And 'I' am this boat, my reason, ego and
Identity on a mind both vast and deep,
As wide as the world, as deep as the deepest seam
Of rock, pulled by a moon that is asleep
Which sets blind currents swirling through its dream.

Bait pots with the smear of time and let them slip
In this boundless, endless sea, then have a snack,
Then winch them up. Images claw and drip.
Take out the good ones, throw the soft ones back
And the small ones, smash diseased shells, then seize
Each one that will bite its own legs off with its claws
And nick it so it's lost its nip. Then sneeze
And toss it in a tank of crowded metaphors.

Then you can sell them to be devoured, this haul
Of Being's dripping symbols. Such small works
Epitomise the vast and boundless deep, so trawl
Where thirty fathoms down great beauty lurks,
Hiding in sand when the currents swirl and free
To emerge in slack-water between the tides,
And I'll pray that the Being that made this sea
Can yield its plenty up these dripping sides.

11 August 1983; revised 19–20 April 1985

Night Visions in Charlestown
(An Ode)

I. DARK NIGHT

I sit on the harbour wall in dark Charlestown
And gaze up at a trillion budding stars
That flutter as a breeze blows gently down
From the sparkling Plough through Cassiopeia, Mars,
And I ask again "What is space? What is night?
What lives beyond death?" and hear my own echo.
This void which scientists cross with a satellite
Has a branchy fullness behind each glow.

In blackest dark I clasp the granite wall,
The sea laps calmly on a shingle beach.
A soft light dances where boats rise and fall,
The wooded cliffs are dark, and out of reach.
Here I can crane my neck and stretch into the tree
Whose blossoms glow, and there a firefly darts
For it is meteorite time. Here my soul can be
A hawk and fly to its higher, leafy parts.

Galileo, Descartes, Newton, Darwin, Freud
Emptied the air of all intelligence,
Made the cosmos a dark, mechanistic void,
Split body and mind, our species and conscious sense.
But now Einstein, Hubble and Penzias stand
For a cosmos full of atomic waves that sprang
From two hundred billion galaxies that expand
With background radiation from the Big Bang.

Our subatomic physics have destroyed
The Materialist paradigm of common sense.
Now Bohm, our Newton, grapples with the Void
Which unfolds fields that come into form, whence
Order unfolds, like Plato's Idea.
So matter comes from nothing, and so do we,
Implicate Oneness budding into air,
Flecking with petals this speculative Tree.

⌐ Our Darwin in morphogenetic fields
Makes Nature live again; a Sheldrake heaves,
The organicist triumphs, the mechanist yields,
One nothing somewhere burgeons into leaves.
Whitehead and Jung affirm, like Einstein and Bohm,
The cosmos is full of waves and infinitely wide.
How can one empty the sea and leave the foam?
Explain the sea-horse yet ignore the tide?

The new philosophy casts all in doubt.
The metaphysical proudly proclaims
That Humanists and Materialists merely shout
Sceptical faiths and lazy, rational claims.
So now I sit like Donne at the dark start
Of a new Baroque Age, when once again
We reach for stars, scrump meanings beyond the heart
Which the fresh soul knows are One, like a daisy-chain.

II. FLIGHT OF THE SOUL TO THE COMING AGE

Now shift perspective. From space our globe's at one,
As the mounting soul floats near the Milky Way;
And whirling round its galaxy, our sun
Is no more a centre than is Christmas Day.
The universe is as vast as the dark round one soul,
Which can travel faster than light to future heights.
Now the dark earth below turns rose-red round one pole
As an Age of global union dawns its delights.

Like old Baroque, I see its sun shine through
Appearance and illusion, the ego's mask,
Dye red the social carnival's ballyhoo
(All dress for parts as on a stage) – its task
To reveal the truth its sunrise mirrors, Light,
And wake souls to a sensual-spiritual face,
To pastoral peace and the bliss of celestial flight
Up this shaman's Tree to a canopy of space.

A Universal Age – Baroque in sunny art!
I think of one who paints peaceful landscapes,
Spanish Teresa's smile, the ecstatic heart,

And as I soar a prophetic vision gapes:
The Baroque started as a Catholic rose –
I see a waving Pope regenerate
All Christendom to rose-blooms, and oppose
New Eastern hordes again at Europe's gate.

I see the nationalistic darkness strewn,
That fragmented, separate time of nightmare toil
Whose reason conquered atoms and the moon,
But lost authority, empire and oil,
Whose states near-perished in an angry shout
As liberal causes broke like a golden bowl,
An Age that reached a dead-end, and cried out
For a replacement vision – for its lost soul.

I see Europeans bring to Charles's town
A sunshine *Zeitgeist*, an Age with a new still –
Their dynamic universe and a lit crown
Like a kestrel hovering on a wind of will.
A new Dark Age is as near as a gust of air
As Islamic terror threatens Europe's gate,
But I see their union overcome despair
As they seek an Age of Hope that they'll create.

I see it blow across the sunlit sea,
A Resurgence of the spirit which will unite
Occupied Christendom's soul with its body
As the Communist darkness fractures into Light!
I see Hungarians, Czechs and Poles declare
For Europe's sun! Though intellect wants proof,
Let the mind seize in beauty a grand Idea,
Let starlight trickle through its rational roof!

I see a space telescope, and the first Voyager,
Now map two hundred billion galaxies
And a lumpy universe in which dark matter
Pulls curving sheets to clumps; and show it is
Like Dyson's and will expand forever, a bowl
Less dense than three atoms per cubic metre – or
It would collapse and vanish into a black hole
In twenty billion years, space-time no more.

⌐ I see a quantum Void, Non-Being kinked
Beneath the four tidal forces which bind
All that is into one; quantum particles, once linked,
Behave as one, join vacuum, matter and mind.
This sea-like Void contains all that exists
And consciousness – those ripples Being craves –
And God, who enfolds what is like morning mists,
Is immanent in the sea that supports all waves.

I see man who evolved from stardust know
A fifth expanding force behind the known four,
And the solar wind, dust blown by our sun, and go
To where the heliosphere ends at the heliopau-
-se so that when the sun runs out of hydrogen,
Becomes a red giant, swallows the earth
In five billion years' time, shrinks to a white dwarf, then
On a safer star man will hail mankind's new birth.

Now I see men who think they're matter, their minds mere brain,
Who are imprisoned in five senses' skin,
Whose earth is a flightless Hell, endured in vain.
But the highest vision of an Age brings in
The next Age; great art does not reflect the 'id'
Of this dark Age, but creates a Sun-Bird's style,
And when the organs of perception have atrophied,
Few can see an Angel peep through an artist's ecstatic smile.

III. THE SOUL AGLOW

I glow on the harbour wall back in dark Charlestown
Like the light on the mast of the fishing smack at sea,
I glow from a visionary power which has folded down
From an implicate nothing-and-One to what buds in me.
Away from all towns I sit in the dark and bask
As if in the church by the sea on Gunwalloe's shore,
I rediscover ancient powers, and ask
To know the tides that lap at my well-lit door.

So hail the Universal Age of Light!
Whose waves flow in from every time of quest,
New rising of Baroque in its own right,

New sunrise for the Holy Roman West!
I look down from the Age with which I glow
And see that after all our questioning breath
Men will see our search as a Way of Fire and know
The Tree-hung star-rose souls that light dark death.

6 August 1983; revised 17–18 April, 20 May 1990

Staffa: Wind

We sit in a small boat which dips in a high
Sea against the tide and, the sun behind, flips wet.
All huddle under oilskins to keep dry
But I, salt on my cheeks, ignore each jet
And think of how I breast a tide each day
And sometimes glimpse a vision as I go.
I look and see a rainbow in the spray,
An arch in the flicking foam of a glimpsed rainbow!

We go to where Fingal lived, hermit of hypes!
Iona's last abbot. We pass the cave
Of basalt rock, it looks like organ-pipes.
The boat stops by rocks, we jump into a wave,
Squelch up island cliffs, tread the green top, edge
Down on black hexagonal columns, so
We reach the great cave, and inch along the ledge
Deep within where the sea waps just below.

Above the boom of the sea as it roars round
I stand where Mendelssohn once stood, and hear
The strange, clear piping of a woodwind sound –
But there is no pipe, it is only the wind and the ear.
The wind I cannot hear plays reed-like round
The ghostly crevices in the rock's rough seas.
I listen for the flow that makes this sound
And think of the quiet wind that makes my lungs wheeze.

My body is, I am rock, cave and deed
And through me blows a wind that makes me pipe
For joy a sound like "*Om*" on a woodwind reed,
That flicks froth that gives my third eye a wipe.
And I am a boat, and at me blows the green-

Filled foam in which I see this windy day
A rainbow that unites seen and unseen,
A rainbow of the mind in corporeal spray.

On my night-sea boatings I can sometimes see
The wind-whipped visions in the water-spray
And then plunge into a deep cave and be
The piping of the wind that sounds all day.
O wonderful wind that gives such sights, please heave –
O wind I cannot see, but can surmise
Through your deeds in my hair and flapping sleeve,
Cleanse my lungs and blow joys to my ears and eyes!

Now I have opened to a diviner wind
Of which the Staffa sound is an echo
And heard a symphony blast, all sound unthinned,
Twelve seconds of swelling *fortissimo*
With a clash of cymbals, awesome roll of drums,
And I have heard the majestic Angels cheer,
But I still think of the Hebridean wind that numbs,
That echoes in rocky pipes the divine Idea.

August 1984; revised 19 April 1985

Sea Force

Sea surges onto craggy Cornish cliffs,
Wave after boiling wave pours round the cove;
Flinging up spray on a dozen rocks, it biffs
And dashes where I sit like Olympian Jove.
What energy keeps its breakers rolling in,
Splashing with surf, thundering from the curl?
Scientists say "It is the moon", and grin,
But I know it's a force, a power, a swirl
That crashes in from calm and froths to shore
And rolls each wave that fumes where the foam droops,
And as the wind blows in the low-bent gorse
I know it is itself, a thudding law,
An elemental power where the gull swoops,
The endless boom and roar of life's tidal force.

18 August 1984

Oaklands: Oak Tree

I look out of my study window at
Green trees in chestnut flower, with candles that
Snuggle round a corner of green field, in the sun
On which blackbirds hop and two squirrels run,
Iron railings, where magpies and jays flit,
Where a woodpecker and a bullfinch sit.
Closer, two goldcrests swing near nuts, like thieves
And buttercups tint yellow between green leaves.

A Paradise, this field, where all aglow
I lay a childhood through a life ago,
Near the shady oak puffed at an acorn pipe,
And watched bees hum in clover when all was ripe.
A log, a pond, a horse, and everywhere,
Nature dances in the flower-filled air,
And among butterflies it is easy to see
A human gathers pollen like a bee.

A Paradise of sunlight and skipping feet
As swallows skim and swoop in the summer heat,
As a robin pecks in grass near children's speech,
The green only broken by the copper beech.
Here birds and flowers and insects perch and run,
And humans grow like berries in the ripening sun.
And tiny heads grow large like bud from stalk,
Like the spring bluebells fluttering round the Nature Walk.

It teaches that man is part of Nature's care,
That a boy can become a man without moving from here,
As a bud becomes the fruit of this apple tree,
Or this downy chick the nesting blue tit's glee,
As a grub hatches from pond slime into dragonfly;
This field is full of transformation's cry,
Of bees and birds and boys and girls and showers,
Observe your true nature among these flowers.

See the great oak like a druid tree – divine,
Filling with acorns that will make a *soma* wine,
And give the sight of the gods to all bound by sense,

Who see merely social faces across the fence.
Your true essential nature must include
This Tree of Life that pours spirit as food
Into the world, like acorns into leaves, and feeds
A horn of plenty that pours out souls like seeds.

30 May 1984; revised 14 September 1993

23

from *Question Mark over the West* (1986–1988)
Question Mark over the West

After Fernhurst we turn up a wooded lane
And drive across Lord Cowdray's estate till
A three-gabled stable cottage and urbane
Line of chestnut trees, facing a wooded hill,
With honeysuckle over the front door.
I stand near a French drain with my cousin and gaze
Across sheep wire and mounded mole-hills for
Wild life, and potter in the house and praise
The white-wooded windows and life of a squire,
Then sit in one wing at the birch-log fire.

And now at night a deep peace in the dark.
We stroll under a brilliance of stars and swoon –
W of Cassiopeia, Plough like a question mark
Or sickle in the sky – and gaze at the moon,
A cusp on its back above a line of firs
And I smell the sweet smell of the earth, digest
The moisture of woods, this idyllic quiet that spurs,
Wonder at the question mark hanging over the West
Like a sickle set to recapture lost ground
And scythe all Western gains without a sound.

The rabbits have eaten the growing shoots,
A fox escaped the hunt up the hill somewhere,
An owl sits on the fence-posts and hoots,
The baaing of new lambs fills the evening air;
A green-topped pheasant sits in the green field,

I hear a gun's report, a squirrel runs,
A hare lopes among hedgehogs; may the gun yield
To the bird by the chestnut fencing. The Englishman's
Country life is as old as Chaucer's day,
The sweet smell of the earth has its own way.

Who would think here of a threat to democracy?
This remote lane through a lord's estate, these woods
Keep at bay the bad news on the TV,
The darkness round our sickle moon, our "coulds".
We who threw up computers and man's quest
Through NASA saucers and voyaged through a comet's trail,
We masters of chips and reason master our West
By carrying homes on our backs as we work, like a snail.
I see the Plough fall in a shiver of stars
And a question mark scythe the fir-trees to stubbed bars.

Before the fire and flintlock guns, we recall
Our roots in our grandmother's garden,
The shed we scooted to, where Percy stood
Over the grinding wheel, sharpening knives,
A fir and frogs in a cellar, the sunlit grass,
"Shut this gate" wood with primroses to each knee,
A bomb blast at the gate and shattering glass;
We made the best of forties austerity
Like the arcade minstrel doll with a hand held out
Who popped a coin in his mouth, we never went without.

This Sunday country air at six hundred feet,
Is heady like wine; we walk past suckling lambs
Up the wooded hill to Northpark Copse and greet
A crack down the blue sky to where a feller jams
Felled chestnut trunks as fencing poles in the ground.
I look between the Downs over the Weald
Towards Black Down and the Pilgrim's Way, which wound
From Winchester to Canterbury across field,
And then we plunge down to Verdley Edge and the chime-
-less clock in the woods that measures a timeless time.

The air is scented with spruce and pine tree,
We cross the road, climb to Henley through beech
Where a stream splashes and pours down the hill, and see

Ears of bud, crocus and snowdrops gush and reach,
Sip draught cider at the Duke of Cumberland
By wisteria, wheel and post-horn, gaze and doze
And watch dark trout dart, turn and dash, get canned
By the pool that collects the spring and overflows
To trickle and splash and gush down the road
With a freedom that our land has always showed.

Over cheese and chutney sandwiches we talk
Of how you settled here – but not how, looking at Mars
That first spring day after a five-mile walk
I saw the night fall in a shower of stars;
Of the peace of a family inside their fence,
Each individual free in the scented air
To think and talk and be, without interference –
And to open their hearts to the One in each easy chair,
So that pinpricks of light pierce from on high
Into this one ball, the mind and inner eye.

Lunch is finished. At four a wet mist sweeps
Up the valley, the horse edges towards the poles
On the leaping flames in the farm as the dark creeps.
In this peaceful country life men find their souls
And live in the shadow of the moon-like One
And go to town to work the West's machines
And then return to enjoy the quiet, the sun,
Or go to the ancient Norman church, grow beans,
Graze sheep under the crooked crozier of the Plough,
The shepherd's crook that hangs in the night sky now.

16 March 1986; revised 23–24 October 1993

At Dove Cottage

I
Once more in Grasmere, I find Dove Cottage,
Go up the garden path and through the door,
Stand in the "houseplace" that was half-kitchen
And half-parlour and look at the stone floor,
Go to Dorothy's bedroom, where she wrote
Her *Journals* – William and Mary's bedroom

Later; see the washstand, jug and bowl, then
William's coffee-grinder in kitchen gloom;

Go up to his sitting-room with bare boards
And gaze at the cutlass chair with pink seat
Where Wordsworth dictated *The Prelude*, 'Leech-
Gatherer', 'Michael', 'Daffodils' – some feat;
Gaze at the wood-framed couch in basket mesh
On which he lay and saw the daffodils
Flash on his inward eye in solitude –
Close to the creative urge in these hills.

I go in to his bedroom and look at
His four-poster – top kept out rats; go on
To the guest bedroom where Coleridge stayed,
Climbed from this window to walk to the Swan
For breakfast, then came back; where de Quincey –
Who came for a weekend and stayed seven months – slept;
Then go to the three children's room, the walls kept warm,
Lined with old copies of *The Times* – inept.

I wander up to the pond where the Leech-
Gatherer sat as still, to catch and sell,
As stone, tiptoe on grass to black water
And look up at the line of Rydal fell.
Among your relics, things you left behind,
I glimpse a spirit who felt for these crags
And sensed the force that rolled through woods and shaped
Your heart, mind and soul more than Union flags.

I recollect the seed-time of your soul,
The schoolroom at Hawkshead which grew your hopes,
And the Solitary's house by Blea Tarn,
A low white cottage under steep green slopes;
And stepping-stones across the fast Rothay
You stepped on to cross to work, like a dam.
And back here at Grasmere I found your grave
By the clear Rothay, near where four ducks swam.

II
Here Wordsworth saw that Nature is alive –
Unlike Newton and the scientific

Materialists who saw Nature as dead
Atoms, not living but mechanistic.
Here Wordsworth felt the mountains move and breathe
And defied science with fresh images
Drawn from his own experience, like, caught
In black ponds' depths, fat medical leeches.

In Dove Cottage I sense the place, the room
Where eternal words came down into time,
Channelled through a poet's consciousness as
He lolled in his cutlass chair, shaped with rhyme
What flowed like the Rothay through his banked page.
I admire this man who knew that the spring
Of man's spirit's immortal, that we're not
Mere atoms that will die and be nothing.

Each decade we renew living Nature,
Proclaim it in a persuasive manner.
In your time you embodied that vision,
As I do now. You were my forerunner,
Full of powerful feeling and solitary –
Your lonely places and lone men. You peep-
-ed at this roadside pool, gathered images
Like a Leech-gatherer from muddy deep.

April 1986/February 1998; revised 24 October 2005

24

from *A Sneeze in the Universe* (1989–1992)
Candleflame Storm

A power cut throughout the village, the darkness shocks
The wind howls, rain lashes the windows,
White surf tears in and foams on the dark rocks.
I huddle without heat where the candle glows,
A roar in the empty chimney, blow on my hand
And sit among the shadows like the Georgian poor
When this cottage was built. The wind that has banned
The TV's noise now rattles the front door
And all is stillness beneath the wind and rain

This December night, and I am still within
And hear the silence beneath the furious storm.
How good that still Eternity should strain
To make us gaze at the candleflame in our skin,
So that we who cower in dark can know Its form.

19 December 1989

Ode: Spider's Web:
Our Local Universe in an Infinite Whole

"Does aught befall you? It is good.
For it is part of the great web of all creation"

MARCUS AURELIUS

I. THE VASTNESS OF THE UNIVERSE

I walk on the dark stones of the harbour wall
And gaze at the choppy foam round two dark rocks
(Gull Island and crag) and the swirling sea recall-
-s the stone swirls where an infinite Zen truth shocks.
The bobbing boats, the harbour lamps that dip
And land, are reflected in the endless deep;
The last clouds blow inland, stars wink and drip
And soon the universe will awake from sleep.

The universe is like a spider's web from here
And stars tremble like drops of suspended dew
On invisible threads that engulf the black hemisphere
And hang like globules under the spider's view.
I gaze at the spiral that holds all in place
And marvel at God the Spider who spans its thread,
At the millions of stars that throb and drip down space,
As the web vibrates with a breath beyond the dead.

There are more stars than grains of sand in this bay.
The most luminous object emits energy an immense
Thirty thousand times as powerful as the Milky Way,
Is sixteen thousand million light years hence;
And can be a young or proto-galaxy, just

93

Eighty-three per cent back to the Big Bang, or can be
A bright quasar embedded in a cloud of dust –
The most luminous star is too dim for us to see.

I think of Bohm who knew Einstein, who knows
The vastness of the visible universe
From equations, who greeted me, then close-
-d his eyes, then said with Einstein's mildness, terse-
-ly: "You can't have a vision of the Whole, it's infinite;
Our universe is a local event, a wave
In a sea of cosmic energy that's implicate.
There's something cosmic behind how atoms behave.

"The universe emerged from the vacuum,
The quantum void which is infinite in space.
Our vision's finite, a view from a room;
You can't measure the immaterial from our time and place.
The Big Bang is limited in importance, as is
Cosmic background radiation, its residue;
I see no unification of the four forces,
There are no prospects for such an optimistic view."

The unified sea foams round two rocks, the earth.
I think of bearded Gunzig with curly hair
Who told how an unstable vacuum must give birth
To a stable universe with an atmosphere:
A quantum vacuum expels pairs of flee-
-ting virtual particles, which return without trace;
Some are transformed into real ones by energy
From the geometric background of the curvature of space.

"A vacuum is unstable and Nature prefers to give
A stable state to a vibrating trembling, so
The energy linked to curvature is negative gravitational
And combines with positive mass to give zero.
It costs no energy to make a universe. But then
The price is entropy, or running down."
So something comes from nothing. Is there anything hidden
Behind physics? "It is not my field," he says with a frown.

I recall the view of a bald Dutch Professor.
As I sat in All Souls he said "We are born to die.
Between, humans make society. An 'I' before
Birth? After death? Fantastical! How? Why?"
The Void's Fire is received in human consciousness
And passed to society; not created by mind.
The human mind that lives in this vast web's "mess",
Did it create these millions of stars that are blind?

II. THE ONENESS BETWEEN THE FIRELIT SOUL
    AND THE UNIVERSE

The mind is the measure of each blind star.
I recall Winchester Cathedral, and the bones
Of seven kings in mortuary chests, and going afar
In the Venerable Chapel, feet on ancient stones,
I said to the Fire, "If you are there, inspire
What Hawking and Gunzig claim is the air,
Come into me," and a terrific surge of Fire
Poured into me, nearly knocking me off my chair.

If the infinite Whole manifests from Fire
Which we receive in our finite brains and see
Then there is within us that which is infinite desire,
Takes part in it, is of the infinite Whole and free.
And as in a hologram the whole's in the part
So in our galaxy the infinite whole can be found,
So in my mind roll the infinite wastes of the heart
Of a bright, eternal vastness that has no ground.

To some there are thirteen signs in the zodiac sky,
One each full moon, for each twenty-eight days,
And Arachne is between Taurus and Gemini,
The spider who spins a thread into a web and sways.
Go within your mind and ascend the universe
And climb the spider's web within the soul,
Look down on the star Arachne, and traverse
And bathe in its translucent glow, and see the Whole!

⌐ The spider that creates also destroys,
Weaving a web from nothing, killing its prey.
This spiral net of stars that traps hangs joys,
A web of beauty across the phenomenal day.
The spiral universe converges at the Pole
Where lurks the transcendent creator Godhead.
Each life is entrammelled in the web of the Whole,
A different shape caught up in the same thread.

Look down and see earth like a round baseball,
The size of a fist held at arm's length, so sublime,
So fragile and finite. Look down and fall
Towards dry, cold Mars. Now travel back in time.
From here the web looks like a ripe fruit tree.
As in a car wash, globes on a windscreen band
When driven by air, then rush apart, now see
The Big Bang's blast, our corner of the universe expand.

Now forward, see Mars' colonisers toil
To give the Red Planet breathable air,
With orbiting mirrors heat the red soil
Till water flows and vegetables grow there,
As the ice melts plant life and forests grow;
And see the pink sky turn a brilliant blue.
The cold planet now has farms, and towns. Oh,
I see a New World for Voyagers with derring-do!

This vast universe, does our consciousness
Fit in or is it just an accident?
Two hundred billion galaxies, each with no less
Than two hundred billion stars – if any less extent
Then the Whole would not have existed a long enough span
For man to exist. The Anthropic Principle!
Astronomy, physics, biology, all centre man
In the planets, electrons, double helix of the web's spiral.

III. THE ONENESS BETWEEN SOUL AND UNIVERSE
    AND THE DIVINE SOUL'S VISION OF THE INFINITE WHOLE

All is interrelated, corresponds perfectly.
Can consciousness be the exception? Is all a mess?

We are the outcome of the universe's symmetry.
Within one law: matter, body, consciousness.
The Fire behind Nature and history shines
Into and through all things, and holds for evermore
Galaxies, matter, bodies, minds, and entwines
Everything in the universe within one whole web-like law.

Like God, the poet sits in a spider's web
As large as the universe, spun from his head,
Waiting for images to float on the winds from the ebb-
-ing beyond and tremble his hung silk thread,
Making him scamper to his winged catch, run round
It, roll it up in a ball, wind it and climb.
He knows a poem is an image caught and bound
In a twisted net of fibrous words that rhyme.

And, hung in the night among stars that drift and flit,
He sees the earth fly into his webbed sunrise
And winds it round with silk and fixes it
In a great web of being, hung with other flies.
And now from the centre of this galaxy,
Woven in light from deepest space, like some
Marble, he holds the earth – white cloud, blue sea –
The earth between his forefinger and thumb!

Gaze at the outward burst of web-hung things
And sense the infinite Fire which moves beyond
And manifests into subatomic strings
And, inseparable from the whole, swirls round this "pond"
's two rocks in this local corner of England,
And with my ego and my infinite soul (and Bohm)
I see the dark whole and local froth, and
Symbolise the infinite in Gull Island's foam.

And I who can see the oneness of sea and sky,
Who can see the Being behind this phenomenal earth,
See also, with X-ray vision, the dark Void, high
Up where atoms unfold from nothing in an endless birth,
Where infinity swells to finite form, like the sun,
Where eternity enters time like a moving sea.
And as I close my eyes and gaze at the One
I hear the wash on rocks of cosmic energy.

⌐ A vision of the whole can be a partial one,
A symbol's fragment of wholeness in a place,
And it can be an inner glimpse of a sun,
Of a Fire like moonlight in infinite timeless space.
So I sit on the wall near dark Charlestown and ga-
-ze on a loving mind that is fifty fathoms deep
And stretches far beyond the Milky Way
And spy with a finite eye on the infinite whole asleep.

2 April–July and 16 August 1991; revised 27 May 1992

The One and the Many

"The One remains, the many change and pass;
Heaven's light forever shines, Earth's shadows fly;
Life, like a dome of many-coloured glass,
Stains the white radiance of Eternity."

SHELLEY

A late night walk. The moon is full
Beside the cliff with a sloping side
That joins the dark sea and curves back
Where its black shadows lap with the tide.

Transfixed on the pier, I stare, I stare
As the moon-like One manifests through space
Into the Being of a silhouette
And its reflection in existing place.

Transfixed on the pier, I gaze, I gaze
At a moonlit void where – mystery! – lurks
A sloping Being and its shadow,
I gaze at how the universe works.

A late night walk, and a spring in my step
As I tread the granite back to my home
And sit agog that the One has shone
Into sloping things that have stained it with foam.

9 August 1992

25

from *A Flirtation with the Muse* (1992–1993)
Imagination: Spring and Sea

How does it work, my spring?
A word bubbles up, a phrase
And then another, linked
And I know I must gush and gaze.

What is this shaping art
That fixes and makes sense
Of Nature's ephemeral tides,
This ordering of evidence?

My imagination wells
From underground with force,
From a subterranean sea,
Imagination's source.

How can my tiny spring
Be filled with sea-wide power
And tap eternal forms
In one small place and hour?

30 August 1992

26

from *Sojourns* (1993)
The Laughing Philosopher

I
Walk up a tree-lined avenue to a gate
And an orange Quattrocento fortress with great
Curved walls and barred windows and a high walk
Where sentries and lookouts stood in idle talk,
Go into an open orange courtyard
Whose arches echo with birdsong and the voice of a guard,

And the summer villa of Cosimo Medici,
Patron to the arts and philosophy.

Here Cosimo held court, limping with gout
Into a long upper room with a ruler's pout
And received the Platonist scholar Ficino
And his Academy, when they all ro-
-de through heat and dust from his small house on a near hill
To report on translations done at the Prince's will.
It is now a nuns' hospital, but the past chimes:
Stand in this place and feel those ancient times.

Here perhaps the Greek Gemistos came the May
He inspired the Pope's banker to revive Pla-
-to's Academy when his doctor's son was six
And had not left medicine for Greek and candlewicks.
Scholars say the Renaissance began to show
When the Ottomans sacked Byzantium's libraries so
Greek books came west, but in fact it was born, we find,
When Ficino became a doctor of the mind.

Here severe Ficino stood and read and ate
As proud Medici sat in pomp and state
Like a Maecenas filled with a divine desire,
And passionately spoke of Plato, Christ and Fire
As like Clement of Alexandria he reconciled
Pagan and Christian teachings, and never smiled
As he brought about a shift in the Christian west,
Brought in a New People with a new quest.

From here he taught Botticelli to transmute
Carnal, erotic love to its divine root:
Sad Venus and the Humanist ideal
Not as mournful shadowy form, but Platonic real.
From here he replaced the halo with a bloom
And expressed Platonic beauty in a womb
And, religious Humanist who believed in Fire,
Secularized the virtuous human with desire.

From here he became a priest and challenged this feat.
Sometimes Cosimo left him to go on retreat

To the Dominican monastery of San Marco
And walk near his cell and watch Angelico.
The Renaissance birth of Venus dethroned Mary.
Now I see Cosimo die in this Villa Careggi.
Ficino reads Plato as he lies sublime
And sighs, "Ah, I have wasted so much time."

II
Philosopher and physician, astrologer, priest,
First and last of the unified men, creased
Ficino saw learning as an aspect of one,
Of incorporeal light behind the sun
Which spread from God, the angelic world, to soul,
Nature and earthly matter, and, being whole,
Paganised the Church for a universal grace –
In Maria Novella, look at his crumpled face.

Downstairs I hear how Gemistos presuppose-
-d the Fire of Heracleitus, under old frescoes –
Temples, swans, gardens, villas and ships, one wrecked –
The Renaissance round my head, and now reflect:
Today a new Renaissance is in the air
As we recover the unity of being where
The mystics and Ficino lived, and see
The universe and soul as one energy.

Last week I sat in my Academy's gloom,
A dozen philosophers in an Uxbridge room,
And spoke to a modern group about the Fire,
To philosophers who know the real and aspire
To change the *Zeitgeist* back to the unified One
That warms each virtuous soul like a sun,
Not back to the atoms of Democritus –
One graceful reality licking down to us.

Alchemists see changes souls undergo:
Blackening (Dark Night) in an underworld of No;
Whitening, *coniunctio* of mind and soul in Light;
Yellowing, ripening of imagination's insight;
And reddening, *unus mundus* of body and soul
And cosmic consciousness, oneness of the whole.

Ficino and I both died from the world and 'me'
To be reborn in our souls and unity.

III
Now in this garden look back at the walls that tease,
The mauve wisteria, small bowled orange trees
Where images hang, touch a Greek goddess, then prowl
To where two boys ride a tortoise and an owl,
And the fountain pool where red fish rise and blow,
Listen to birds, pick and taste leaves and glow
With the smell of scents, all senses like a choir –
See pink chestnut candles like a mind on Fire!

In our Universalist time, when the Fire and
Incorporeal Light blaze across our land,
My books echo Ficino and reconcile
Western and Eastern Fires in a new style.
I must not be a preacher in a church
Or lecture on the Fire as a pentecostal search
As my six works show the universe's law
In an interlocking picture, like a child's jigsaw.

In a picture in Milan by Bramante
Two philosophers stand by a globe, one sad, one gay.
Democritus knew atoms before Rutherford's ball,
He laughs because men believe transience is all.
Heracleitus weeps as all believe "everything flows"
And no one sees the Fire – which he himself knows,
And so should smile. Sad Ficino, laugh and inspire:
For all is flux, but underneath – the Fire!

1–12 May 1993

Secret of the Muse

That you are a sweet Muse, I know
But which one are you? Which of the nine?
When I am with you I don't care
Which as you make me feel fine.

You seem to be the lovely Erato,
Playing a lyre, smile like a purr,
Muse of lyric and love poetry,
And you are erotic enough to be her.

Then you seem to be Polymnia
Of many hymns with your pensive look,
Muse of all sacred poetry,
But then it seems you hold a book

And I think you are Clio, the Proclaimer,
Holding a date-filled chart-like scroll,
Erudite Muse of world history
Who knows how civilisations unroll.

Or are you heavenly Urania,
Holding a globe, a star, a purse,
Muse of astronomy and the One
That is hidden behind the universe?

But I know you are Calliope
The beautiful-voiced, holding a tablet:
Muse of heroic epic poetry
Who tempts me towards the task I was set.

Like a chameleon, my Muse,
You loom and dissolve and change your shape
And are all Muses, each by turn,
And leave their gifts near where I gape –

Even well-pleasing Euterpe,
Muse of music, playing her flutes,
And the songstress Melpomene
With her tragic mask and tragedy's fruits;

Whirler of the Dance, Terpsichore,
Muse of lyre-dance and choral song,
And blooming Thalia, comedy's Muse,
Holding a comic mask in a throng.

Muse, I know you are all nine Muses
And channel their father's power to me,

But most you are Calliope
Who becomes Erato to tempt me with glee

As you know my impossible task ahead,
To think of which makes me feel ill,
Six years of toil on a vast epic
That will be worthy of Homer and Virgil.

29 August 1993

27

from *Angel of Vertical Vision* (1993)
Man (Or: God the Artist)

What a marvellous thing is man,
Two eyes, two nipples and
A nose, a "thing" balance
Two arms, two legs – just stand

And gaze in the mirror;
Ten fingers and ten toes,
What symmetry and proportion
The design of man shows!

And how economical is
Each orifice and lip,
Two ears, two hands, two feet,
And stomach and scrotum dip.

What does the design say
About the designer's mind?
God or evolution or Light
Is an artist who can find

Balance and symmetry,
Proportion and design
In a network of functional veins
That criss-cross round the spine.

3 October 1993

28

from *A Dandelion Clock* (1994–2004)
A Dandelion Clock

I walk up the quay for papers
And stop: a golden dandelion
And, spores in a ball, a fluff clock;
Two stems in grass, one root – rust, iron.

I look transfixed. A golden sun
And downy seeds – white stars that blew –
Joined: the Light and its universe
A wind like a Big Bang can strew.

And then I see Light in a soul,
Myself and my works, one round ball
On waste ground in a public place,
Fluff spread on the wind, scattered – all.

And I am sad for men pass by
The dandelion without a look
And winds will blow my works past men
Too busy to notice each book.

Next day I pass. A stormy night
And winds have whined and howled and moaned,
And now my clock has blown, the fluff
Has gone, as if I'd died dethroned

And my works had been scattered from
Their home in a round One that blew,
And all that's left is a gold soul
And a stem where my works once grew.

Then I think of the universe
And the galaxies that drifted
To stars. My works have shown the One
Like spores that crowd around my head.

13 April 2003; revised 22 October 2005

29

from *The Warlords Part One* (1995)
from The Warlords
From D-Day to Berlin

[A D-Day Soldier reflects]
(D-Day Soldier)

D-Day
Soldier:

For two nights we tossed on the choppy sea.
It was full of ships and craft, surely the Germans
Would see us and bomb us from the air?
The storm soaked us as we huddled on deck.
No one said much, we waited, seasick. Then
At H-hour a barrage from our Navy ships.
We scrambled down long ropes, packs on our backs,
Clutching rifles near tied gas masks, and jumped
Into assault craft, a ribbon of shore ahead
Gleaming in the early morning sunshine,
With little puffs of smoke from our Navy's shells.
Dipping, swaying, we crouched all tense and looked,
We approached through fire, bullets whipped up the waves
And clanged our sides. We nosed through floating bodies
Towards the smoke. A German plane roared down
And strafed the crowded beach, men and vehicles.
In that moment each one of us was afraid.
Yet we all showed courage. Bang! Down went the flap,
Out, we jumped into three feet of cold waves
And waded through the bullets and corpses
To the sand at the lapping water's edge,
Then dived as the plane whined down and raked our path.
"Mines," someone shouted, "stick to the matting."
We ran doubled-up under sniper fire.
The man beside me on the landing craft
Fell at my side, shot through the head. We gathered
At a muster point at the top of the beach,
And I saw a German soldier dead in a tree.
We were given provisions, and then ran on
Towards a house and fields, we advanced....

[Stenographer on Hitler]

(*17 June, morning. Margival, near Soissons, Hitler's reserve HQ,*
Wolfschlucht 2. Hitler, Rommel *and* von Rundstedt. Jodl, Schmundt *and*
others. Stenographers.)

Stenographer: This man is the terror of the world. Four Focke-
Wulf Condors flew him and his staff to France,
The entire fighter force along the route
Was grounded, anti-aircraft batteries
Shut down. As he drove from Metz airport to here,
Luftwaffe fighter planes patrolled the highway.
He has come to boost the Field Marshals' confidence
After the reverses in the battlefield.
All men tremble at the power his conquests brought.
I look forward to seeing what the man is like.
I am sure he will have Rommel quaking too....

[Chorus of Auschwitz prisoners]
(Chorus of Auschwitz prisoners)

Chorus: What will become of us? Who will help us.
We hear that Montgomery has landed,
Normandy is a long, long way away.
How many months will it be before his troops
Have captured Berlin and reached here? Where are
Zhukov's men? Last month, eight thousand were killed.
This month, some two hundred and twenty-five
Thousand, mostly Jews sent from Hungary.
We know, we've seen them, we drag the bodies
From the gas chamber into the crematorium
Next door, we burn them and bury the surplus.
Each day prisoners are taken out and shot
Before the killing wall next to block eleven,
And more are hanged on the portable gallows.
Montgomery, make haste, help us, help us.
We cannot wait more than a few more weeks.
It will be our turn soon. Help us, help us....

[Montgomery in his caravan, praying]
(Montgomery *in his caravan, praying.*)

Montgomery: O Lord, who helps the righteous in peace and war,
O Lord of Love and Light, O mighty Lord,
I have flung a quarter of a million men
Across the Rhine to thrust towards Berlin
And root out the Nazi evil around Hitler's power.
O Lord of Light, fill me with your wisdom,
O God of Light, come into me now, come.
Purify my thinking, so my decisions are right,
Exonerate me from the deaths I cause.
I submit to you the power I have over men.
Guide me with your power, you ah! bright Light,
Guide me with your Providence. Thy Will, not mine,
Be done. If it is Thy will, let me have
The victory, let the Germans surrender to me
As your chosen instrument doing your will.
Not to the Americans, but to me.
Let me cleanse the earth with the Light you give me.
And after its moral cleansing may the soil
Return to your beauty, devoid of tanks
And guns and shells, the machines of war
Which so disfigure your simple paradise.

30

from *The Warlords Part Two* (1995)
from The Warlords
From D-Day to Berlin

[Truman is told about the atomic bomb dropped on Hiroshima]

(*6 August. The cruiser* Augusta *returning from Potsdam.* Truman
and Aide.)

Aide: I have an eye-witness report from Hiroshima.
The uranium bomb was two thousand times the blast
Of the heaviest bomb ever used before.

Truman: Describe what happened.

Aide: A flash and with a roar
            A yellow and orange fireball rolled and shot
            Eight thousand feet into the sunny air
            And turned into a ten-mile high column
            Of black smoke, a mushroom cloud rose and hung,
            And as the great wind dropped, on the ground
            A flat desert where there had been a city,
            The roads like tracks across endless waste ground:
            Hiroshima has disappeared, and in its place
            Rubble, ruins, twisted metal and people
            Horribly burned, lying still, stirring or
            Groaning and crawling or just sitting dazed.
            Over ten square miles a thousand fires blazed,
            And a hundred thousand may have died at once.
            Birds had burnt up in mid-air, and people's brains,
            Eyes, intestines burst, their skin peeled, and some
            Burned to cinders as they stood. Others had
            The print of their clothes burnt onto their naked backs.
            It was awesome. Sir, this new weapon which
            Makes a thousand-bomber firebomb raid look
            Insignificant, has in one blast outmoded
            Six years of war, which must now be strikes like this
            That can wipe out half a country without warning.
            A new terror has arrived, that makes one yearn
            For the sort of world war we have just seen
            Where hatred has a limited radius,
            That of a conventional high explosive bomb.

Truman   (*with awe*): This is the greatest thing in history. We had
            To drop the bomb, I had a report that
            Half a million Americans would be killed
            If we were to invade Japan. General
            Marshall and I are quite clear it will stop
            The Pacific war before the Russians reach
            Japan, which we can occupy alone.
            We have learned from Berlin, where the Russians
            Occupy half to our quarter. The hope is that
            This bomb will abolish war because no one will
            Invade another's territory and risk its use.

Aide: So long as Stalin doesn't steal it from us....

[Montgomery marginalised]

(*December. Lüneburg Heath.* Montgomery *standing alone on the heath.*)

Montgomery: Marginalised, I was marginalised,
And with me Britain, and as a result
It's an American-Russian world now.
Did the Americans do it deliberately
To advance their power, or were they just blind?
In not going to Berlin, was Eisenhower
Just being fair, too trusting and naive?
Or honouring a deal that Roosevelt made
At Teheran with Stalin, to secure
A Russian offensive that would coincide
With my *Overlord*: Berlin in return for attack?
If I had led the Allies into Berlin
Before Churchill met Stalin at Yalta,
I could have held back the Communist tide,
All Europe would be Anglo-American.
Now the Soviet Union surrounds Berlin
And controls Poland. If my way had prevailed,
This would not be so. Does it matter now?
Yes, for many millions will not be free.
Or is there a stability I don't know about,
Is there now a secret east-west accord?
I can't believe that. Once again, I have been proved right.

(*Silence.*)

I sometimes question what my battles were for.
Was the world a better place for what I did?
Yes. I pushed back Fascism in North Africa
And Italy and North Europe. But as fast
As I rolled it back, Communism took its place.
Hitler was Overlord of Europe till
I invaded Normandy. Who's Overlord now?
Not Eisenhower; not Churchill, nor me, we
Were marginalised. Europe is now divided
Between Truman, all-powerful with his new bomb,
And Stalin, whose huge Red Army has occupied
The east and who cannot be dislodged by
An atomic bomb. Stalin is Overlord –

Apparently, for the real Overlord is you,
My guiding, Providential, loving Light
Without whom Hitler would have won this war.

(*Silence.*)

Now America is an atomic power
Thanks to German scientific insight,
And Russia will soon be one too, warfare
As I have known it is of the past, finished:
Operating from mobile caravans through scouts
Close to the battle front, like Marlborough
Or Wellington or Napoleon. War
Is now a distant nuclear missile threat.
And where does that leave Great Britain? Not great.
The body of our European civilisation
Has suffered a malignant cancer, which has been cut out
With our consent by the surgery of two other
Civilisations: the American and the Russian.
Now, after our civil war, we are convalescing
And our health will be restored.
But no more have we the energy for empire,
No more is our role in Africa or Asia.
Empire is at an end. We have ended
An imperial phase in our long history.
If that had to happen, then the civil war had to too.
Now the British Empire will collapse for we've
Bankrupted ourselves to recover from Hitler,
And a new Europe will grow out of this ruin.
I, who rule a quarter of Germany, consent
That German people should be in our new Europe
In which Britain, an island, will be different....

(*Silence.*)

For over a year I implemented a plan.
Now there is no need for it any more
I feel slightly lost, a warlord without a war.
I must live again without a plan, I must find
My meaning in God's world, beneath reason.
I must look for the plan in the universe,

Rather than Rommel's, and there is as much
Deception and subterfuge, God is a General
Who guards his secrets from his troops' eyes.

(*Silence.*)

Under the atomic bomb the world will draw together.
There is a need for a new philosophy
Which embraces all mankind, all religions,
A metaphysic for the United Nations.
The only way I can live without a plan
Is to piece the potsherds of the universe
Into the tessellated urn from which they came
And, like an archaeologist, know its pattern
In the fresh air of the universal sunshine....
But I have moved beyond war and conflict,
I look for opposites being reconciled.
I hope my son and Rommel's become friends.
And I ask of future generations
Not glorification or triumphalism,
But sober assessment, and credit where due.
More than Lawrence of Arabia, like the moon I drew
Tides of men, and flung them like a stormy sea
Up the beaches across the Channel, towards here.
Like Marlborough, I never lost a battle.
I stood for a Britain that had greatness.
I was a potsherd in the larger pattern,
A fragment, an episode, a chain of events
In the unfolding process of our history;
But I am proud of what our deeds achieved,
How our courage transformed our time, our Age,
And in the stillness of the trees, round this heather,
In the ghostly moaning of the winter wind
Which sounds as if the dead are gathering,
I hear the million men of *Overlord*
Roar their approval for a job well done.

31

from *Overlord* (1994–1996)
from Overlord: The Triumph of Light

[Book 1, lines 1–49, 102–151, invocations to the Muse Calliope and forerunners on Overlord]

Tell, Muse, of tyranny and millions killed,
Of the pinnacle of the world's power
Among mountain peaks and green slopes, of cruel
Destruction of cities, and whispers of
A Nazi atomic bomb. And tell of
The rise of Eisenhower and, with Christ's help,
The defiance of his supreme command
And opposition on the battlefield
Of Montgomery and Zhukov which led
To the liberation of Europe from
Nazi tyranny, the fall of Berlin
And the defeat and death of Hitler, who,
With counter-symmetry and chiasmus,
Plunged earthwards when he lost Satan's support
Like a falling star with a burning trail.
And tell of Light's triumph over Darkness
Though Satan's guile nearly outwitted Christ
Through his wily disciple, Stalin, and
Near spoilt God's plan for the millennium.

Tell, Muse, of plans and battles, commanders,
Of ambition and conflict, as the day
Of decision approached that would decide
Who would be Overlord of the whole world,
Whether Hitler, Overlord of Europe,
Commander-in-Chief of German armies
Whose genocidal rule of gun and noose
Conquered his neighbours in a new empire
Till tyrannicides challenged him, to bring
In a post-Nazi regime with Rommel
Or Beck as Head of State to end the war;
Or divine Hirohito, prisoner of
His murderous Army Generals, Overlord

Of Asia, Hitler's sole ally now that
Mussolini was gone; or Eisenhower,
Supreme Commander of Allied Forces,
The man who more than any other ran
The war and planned an Allied victory
And brought about American world rule;
Or Montgomery, implementer of
Operation *Overlord*; or Roosevelt
Or Truman, leaders of the world's foremost
Rising power; or proud Churchill, who still held
The British Empire that ruled a quarter
Of the colonial world, and who had stood
Alone when Europe fell and, brave, defied
The cruel dictators' might; or bland Marshal
Stalin, co-ordinator of Russian
Forces which were led by Marshal Zhukov,
Who sought world power for a land of peasants....

O shades of my forerunners, o Homer
Who showed gods beside heroes on the plains
Of Troy; o Virgil, who told of the dark
Fortunes of Aeneas, both on earth and
In the underworld; o Romancers, who
Sang of the search for the Grail, the chalice
That shone with pure Light; o Dante, who with
Virgil passed from dark Hell to Paradise;
O Marlowe of the warlike Tamburlaine,
O Shakespeare of *Henry the Fourth* and *Fifth*;
O Donne, who judged the new philosophy
And science of a sceptical new Age,
And abandoned *The Progresse of the Soule*,
An epic work on the scale of nature
(From first apple to Queen Elizabeth);
O blind Milton, who lamented the lost
Paradise of Satan-Cromwell's England,
Who justified the ways of God to man;
O Marvell, whose Garden was Paradise;
O Dryden, who showed Monmouth's rebellion;
O Pope, whose sylphs guarded Belinda's lock;
O Goethe, whom Weishaupt called Abaris,
Who created Faust as illuminate;
O Blake, whose Hell was a great energy,

Who wrote of Milton and of higher worlds;
O Coleridge, who opposed Newton's mind
As passive, "mere materialist", and
Reconciled physics and metaphysics;
O Wordsworth, who pondered an epic on
King Arthur and, listless, recoiled and drooped;
O Shelley, who revealed the One as Light;
O Tennyson, who wrote of Arthur's wars;
O Hardy, who recreated the wars
Of Napoleon – I beg you, help me.
O Pound, who saw the decline of the West
And hinted at a deeper meaning, you
Who sat under a Rapallo full moon
And urged me to begin this task which I
Have now pushed aside for twenty-five years,
Who stood and gripped my hand, passed on the power
Of Calliope's art – I salute you.
And all who wrote of the great battles of
History: Troy, Actium, the Spanish
Armada, Trafalgar, Waterloo and
The Somme; as I gaze at a hedge I see
I grow a white vision like a wild plant –
Please come to my aid with heroic verse
In twelve books like twelve leaves on the stem of
Jack-by-the-hedge (garlic mustard) which grows
Wild in hedgerows and ends in a white flower.

[Book 1, lines 939–944, 989–1009, D-Day]

The greatest invasion fleet ever sent,
Five thousand ships, bobbed in the still dark waves
Off the fortified coast of Normandy.
From the shore it resembled a distant
Flock of dark sea-birds caught in the storm and
Riding out danger on the choppy sea....

D-Day, day of decision, departure,
Disembarkation or defeat, D for
The Day (*en Français J-Jour*) and H for
The Hour, which fluctuated on the coast
Like high tide. Half light, the tossing sea was
Filled with assault craft. Sea-sprayed, men hunched in

Helmets and packs, rose and fell, surged forward.
Hearts in mouths, none spoke. All looked at the beach,
A distant line of sand, holding rifles,
Moving forward stealthily as a fox
Approaches a farmyard, creeping at night.
Who would be dead in a few minutes as
H-hour approached? What hand-to-hand combat?
The infantry went in, silent heroes.
Splash! Down went the flap into a ramp. Choke
With admiration and awe as each stood
Up and jumped into three feet of water,
Rifle held up, the cold chill of the sea
Shuddering through, and waded forward as
Machine-guns chattered like awakened geese
That honked indignantly in the silence.

[Book 2, lines 1–62, invocation to Milton]

O Milton, who at fifty-six years old
Left the plague of London for this Chalfont,
This rural cottage of a regicide,
Fleetwood, found by Thomas Elwood,
And, blind, lived in this study at the back,
Bed near the fireplace, diamond-lead windows,
In depression, convinced you had wasted
Twenty years on political pamphlets,
Twenty wasted years given to public life,
For your Paradise to collapse, for all
You stood against with such moral courage
To be restored, which would have cost your life
Had not Clarendon and Marvell saved you;
And, with (like me) a few short poems done,
Having been Cromwell's Latin Secretary
(A Hansard in universal language
To inform all nations of what Cromwell
Had said, almost Foreign Secretary),
And having read all history, literature,
Philosophy and science, and become
A polymath (politician, linguist
Of six languages, mathematician,

Organ-player, singer and gardener),
Who took up the epic you first dreamt of
In Italy and set out in *Mansus*,
And pushed aside for twenty-five long years
(As long as Virgil pushed his task aside)
Except to make a list of cast and notes
Before Cromwell's fine Paradise was lost,
In a workbook before you went blind in
That dreadful year when your wife and son died;
Who, sitting in bed, pacing this wood floor,
Sometimes groping out into the garden,
Waking at four, dictating at noon to
Your wife, daughter or amanuensis,
Sitting, one leg swung over the chair arm,
At perhaps fifty lines a day, finished
Paradise Lost in just over six months
From July sixty-five to January
Sixty-six, shuffling out after "milking"
To eat in the kitchen with your (third) wife,
Elizabeth Minshull, sit on these tiles
Before this fire, or on the brick floor of
This parlour to receive guests; o Milton,
Renaissance man, you who wrote three-quarters
Of your poetic work in the last eight
Years of your life, having reached fifty-six,
As I stand in your study by your quill
And lovingly finger your desk and stools,
I feel your presence and sense its power,
Standing by the fireplace I invoke you,
Sense your encouragement – o blind Milton,
Act as intermediary between
Me and the Muse, help me, send me blank verse
From a source as deep as this well, as sweet
As that green hill, chewed by cows till milking;
Your Satan, like Cromwell, rebelled against
God like a regicide and did not seek
To rule mankind through a New World Order
Like my dark Satan, but inspire me now
I tell of Stauffenberg's rebellion and
The cosmology of Heaven and Hell....

[Book 2, lines 92–183, the seven Heavens]

Tell, Muse, how Heaven is, and how the veils
Fold round the rose where Christ is found, all love.
In seven rings of increasingly bright Light,
Seven levels, each veiled from the next one,
Each miles wide and merging into the next
So seven seem one as seven ridged fields appear
Part of one landscape, or as on the green
Tiered terraces of Glastonbury Tor
Seven spiralling paths wind up one hill;
There were seven Heavens for departed
Human spirits, and in the empyrean
Above, high Angels shone, Cherubim and
Seraphim, Christ, St John and St Bernard,
And beyond them, the great dazzling brilliance
Of the most radiant Light, the Fire, the One.
In the first Heaven or first ring of light,
Behind the veil that hides the Light of God,
Enfolded in bliss, spiritually
Awake, basking in Light, dwell those who have
Glimpsed the Light in their life but who have been
Inconstant to it, like Shelley, Omar
Khayyam or Michelangelo, who have
Pursued other passions though open in
Their intellectual vision, now content
Among the lower Angels who visit
Mankind as messengers. In the second
Heaven, behind another veil, dwell all
Who have opened to the Light in their life
And seen their destiny, the purpose of
Their existence during blissful oneness,
And preserving the view of their senses,
Have become leaders in their active life
Like Cromwell or St Paul; now full of joy
In the blinding Light. In the third Heaven,
Behind its veil, dwell those who through God's love
Have risen in their life to mysteries
Of creation; who have understood through
Prayer how the universe turns through cycles,
How all is process and growth through the Light,
Like Heracleitus, Plato, Plotinus,

Philosophers who knew the Fire of Love,
Now serene among Principalities.
In the fourth Heaven, behind its veil, dwell
The spiritual Masters, who in their lives
Regularly saw the Light and, being
Teachers, taught it and showed mankind revealed
Wisdom, like the mystic theologians,
Teachers and historians like St Clement
Of Alexandria, Bonaventure,
Dionysius, Suhrawardi or
Padmasambhava among the Powers. In
The fifth Heaven, behind the veil that hides
It, dwell those who, knowing the blissful Light
Have in their lives approached near the divine,
And praised God from their love of creation,
While having carried forward the Light through war
Like Charlemagne, Bunyan and John Wesley,
Among the Virtuous. In the sixth Heaven,
Behind its veil dwell all the just who have
Been filled with Light and Love from the Most High
And balance mercy and divine justice,
Their vision of what is equitable,
Like Pope Gregory the Great or Cassian,
Filled with righteous peace among Dominions.
In the seventh Heaven, behind the last
Veil dwell, closest to the Great Creator,
All the best contemplatives, who have known
Light in its greatest luminosity,
Pure spirits who in their lives made contact
With the highest Creation, true mystics
Like Sankara, Bayazid, Al-Hallaj,
St Gregory Palamas, de Léon,
St Hildegard, Dante, Meister Eckhart,
St Teresa, St John of the Cross, Blake,
Julian of Norwich, T.S. Eliot
Among the Thrones.
                    Beyond these seven Heavens
Is the empyrean, where the Light is
Dazzling, where Christ dwells in the centre of
A celestial, sempiternal rose,
Surrounded by saints, Augustine, Bernard,
St John the Beloved, and the Virgin

Mary, and the coalition leaders,
Founders of minority religions,
Zoroaster, Mahavira, Lao-tzu,
Krishna, the Buddha, Mani, Mohammed,
Hui-neng, Eisai, Dogen, Nanak and Fox,
And Cherubim and Seraphim, a Rose
Of Light whose petals form the scent-like home
Of the Love that invades the universe.
As bees nuzzling in a rose, the Angels
Were honey-gold in the Light of Heaven.

[Book 2, lines 502–709, the seven Hells]

In seven rings of increasingly dim dark,
Seven Hells lurk like dark descending caves
To which all souls are drawn by the degree
Of shadow or darkness in their nature,
Seven levels, each veiled from the last one,
Each miles wide and merging into the next
So seven seem one, as seven caves appear
Part of one long cavern in Wookey Hole –
Through which, underground, flows the River Axe
Whose million-year-old swirl has carved chambers
Where clear green pools lie under stalactites –
When seen from the path that leads down into
The fissured limestone walls of the last cave.
Beyond a dark wood and a vestibule
Where slump, heads bowed, the souls of the futile,
Who, rejecting and rejected, wait, bored;
In the first Hell, in gloom, among horseshoe
And pipistrelle bats hanging from the roof,
Dwell those who can be rescued, virtuous
Heretics with rational-social outlooks,
Who were proud with a high opinion of
Their merits, exalted and arrogant,
Novelists, dramatists and poetasters,
Rationalists and humanists, scholars,
Positivist philosophers, their dupes,
And reductionist scientists, and theirs,
And sceptical materialists, who,
Though agnostic or atheist and not
Aware of the Light, have led blameless lives –

Democritus, Newton, Darwin and Freud –
With souls of pallid greyness, along with
School inspectors, teachers, doctors, dentists,
Police and all who ran the State system,
Insurers, traffic wardens, the blameless
Church-goers who sang hymns and said rote prayers
And missed the Light, the essence of all faiths,
Because the vicar was not mystical,
And here dwell many vicars in this murk,
Archbishops, Cardinals, ministers, priests,
Who recited mechanical prayers from
A book, and missed the vision of the Light.
Here each endlessly proclaimed his creed and
Knowing it was wrong, felt dissatisfied.
In the second Hell, in darker torment,
Dwell in dampness the lustful, all who have
Been attached to their sensual desires,
Slaves to the need for gratification
Rather than masters of their deep passions,
All who had self-indulgent appetites –
Messalina, Casanova, Harris –
The incontinent who lacked discipline,
A ring of whores and Don Juans, whose itch
Or ache kept them in body consciousness,
Which used others as objects, instruments,
So their souls were never lit by a ray
Of Light and never grew. And also here
Were lovers and mistresses whose desires
Distracted them from truth during their lives,
Who broke up others' unions, brought grief
To others and deprived them of the Light,
Government Ministers, Princes and Kings,
Nobility and workers side by side,
Their souls unreachable like nuts in shells;
Here they itch, twitch and ache without relief.
In the third Hell, in still dingier gloom,
Dwell the gluttonous, all who preferred food
And drinking and loud laughter in taverns
To contemplation which opens the soul
To the Light and starts its growth, like a shoot,
All who surrendered to their appetites –
Lucullus, Henry the Eighth, De Quincey –

A ring of social hostesses and guests
Addicted to alcohol, nicotine,
Drugs and time-wasting, passing many hours
In hazy consciousness, an illusion
Of togetherness: here hunger and thirst
Torment them in their perpetual fast.
In the fourth Hell, in even darker murk,
Dwell the hoarders and spendthrifts, all who had
A selfish appetite for money, and
Were avaricious, greedy for their gain,
Were misers or extravagant spenders –
Midas, Rothschilds, Rockefellers and Ford –
Attached to their greed, too busy earning
Fortunes or shopping, using merchandise,
Cars, computers, lazy sun-holidays –
Profiteers, property developers,
Bankers, stockbrokers and solicitors,
Stock exchange players and estate agents,
Lawyers, accountants and tax inspectors –
To contemplate and open to the Light
And journey up the Mystic Way, progress,
Their acquisitive consciousness having
Barred them from growing their souls; here, endless
Craving to hoard or spend, unsatisfied,
Leaves them in permanent numb frustration.
In the fifth Hell deeper in darkness and
Egocentricity and selfishness,
Dwell the wrathful, all who have assaulted
Or attacked others in fits of anger,
Who did not learn to control their temper,
Disputed heatedly, felt bitterness,
Felt scorn and yearned for revenge, and believed –
William Conqueror, Philip the Second –
Humiliation must be answered, who
Were quick to take offence, so did not seek
Quiet or meditate to bring in the calm
The Light gives, serenity and peace that
Passeth understanding, political
Agitators, demonstrators, MPs,
Football crowds and players, beer-drinkers and
Revolutionaries whose consciousness
Was too much on society or men

To be transformed by Light; here, endlessly
Stirred to rage by no cause, and unable
To express it, they boil and seethe within,
Simmer as if insulted, discontent.
In the sixth Hell, in deepening darkness
And self-assertion, caring for no one
But themselves, as if locked in a dungeon,
Envying the good fortune of others,
Resenting and coveting beauty, wealth,
Dwell the violent, all who have struck a blow
Against their neighbours, robbers, murderers
Who have injured fellow human beings
By theft or bestial bodily assault –
De Sade, Dick Turpin and Jack the Ripper –
And the fraudulent who out of malice
Have tricked their neighbours, cheated or swindled
Them of their earned savings, being attached
To advancing their own interests and not
Opening to the Light's gentle calm and
Loving their neighbour in the unified
Vision, violently separating
Themselves from the Light's truth; here too are found
The tyrants who had tens of thousands killed,
Who could not complete their divine mission –
Robespierre, Napoleon, Lenin and Haig –
And suicides, who out of self-hatred
Ended their own lives, ignoring the Light
Which reveals to all men their destiny,
And all who have been violent towards God,
Nature and art, who have gouged out the earth
Or damaged paintings, both God's creation;
Polluters and wilful hewers of trees.
Here an endless desire to harm fills all,
But they cannot express it and so feel
Frustrated, murderous and unhappy.
In the seventh Hell, in night darkness dwell
The spiritually slothful, the most
Ignorant who deceived their neighbours, who
Were not misguided but deliberate,
Fraudsters who falsified reality,
Who corrupted and perverted others,
Panders, pimps, seducers who degraded,

Flatterers who exploited rank desires,
All who made money out of the pure Light,
All fortune-tellers who used psychic powers
And magic to foretell the future known
Only to the Light and who stole money
Out of public office, betraying trust,
All hypocrites who misled others' souls,
All thieves who stole from others, all who
Advised others to practise fraud and sowed
Discord in religion, town, family,
All falsifiers of accounts, and all
Who were brutal with a deceiving smile,
Who authorised foul genocide, all who
Were separate from mankind, practised Satan's
Deceit and so are closest to Satan,
To the Lie which would falsify all truth –
Cagliostro, Marx, Illuminati –
And farthest from opening to the Light,
Their attention on corrupting others.
Here a perpetual yearning to gull
Others fills their minds without expression,
And their craving to chat is unfulfilled
And leaves them endlessly discontented
And miserable. In all seven Hells
One glimpse of Light can take a spirit out
Of Hell and put it in the first Heaven;
As in the dark regions of Hell no light
Penetrates, redemption by Light cannot
Be expected.
             Beyond these seven Hells
Is pitch darkness of chaos, where light is
Absent, where Satan dwells in the centre
Of a thorn, guarded by prickles, hanging
Like a bat (as his form Odin hung on
The World Tree), near a cesspit where all waste
Matter decays before, recycled, it
Flows back into existence; surrounded
By Arch-demons, forms his emanation
Spawned in fornications, incarnations
Both aliases of himself and children,
Such as Baal, Sammael, Beliar, Abaddon,
His Hindu-like manifestations as

Idol, seducer, fornicator and
Destroyer; and by all his disciples,
Simon Magus, Roderic Borgia (Pope
Alexander the Sixth), Adam Weishaupt,
Eliphas Levi, Aleister Crowley,
Rasputin; in a thicket of Darkness
Whence, like the Axe through underground caverns,
Decomposed, broken down into new forms,
Its force and consciousness again released,
Matter flows out into the universe,
Polluted with deception and falsehood.

[Book 2, lines 2187–2194, 2203–2241, the two forces in the universe]

The universe is governed by two laws
Which are opposing forces held at one:
The expanding Fire and speed Hubble found
That counteracts gravity as Newton
Thought, and spits out galaxies like bonfire
Sparks; and the contracting Darkness and wreck
Of decaying Dark Matter and black holes,
Destruction and evil....
Each force has its own law, and each one has
Its time. Look at expansion, and the age
Of the universe is sixteen billion
Years; (and the most distant galaxy known
As 8C 1435 + 63
Is fifteen billion light years away, and
Contains stars that were old when their light set
Out); look at decomposition – the stars –
And the age is eight to twelve billion years.
Time is many sequences of events.
Out of white holes (one near this earth) pours stuff,
As from a Roman *cornucopia*;
Into black holes like drains stuff disappears.
Both forces are in balance, birth and death,
New and old, light and dark, plus and minus.
God the zero Fire holds all opposites:
Zero equals plus A plus minus A
$(0 = (+A) + (-A))$,
The universe both expands and contracts
And thrives on the tension between forces,

The balance Newton sought and Einstein found
(The cosmological constant), and then
Doubted, the tension that balanced Hitler
And brave Stauffenberg, who was cheered in Heaven;
Nazi tyranny and brave Eisenhower
Despairing at Montgomery's slowness,
Moving his headquarters to Normandy....
God, Fire, contains what reason separates,
Making one two, truth into illusion,
Reducing the whole to conflicting parts,
Laws, forces, Heaven, Hell, Christ and Satan,
The sea to eddying currents and tides,
A multiplicity of opposites
Which intuition restores to a whole,
Seeing all division is of the One.
God, Fire, shows difference is deception
And unites and blends the Darkness and Light.
God, Fire, includes the Darkness and the Light.

[Book 5, lines 1–102, invocation to Dante]

O Dante, you who were born in Florence
Near the Duomo in this tall dark house of
The Alighieri in this narrow street,
With arched front door and barred windows, in twelve
Sixty-five, descendant of a Roman
Soldier who settled on the Arno and
From the Guelfs who expelled the Ghibellines
From Florence at Benevento, and whose
Leader, Boniface the Eighth, blessed you in
A crowd; you who first met Beatrice, Folco
Portinari the banker's daughter, at
A party at Casa Portinari –
She lived in the *sesto* of San Piero –
Where, nearly eight, Bice (diminutive
For Beatrice) wore a bright scarlet dress, and
Who next met her down by the Arno near
The Ponte Vecchio when you were both
Seventeen, and she greeted you with charm,
Wearing pure white, walking with two ladies,
And you saw her as Love, the Virgin, and

Stood on summer evenings by this stone south
Of the Cathedral in this Piazza
Del Duomo, near twelve and thirteen, and, hurt,
Suffered the pain of seeing her marry
Simone de' Bardi – at the same time you
Married Gemma Donati, to whom you
Were betrothed six years – and then die in June
Twelve ninety, and had the idea of your
Divine Comedy beaten out of you
By grief for the loss of your first love, as
You, a Cathar Pure One, mourned the passing
Of Pure Love; you who then opposed the Pope,
An unscrupulous, imperial man
Dedicated to papal tyranny,
And led a White mission to Boniface,
Who detained you while Charles of Valois's
Black Guelfs re-entered Florence, and who then,
With fourteen other Whites, was condemned to
Be burned to death in March 1302
For bribery, as you heard in Siena,
And knew exile on "another man's stair",
Rueful that great poets are not read by
Philistine governments, who would suppress
Their truthful eye and universal voice
For ephemeral topicality,
And, travelling between noble houses
In North Italy, in Casentino,
Verona, Lunigiana, with Virgil
As your guide (the forerunner to Beatrice),
Described the souls of Hell and Purgatory
In *terza rima*, and soon left behind
Political crises that kept you from
Rising above the fallen world, and, in
Exile from your beloved Florence, found
A heavenly city through your Beatrice;
You who showed the damned in Hell – neutral souls,
Virtuous pagans, simoniac Popes,
Francesca da Rimini, Filipo
Argenti, Farinata Uberti,
Piero delle Vigne, Brunetto Latini,
Ugolino – and every cruelty,

Every conceivable torture, every
Harmful act humans are capable of,
Campaldino and Caprona battles,
Atrocities on Albigensians,
A million of whom the Pope massacred
(The clergy not "shepherds" but "assassins"),
The sad effects of Satan in human
History, and finished just before you died
In Ravenna; you who knew Hell on earth,
Reflected the savagery of your Age,
Temporal tortures in the eternal,
And gave them a divine significance,
You who, a Protestant before your time,
Were Cathar in turning against the Pope,
Were Supreme Pontiff of that defunct sect,
You who hoped the German Emperor, Henry,
Would overthrow the Pope and then restore
A purified Christianity, who
Wrote your *Divine Comedy* to exalt
Your faith in the Cathar religion (like
The House of Aragon, Counts of Toulouse)
And heap abuse on meddlesome Popes who
Persecuted the Albigensians
And intrigued your exile, so you consigned
Odious Boniface the Eighth to the eighth
Circle of Hell – help me now that I must
Narrate the greatest evil of our time,
Of our cruel century, and how it happened,
The extermination of a race in
Death camps as desperate as your inferno,
Premeditated killing in Auschwitz
Where the Illuminati's guillotine
(Malthusian Grand Orient's instrument)
Became gas chambers through inventiveness,
Manned by the victims, under the SS,
The Schutzstaffel or Protection Unit,
Who, robot-like, always obeyed orders.
Help me as I tell of the revolt that
Brought an end to gassing in one thousand
Six hundred and thirty-four factory-like
Concentration camps and to genocide.

[Book 5, lines 3298–3359, Auschwitz]

In life as well as camps such as Auschwitz
Individuals achieve the greatest fame
Or notoriety when position
Lifts them above anonymous faces.
Roza, the organiser of the theft,
Was now as famous as the camp hangman:
Jakob Kozelczuk, who, having arrived
From East Poland over a year before,
Was now the bunker's attendant, jailer,
Who kept the cells in order and led out
(When they had undressed in the lavatory
And their name in indelible pencil
Was written on their naked bodies, to
Facilitate identification
Before the crematorium ovens)
The victims to the Black Wall, named from its
Black cork insulating plates, in the yard
Between blocks Ten and Eleven, where, before
Grabner, the Political Head, they were
Shot in the back of the head in pairs. He
Grabbed each pair of skeletons by their arms
And at the double hurried them over
To the Wall of Death and stood between them,
Still gripping each at the scrawny elbow,
And made each kneel on one knee, then one rise,
Head to the Wall, not looking to one side,
Unable to stand upright after months
Of crouching, famished, in a stinking cell.
As a pied wagtail on a sea-wall bobs
And dips its tail and bobs again and then,
Running, dapper, wags its tail up and down,
So, to and fro fussed dapper Kozelczuk.
Nearby a prisoner stood, holding a spade
And, strutting slowly like a carrion crow
In black plumage, in black above his prey,
With short air pistol or small-calibre
Rifle so no sound carried to those who
Lived on the main road just beyond the Wall,
The executioner, generally
Gestapo chief Palitzsch, menacing with

His gun behind his back, shot each in turn
In the back of the neck where the spinal
Cord enters the skull. When each had fallen
With a groan, as blood ran in a thin stream
The executioner put a boot on
His forehead, pulled up an eyelid to see
If the eye was motionless, and if there
Was a gurgle, shot him again in his
Eye or temple. The corpse-carriers, with
Fear in their alert eyes, and with speed, then
Loaded the corpses on wooden stretchers,
Ran them to the other end of the yard
And threw them, blood still trickling down their heads
And backs, on a mounting pile of corpses
By a far wall where a swarm of flies buzzed.
The spade-holder shovelled sand on the blood.
Kozelczuk fetched and led out the next pair.
Most guards saw men as vile material that
Could be stilled with one shot and in an hour
Reduced to its component atoms and
Returned to the earth mixed with clinker and
Ash.

[Book 5, lines 3489–3511, why did God allow Auschwitz?]

God, Fire, from which all forms at first emerged,
Transcendent One and immanent Light, is
Like both the silence in a timeless cave,
Eternal stillness in whose sea we are
Like white wave-crests, with which we are at one,
As in Capri's Blue Grotto's blue-white light,
And the loving tide in which we all live,
With crabs and shrimps, starfish and all creatures;
The current that carries us through our time,
Gently pushing us to warmer waters,
Sad that some men are predators who hunt
And devour their brothers in great numbers
As sharks kill shoals whose souls dwell with the Light,
But, ever moving history forwards, glad
That men as brave as Dorebus resist,
Fight back for universal peace and right.
"Why did God allow Auschwitz?" you ask. So

Evil energy could be neutralised
And souls made pure by suffering could crowd
Into Heaven's tiered amphitheatre and,
Released from the fierce gladiator's sword,
By their endurance chord Europe's discord,
Express hidden harmony in one choir.

[Book 6, lines 1–56, 117–136, invocation to Homer]

O Homer, you who, though blind, wrote the first
Western literature about your hero
Odysseus, King of Ithaca, who won
The ten-year long Trojan War by a trick
And who then journeyed home for ten more years
And killed the usurpers in his palace,
So many places claim your birth – besides
Ithaca, Smyrna (now Izmir), Chios,
Colophon, Pylos, Argos and Athens,
Salamina in Cyprus, Rhodes, Kymi –
From 800 to 550 BC,
And learned men assert that you were just
An oral tradition, not a person.
Yet I intuitively sense that you
Grew up here in Ithaca in the eighth
Century and absorbed your local legend,
Odysseus, and detailed geography
Of the island you first knew as a boy:
The Cave of the Nymphs with a round hole in
Its roof for nymphs and gods to enter, and
Just a slit for mortals, where Odysseus
Hid Alcinous' treasure; and the Hill
Of Hermes, Pitikali, where his great
Palace was, from which three seas can be seen –
The Ionian, Tyrrhenian and Gulf
Of Patras – by an ancient round stone church,
And, across Polis Bay, Asteris isle,
Daskalio, where the suitors sought to lure
Telemachos. I feel you visited
Troy for local detail and sat where I
Sit now on this hot July afternoon,
Wind in my hair from the Scamander plain
Where Achilles once camped and heroes fought,

By the altar of Alexander's late
Temple of Athena, and looked back as
I do at the east gate where the Greek Horse
Was brought to the approach and dragged inside,
Barely big enough for a few men to
Hide in, then up the steps to the royal
Palace where it stood as a wheeled trophy;
And, before you went blind, while you could see,
Gazed as I do now back at house VI E,
Paris's well-walled house ten yards down steps,
Where Helen lived, the prize for whom all fought.
From this vantage point, then a stone terrace,
Where I sit now, your Helen sat and watched –
Content with Paris, flattered and troubled
Just ten yards up the steps from her front door –
A thousand ships gathering to rescue
Their kidnapped queen and take her back to Greece.
You too wanted to show war is absurd,
That thousands died so Helen could go home,
A war that Zeus wanted so he could curb
The overpopulation of the earth;
You admired their exploits and bravery,
Not the futility of ten years' war....
O Homer, you who were so wise on war
And understood its folly, how brute force
By one side is matched by its opponents,
Whose stance was neutral between Greece and Troy,
And who understood how deviousness
Wins wars, as I sit on a stone and gaze
Across the plain to the distant blue sea,
My tongue parched at the end of a hot day,
July sun warm on my left cheek, the wind
Whipping from the sea and drying my sweat,
Sparrows chirping, cicadas sh-sh-ing,
A tractor cutting an early harvest,
And wonder how the Greeks found wood from dry
Olive trees and made a Trojan Horse on
That dusty plain, and see your Troy VI and
VII A, blanking out the rest, and dream –
Help me now that I tell of Hitler's trick,
How he deviously hid an attack

Behind a feigned defensive *"Wacht am Rhein"*
To stun the Allies into surrender.

[Book 8, lines 1–10, 81–188, invocation to Virgil]

O Virgil, who wrote of the dispossessed
Though schooled by Epicurean Siro,
Who lost your Mantuan farm to soldiers
Of Antony and Octavian after
Dread Philippi in 42 BC,
And, hating the turmoil of the civil
War, shy, retiring, lived like a scholar-
Recluse and wrote of Arcadia's idyll,
Spent five years describing the pastoral
Theocritus' shepherds in ten *Eclogues*....
I find you in Naples in your empty
Tomb, a *columbarium* high against
A sandstone cliff like that at Cumae round
The Sibyl's grotto, next to the Via
Puteolana and Agrippa's arch
And tunnel for the road (called the *Crypta
Neapolitana*), whose level has
Since been dropped, leaving your tomb in the air,
The tunnel high; here, between one and two
Miles from the *Porta Puteolana*
(Or *Cumana*), the site marked by an arch,
Near your villa which lay in the gardened
Villa Communale by silver sea,
Which you acquired from your tutor Siro,
Near which in eighteen nineteen a small white
Temple was put up with a white bust of
You long-haired, blank-eyed; here, having walked round
Santa Maria di Piedigrotta
Under the railway bridge next to traffic
Thundering through a road tunnel, I climb
A steep grove filled with sacred leaves, the bay,
Past Leopardi's tomb and climb up steps
Lined with delicate blue jacaranda,
And pass a Roman aqueduct and cross
The top of Agrippa's tunnel, descend
To a yellow reticular doorway:

A long window, a hole above it, two
More in the roof and ten niches for urns,
In one of which is a spray of dead bay
Leaves. Outside a train hoots, a distant roar
Of traffic rises and falls, but here you
Who knew Octavian and sang of peace –
Who admired his charisma, embodied
Him as Aeneas, a man burdened by
Responsibility, sustained by will,
And saw him as ruthless in pursuit of
His duty, had him acting cruelly
On the last page as he butchered Turnus –
Rested quietly till Robert of Anjou
In the mid fourteenth century sought to save –
Christianise – you (as did Dante when he
Made you his guide through Hell and Purgatory),
Holding that your fourth *Eclogue* prophesied
The birth of Christ rather than the child of
Antony and Octavia, sought to
Bring you to Heaven, and removed your ashes
To the Castel dell' Ovo's chapel, whence
You look across the sea from the causewayed
Island, and dream of this sweep of Naples
Which holds your villa and this tomb. Outside
The sunshine falls on an ivied wall; here
A metal stoup for water, and a fit
Memorial for the creator of
Aeneas. I leave and climb and lean on
A wall and gaze down at the weeds growing
From the top of your rounded tomb. Guided
By Tasso's friend Manso, Milton may have
Come here in 1637. Pigeons
Fly in and out of the grottos, and I
Recall you saw literary toil as much
A public service, believing the man
Of letters served his country by writing
Worthily about it, as soldier's toil
Or statesman's. I ponder your account of
The underworld, where your hero (crossing
Acheron, Cocytus and swamp of Styx,
More foul no doubt than swirling Rhine) found truth –

O Virgil, help me now that I tell of
Eisenhower's visit to the underworld,
And how it was foretold that he would lead
America, cheated at Yalta, to
A world peace, a universal concord
Mankind would rejoice at, help me as I
Embody a new mood in Eisenhower,
Show a new American way of life,
An ideal form of world government, that
Will end all wars, use the nuclear bomb
To bring in a *Pax Americana*
That will outlaw strife and bring peace, help me
Portray America's divine mission
To civilise tyrannical mankind
With democratic values and allow
Each region's inherited genius
To grow again – a rich harvest of peace.
You who wrote "*audacibus annue*
Coeptis" ("favour my bold undertaking"),
A reference to the Golden Age in which
The Saturnine kingdom (Osirian
As Saturn was Osiris's father)
Will return, rule of Osiris-Satan,
And "*magnus ab integro seclorum*
Nascitur ordo" ("the great series of
Ages begins anew"), two phrases which
Are echoed on the one-dollar bill as
"*Annuit Coeptis*" ("He – God – favoured our
Undertakings" or "our enterprise is
Crowned with success") and as "*Novus Ordo*
Seclorum" ("new order of the ages"
Or "new social order" or "a New Deal"),
And which, combined, give, "Announcing the Birth
Of a New Secular Order", and so
"New World Order" (of Osiris-Satan),
Help me show that the crossing of the Rhine
Would end in the New World Order Christ wants.
As I leave your Augustan calm, under
The railway arch, traffic, choking with fumes,
Thunders past and I am sad to return
To this order's belching, polluted Age.

[Book 8, lines 1598–1622, 1642–1663, 1732–1779, 1788–1809, Eisenhower visits Hell]

Hell and Heaven are in a fourth dimension,
And are separated from earth by just
A tunnel like a worm-hole, that connects
The physical to immaterial worlds.
Hell and Heaven are very near the earth
Once the transition to the Fourth is made.
The starting-point for all is where we are,
And the crevice to Hell and Heaven is found
Between our eye sockets and cranium,
Between our forehead and jugular vein.
Each has a tunnel to a world of Light
And thence branching tunnels to Light and Dark,
To one of which each goes after Judgement.
Hell and Heaven are behind a veil which those
Who are near death go through and accident-
Victims who die for five minutes and then
Revive recall, telling how their spirit
Rose above their body, suspended near
The ceiling, until it rushed like the wind
Up a tunnel towards a bright light which
Spoke to it, turning it back towards life
As its time had not come for it to die.
Satan cannot harm anyone within
A cathedral, church, temple or mosque, but
Christ's protection does not extend outside....
Eisenhower, passing between dimensions,
Not geographically journeying
To a four-rivered place, entered the cave
Of his unconsciousness and – having seen,
Without regret from above, his own dead
Body lying on the dry stones as if
He had discarded a used garment that
Still had wear in it, and finding he could
Float through solid walls in his spiritual
Body, drawn into thick dark – like water
Gushing in a subterranean torrent,
Rushed up a tunnel, accompanied not
By the black-clad nun, who had vanished, but
The Smiling Angel, who was now "alive",
A form Satan assumed to deceive him.

At the dazzling reception point, Angels
Stopped him politely, like immigration
Officials in a new country who looked
At the tell-tale passport of his aura.
The Smiling Angel conferred with the group,
Then both proceeded to a new tunnel
Which strangely sloped downwards like a wide drain….

There was a commotion. As Eisenhower
Puzzled over his conundrum, he saw
A shade push forward who, familiar, spoke
In a voice choking with frustrated love:
"As I died, I thought I'd never see you,
Dwight. Now three years have passed since that March day,
And once again I feast my eyes on you
Who I so much admire. But please beware.
They are deceiving you, my son, you are
Not in Heaven but in Hell. You are now in
The first ring of Hell and these charlatans
Have been brought up from the lowest ring to
Deceive you with their lies." Eisenhower stared
In disbelief at the gaunt shade, and then,
Overjoyed, moved to embrace his father
And, lacking a body, blended into
His mist, felt his own being drawn to him.
"How are you, father?" he murmured. "But if
This is Hell, and it's certainly gloomy,
Why are you here, you who lived for the Church
As one of the River Brethren, and then
A Jehovah's Witness? Why aren't you in
Heaven?" To which, sadly, his father replied:
"The Light, Dwight, I never saw the Light. I
Read the *Bible* and prayed. That's not enough.
No matter how blameless a life you lead,
No matter how poor you are – and we were
Poor; if you have not opened to the Light
You must wait here for the experience.
I cannot progress till I have opened,
And I do not know how. I try – in vain.
Believe me, for I speak from bitter grief,
Nothing in life is as significant
As opening to the Light. I have earned this

Miserable existence. To my great shame
I remember whipping you when, banned from
Trick-or-treating on Hallowe'en, you cried
And beat an apple-tree trunk in your rage
Till your fists bled. Your mother put salve on
Your torn hands and read from the Bible: 'He
That conquereth his own soul is greater
Than he who taketh a city.' And now
You are a conqueror of cities while
I abused you and never saw the Light
And so am here in this murky darkness."
Overcome with sorrow and sympathy,
Eisenhower spoke: "No, father, you did not
Abuse me, I deserved your punishment."…
The Smiling Angel, reaching for his arm,
Tried to escort Eisenhower away from
The old man, who shouted: "Beware, they are
Telling you wrong, passing on Hell's ideas
As Heaven's to deceive you. They want Russia
To run the world as proxy for Satan
And the murderous Illuminati.
They want America to lose the war,
Stalin to take Berlin. They promise our
United States will triumph in the end.
But they do not mean that. They would bring in
A world government that has Hell's approach
To people: genocide. My son, you must
Become President to prevent such things.
You *will* be President. And there will be
A world government that has Heaven's approach
To people: freedom and humanity.
It will bring in universal concord.
It will look back to you and invoke you."
The Smiling Angel made a sign, and now
The old man was hustled away, shouting,
As if he had heckled a dictator.

[Book 12, lines 363–374, the poet nears the end of *Overlord*]

Through my Cornish window, the sea rolls in,
White wave upon white wave heading to shore.
A full moon shimmers a causeway of light,

And seeing each long wave curl, turn and break
And foam up on the sand, drawn with a fine
Inevitability, a tide in
Me is tugged and I know I will complete
The rolling succession of crests in this
Vast work, I feel a sense of peace, flecks of
Achievement, and I rejoice in the sea
And the moon that governs it, in my works
And the bright moon that draws them out of me.

[Book 12, lines 2541–2546, 2579–2695, Eisenhower sees dunces sitting in the 'Museum
of Monstrous Dunces' in an annexe of Purgatory]

Eisenhower came to a foyer that seemed
To be an annexe of Purgatory.
His guide said: "Do you know who I am?
I was your enemy, I had one eye
And one arm, but I tried to kill Hitler.
Count Stauffenberg at your service, General....
...I must talk about Purgatory,
And this 'museum', which is a special one.
It is possibility, it does not
Exist. Like virtual reality
On earth – which is itself a tendency
As it has not yet been discovered – it
Brings images to your eyes which seem real
But are not there; they're virtually real.
It may seem that we have travelled through time
But we have not. We are still in our time.
But Heaven's forecasters have put on display
Identikit types who are expected
To live on earth and follow a wrong path.
Here we are in the next century among
Projections of some men who might reach Hell,
Predictions of great men who're scarcely born.
There is freewill, this is the only way
We can visit and learn from the future.
If you visited them in Hell you would
Find them drawn from all rings, not one alone.
Here they are in a kind of museum
We call the 'Museum of Monstrous Dunces',
A living waxworks of types yet to be,

To serve as a warning to all spirits
Of how it is possible to go wrong,
How the earth's culture was captured by Hell
And what must be reversed now Heaven commands.
See how the Millennium ruined the great."
In the misty twilight Eisenhower saw
A row of shades sitting in dunces' hats,
Pointed magicians' cones that were opaque
But also transparent, dunces whose names
He did not know though names hung round their necks.
Of four who sat together Eisenhower
Asked, "Who are they?" His guide replied: "The first
Was a neurobiologist who had
An astonishing hypothesis, that
Mind is but brain and there are no spirits,
That death is nothingness and extinction.
He has found out he was wrong, and sadly
Sits contemplating his life's big error.
The second was a neo-Darwinist
Scientist who was physicalist and
Denied spirit. He also sits and stares.
The third one was a cosmologist who
Had a wasting disease. He too denied
That spirits borrow bodies during lives
And he too wears a dunce's cap and broods.
The fourth was a philosopher who was
A linguistic analyst who spoke of
Language, truth and logic and advanced his
Verification principle to show
There is no spirit and to debunk all
Metaphysics. He too found he was wrong."
Another row of dunces caught his eye.
Four shades of yellow hue like a foul smog
Sat sadly on a bench. "Writers," his guide
Said with evident loathing and contempt.
One flailed like a windmill with shade arms and
Stamped shade feet up and down and kicked out and
Spewed a tirade of vituperative
Abuse. "Is he angry?" asked Eisenhower.
"You can say that again," his guide replied.
"He embodied the vice of anger in
His plays and derided positive thought,

His life's work showed negative emotion.
Now he sits in a corner like a child
Who has had a tantrum and must learn to
Cool off." The sulking man had a spade beard.
Beside him sat, grimacing, a bald shade
With myopic eyes and an expression
Of disgust, hunched and slumped as if depressed.
"A poet," said his guide with some pity.
"He polished all his lines until they shone,
But what they said snivelled about bedsits,
Work and pensions, wimpishly complained and
Whined querulously and held life to be
Meaningless, death the end. He never found
The truth about his spirit. Even now
He has not learned, and drivels as in life
But in a technically accomplished way.
He sees he was wrong, but cannot reform."
Next to him sat a grumpy curmudgeon,
A churlish shade with a miserable look
Who snarled at other shades, with bloated eyes
And double chin. "His novels," the guide said
With disdain, "were colloquial and knocked
All phoniness, but he never lifted
His ego to find his spirit and was
Far worse than those he ridiculed. He spent
Much time in his club drinking and talking –
How phoney that seems when it's viewed from here –
And ignorantly said he hated God
And taught the youth that nothing survives death,
And now he's found that his world-view was wrong,
That misanthropy is a great error,
That the law of the universe is love.
He never found any laws except rage.
What a trio! Angry, whining, snarling –
Each dunce a spoilt child with nothing for youth,
Nothing to say, no truth to show save his
Ugly soul to a culture that has lost
Its sense of beauty, reflects ugliness
As in a mirror." Eisenhower asked, "And
That one who looks baffled?" His guide replied:
"A vain colon, rude about England, who
Saw Mohammed in terms of Satan, and

Confused Heaven, where Mohammed is, and Hell.
He was seriously confused but was
Held to write with magic realism
Which meant expressing what is ordinary
As something pretentious. A hopeless case.
And now he has found out that he is wrong.
But don't waste time on these erroneous scribes.
Over here, these four will interest you.
They are truer monsters of a culture
Captured by Hell, replete with ugliness."

[Book 12, lines 2781–2825, Eisenhower approaches Purgatory]

At first Purgatory seemed hidden in mist.
His new guide greeted him: "Welcome, General,
I heard about you inside Auschwitz. You
Can probably tell I was a woman.
Until last January. I was hanged there
By the Nazis for helping Jews escape.
My name was Roza Robota." The name
Meant nothing to Eisenhower, who nodded.
They both moved on and the mist now lifted.
Eisenhower found himself on a high hill
That overlooked a plain quite like Falaise,
A long, wide meadow full of wild flowers
Where stood or sat millions of shades as if
In an open-air concentration camp.
"This is an annexe to Heaven?" Eisenhower
Asked his escort. "This is Purgatory?"
"Yes," said his guide, "it is outside the walls
Of blissful, subtle and fine Heaven. Here
All who have glimpsed the Light receive further
Training until their spirit-bodies are
Subtle and fine enough for them to be
Drawn on into Heaven as they desire.
But you have come here at a special time
(I mean 'occasion', it's eternal here).
This is a reunion for all who died
In Hitler's Holocaust. All these spirits
Were starved or shot or hanged or gassed to death.
All lines of Jews who ran to the edge of
A deep pit and knelt to be shot so they

Fell onto a deep pile of bodies; all
Who were herded into gas lorries or
Gas chambers; all who expired in Auschwitz,
All who were hanged like me or were butchered
At the killing wall or in the bunker,
And all who were victims of Hitler's Hell
In sixteen hundred other camps – all these
Are gathered here before us now, and see,
Angels move among them to help open
Their centres to the Light so they can move
On to Heaven. Purgatory is like
A reception centre for refugees
Where papers are processed and permits given.
It is a transit camp which they vacate
When they move on to Heaven. You see that few
Victims of the Holocaust are in Hell."

[Book 12, lines 2940–2954, 2965–3022, 3335–3398, Eisenhower visits Paradise]

Each tier of Heaven undulates like chalk downs
And seems cloudlike when suffused with sunshine,
And now alighting in the first Heaven
Eisenhower found himself in a great crowd
Of excited shapes who shone radiantly
On a summer meadow brilliant with Light
From a source hidden in its great brightness.
All was balmy, all were happy as if
A great crowd at Ascot milled in great space,
Awaiting the first race in pleasant heat.
All round were study-rooms and lecture-halls
But now like students sitting in the sun
All were content to be at peace, pleased at
Their liberation from the earth or Hell
And their attainment of this Paradise....
There was a path that wound its way around
As on Glastonbury Tor, only the scale
Was more like Mount Vesuvius, and each
Of the seven levels was separated
From the one below by a veiling mist.
They did not walk or climb, but floated up,
Effortlessly in their weightless spirits,
Not arduously with dense, weary feet.

As they ascended he saw tiers as downs
With shapes on them seen from a great distance,
He saw little detail through each white veil.
At last they alighted on the top rim.
He found himself on a protruding rock,
On a vantage point that looked down on all
Who were gathered in the brilliant sunshine.
And now what he saw made him cry aloud
With awe, surprise and delight. For, through veils,
From the summit of the seventh Heaven
He saw all lower rings of Heaven as
Petals of a great rose filled with spirits,
Their undulating folds like upland hills,
As soft as clouds and perfumed with wild flowers,
And, bright in the centre, dazzling, stood Christ
On the stigma of the central pistil,
While on the anther of each stamen round
Him were all his Angels and saints, founders
Of the earth's religions and their martyrs,
Shimmering and rippling with Light as when
The sun plays on a limpid satin sea
Which turns now blue, now gold, now silver in
The evening cool. There was one network of
Light, to which all (Bonhoeffer too) were joined,
Light shining round the head of each, haloed
Power, and when Christ spoke from his central perch
On the stigma of the great Rose of Light
(Whose ovary of Fire and stalk, the source
Of the brilliance, emerged from God's darkness)
All heard him, for all shapes were beings in
The Light of Being that permeated
All spirits and shone through and into them,
Which in turn shone back into it so all
Was one glow of Light and great joy. Here in
An endless present like a summer's day
They never tired of, content in the now,
Basked spirits with the brightest bodies while
From fixed positions, as in the UN,
They held conferences for all Heaven
And advised Christ with influential views
And lobbied till a consensus emerged
That preserved harmony throughout Heaven.

As lights leap on a blue sea in summer,
As if a thousand fish surfaced for air
And blew a bubble or kissed the sunshine,
Or as in evening a sea turns silver
And satin smooth on which a russet sky
Flecks bars of pink and the evening is still,
So, now excited, now calm, the spirits
Of Heaven waited to listen to Christ.

Now joyful Heaven gathered round dazzling
Christ Pantokrator, all celebrating
With beaming smiles a new Era of Peace.
Gone was the threat to end embattled Heaven,
Now all spirits in all levels could grow
Like wild flowers in a summer heat. All was
Bliss and process of self-perfection. All
Could now develop their talents through thought
In libraries and pleasant interchange
As spirits sought out past giants and learned
From Plato, Shakespeare, Michelangelo
And Beethoven between openings to
The Light. Just as at a weekend conference
Five hundred still in bodies listen to
Lectures intently, and later loiter
In the foyer, browse through books, walk to eat
And sit on grass and bask in the warm sun,
And each morning come in to the group hall
Past cherry and magnolia blossom
To meditate before breakfast and leave
Aglow with Light to climb steps like new monks,
Floating on silence like water-lilies,
Alive in beauty to all beauty, and
Pure spirits in their forgotten bodies,
So the Angels attended talks by all
The most advanced spirits who left their mark
In philosophy, literature, art and
Music, and turned out to be right, and then
Stood and loved in small groups, exchanged thoughts and
Shimmered their brilliant auras in greeting
And sat in the large meadow and basked in
The blinding Light that shone into all hearts,
And sat and soaked it in, meditating,

Praying energies that vibrated out.
Paradise was learning, growing, being
Flooded with Light, not being still; moving
Forwards, upwards like rose-buds unfolding,
Pushing towards the sun into rosedom,
Till a scented, satiny bloom brought joy.
Paradise was endless thrusting and peace,
Opposites in perfect balance. Angels
And spirits mixed freely; spirits aspired
To be Angels, and Angels advisers.
Heaven was endless potentiality,
Angelic possibilities and Light
In sunlit meadows on a summer's day.
All was happiness and delight, and no
Suffering or body-desire troubled
Their serene bliss, union with the divine.
Paradise was a pleasure garden where
Spirits grew like roses in happiness
That was felt sensually, though spiritual,
As rest and refreshment in changelessness
After the many changes on the earth,
Its pains and insecurities, dashed hopes
And bottomless despair when seen falsely.
Paradise shone out as a paradox,
Of changeless change, unceasing summer Light
In its garden, meadowed environment,
But endless spiritual development
And prayer of plant-like beings, ceaseless growth.
Here was the source of Infinite Light which,
As Eisenhower now saw, flowed into man
And as divine love rules the universe.

[Book 12, lines 4900–4923, 4945–4958, 4965–4995, Christ visits the poet]

Christ smiled for all was now well with the earth.
He alighted in an Essex village,
In Great Easton's churchyard, by the church porch,
And walked down to the war memorial,
To pay his compliments to this poet
Who had volunteered to reflect the Light
And revive medieval vision in
A tale of war and modern life that points

Like a signpost to Truth (which was concealed
By false men in our secret century,
In a dark time when evil was rampant)
For pilgrims to seek on foot by their own
Efforts, down an alley, across a stile,
And glimpse it as the sun of all men slides
Behind the rolling green pastures' skyline –
To this reluctant, volunteer poet
Whose mission was to spread the Light through art
And revive it in a modern epic,
Hopeless, forlorn task, doomed to sure failure.
In the church across the green, which has red
Roman tiles in its walls, a reredos,
Central panel, triptych without hinges,
Shows Christ crowned, throned in majesty, with six
Gold-haloed apostles each side on screens....
And from the Norman church a peal of bells
Rang out as if to salute Christ's Kingdom,
Rolled across the green and surrounding fields,
Across the Saxon fort and the Swan pub,
Through willows and past sheep, across the stream
And the green fields towards Tilty, across
The footbridge over the river Chelmer,
Ringing in the millennium and New Age,
Carillon of five bells, like my five themes:
Christ's triumph over Satan, Eisenhower's
Over Hitler, liberated Europe's
Over tyranny, Heaven's Millennium's
Over Hell's, and Light's over Darkness – all
Ringing the changes of one five-belled peal....
The bells pealed round the Essex countryside
For all to hear them like a poet's tongue
(Which rings out words for all across rooftops)
As if God spoke in joyful majesty
Through sounds my Muse tolled from His Rose of Light,
Claiming to be Overlord over five
Contestants – Eisenhower, Hitler, Stalin,
Roosevelt, Churchill (all Rockefeller dupes) –
Through two higher forces that served Him like
Day and night or life and death: Dark and Light,
Christ and Satan; speaking for Paradise.
Paradise called like a bell-ringer's chimes,

Washed through the air with Heavenly harmony.
I sat nearby in the timber-framed Bell,
Filled with the purling of eternity,
Jack-by-the-hedge's white flower in a vase,
Warming myself at my fire-dog which showed
A lion and unicorn through glowing logs,
Musing on the mystic tradition of
Augustine, Hildegard, Bernard, Dante,
Julian of Norwich, and a new Light
Which shone a brilliance above my dark mind,
Musing on how the Mystic Way is quite
Separate from the Dark Way, and opens to
The Light of Heaven, not false light of Hell,
And seeing him gaze into my window
I beckoned Christ to share my leaping hearth,
And thought I heard a thousand Angels shout.
Christ spoke: "The Triumph of Light's now assured."
Christ, Paradise is here, in my beamed house!

2 June 1994 – 23 November 1996

32

from *Classical Odes* (1994–2005)
Book One: A Tudor Knot

At Otley: Timber-Framed Tradition

Flailed hedges bud, corn shoots are a lush green;
The Suffolk countryside has burst with spring.
As I drive up Hall Lane the brown woods screen
The four tall double chimneys and nuzzling
Gables of this studded red brick and white
Moated Tudor Hall. A willow weeps where
Ducks splash in green. The high hedge is alight
With the last sunshine in the languid air.

I peer through an arch at the rose-garden,
Cloven Pan, croquet lawn, budding chestnut.
Beyond the vegetable garden I then

Peep into the high cage where peacocks strut.
One fans his tail: false eyes like works of art.
The nuttery is dark but lilies glow
From H-shaped fishponds (or stews) where rudd dart
Down to the viewing mound and barn below.

I turn the ring on the studded front door
And stand in the mullioned Great Hall and gaze
At the ancient brick screened cross-passage floor.
Adam de Otteley in Crusade days,
The Cresseners and then the Gosnolds sat
On a raised dais in an earlier hall
And fed guests. John Gosnold the Second, at
Henry the Seventh's reign's start, beamed the far wall.

Robert the First rebuilt and carved "RG"
Round the now walled-up ancient entrance and
Added "RA" on beam brackets when he
Wed Agnes in 1506. His grand
Linenfold parlour wall-panels predate
The "hung linen" of Lavenham Guildhall
Built by his cousin. Heir to "R's" estate,
An old Robert the Third stares from his wall.

Upstairs in the Banquet Room "R" built, my
Bedroom, Robert the Third aged twenty-four,
Fair-haired, and his bride Ursula, sit high,
Naked, columned, between the arms they bore,
Gosnold and Naunton escutcheons, beside
A Green Man who blesses their flowered union
In 1559, mark of "R's" pride –
They moved in when he died some twelve years on.

I descend the stairs that are scratched and scored
By spurs Colonel Robert the Sixth wore at
The siege of Carlisle, where, Royalist, bored,
He survived nine months eating dog and rat.
He fought on the wrong side and was then fined
By Cromwell's men, who filled parts of the moat.
I gaze at the deed Robert the Seventh signed,
Which sold the lands. The Hall went like a coat.

No more bowls and cock-fighting, cheer and shout,
In the "Plahouse" under the Banquet Room.
For two centuries the Rebows let it out
To farmers who barely wielded a broom.
And so, miracle! Much is still intact
And this Hall is a living monument
To a family who were at court, backed
It as JPs and had a landed bent.

Here Bartholomew's voyages were planned.
In 1602, funded by the Earl
Of Southampton, he reached Virginia and
Named Martha's Vineyard after his small girl,
And perhaps sat at this hearth with Shakespeare –
Who based Prospero's isle on his new world tale
Of springs, sassafras logs and Indians there:
Caliban knew the Vineyard Indians' trail?

Five years later he returned and founded
The first English-speaking settlement in
The US at Jamestown, which he then led
Until his death of swamp fever. A thin
Stockade had then colonised the US
Thirteen years before the *Mayflower*, a base
From which to chart America's progress.
The USA began round this fireplace.

And now I am custodian of these beams,
Part of our manorial heritage at
One of Britain's top twenty (so it seems)
Historical houses, I am glad that,
Instead of sailing abstractly across
An unseen past of submerged homes and art,
I have found actual ancient rooms to toss
And anchor in as I voyage the heart.

The mind is larger than uncharted seas
And I have always been a voyager.
History is vaster than five continents' trees;
We grow in woods and make a Hall's timber.
The literary night flits with ghosts that

,oom and retreat, and I am glad the days
Have brought me to a room where de Vere sat
With Southampton to plot empires – and plays?

Night. I leave my gabled chimneys and grasp
Timber-framed Tradition shuts out a crowd
Of brilliant stars. I look upwards and gasp
For this year's comet, Hale-Bopp, trails a cloud
Of bright gas that might cool to fragments, bump
And cluster in galaxies. One pace, mark,
And Tradition's chimneys obscure its clump
With age-old warmth and shelter from the dark.

8–9 April 1997

Pastoral Ode:
Landslide, The End of Great Britain

I

I wander round this Tudor, timbered Hall.
The setting sun shines spangles in the glass
Of leaded windows set in a brick wall.
I feel it in the air, eighteen years pass
Like the long shadows on the croquet lawn.
In the still evening I detect beside
My open study window and calm scorn
A shifting in the nation, dark "landslide".

Night's shadows creep, the sunlit garden fades.
Eighteen years of a certain kind of rule
Are ending. Cold war and armed truce are shades;
In place of missiles, hospital and school.
The country needs renewal, a safe switch
To a fairer society, have-nots
Doing better without hurting the rich;
A new energy, free from backbench plots.

I feel it in the breeze, a mood for change.
The people have turned against long tenure
For a fresh approach, rejecting as strange
Smears, lies, divisions and corrupt behaviour,

Impatient with State cuts and expecting
An end to cash shortage and mass pay freeze,
Certain taxes will go down, resenting
Division, splits, scandals and endless sleaze.

The people have forgotten it went well,
How unions were tamed, the pound made strong,
How living standards rose, inflation fell,
The victories won in wars against the wrong,
How privatising, market forces so
Transformed the weather they prolonged daylight
Till this illusion that the sun must go
Spread across the land like these shades of night.

A peacock honks from dark silhouettes, tense.
A world government Group has planned to scoff
At and steal our national independence,
To break up the UK by splitting off
Scotland and Wales as European states,
Finishing with the pound, stopping our boom,
Bringing back union strife. A tame press baits
One side with its scandals and foretells doom.

The gloom is real, the vision has now gone.
The regicides ditched conviction, belief,
Loyalty to an idea and passion
For the pragmatic posture of a chief
Who linked with personalities and hoped
For human loyalty and was let down
When they, still fighting for an idea, moped
And betrayed him with this pretender's frown.

I think, walking under the early stars
(Looking for a man in a ruff, his head
Tucked under one arm), knowing *their* press czars
Manipulate opinion round their dead,
Surely the public cannot trust this dressed
Demagogue who has like a hatched cuckoo
Pushed all the other eggs out of their nest
And opened his mouth to devour and chew.

I rest on centuries' quiet in the Great Hall,
See our nation's history in adzed beams, bide
Time. I switch on the television. All
Exit polls predict a Labour "landslide" –
Into the sea towards Europe. I go
To bed, watch a screen and count swings, like sheep,
Of eleven to fifteen per cent. I know
What the outcome will be, and fall asleep.

II
A cuckoo calls. I wake and grope a hand
To the bedside radio and now hear
That this upstart who has said "Trust me" and
Has hatched by policies already there
In the old, reused nest, has won with ease
By a hundred and seventy something seats.
The people sought to punish splits and sleaze,
Not give unchecked power to these pious cheats.

I walk with painters and a builder, chat
With an electrician and leaded glass
Repairer, who do not refer to that
Result as if nothing has changed the grass.
Bees swarm round their queen on a white post, twined.
A beekeeper lifts them with his bare hand,
Puts them in a box and leaves some behind.
So Providence removes a clustered band.

A blazing day and on my lunchtime screen
In the moat room, French windows wide open,
Our Prime Minister calmly ends a scene
And says that he will leave the stage; and then
The pretender arrives and grasps raised hands
That happen to wave issued Union Jacks.
A hired crowd: such "public opinion" bands
Bode fierce manipulation, and the axe.

Late afternoon. A cockerel struts and crows.
Small midges dance above grass by the moat.
I sit in the open study windows
And recall a Shetland ram and a vote
At a show for first prize in a rare breed.

Penned in by sycophants, with two curled horns,
That scornful long-haired ram waited to lead.
So had our lost leader waited on lawns.

Wild bees and wasps nest in our viewing mound.
We have a trusting public, who believe
There is no danger in our hillocked ground,
That well-strimmed promises do not deceive.
Our new society hums like wild bees
That menacingly buzz to guard their nest,
Which looks harmless in an afternoon breeze
But contains lethal stings that can arrest.

A Bilderberg agenda rules this crowd.
Like actors politicians recite scripts
Under the direction, as from a cloud,
Of a global *élite* in bankers' crypts
Who want a European Union
And urge our politicians to agree
To hand their power to bankers to bring on
A single European currency.

I walk past the nuttery urn and stand.
A bunch of Scotsmen now hold all the main
Offices of State in the UK, and
Will give the Scots and Welsh Parliaments plain
Self-rule, break England into regions – eight
Linked to Europe through county councils to
End all national borders and integrate
Our nation in supranational EU.

A naive optimism is abroad,
Settling the Irish problem is now right
As if IRA hard men, overawed,
Will surrender, give up their century's fight.
They will seek a united Ireland in
The new United States of Europe, scent
We now have leaders who will not bargain
With realism, but with wish fulfilment.

Here by the moat under a chestnut tree
With candles I ponder. Our nation's gold

Will now go to Frankfurt, and there will be
Nothing to back our pound, which must be sold
For inflated euros as we unroll
A Union of fragmented nation-states.
I see a country Rockefellers stole
From Rothschilds while our Englishness deflates.

By hanging fragrant wisteria I mourn
The New World Order's rule, towns ringed by moats,
Motorways where tanks can move in at dawn,
Besiege the people, keep them out like goats
If they are driven to the countryside;
Where, hospitals and camps heaped in ashes,
A populist leader with a landslide
Reaches out to a crowd he oppresses.

Indoors I linger on the landing by
My framed seven-foot chart and print of Canute
Commanding the sea to retire. Now my
Nation-state is provinces in a mute
Centralised Europe which floats a slick top
Of grants, policies, laws that all seem strange,
Like King Canute I see but cannot stop
The tide that creeps in and wets us with change.

The UK this momentous day has been
Sold to a United States of Europe.
I take no pleasure in having foreseen
On my chart twelve years back the sickening drop
To our civilisation's newest stage,
Along with Communism's end. I see
Our tradition invaded and rampage
Like our fishing fleet into slavery.

Will the change last or perish with the hours?
The purpling of meadows is seasonal.
The rarest minds, like the rarest wild flowers,
Are ephemeral and perennial.
See a thousand faces droop from stems, blow
Like purple snake's head fritillary bells
In Framsden's mottled green water-meadow
Where each spring hang transient, perennial smells.

155

⌐ Time creeps as on the face of an old clock.
Cogs turn, pendulum ticks and lowers weights,
The long-case hand moves discreetly, tick tock,
Past painted peacocks, floral scenes, estates,
The moon a woman's red-lipped face half set.
The hand ticks with the tyranny of time
And on the hour, with a whirr of cogs met,
The ting-ting-tinkle of a high-pitched chime.

Ducks swoosh by white lilies, quack their advice.
Like Marvell and Voltaire I will retreat
Into my garden, Suffolk paradise,
This end of Great Britain, sit on a seat,
Put the moat between myself and the world,
Leave the affairs of State to come unstuck
In an impostor's hands, Euro-flag furled,
And feed chickens and peacocks, and breed duck.

I will retreat into the distant past,
Recreate history as a Tudor knot
And medieval herb garden, contrast
The apothecary's rose and the shot,
Splashed blush-white of Tudor *rosa mundi*,
Learn falconry and Tudor bowls and thought,
Study the Virgin Queen's progresses, try
To ignore the dreadful things done at court.

I will keep hawks and bees and watch wheat grow
In farmers' fields by bridle-path and lane,
Listen to the cuckoo where cowslips blow,
See gold fish spawn in splash-ripples like rain,
Look for rabbits at dusk, savour the balm
By ponds aglow with lilies, gaze at stars,
Write odes as if this were a Sabine farm
And ignore conquered ninnies' blind hurrahs.

1–26 May 1997; revised 2 July 1997

Contemplations by a Sundial

I sit by a sundial's stone pedestal
And watch a shadow creep from its gnomon
Round Roman numerals and a central
Compass with eight points, aligned to the sun.
One end is empty, older dials are so;
And on the plate, among the tossing flowers,
A rustic Elizabethan motto
Proclaims: "Amyddst ye fflowres I tell ye houres."

How simple, to tell the hour of the day
By a sun's shadow on a flat surface
Marked with a diagram of hours which splay.
The length of days varies as seasons chase
And so hours varied in length with each change
And were known as "temporary hours", in length.
The Greeks and Romans used such time till strange
Arabs introduced "equal hours", with strength.

As many times as the eight winds have been:
Apparent solar time of sundials; shocks –
Dynamical, sidereal (true, mean);
Mean solar time of seventeenth century clocks
Local to prime meridian's time zones;
Daylight-saving; co-ordinated chime
Of universal time; atomic tones.
With so many times what, I ask, is Time?

Time cannot be seen. Only its effects –
As ripples on a pool or tossing trees
Suggest a wind – wrinkle what glass reflects,
Turn the air chilly with a cooling breeze,
Corrode metal, cause buildings to decay,
Thickets to turn to jungles, flowers to droop.
Time is the passing of each blue-skied day,
And slow ticking of waddle into stoop.

Time is a succession of events. Ten
Thousand million million million have bred
Each second since the moving One knew when.

Past events are not obliterated
But added to by all present events.
The past always persists in the present.
Space is the order of co-existence,
Time of succession, of events now spent.

I contemplate by my sundial, and gaze.
In medieval times a dial was grass,
A human body its gnomon to laze
And cast a shadow on its maze, and pass.
Now I sit with the sun upon my back,
My head a stick with contemplative eye,
And show time as my shadow moves in black
To the course of the sun across the sky.

I tell the hours by how my shadow creeps
As, wrapped in contemplation, I reflect
On the sun which created Time and peeps
At its universe, cause at its effect.
I sit with the Light behind me and feel
Its warmth rise up my spine, cast a shadow,
My silhouette, on the earth's surface, steal
With dark outline, hint at the One's bright glow.

I am a sundial in a sun as bright
As ever did shine on these rustic flowers.
I am a gnomon who receives sunlight
And shadows it so all can see its hours.
I am not measured by my sunlit side
But by the shadow I throw from the One.
I tell hours and proclaim, eternal guide:
"Behind each shadow reigns a glorious sun."

30 July – 4 August 1997

In Otley Hall's Medieval Gardens

I walk the grounds of Tudor Otley Hall
And gaze at the herber, its brick seat wall
And periwinkle cushion, pegged lattice

With medieval herbs, quiet for bliss
Designed to recreate 1260 by
Sylvia Landsberg's manuscript-garden eye.
I look across the mille-fleurs wild meadow
And twelve-tree orchard to a Mound aglow.

I climb the winding path to the Mound's peak
Where as on a ziggurat old gods speak.
Henry the Eighth's courtiers put flags on Mounds.
I reach the top and look down at the grounds,
Across wheat to Otley church, spire like thread,
Where like the Gosnolds my son will be wed,
And across ploughed fields to the moated wood
Where five thousand doves coo-ed, the Gosnolds' food.

I descend and walk through rose-tunnel cuts
Where vines and roses twine round chestnut struts
Bent into curved arches on iron frame,
Tied with tarred rope as in old days, the same.
I pass the Wolsey's-ceiling raised parterre,
Maggie Howarth's pebble-mosaic square.
Near orchids the sundial proclaims its trade,
"Amyddst ye flowers I tell ye hours" – with shade.

Arched like a medieval cathedral,
The hazel nut-walk leads to the central
Looped knot in the Knot-Garden of Princess
Elizabeth's prayer-book, box-hedged, endless,
Edged with four *fleurs-de-lis* and Tudor flowers.
A white ball stands for the One that pours hours,
Twenty-five herb beds stand for the many
Civilizations of global history.

Gaze at the Tudor knot: from the One, see,
Infinity signs crossed, eternity
Pours into time's, compass points, four arrows;
Now UK's twenty-five counties propose
A nation-state; now one of twenty-five
States fractured so USE regions thrive;
A tangled Tudor knot, the English fate
In now a European, now global state.

⌐ I sit as in a Zen garden's stockade
And reunify knowledge in the shade.
A garden states a truth in herbs and hours:
History, physics, philosophy in flowers.
Here what Pre-Socratic Greeks grasped and spun
(Heracleitus, Parmenides), the One,
Is given dramatic substance in plants' calm,
A philosophical garden of charm.

It says what Gothic Notre Dame's north rose
Attempts with thirteenth-century glass that shows
Thirty-two petals radiating out
Like civilisations that gush and sprout.
To the medieval mind, sun shining
Through stained glass is like Light penetrating
From outside One to central earth and soul –
Or from One stem out to make many whole.

I walk on to the croquet lawn and heed
The two thatched summer-houses with new reed
And the white dovecote where four fantail doves
Sit in holes, peep and wink above foxgloves.
I detour to the six white geese that glare
And squawk with glazed eyes, orange beaks in air,
Expecting a handful of scattered corn.
Four herbaceous borders adorn the lawn.

I wander in the rose-garden and smell
Tudor roses which last three weeks and tell
The modern breeds mixed in. Under the grass
Is the courtyard where players of good class
Put on plays when the Earl of Essex came,
Before he was beheaded in great shame.
Where the moat meets the causeway from the lane
I tread and fifty fish turn like thrown grain.

I wander on, taking the moat walk by
Curtains of splashing water, pumped supply
From bore hole three hundred feet underground,
Aster and secret shrub gardens, go round
To the hostas around the water-trough
That was pulled out of the moat's silt just off

Where the kingfisher darts, probes the banked flood,
And sometimes the grey heron waits for rudd.

I amble through the woodland walk to where
Blue and white peacocks fan their tails and stare
And pass on to the pool and lilies' bliss
Where goldfish wink their fins and blow a kiss
And the dry garden which boasts banana,
Where Red Admirals land on sprayed buddleia.
A rabbit bobs where yellowhammers flit,
A nightingale warbles near smart coal tit.

And now, near woods that ninety hollies share,
I look back at the inner stew pond where
Ninety yellow iris (*fleurs-de-lis*) stun,
Send their spears up into the blinding sun,
See many gables and tall chimneys vie
And the Tudor house floating in blue sky,
And I am happy in this Tudor place
Far from England's decline and soured grimace.

The present time is lean, our grandeur's gone,
But in our long history it's a season.
Our civilization's reached a great age,
Tudor halls focus on its youth, encage
Growth from spring through summer's imperial aim
To the autumn of what England became.
These gardens that state the One as did Greece
Convey the essence of old English peace.

Here by the moat, weeping willow forlorn,
A hundred ducks wait to scoop up thrown corn.
The mood is timeless, could be the Crusades,
Quintessentially English, never fades.
Here contrasting gardens and periods merge
As parts flow into whole without a verge.
Here the One's known like a Graeco-Roman bowl:
One garden poured into one round-rimmed soul.

Written 2, 19–20 June 1999; revised 25–26 December 2000; 11, 15 April, 2 May 2003

At the Bourn Fête: Ancestors

People stream past towards the ancient hall.
I spot our greeter standing on the slope,
Shake hands and walk round the side to the back
Where a crowd mills round stalls, stand by a rope
And, introduced, stoop by the microphone
And describe how John Hagger became Lord
Of the Manor and built this house, and then
Declare the church fête open. All applaud.

I judge paintings of a rose, then wander
Round stalls, pick up a booklet with a crest
And thrill – for now I read, crowds meandering,
That John Hagger was Cambridge's largest
Rearer of sheep who had two manors and
Eight hundred and twenty acres, demesnes
Round Bourn. My business sense and love of sheep
Are atavistic. They are in my genes.

He bought the manor of Ragons or Dives
In 1554, more lands in Bourn,
Then two estates from Chuter and Turpin,
And Crede, then one from Tryte with waving corn.
In 1589, the year he died,
He bought Monk Fields, and, with a woolman's weight,
The manors of Riggesby, Burwash and
St. George in Bourn, once in Picot's estate.

So now I understand! I'm in his mould.
Land and "wool-growing"'s what my forebears did.
The echo's in my mind, I fled from it.
I come from Cambridge stock, but Essex hid
My rootedness there for some fifty years.
I feel ancestral peace when I look out
And see thirty sheep in Great Easton's field,
Yet somehow went to Oxford and learned doubt.

Did I inherit my love of the sea
From Admiral Hagger, whose naval victory
Electrified his time? Do I have his

Proclivity towards the Admiralty?
Another ancestor, Mrs. Burton,
Had a dame's school (I have her warming-pan),
Lived to be a hundred, while a Harding
Wrote for *The Times* and was a literate man.

Businessmen, spies, schoolmasters, journalists
May be products of an ancestral gene.
Am I a conglomeration, genome,
Of echoes of past lives I have not seen?
In the same way, I send my influence
Down generations to a future pen.
All generations are connected in
A line that repeats victories of dead men.

I walk on through the fête and work the stalls:
Cakes, books, bottles, plants, band, tug o' war last.
People mill round two sows, snouts through their bars.
All are interconnected to the past,
All from ten families, Cro-Magnon tribes.
All various people are similar, all –
These ones smiling, those ones berating – like
The chimney-pots that rise from old Bourn Hall.

The fête raises cash for the Fabric Fund
That maintains the church structure in good nick
So lead, mizmaze and pillars are guarded.
The fête also embodies the fabric
Of a community where all know all.
Four hundred rub shoulders at stalls, in toil.
All interconnect within one pattern
Like the dead lying in the churchyard soil.

1 July 2000; revised 29–30 January 2001

At Tudor Otley Hall: The End of England

I wander in the grounds in evening sun.
The measurers have gone, it can be sold.
All I have to do now is give the word

And this place which runs at a loss, so old –
Vibrant with Tudor history – may go
To someone who wants it to be homely,
Who'll shut the gates to the public and brag
That he's now got America's history.

I look at a long line of marigolds,
Study the Tudor kind that Marlowe knew,
Walk in the summer vine-and-rose tunnel,
Smell the scents of flowers that waft through the view
And look back at the distant chimneyed Hall,
And know I will set a future work here
Which I glimpse ahead as once in Pisa
I saw what I'm now completing this year.

I sense a work about England. This Hall
Smells of Merrie England's heyday, the crown
And the Utopian call that took Gosnold
To found his settlement, die in Jamestown.
I see us moderns gathered for the rites
That will end England, split it into eight;
See this place with departing eyes, lament.
I'll turn it to images that won't date.

I drive to Essex, sleep, wake in turmoil.
The film I wrote five years back floats through air.
How galling to sell to an ignorant yob
And then be asked if scenes can be filmed there.
I am in anguish, have to choose to change,
And do not want to choose to let it go.
Yet I must let go and write what I've seen.
I have to leave to distance what I show.

I talk to Ken who administrates schools
For me, helps run my properties as well.
I say film access must be written in
The contract. He says, "You don't want to sell."
We talk. He says, "Why not leave it a year?"
If I were to a great weight would be clawed
From my mind. I know accountants see costs,
They have no vision, they can be ignored!

And so I'm faced with a free choice. I don't
Have to go, but it's losing funds; must bow,
And next year there'll be a war on Iraq.
It would be wise to get shot of it now,
Cash in my investment and walk away.
I'm free to choose what I'll become, I grip
My desk, aware of choice, of my being.
I choose to relinquish my ownership.

Now at Great Easton I look at reaped fields
With machine-cut bales of hay that await
Collection on a tractor's wire trailer,
And I'm at peace, I'm master of my fate,
I know my choice was right, that I'll soon be
Too old to drive up and down the A12.
Otley Hall is simply in the wrong place.
I've Essex memories which I must delve.

I see, in this house, a bound sheaf of corn
Pargeted outside on the entrance wall,
A great work of poems bound by one theme:
The end of England in that Tudor hall,
Which shows tradition, continuity
By which to measure England's quick demise
And I, the poet of decline, am now
The poet of the anguish that will rise.

I see a wingèd horse, soaring vision.
I who at twenty was a Romantic
Poet of youthful solitude, imaged
Subjective anguished growth that's organic,
And by forty was in a Baroque phase,
Mixed spirit and sense, caught dynamic flow,
The metaphysical that's behind all,
The rayed Sun in events and soul aglow;

Have now, past sixty, grey, turned Classical,
Build social poems, sound formal beauty
From my tongued bell on country house, ruin,
Peal in proportion and with symmetry,
Near gardens that display the One in plants,
Patterns like balanced buildings, columned prose,

Objectivise poems like stone *façades*,
Ring out *mores* past balconied windows.

Like Shelley, Keats and Byron I have trod
Italian, Greek and European roads.
I am more European than most English,
I sing Tudor tradition in my odes.
I will embroider on its tapestry
Of voyages to the New World, and show
The greatness of rural England beside
The richness of Europe's cultural glow.

Conceived 15 July 2002; written 20 July 2002; revised 21 October 2002; 3 February 2003

The Conquest of England

I
I sit and look across the sea to France.
Framed by my window, both sides of the bay
Recede in mist that masks the horizon
Where leaders have been meeting to display
With some secrecy that all decisions
Have been snatched from our side of this calm sea
And dropped beyond the wobbling reflection
Of a moored yacht and beyond Normandy.

There is a new EU constitution
For a new behemoth of three hundred
And seventy million folk, one state stretching
From Galway to Gdansk, and German-led.
Chaired by d'Estaing, a convention will tell
What two extremists drafted as our fate:
A new set of rules to unite Europe
And bind all states into a superstate.

Habeas corpus and a thousand years
Of English legal history will be wiped
Out by European law, and we will find
Our foreign/defence policy's been swiped
And's now anti-American, our tax
Will rise to Europe's, businessmen will pay

For the ten new, poor countries to catch up:
International socialism has sway.

Each state will make over its sovereignty
And some powers will be delegated back;
But not public health, social policy,
Transport, justice, agriculture, a stack
Of energy, environment and trade
Powers we've lost. Article 9 stipulates
The constitution will have primacy
Over the law of all its member states.

Article 46 makes clear, to leave
The EU without permission will be
Illegal. Secession must be approved
By two-thirds of member states. Now I see
A third can strip a seceder of all
Trading rights and cash, currency reserves
Held by the European Central Bank.
We forfeit our savings! This Europe swerves!

I scan the papers, digest the comment.
It's a prison clause, the union is not
A voluntary one we're in, it's the end
Of parliamentary sovereignty. I jot:
Our democracy would be abolished,
All would be within Brussels' competence.
I see Putin sitting beside Chirac.
We may be run by Russian "common sense".

This draft will go before the convention
Of a hundred and five. There'll be a new
Treaty of Nice when all the twenty-four
Other states could create – and then pursue –
A union and marginalise Britain
Who, sucked in, could in just nine months deflate
From being liberators of Iraq
To twelve regions in a conglomerate.

Is our future as the fifty-first state,
An island offshore from America,
Independent of Europe, self-contained,

Our currency tethered to the dollar?
Our fishing and farming free from quotas?
The American mind first set its prow
From East Anglia and voyaged to Jamestown –
Is it not fitting we should join it now?

But we've not liked its attack on Iraq,
Don't want to share its world hegemony,
Suspect that the *Pax Americana*
Is an oil-grabbing war on tyranny.
The US came in late in two world wars
When we gave it British oilfields as bribes.
It ordered us to abort Suez, yet
Expects support for war strikes on poor tribes.

Should we continue alone as we did
When we built two empires and ruled the waves?
We're the motherland for the Commonwealth,
We're still loved – we fed the backward, freed slaves.
Our empire's improved the lives of natives,
Our liberal capitalists expanded,
Created a global economy –
Can we not trade with all and stay ahead?

Again, we drive on Bodmin's misty moors,
An undulating green land with some sheep
And distant hills, our pleasant English land:
Sporadic farmsteads, well-cared-for woods sleep;
Granite stones, clumps of gorse, cows in walled fields,
The glory of the English countryside,
Its produce like our pension fund still ours –
I look on it with heavy-hearted pride.

I drive down Devon lanes with buttercups
And green hills smiling in the morning sun,
Grass shimmering-green, to an old stone bridge,
Past a horse, farmhouses and a hen-run,
Ivied sheds and trim flower-bordered lawns
To the stannary town of Tavistock,
Walk by the Tavy's weir that froths silk strands;
Abbey walls, arched bridge to the market block.

I taste creamy Brie in the old cheese shop,
Then drive across Dartmoor to Two Bridges,
The English sun warm on my cheeks, hedges
Pinked by wild flowers, up to the tors' ridges:
Boulders buried in green, small wild ponies.
We stop and munch our lunch on a knoll. Still,
I hear the cuckoo from a wooded copse,
A nightingale trill from behind a hill.

We turn off for Chagford, a narrow lane
With harebells in the hedgerows either side.
I stop at the Three Crowns, stand in the porch
Where Sidney Godolphin was shot and died,
Savour the remote village and thatched walls.
England, I love your hills and leafy ways
Which Montgomery and Churchill defended –
I brim sunshine and a patriot's praise.

II
I stretch out in the warm, late April sun.
A heatwave from the Sahara: blue sky,
Cloudless, a haze above the sea, my cheeks
Warm, shoulders, arms, body, legs and each thigh.
I feel the sun permeating my flesh,
Imbuing it with healing vitamins.
I bask and soak it in, red-brown go in,
See the nightmare that's happened in Athens.

On TV, in the Stoa of Attalos,
Near colonnades Socrates and Plato
Spoke from at the height of Athenian
Democracy, our nation's dealt a blow:
Ten new nations are welcomed to Europe,
And (bathos) Blair stands up and speaks for three
Minutes, exalts their new-won freedom from
"Dictatorship and repression" with glee.

Elsewhere in Athens rioters now fight
A street battle in protest against Blair,
Calling for peace by bombarding police
With petrol bombs and stones flung through the air.

Policemen fire tear gas, agitators
Put on goggles and ventilators, spread
Across Constitution Square, hurl rocks while
Europe's new constitution's presented.

The ten thought they'd be in a rich men's club
But find a deep division between those
Who hate America – France, Germany –
And those who're with the coalition's pose,
Regime change in Iraq. The new boys don't
Want to displease America's rulers
Who liberated them from the Soviets,
But don't want to displease their new masters.

The deepeners are aghast, the wideners
Have linked poor countries with no welfare scheme
For their elderly and improvident
To their tax systems, so rich countries cream
Tax from their bourgeoisie to pay pensions
For Bulgarians, Turks, Cypriots, Maltese:
A socialist Europe where wealth's transferred
From the landed to ghettos overseas.

"Democracy, freedom, the rule of law
Unite the EU," Blair says. An imposed
New constitution will abolish all
Twenty-five nation-states, which will be closed
States in a superstate, their assets locked
In Frankfurt's Central Bank. And then? To free
Them two-thirds must vote – or seceders lose
Them with trading rights. Some democracy!

He's proposed the new superstate should choose
A President whom the White House can call.
He wants this time-span job: no Parliament
To be questioned by, no Queen and no fall.
I grasp the posturer's attacked Iraq
To create an image that he is pro-
Nation-state while he dumps the pound for: not
Presidential ambition – the euro!

I grasp his "courage" that attacked Iraq
When his party, country, Europe opposed
Was to con us into supporting him
While he sold British interests and bulldozed
Parliamentary sovereignty and tax
To be run for the world government's gain.
I grasp he is the quisling of our time,
His betrayal's an indelible stain.

He signs our nation into superstate
With one President, Foreign Minister.
As a wind rustles a field of gold wheat
I hear the British people's quiet anger.
There have to be trade union rights – to strike.
Now Britain's voice speaks from the vaults of banks
And must be diminished, and this traitor
Still poses as a hero against tanks.

A new Norman Conquest is in the air.
We are now just one voice in twenty-five,
We're recreating a Soviet Union
In Europe, a new union that will thrive.
Many have tried to end the English power –
Spaniards, French and Germans. Now a Briton
Has succeeded where all others have failed.
What can we do? Riot? The glory's gone.

III
Dusk gathers on the land. I look to sea.
It's so calm beneath my evening window.
Beyond the clouds a clear pale azure sky
With hints of pink. Gulls flap, wheel to and fro.
My cormorant has stopped diving for fish.
All is so peaceful, tranquil, this May day.
I look towards Europe, to the skyline,
Disturbed: my country's no more round this bay.

Across the newspapers, "Europe sets out
Sweeping new powers" and "EU issues draft
Constitution". On all sides there are fears
Sovereignty's lost. Just "tidying-up"? That's daft!
Blair's had the preamble's "federal" struck out

But a more-than-federal state looms sullen
Like the dark clouds above me, dimming light.
The Sun proclaims, "The End of our Nation".

I read the headlines with numbed foreboding.
Britain ruled from Brussels, two million jobs
Will go, Frankfurt will set all interest rates,
Bureaucratic inspectors will, like yobs,
Prowl, scuffle, mug our purse. The Queen will go
Next, the Head of State will be elected.
All Churchill and Montgomery fought for's
Been surrendered as if Hitler weren't dead.

Light fades, the sea turns grey, gulls shuffle, stand
On rocky bar and breakwater and stare.
All the certainties I knew as a child –
Gone. A new legal code, guilty as air
Unless proved innocent. A thousand years
Of long English tradition now buried.
I, the chronicler of Britain's decline,
Am sad I was alive when it ended.

And yet this ending was not unforeseen.
Fifteen years back I put the United
States of Europe on my long chart. I wrote
A verse play on a Prince's choice and dread.
Ignored! The Establishment ignored me
And now they're finding out that I was right.
I wrote of regions replacing England.
The new treaty's unveiled them to our sight.

I foresaw it and warned an Earl, who leapt
Onto the woolsack in the House of Lords
To object that it's been packed with yes-men
To vote through these constitutional frauds.
Our Prime Minister's in with foreign powers,
Is internationalist, would give our land
Away without a vote – his masters' will.
The Earl's act shines across this murky sand.

The light is fading fast, the gulls now sit
On water like ducks, ready to take wing

To their nests in the nearby cliffs, a moth
Flits past my window in its foraging.
A peaceful, tranquil calm but I'm troubled,
  see someone shooting our traitor who
Is doing to our country what Philip
Of Spain, Napoleon, Hitler could not do.

And inwardly I'm filled with a quiet rage
For I'm powerless. What can I do but mewl?
Bilderberg have us by the throat, we have
To submit to a time of foreign rule
By diktat as compelling as conquest,
The Queen brushed aside in our Cromwell's swoops,
A revolution that – though mere paper
Constitution – is more crushing than troops.

The dark has gathered, I can hardly see
To write these words in my sea-view window.
The gulls have merged into the twilit mist.
The Queen, remote, aloof, who chose to go
And unveil a street sign that lacked planning
Permission and had to be taken down
Instead of Gosnold's statue Ipswich planned,
Is shaken, but's not defending the Crown.

That's at the heart of it, we're all dismayed
At our indifferent Royal Family;
Their independence, which they won't defend,
Should be our guarantee of liberty.
They sneer at us and patronise, ignore,
Look with superior airs and did not heed
Our warnings and are now in shock. Too late!
You should have listened long before the deed!

Now snails are creeping on the lamplit lawn,
And little flying midges cross the bay
And there's a misty blur on the skyline
Which could be land, Europe floating this way.
It looks like a far bank seen from a ship
In a wide river, and I swear it's France
Drifting towards us: continental drift
Encroaching on our independent trance.

⌐ I think of wartime England my parents
  Knew, the brave land young men fought for and died;
  I think how I'm English and wear my birth
  As a badge of honour with Essex pride.
  I knew we'd be here that election night
  Six years ago, but few agreed with me.
  They trusted the grinning young globalist
  Who'd captivated – captured my country!

  The birds have gone, the lights are in windows
  Across the harbour, men walk dogs, in awe,
  Saunter or stand in half-light, unaware
  Their future's been snatched as if by a war.
  The seaside village with one shop is quiet,
  A fisherman is unloading his boat.
  All think of the end of a long day's work,
  No one thinks of the Channel as a moat.

  And I'm a dislocated dissident.
  I've opposed those who are running our land,
  And soon I'll oppose those who take it on,
  French-, German-speakers who have for long planned
  To confiscate our wealth, spread it around.
  Most Europeans do not have our slate,
  The provident must fund the improvident.
  Thrift does not pay in the new superstate!

  The Earl of Pembroke and the *Kaskelot*
  Have port-hole lights below their six tall masts.
  A couple walk across the harbour bridge,
  Their footsteps echo as the twilight lasts.
  Gull Island shimmers in the glassy sea,
  Walkers on the pier look out from a lamp
  And at a light beyond it on Ropehawn
  On the Black Head above a far boat ramp.

  And now the crab-pots have been lost to dark
  And half the boat that lists as if it fell.
  The sheep on the hillside have disappeared,
  The outside drinkers are in the hotel.
  All's dark and quiet, the roundhouse still under
  Flagpole, the battlemented fort and sand

174

hat's Smeaton's harbour's black, but not as dark
As the night that's settled over England.

2, 17 April, 27 May 2003; revised 9–12 August 2003

33
from *Classical Odes* (1994–2005)
Book Two: In Europe's Ruins

On Delos: Island of Apollo

From the boat I'm rowed to Mykonos, find
A half-a-crown white house after a hunt,
Sleep to braying donkeys, then breakfast on
Bread, butter, honey on the waterfront,
The blue-indigo choppy by my feet.
The boatman calls he's leaving from the quay.
I leave my breakfast unfinished and cross
To green Delos: the Athenian Treasury.

I land at the mole below the Sacred
Harbour, find the Sacred Way, walk, exult
At the Hieron, Sanctuary of Apollo.
Ionians settled here and brought their cult
Of Apollo, god of light and music,
Under Naxos' rule made this place the first
Religious centre of the Ionian League
Till Athens "shielded" it from Persia's worst.

I find the late seventh-century-BC House
Of the Naxians and see the marble base
Of the immense statue of Apollo
That once stood here, read the archaic face
That's inscribed "I am of the same marble,
Statue and pedestal" – hinting a gloss:
That divine and earth's forms are of the same
Material, the oneness of the cosmos.

Three temples to Apollo stand nearby –
The oldest one was where the Treasury

Of the Delian Confederacy was stored;
All under Athenian hegemony.
Here to this precinct came famed Nicias
On an embassy, bearing a bronze palm,
Which blew over with the immense statue.
Storms don't exempt celebrity from harm.

I see the Stoa of the Naxians
(Sixth-century), where was kept the bronze palm-tree,
Head past the Sanctuary of Artemis
And monument to naval victory
Which housed a trireme, for the Sacred Lake,
Linger at the Temple of Leto, go
To the seventh-century terrace of five lions
Who in Naxian marble still watch for foe.

They guard the sacred place where Leto bore
Apollo and Artemis, wide awake,
As in Karnak sitting on their haunches,
Front legs upright, facing the Sacred Lake
Which held swans, geese sacred to Apollo.
I return via the Theatre-Quarter tasks:
See several houses, and Cleopatra's,
Mosaics of Dionysos and masks.

I see Mount Kynthos, where the sanctuaries
Of Zeus and Athena stood, the grotto
Of Herakles, the august Heraion
And sanctuaries of foreign gods below.
I look at the Harbour Quarter, at old
Warehouses, then sit by the choppy sea
In wind and see it all in its heyday,
Blank out what's late, see only fifth century.

All that happened forty-three years ago.
Now it seems as if it were yesterday.
Since then I have become a stonemason
Of sorts in my workshop's Pheidian display.
I hew a marble block to rough outline,
Then chisel, fix the rhymes, bits disappear,
And slowly a face is brought from the stone,
An image that was waiting to be clear.

Once the shape is revealed, I work round it,
From top to bottom, from bottom to top,
Beat chisel with the mallet of my ear,
Shave off words like chippings, know when to stop,
And then polish so each contour is smooth,
Check for unsightly wrinkles, leave all smart,
Stand back and judge if my new Apollo
Reveals Beauty through my stonemason's art.

Delos, top-sacred, burglar-proof war-chest
For the Confederacy's silver talents
Levied by Athens for all the islands,
The anti-Persian Ionians' defence,
Inspires awe at its sacred history,
But it's not tribute that has my tribute,
The money Athens hoarded for its use,
But the seat of the god that I salute,

The "invisible" isle, twice purified,
Uninhabited – no births or tombs – so
Unsoiled by human contamination
As birthplace and dwelling of Apollo,
God of Light, sun, poetry and prophecy,
Of measured words, the face I hew from stone
Whose sacred isle was corrupted by wealth,
Whose unseen mystery became seen and known.

Conceived 9 September 1958/22 July 1996, written 22 August 2001

By the Arno, Pisa

I take a bus to the brown wide Arno
And walk along the waterfront to where
Shelley lived near the large *ponte* and wrote
'Adonais' about Keats, in despair.
I wander via the tiny Templar church
Across the river to the other side,
See where Byron lived in Toscanelli
And see them meeting after poor Keats died.

⌐ Shelley suffered in Italy. He brought
Allegra to Byron's Venetian home.
Byron gave him and Mary a villa
Where their baby girl Clara died. In Rome
William died as at Caracalla's Baths
Shelley wrote part of *Prometheus Unbound*.
They returned here with a new son, Percy –
Allegra died and then Shelley was drowned.

I stare at a Roman wall, sense the ghosts
Of Shelley and Byron, and think of Pound
Who wrote *Pisan Cantos* while detained here,
Welcomed me at his mountain home I'd found
In Rapallo twenty-three years ago,
Urged me to make a start on my epic
Which I'd outlined to him: "If you can see
It, you can do it. Seeing it's the trick,

It's half the battle. It is like making
A table. It does not matter which leg
You start with so long as the table holds
Up. T. E. Hulme said to me" (one leg's peg)
"'All that a writer has to say will go
On half a side of a postcard; the rest
Is application, elaboration.'
Have you got that application – and zest?"

I gaze at the Arno. Red and orange
Houses shimmer in the water at me
In the warm afternoon. A high feeling
Elevates me, I sense my destiny –
To write an epic like Virgil's, Dante's,
Homer's and Pound's. Like Virgil I have shirked
A huge task for twenty years: to pattern
The war in verse, dark Hitler's fall reworked.

I must begin by the Arno's mirror
Which Dante knew in Florence, and Pound knew.
I must bring together the Fire, history,
Cosmology, science in a new view,
All disciplines patterned in one verse work
With the novel eye of Galileo,

Who had a new view of the universe
Here in Pisa by this same brown Arno.

  shudder for my achievements so far
Are but preludes to this impending task,
A clearing of my head for what's to come.
  must portray, wearing a tragic mask,
Universalist world history in verse,
The height of goodness and depth of evil,
The struggle between Christ's and Lucifer's
New World Orders; vision, heroic will.

Elevated pure feeling wells up, wets
My eyes. I tremble with intensity
At the enormity of the huge task,
At what I have to do to embody
All Western civilization's culture
In one twelve-book poem. I quiver in
The exalted vision of perfection
And my inadequacy to begin.

I sit in a bar on the Lung'Arno
Mediceo, near where Byron lived two years,
Sipping a glass of tea, for ten minutes
On and off my eyes mist over with tears
Which I blink back, now knowing deep within
The next phase in my work. I've had, I grasp,
The equivalent of when Dante saw
Beatrice by the Arno, felt his task's clasp.

I sit by the Arno and sense a call,
Know with awed certainty what I must do,
And after my epic I see I must
Make the Italian and Greek pasts run through
My verse, as Shelley and Byron once did.
I take a taxi to my luggage, lurk,
Sit on a fountainside waiting to go
Back to England, knowing my future work.

O Pisa, besides the Arno's mirror
That reflects coloured houses that shimmer
I've found a spring of creative feeling,

Imagination wide as a river
That can reflect the world and universe,
And I know the roots of our Europe grew
In the Greek-Roman and Renaissance worlds
With certainty Shelley, Byron, Pound knew.

Conceived 3 May 1993; written 21 August 2001; revised 20–21 July 2002

Summer Palaces

I
Outside Charlottenberg's winter palace
The Hohenzollern King in Prussia, lace-
Clad Frederick the First, looks at Queen Charlotte
And the son he, the Elector's son, begot,
The Soldier King Frederick William the First,
Who doubled the Prussian Army and burst
With rage at his son's poetic tastes, then,
Suspecting him of having a fond yen,
Put him in prison and condemned his friend
To beheading outside his wall – some end.

I find Frederick the Great in Sanssouci,
His summer palace at Potsdam, where he
Lived *sans souci* with greyhounds, "free from care",
A philosopher-king who had Voltaire
Living in for three years, dining aglow,
Sitting outside the Prussian Rococo,
Above the six-tiered terrace where grapes bend,
Under a spoked sun at the trellised end,
Above the fountain with Roman statues,
His kingdom shrunk to garden gods and muse.

Enlightened man of French culture, aesthete,
He built his single-storey palace seat
In a vineyard. Cherubs and grapes, at home,
Surround windows of the central green dome.
Cherubs and vases decorate and mock
Each Corinthian column, in Baroque
Restraint rather than exuberance. All
Is detachment, simplicity and fall,

Classical will to cultivate and be,
A garden in pensive tranquillity.

Reliefs illustrate, in his Orangery's
Ovid Gallery, Roman elegies.
Chinese musicians grace the tea-house wall.
Eighteen marble statues represent all
Arts and sciences by the Rococo
Art gallery. He is buried below
The terrace as he wished, by six Caesars,
Flora and Zephyrus (west wind), near stars.
There is an inscription on a flat stone:
"The philosopher on the royal throne."

And now I see the decline, Wilhelm wave
From his Berlin window, the Kaiser grave
Above the square where books would burn like straw,
At people he was leading into war
And, when the Hohenzollerns had to go,
Republic hailed from a Reichstag window.
He went into Dutch exile, and his son
Returned the day the Munich *putsch* was done.
The Crown Prince in Potsdam's Cecilienhof
Backed Hitler till the Russians saw him off.

II
I go to Vienna's Belvedere palace,
Built by Prince Eugene of Savoy, whose place
In history came from turning back the Turks
From the city gates and Europe's earthworks
In sixteen eighty-three. Its roof now jars:
Three Turkish tents between side cupolas.
Here Maria Theresa held a banquet
For her doomed daughter Marie-Antoinette
Who was engaged to the Duke of Berry,
And would die with him as sixteenth Louis.

In the Hofburg Maria Theresa glides,
Again in the Schönbrunn palace – that hides
"Beautiful spring" – which she made her summer
Residence where her sixteen children were.
She held the Habsburg lands others would seize –

Bavaria, France, Prussia and Spain – with ease.
I see her four-poster and conference room,
See a thousand servants bow and her groom,
Franz the First, German Emperor, at her side.
She wore black for fifteen years when he died.

I see the family group, her children's place
On the floor at her feet, and search her face
For the loss of Silesia and Poland.
Mozart gave his first concert in this grand
Mirror Room, a child prodigy, and jumped
On Maria Theresa's lap, kissed and bumped
Her cheeks, spoke of "Papa" Haydn, engrossed.
Here Baroque and Rococo reached their most
Exquisite in painting, sculpture, music –
For forty years culture was plethoric.

Here came Napoleon, he lived here for
Four years married to his second wife, raw
Marie-Louise, daughter of Franz the First,
Who bore him a son whom she fondly nursed,
The Duke of Reichstadt destined for a throne.
He played in the formal gardens alone.
Here, stuffed, is his companion, which brought bliss:
A crested lark. He died aged two in this
Room where Napoleon slept, awed at his task,
And here is a painting of his death-mask.

I see the decadence, sixty-eight years
Of Franz Josef's rule, tragedies and tears:
His brother Maximilian shot in
Mexico; Rudolf, lovelorn Crown Prince, thin,
Shot in a Mayerling suicide pact;
Elizabeth his wife killed when attacked
In Geneva; the Archduke, now his heir,
Who for twenty years lived at Belvedere
And knew its marble hall, shot by a Serb
Who triggered the First World War on a kerb.

When, after walks with Katharina Schratt,
He died in this Schönbrunn room – I gaze at
A painting of him on his death-bed – Karl

he First, a nephew despite low morale,
succeeded him till the end of the war,
And his son Otto, then, was barely four,
Who, an old man, took Mass, standing, with me
in a Prague church, the King of Hungary,
Emperor of Austro-Hungary, and more:
The uncrowned Holy Roman Emperor.

II
The Summer Palaces at Potsdam and
Vienna saw the greatness of the hand
Guiding Hohenzollern and Habsburg State,
The war between aesthetes Frederick the Great
And Maria Theresa, who honoured each
Other as they struggled for power and reach,
Protestant Prussia, Catholic Austria's shrines,
High art in both, end of dynastic lines;
Saw Wilhelm and the Crown Prince abdicate,
Karl and Otto share a similar fate.

The imperial cities of Berlin and
Vienna were full of beautiful grand
Baroque buildings, showed a culture in stone:
First the low style, and, once the Turks were thrown
Back, relief and a high style with ornate
Decoration, symmetry, soaring state.
The Hohenzollern-Habsburg war inspired
Europe's finest buildings, her spirit fired.
And Summer Palaces with gardens gave
Europe a summer, art that scorned the grave.

What was the Baroque? Architecture's dreams
Of boundless possibilities, what seems
Opening to a beyond (what's real now prime),
Revealing the limits of space and time,
Transcending divisions (sacred, profane,
Temple gates, triumphal arch on one plane),
Seeking harmony in movement, heightening
Awareness, the One intoxicating,
Blending regular and irregular,
Merging all arts to know joy in order.

⌐ Enhancing a sense of the One through flight,
It images sunbursts of radiant Light
(Hugest in Vienna's St. Charles's span).
It ranged from Naples to Rome and Milan,
Brussels, Antwerp, Madrid, Bourbon Paris,
Sense and spirit in unison, in bliss.
At first Habsburg and Catholic, it spread
To Protestant German lands and fed
Imperial grandeur, the oneness of all.
It has come again in a new form's call.

The Russians have gone, as after the Turks
There is relief throughout Europe. In works
A new baroque style is now emerging
That combines sense and spirit (vision's wing)
And looks beyond what seems and knows the real
As sunbursts of radiant Light that reveal
What unites still and moving, large and small,
Finds harmony, order, meaning in all,
Rejects the functional for the fired heart
And brings in a Universalist art.

A new style has burst into old Europe's dreams.
I mix British and European themes,
Like Virgil pastoral and epic frieze,
Adorn beyond what seems, both teach and please.
Away with drab, spiritless glass and stones,
In with what shaped Europe's greatness from thrones.
Let Summer Palace gardens include flowers
From a high culture's dream of divine hours.
Like Voltaire in his Château de Ferney
Plant chestnut and beech avenues, and be!

Conceived 21 and 29 July 1994; written 29 July 1994; revised 26–27 July 1997

Auschwitz and Immortality

Wheat fields, a barbed wire fence, a guard house or
Tower we climb, sentry watch-posts. From a square
Turret we gaze, appalled, numb. Barracks for
Women on the left, men on the right, bare.

A railway line divides round a ramped goods
Platform. A guard hut. A recorded glum
Voice says the gassing was done in the woods
Near ruins of a crematorium
Blown up by guards. I linger at this shrine.
Wild flowers grow in the sleepers of the line.

I listen for the jar of the train, and
The trudge and rasp of suitcase on the ramp,
The fit picked out to slave with a waved hand,
The shuffle till the rest (three quarters) tramp
To the "bathhouse", strip off their clothes and learn
Too late that the showers squirt gas, not water.
I hear them dragged next door by slaves who burn,
Earn freedom by loading each cadaver
Into an oven, dump ashes in ponds
In the woods: Auschwitz One's lost vagabonds.

We drive past slave factories to Birkenau,
Auschwitz Two, and meet our old Polish guide,
A white-haired inmate of nearby Plaszow
Who knew the sadist Goeth and those who died.
We follow on a path to the main gate,
Read *Arbeit Macht Frei*, Work Makes Free, with awe,
Take an avenue through three-storey great
Brick blocks where prisoners lived, enter block four.
The walls exude Polish and Soviet fear.
The Jews from East Europe were settled here.

We wander round blocks and see narrow racks
On which five people slept, their filthy straw,
The rows of unprivate toilets, the packs
Of Zyklon B gas crystals, and the raw
Piles of things that were stripped: hair turned grey by
Gassing, spectacles, shoes, luggage all named,
Shaving brushes, wooden limbs – so to die
They hopped, stood on one leg. Our guide, inflamed,
Tells of the biggest centre, from such clues,
For mass-exterminating Europe's Jews.

We glimpse Commandant Höss's house outside,
Pass medical blocks where Mengele's sneer

Experimented on prisoners, and stride
Through a courtyard to the Killing Wall where
Twenty thousand Poles were shot or hanged on
Mobile gallows, and Block Eleven, death block,
Where courts tried and sentenced, the washroom wan
Prisoners stripped in to be shot, still in shock.
We go down to basement cells where, before
Execution, Christ was drawn on a door.

Now we stand in the hot assembly square
Where the SS counted prisoners, and gaze
At the gallows where one day, in such air,
Twelve Poles were hanged at roll-call. The guide brays,
"Now we go to see the gas chamber, and
Crematorium." At a grassy hill
With brick chimney we go down a shaft, stand
In a long barrow, the concrete, cold, still
Bunker where a million died, in dismay
At three ovens which burned hundreds each day.

We stand at the rebuilt gallows – a wood
Box, uprights and bar, iron hook for a rope –
On which, till the box floor fell in, Höss stood,
Like the gallows on which thousands lost hope.
Two attempts were abandoned as a mob
Tried to lynch him. The next dawn, with no din,
He was hanged. Himmler had said of his job,
"Existing extermination camps in
The east cannot work on such a scale, I
Have now designated Auschwitz to try."

The grey soil beneath the roots leaves me tense,
The dust on my trainers makes me feel ill.
Here, from *Mein Kampf* to Wansee Conference,
A wish to kill all Jews became a will.
Of eight million, over five died at walls
Near as many non-Jews during the war.
The systematic death-process appals.
How can man see man as a clawed, jawed maw,
A beast before a killing wall, a thing,
And not feel for a naked soul in skin?

rom common origin in One Fire's mind
ll creatures manifest in brotherhood.
hose in peaked caps who "thingise" humankind
)o not see we are sparks from the One Good.
emoved from the Whole by uniforms, shrill
llegiance to a part their reason chose,
ll who would torture, suffocate and kill
)ur human brothers, spill blood or stop nose,
)eny common humanity in skin,
emove their souls from the One Light they're in.

Iell is separation from what is real.
Ieaven floods with energy from the All.
Iell can be where frowning firing-squads kneel,
Ieaven can shine through staked smiles before a wall.
ll mankind is one, fish in dipping waves.
ienocide, like a fisherman's crowbar
tains red the souls of all who fill mass graves.
ictim everywhere, be assured you are
n immortal spirit, shaped like bright rays,
hat goes on in glory to Being's next phase.

onceived 24 July 1994; written 26 July 1994; revised 29 May – 7 June 1997

In Byron's Ithaca

rom the ferry I probe wild Ithaca,
he rugged sights that blind Homer once saw:
he Korax rock or Ravens' Crag, the Cave
)f Eumaeus the swineherd who lived raw,
Vatered his pigs at the spring or Fountain
)f Arethusa; and as we enter
athi harbour, look for the Nymphs' Cave where
)dysseus hid the Phaeacians' treasure.

Ve dock and I wander out from the quay
mmersed in Homer – the pigs swilled acorns
nd black water, bees hived in the stone jars
n the naiads' cave; rosy-fingered dawns!
pass under, no! – Byron's bust in stone!
m shocked, then grasp: the British ruled this bright

Ithaca from 1809 before
He went off to Messolonghi to fight.

I bargain with a driver, set off round
The island – the Cave of the Nymphs, a pit
Four kilometres off up a steep track,
Through loud cicadas. I squeeze through a slit
On the north side, descend steps to the floor,
See the smoke-hole in the roof where gods could
Enter. Here Odysseus hid the gifts from
Alcinous. I stand where Homer stood.

We drive past Phorkys cove, where Odysseus
Landed, to Mount Aetos (one site for his
Castle), across Agros, Laertes' fields,
Up a steep slope, then skirt Odysseus's
Birthplace on Mount Neritos (in a cave)
To Polis Bay, alternative landing
Spot, where Tennyson's Ulysses set sail
In his old age for western stars, yearning.

I see the island of Asteris where
The suitors tried to lure Telemachos,
Go to Stavros and Pelikata's Hall
Of Hermes, seat of Odysseus' palace
Which has a view of three seas as Homer
Describes, and the museum's Mycenaean
Pots, and Odysseus' "drinking cup" with ringed
Stem for fingers – grip – found in a broken

Cave I visit in Polis Bay, collapsed
By earthquake. I stand near the sunken mole
Where Tennyson's Ulysses would have stood,
Then pass near Melandros spring's gushing hole
And Homer's seat, where he taught his pupils,
And then go back to Phorkys where Odysseus
Landed to be away from the suitors,
Disguised as a castaway, and thanked Zeus.

I swim from sharp stones in clear cool water,
My clothes piled by an olive trunk in heat
Where sailors laid Alcinous' treasure,

Then lie where Odysseus lay in a sheet
Of linen, and muse on the poet who
Brought me, blind Homer of the wine-dark sea,
And again see Byron's face, am haunted
As much by him as by *The Odyssey*.

Like T.E. Lawrence, a British agent
Who led the Arab revolt against Turks,
Byron supported the Greek freedom-fight
Against Turkey and *lived* while writing works.
He came to Kefalonia as agent
To represent the committee in Greece,
Spent six weeks in Argostoli, then moved
To a healthier, prettier place, for peace.

I think of the house in Metaxata
Where Byron spent the last four months before
Leaving for Messolonghi, with its view
Of the plain, castle and Mount Aenos, saw
The ivy that's survived the house's wreck
And the rock he sat on in Lakithra
Near Mycenaean tombs and, inspired, wrote
Unaware he'd soon die of a fever.

I used to think Byron an egotist,
An Augustan, not a true Romantic,
But now fondly recall polished stanzas,
Wit, turn of phrase and easy rhetoric,
Models for my own verse, and, philhellene,
The love of Greece and Italy I share,
And reckless urge to fight tyranny, be
A British agent for freedom and dare.

O Byron, rediscovering you here
In Vathi, your alertness to the hour,
I bow before your bust and to your heart,
To racy narrative and pulling-power,
To you as a British secret agent
Resisting the imperial power with thrills
And sitting on rocks and scribbling lines
That will be as immortal as the hills.

⌐ And despite your rational, Augustan thought
Your material's acutely Romantic.
I honour you for your dashing panache,
Stanzas dazzlingly accomplished yet strict.
Through your philhellenism I bear fruit
On the much-gnarled Romantic olive tree,
Rooted in the classical and Nature:
Ruined stones and the sparkling Phorkys sea.

Conceived 22 July 1995; written 22 February 2001; revised 28–29 March and 31 May 2001

At Virgil's Tomb

I take a taxi from Naples and reach
The Porta Puteolana, pay – I wave –
Under Santa Maria's railway bridge,
Through the bay grove past Leopardi's grave
Climb to a Cumae-like sandstone cliff-face,
Cross the top, jacaranda in blue bloom,
Of Agrippa's tunnel, descend steps and see:
Virgil's reputed reticular tomb.

It once stood by the road, but's now high up.
It seems a family *columbarium*
With weeds round the roof's two holes. I enter.
It does not seem one man's mausoleum:
Ten empty sunlit niches for ash-urns,
A long window, three air vents and a door,
A metal water stoup. "*Hic Vergilius,*"
I read, "*Tumulus Est.*" A sandy floor.

Taken ill in Megara, Virgil died
In Brindisi, where his ashed bones had been
Raked from the pyre and brought (Donatus says)
To Naples and placed in a tomb "between
The first and second milestones of the *Via
Puteolana*" near land he had bought or
Inherited from Siro, where a white
Temple to Virgil was built, that I saw.

Was this the place? Where did the *Via* start?
 muse on words a friend (Horace maybe)
nscribed here, Virgil's last dying distich:
'Mantua bore me, Calabria snatched me,
Naples holds me. I sang pastures, fields, kings."
Statius, Silius Italicus enjoyed
This place, as did Petrarch and Boccaccio.
It fell into ruin and was destroyed

In the time of Robert of Anjou, who,
Holding that the fourth eclogue prophesied
The birth of Christ, not of Antony's child,
Ordered that Virgil's ashes should reside
In a wooden casket in a chapel
In Castel dell' Ovo where the Siren
Parthenope landed, causewayed island,
So he could be Christianized, brought to Heaven.

A train hoots, the traffic roar is distant.
I sit in glorious silence, quite alone,
And ponder the soul of Virgil, who knew
Octavian, on whom Aeneas was grown,
Celebrated peace and guided Dante;
Gaze at the arch and the steep grove outside,
A place fit for Aeneas's creator.
Someone's left laurels that have shrivelled, died.

I trace my origins as a poet
Back to this place – many of my school hours
Were spent translating bucolic *Eclogues*,
Rural *Georgics*, *Aeneid*'s herbaceous flowers,
Whose scents, entering my soul, later inspired
Me to create my own epic garden.
As much as any he was my mentor
And guided my pastoral and martial pen.

I leave and walk back down through the bay grove.
The shock of traffic thunders through the arch,
Choking with fumes; the modern world returns
With a roar that assaults me as I march.
But I am still lost in that peaceful tomb
And muse on Virgil's burned bones and the verse

That outlived Augustus's world Empire,
Will last as long as gold coins in his purse.

O Virgil, you lived through civil unrest
And saw at close quarters Augustan peace,
The ideal life of shepherds and farmers
And soldiers who return to ploughs and geese
That I now see in arable Essex
And Suffolk and, too, catch pastoral and war;
You caught the *Pax Augusta* Caesar dreamed
In fine sculpted verse that fills me with awe.

Conceived 18 October 1995; written 19 August 2001; revised 22–23 July 2002

At Horace's Sabine Farm

Near Licenza I take a dusty track.
We park, get out and I see, deserted,
Low walls below green foothills with small trees:
Horace's Sabine farm, villa gifted
Him by Maecenas. I wander through twelve
Rooms grouped round an open courtyard with square
Water, above gardens and swimming-pool.
It is serene: grass, wild orchids, clear air.

Some of the low walls enclose mosaics:
The bedroom floors. I stand on one labelled
"Horace's bedroom". Was this the room full
Of mirrors so he could, with desire swelled,
See his sex acts from all angles? I note
The net walls and see lead piping that awes.
It channelled water from the square court pool
Under neighbouring rooms' mosaic floors.

Here Horace turned his back on busy court,
Ran his estate with a foreman, eight slaves;
Wrote *Epodes* and *Odes* modelled on Pindar
In Sapphics and Alcaics, Greek enclaves
Learned as a student in Athens. He'd fought
At Philippi, and met Maecenas through
Virgil. A girl brings a Visitors Book.
I leaf; one a day mostly, some days two.

I wander up to the Bandusian spring.
The cool brook gushes down by the track's twist.
I dip a hand in, scoop and taste limpid
Water "clearer than crystal". On my wrist
I have a leech, flick it off and recall
How thirty-nine years ago I came here
And drank at this Muse's spring and became
A poet. That day clings like a leech, near.

I recall clearly standing with schoolfriends
And Peter Croft, Latin master long dead,
Young with hooked nose, bleary eyes, stick-out ears.
"The water's pure, you can drink it," he said,
And so we did. I wander up with ghosts –
Green hills all round, bamboo, crab apples, twee
Farming – to the rocky fountain Ninfeo,
Fifteenth-century, built by the Orsini.

And now I sit at school two weeks before
The end of term – Croft then the party's purse –
On a seat on Lower Field in March sun,
Reading *The Faber Book of Modern Verse*:
'The Wreck of the Deutschland'. Suddenly I
Knew that despite my classical background
I was to be a poet, had been stirred
To a life-long vocation I'd just found.

That perception which led me to read Keats
And Shelley that cricketing summer, blank
And turn away from Law and read English,
Was ritualized, chalice-like, when I drank
From this spring, which seemed to flow underground
From the Muses. I'd communed, drunk romance,
Immortal liquid, and now part of me –
My soul – needed immortal sustenance

From the poets of Rome's Augustan Age.
I walk down to the villa's swimming-pool –
Clearly outlined in grass – and see Horace,
Maecenas, Virgil dip and play the fool
Though under pressure to hand in good verse,
Reflect I've followed Virgil most, yet see

My works reflect bits of Virgil, Horace
And Ovid; all go back to the Big Three.

O Horace, friend of Augustus, you filled
Your works with lovers he excused (to see
Latin lyrics that rivalled Greek lyrics
Though he'd campaigned against adultery).
Were you really dissolute, or were they
Make-believe lovers in literary forms?
He chose you to write the 'Secular Hymn'
And so, as his laureate, to convey norms.

Your Greek sophisticated sadness mixed
With your Italian vigour, rhetoric
(Like my Englishness and Europeanness).
You did not look back to the Republic,
Saw religion as a social practice,
Content to be Augustus's laureate,
Balance love, friendship and enjoyment; death,
Bloodshed and duty – the private with State.

Conceived 24 September 1996; written 18 August 2001; revised 24 July 2002

In Dante's Verona

I
I walk streets of Verona with a guide
After the worst of the heat, and hear how
The Veronese were Ghibellines, who'd been
With the German Hohenstaufens, and now
In Dante's time banned the Guelfs who were with
The Pope (who could not enforce domicile).
Dante visited the Ghibellines here
Three times after his disgrace and exile.

As a White Guelf he had opposed the Pope's
Ambition to rule the Holy Roman
Empire and expand Papal territory
And, sent to San Gimignano to plan,
Solidified the Guelf League for its war.
When Charles of Valois arrived at Florence

The Black Guelfs' HQ), Dante was chosen
Ambassador to make the Pope see sense.

While Dante was in Rome, Charles had entered
Florence, allied with Blacks. Whites, though absent,
Including Dante, were accused and fined
For Ghibellinism, embezzlement,
Opposition to the Pope and Charles –
Payment in three days. He could not return
From Rome to pay in time, and in default
He and fourteen Whites were condemned to burn.

Now in exile, Dante contacted most
Pro-Ghibelline families and came here
To the della Scala, planned his return.
I stand by the Scaligeri's palace where
He stayed with Bartolomeo Scala
(Now a police station) in 1303
And see the stone staircase where he first saw
The ruler's brother, the young Cangrande.

His great-great-grandfather Cacciaguida,
Speaking as shade in 1300 (in
Canto 17 of *Paradiso*),
Had foretold the first refuge he would win:
At the court of the "mighty Lombard" who
On a ladder bears an eagle. He'd see
A youth with him who would become famous,
In whom he could place his trust: Cangrande.

Now he urged Albert the First, German King,
Habsburg Emperor, to come to Italy,
Regarding him as a Roman Emperor
Who ruled with a divine authority:
"Come see the Capulets and Montagues" –
Feuding families, neighbours who'd had words.
I sit in the Piazza delle Erbe
Which Dante saw and watch caged singing birds.

At La Lastra the Whites and Ghibellines
Lost. He went to Bologna for a span,
Until expelled, then Lucca whence, sustained

By the thought of the great work he began
In 1308, he moved on, living
In noble houses in North Italy,
Their bread bitter, tread on their stairs heavy.
Exiled, he sought a heavenly city.

After the rift between the Emperor
Henry and Pope Clement the Fifth, hopes dashed,
He returned to the Lord of Verona,
The twelve-year-old youth he'd seen, unabashed
Cangrande the First who'd now made a great
Ghibelline state of the north's ruling rooms.
I see where he stayed with Cangrande in
The castle opposite the Scala tombs.

Cangrande's military activities
Had become legendary, his conquests matched
By his tall beauty, graceful speech and wit.
Noble, courteous, clever, he had attached
Brescia, Vicenze, Padua, Cremona,
Parma, Reggio, Mantua, Treviso.
He aimed to unify all Italy,
Gave exiles homes, patroned their art for show.

II
In a letter Dante dedicated
Paradiso to him, sent him the fair
Copy, half a dozen cantos a time.
His wanderings in poverty, threadbare,
Had ceased. Now he had a base for his work.
He opposed the Pope as Cathars had done
And consorted with his foes. Cangrande
Was a hunting greyhound, "*cane*", a pun.

Now he recalled Florence's Duomo square
Where, between 12 and 13 now, he stood
On summer evenings, walked round the corner
To the house of his birth and childhood
In his medieval street, windows grilled,
How by the Ponte Vecchio he did see
Radiant Beatrice near the splashing Arno
And was inspired to write his *Comedy*.

stand by San Zeno's Basilica
Between a Romanesque campanile
And tower, go inside and look back and gaze
At the white-mauve rose window's shimmering ray
Suggesting ethereal heaven, glimmering,
A twelfth-century rose window that shows
The Wheel of Fortune Dante saw and used
As Paradise's "sempiternal rose".

The breach with Cangrande came suddenly.
The warlord entertained his troops crudely.
A jester told dirty jokes, did a mime.
As Dante winced, Cangrande said cruelly,
'I wonder why this stupid fellow knows
How to please everyone when you who're meant
To be wise can't please them at all." A boy
Heaped bones at Dante's feet, a mock present.

Now his last visit, to Sant' Elena.
I see where Dante, as philosopher
And scientist, debated with great minds
In Cangrande's presence, whether water –
In streams, rivers, ponds, lakes, seas and oceans –
Is higher than the earth. Dante maintained
That nowhere in the world can the level
Of water be higher than earth that drained.

I sit again in Piazza dell' Erbe
And think of how he caught malaria
In Venice and, having borne a vision
All round Italy, died in Ravenna.
How practical was his diplomacy,
How well he bridged Nature and the divine.
I gaze at the winged lion, emblem
Of Venetian rule and the mystic line.

Santa Maria Antica. I stand
Beneath the tomb of Cangrande, his dust
In his reclining figure, the ladder
(*Scala*) imaging ascent, upward thrust.
At the end he only had Verona
And Vicenze, but I admire the way

He presided over the revival
Of this city's artistic interplay.

O Dante, like Shakespeare later, you made
Universal types from historical
Figures and blended them with your vision
In 1283 of an aureole,
The Light's three-sphered Trinity, "Eternal
Light" who dwells in itself alone, and knows
Itself, the Light seen when one's consciousness
Swoons beyond thought into the mystic rose.

O mystic Dante, who spent a lifetime
In working out the deep implications
Of your 1283 vision, I too,
In 1971, had some visions
That took me decades to unfold in books,
That fill my philosophy with ferment,
My history and my literary works.
I stand by your statue and nod assent.

The Light exists within itself alone
And it is a mystery of the meaning
Of life that it can shine into our souls
In times of need or of its own choosing,
Change us with its fathomless, clear substance,
Its single, changeless form. O Living Light,
Philosophy, history, literary works
Are worthless if they ignore inspired sight!

Conceived 20 July 1998; written 5, 10–11 February, 8 August 2001

34
from *Classical Odes* (1994–2005)
Book Three: A Global Sway

At Troy VI

I enter by the east tower and am by
Troy VI, which Turkish archaeologists say
Was Priam's city: yellow blocks. I walk
Past the east wall and reach the east gateway
Where hung the Dardanian Gates no Trojan
Returned to when Achilles stalked; explore
The small rooms of Troy VIIA where US
Archaeologists find the Trojan War.

I pass the Troy VI *megaron* houses
And look at the north-east tower and cistern;
And Temple of Athena – victors' god –
Where Xerxes slaughtered a thousand oxen
Before his invasion of Greece; Troy I's
City gate and wall; the ramp of Troy II
Where Schliemann found Helen's treasure and thought
It was the city where Achilles slew.

I pass the VIM building, perhaps once
The royal palace in view of its sprawl;
And a sacred precinct to Cybele;
And walk back along Troy VI's block wall
To the Great Tower, look through the Scaean Gates,
See their sewage channel; house 630;
The pillared house; where old men sat and watched
Helen stroll along the rampart deftly.

I return full circle to the east gate
Where the Trojan Horse was left and wheeled in;
It's narrow so the Horse was long, not wide –
Held six to open the doors from within.
This gate was nearest to Scamander's plain,
Had no sewage channel to catch Horse wheels.

The Greeks would have left the Horse on this sand.
I see them tug with ropes, lean, dig in heels.

I reach VIC and VIE, the houses
Of Paris and Helen, perhaps. I climb
Ten steps and sit on Athena's altar,
Peer for distant blue sea, Greek sails – springtime!
Round here was surely Helen's high terrace
From where she saw the Greek army arrive,
The thousand ships anchor, men disembark
And cross the dusty Scamander, and drive.

I sit in the hot sun, pad on my knee,
Scribble my impressions – while my neck burns.
The cooling wind across the plain tempers
The heat, dries my sweat. My shadeless heart yearns,
I am drawn to this place and brave the sun.
My tongue's parched at the end of a hot day.
I peer for the Achaeans' harbour where
They beached their ships in Cape Sigeum's bay.

I see the wood Horse dragged through the east gate
And up the ramped steps to the walled beauty
Of the fifty-bedroomed royal palace
Where it is set up as a wheeled trophy,
And think, as I look back to house VIE,
Zeus wanted the Trojan War to prevent
The overpopulation of the earth;
A goal our Bilderbergers implement.

This is where it all happened: the *Iliad*,
The departure of Odysseus, the course
Of Agamemnon, the flight of Aeneas
Which led to Rome's founding. This was the source
Of Greek drama and verse, it feeds my soul
Which feels its warmth as my neck feels the sun.
This ruin bore and haunts our literature.
The literary West was here just One.

The war? I see Trojans as Luvians who
Spoke different languages, Homer avers.
I see the Greeks come in twelve hundred ships,

Each with a hundred and twenty warriors.
The Trojans had one tenth of the Greek force.
An unequal contest dragged on ten years
Till the Greeks sacked this place, pulled down its walls,
Began Western expansion, Eastern fears.

Conceived 15 July 1995; written 25 August 2001; revised 30–31 July 2002

35

from *Classical Odes* (1994–2005)
Book Four: The Western Universe

In Cornwall: A New Renaissance

I
Cornwall, conducive to poetic trance!
I stare out of my window at a sea
Half-sunlit, half-choppy that laps, below
My window, a wall twenty yards from me.
I look and spot my cormorant diving
Beneath the inky waves for fish. Now I
Have returned to my work, am lost. The sea
Helps me to concentrate and unify.

The sea is like my mind. Spread round the bay,
Reaching the horizon, it's vast and deep
Yet is ever changing, sometimes as calm
As a lake, tranquil with lights flashing, steep
Sunlight splashing off it like heavy rain.
Sometimes it is stirred up and breakers roll,
Crash, pour over the pier and dash up spray.
Heedless of its mood, my mind's a still bowl.

Sash-windows up, fresh air gusting gently
From open sea – Channel and Atlantic,
Oxygenizing my poor labouring lungs
Charges me with energy so I'm quick,
Alert, write sixteen hours with little breaks,
Always clear-headed. This open-air, plain
Regime is like writing on the beach, I
Am close to elements: sun, wind, mist, rain.

⌐ I work unaware of its moves, yet sense
  Its presence like a deep unconscious mind
  Torn from behind my eyes, out there to see.
  The tide keeps me company. I write blind
  And come to and notice the tide's gone out,
  People are playing on the beach, gulls stroll,
  Or else, tide in, I see boys skimming stones,
  Then I return to deep within my soul.

  Why do I do this, spend my time each day
  Drafting a poem, polishing it twice?
  I sharpen my thought, hunt for precise words,
  Make a statement in language that's concise,
  Associate a place with a giant,
  See poems as cross-disciplined, in rhyme,
  Mix disciplines, felt thoughts, in a fresh whole,
  Imaged perceptions that can withstand time.

  But why do I do this? I have been blessed
  With wives, children, worldly success and looks,
  I own three schools and a large country house,
  As many properties as I've done books.
  Millions come in and go out every year.
  I have a need to keen clarity, search
  For new ways to relate to and present
  The One in words, as some need prayers in church.

  The One's apart from all religions, creeds.
  As there is no church to which I can go
  My words reveal a new metaphysic,
  Channel the Light, define soul like Plato.
  I embody Truth in daily poems.
  While others repeat prayers, chant mantras, shout
  At football matches or do hard crosswords,
  I find new angles on what life's about.

  I experience something that's ordinary,
  That hints at the One, and reflect and frown,
  Feel it more intensely than others do
  So it takes root and I must note it down
  And dismiss it from my immediate mind,
  Like classifying and filing, a bit

Like discarding in something memorable.
It finds me, I don't go in search of it.

I see and feel with an intensity
Others don't seem to have things they don't meet,
Forget, aren't haunted by. My poems grow
Out of my sown unconscious like gold wheat
As I reflect on the experience.
Writing harvests what's thrust to consciousness,
Purges like a confession to a priest,
Wipes clean inner eye's screen and reaped *largesse*.

It's like watching seaweed and driftwood washed
Up onto a beach by a wave-led tide,
Images strewn along the water-line
To be beachcombed, picked up, brought back and dried.
Sometimes the sea throws up nothing but due
To atmosphere sends up a mist that rolls
In from the deep, the unconscious envelops
In a cloud of unknowing to feed souls.

A sea-mist is creeping in from the sea.
The Truth is hidden from the mind, concealed
When vapour separates it, comes between.
The mist rolls in upon the house, the field.
I'm a poet of sunlight seen through mists,
I flash flecks of sunlight like splashing rain.
I love it when evening sea turns silver,
Streaked orange. Now fog's obscured the sea-plain.

It is dark now, the fog is thick and dank.
I slip out for a walk, stand on the pier.
The sea-cliffs on each side of the harbour
Are shrouded, a lamppost's light gives some cheer,
It's pale in the wisps that screen the village.
I have been writing in this sea-fog cloud,
Striving for clarity at my window
As waves pound on shingle whose drag is loud.

II
Next morning in my window, with the surf,
I think of the Renaissance that combined

Christian and pagan, how Ficino held
The Light's available to all mankind
At all times. I think how I have restored
Universals to philosophy's blur,
The universal Light to a cosmos
That's been reduced, by logic, to matter.

A new Renaissance is here, new rebirth.
We look at history as a whole, reverse
Modern philosophy so it reveals
The Light that created the universe
And literature so it glows the beyond,
Shows the One in a wave's curl and tranced sight,
Sees body as the rib-cage of the soul.
A revolution's restoring the Light.

Downstairs, yesterday, I have, between feeds
And sleeps, played with my new grandson, a whole
Who lies shaking his arms, kicking his legs,
Intent, clutching a finger, a new soul;
And I also talked on the phone at length
About restoring the soul to our time.
People are gathering, a plan's being made
For a Spirit of the Age that's sublime.

The sea, a baby and my pondering soul
Are all in one accord and hail the One,
Restore purpose, show that Supreme Being
Cares for various humankind like the sun.
I scorn materialist man-made teachings
That a third of men should be starved, made ill
Or killed in war. Metaphysical love
Pours the One's compassion, its tides and Will.

The lunch-time News announces the shock news:
To this murky backwater of the south-
West, our PM, Blair, and his wife will come
To help tourism back from foot-and-mouth
(Which stopped at Devon, did not reach Cornwall).
A small crowd waits by the Pier House – young, old.
I wander over. No one knows the times.
The media circus know – they have been told.

Three cars arrive by the shipwreck centre.
The Blairs go in, sit with two Tourist Board
Reps five minutes, emerge, grinning. He signs
Autographs. I stand under trees unawed
With Matthew. Blair stops, stares at me, a look
Of half-recognition. I stare my mind.
They walk twenty yards, a small crowd round them,
To a long camera line, pose, dock behind.

The vicar's waiting at the Pier House door
To greet the visitors and serve them tea.
Drawn by him a large crowd is strung along
The road across the dock that slopes to sea,
Who to a camera resemble tourists
Among media vans, having braved the rain.
The vicar's been three hours at the wrong place.
He's wasted his time, he's waited in vain.

Open-necked, sun-tanned, embracing, grinning,
On holiday with media profiles,
They stand with their backs to the dock and preen.
A hundred flashes catch their sincere smiles.
The papers will say they had a cream tea,
Chatted to smiling folk on holiday,
That there were many tourists. Then they're off.
Government by camera. I turn away.

Minimalist – the bare-minimum time
To convey the impression they were in
The village a long while. They barely glanced
At the dock, did not tour a ship, see tin,
Get briefed on china clay, go to the beach,
Walk round. They had no interest in the place
Save to be snapped drawing attention to –
Linked with – a glossy port: image, surface.

Back in my window I return to less
Light-weight things than image and photo shoot,
Trivialising for impression, con trick
That has replaced arguments that refute.
I forget this new-world-order mouthpiece
Who sees himself as a Bilderberg sage,

Who deceives on the material system
And ignores the true Spirit of our Age.

In my mind I'm on the Lizard (*Lys ardh*,
"High place"). Sun bounces off sea with great glare,
By couch-grass I see the rocks off the reefs,
The one visible outcrop – stratum bare –
Of the Normannian plate that collided
With "Cornwall" three hundred and seventy-four
Million years back over oceanic crust
And thrust great Lizard rocks from the sea floor.

I move behind outer image, surface
To the inner mind as deep as the sea
That's filled with images like sea-creatures –
Crabs, eels, strange starfish, the anemone,
And ignore camera crews doing intros
And leave wordly distraction for the calm
Within the Light's Universal Idea
Where ideas float like jellies that alarm.

I am with the Light which lasts for ever,
Not transient puppets employed to betray.
A Revolution's coming in all thought
That will see culture as a mystic way,
Restore the view the giants lived by who
Tower above the pygmies who run our State;
A new Renaissance that will hold up quests
And question our notions of human fate.

14–15 August 2001; revised 16–18 August 2001; 2–3 April 2005

Among Loughton's Sacred Houses

I park in Brooklyn Avenue, a long
Way back from the High Road, linger, loiter
Outside the house I came to when just three,
Semi-detached with a concrete area.
I recall sitting on the stairs inside,
Could go up on my bottom, heaved and strove.

see myself sitting in my high-chair,
My mother in the kitchen, by the stove.

hear a deep voice on the radio
Read the war news, then see myself in bed
Listening in terror after lights-out for
Doodlebugs, and once heard in mounting dread
A knocking underneath, a broken spring.
thought there was someone below my feet
And was too paralysed by fear to look,
And cowered in the safety of my sheet.

And I came to this gate with my father,
Where I'm standing, fifty-nine years ago.
The sky lit up with a white flash, windows
Behind broke, bits of glass fell, lay below.
see my father turning in the dark,
Saying "Come on, back in" in a low shout,
Limping-running back towards the front door
While I chant with glee, "The windows are out."

A string of bombs had hit the cricket field.
We lived in the V-bomb corridor then.
My father told me stories at bedtime
Of "Peter and his dog", when the siren
Went off at the police station – air raid!
And I was led by hand to the shelter
Somewhere downstairs in there, lay on a rug,
Was read to as we waited for thunder.

From here I walked to school, first Essex House,
And then to old Oaklands across the road;
And walked back with Robin Fowler's mother.
My shoelace came undone *there*, as she strode
By her bike she stooped and tied it. That night
I tried, fumbled lace and mucked up my bow.
In old Oaklands garden I lay inside
The Morrison shelter in the sun's glow.

Grandpa, white-haired, one finger missing, came
And sat gnarled by the fire, and one lunch-time
Went to the shops in fog, did not come back.

I was sent out and found him, nose in grime,
Towards the High Road, lying on the ground.
He had stumbled and cut his head. I "woke"
Him up and led him back through the thick fog,
Bleeding, now wonder: did he have a stroke?

I see my father's study, he sits by
A desk, green curtains drawn, light on. I stand
While he tells me the twins have died. Will I
Help tell my younger brother, hold his hand?
Filled with importance and responsible,
Wondering if I should grieve, they'd not known me
As they'd never left hospital, I nod,
Am haunted by that room which I still see.

I drive to the school my grandson went to
And stand outside the green home we bought, see
Myself hold a grey battleship. Up there
Wires hung from the skirting-boards, ARP
Telephones had stood on the bare floorboards.
A hot May afternoon, and I hear words
From my birthday party in the garden.
Robin Fowler gave me a book on birds.

I said, "I've got this book." "No, you haven't,"
My mother said menacingly, laying
Jammed bread on a clean, white tablecloth I
Sat at with other small children, watching.
A blob of damson jam dropped on the cloth.
I see my mother in a summer dress
Pinch salt and rub it on the purple stain.
I could lean in and rub the salt, touch, press.

I see the bedroom where I used to read,
Up there on the right, where I dreaded creaks,
The streetlight reassuring on the wall;
And then I moved to the back room that speaks
Of my brother. We shared a black cupboard –
Rickety, a door catch that clicked
And whispered round it from our twin beds till
One of our parents called up, "Go to sleep."

recall being ill and the gas fire
By which I would read all Dostoevsky.
Or Walker came, I ate arrowroot,
A poached egg on mashed potato. I see
My mother cook on the old kitchen stove,
Red and black tiles on the floor: Welsh rarebit,
And on Sundays a sizzling sausage pie;
High tea at six, the nursery dimly lit.

As I had younger brothers and sisters
Nurses came to stay, my former bedroom
Had a bath, nurse's chair and baby clothes.
I saw a baby being bathed in gloom,
In a half-oval white bath that slotted
In a metal holder on folding legs,
Filled from a blue enamel jug's water
Boiled on the coke boiler near piled clothes-pegs.

I think of summers in the back garden,
The grey enamel tub we put pears in.
My father up a ladder hands pears down
For me to pull off twigs and leaves, wipe skin;
And also apples from the apple-tree
To take to the cellar, arrange in rows:
First pears, not touching, topped with newspaper,
Then Cox's orange pippins above those.

I recall how we dressed for church in suits –
The clock ticked too slowly on the church wall;
How we walked to my grandmother's and sat
In her large pink armchairs, while in the hall
Her clock struck each hour's quarter sonorously,
And told our news, my aunt nearby, her skills
No longer at the London Hospital
Where I saw Queen Mary by daffodils.

I stand in Station Road, mind in nursery.
I sit left of the fireguard and coal fire.
My mother holds her hands towards the coals,
I feel warmth on my cheeks as I aspire.
Coals glow red-hot, orange, I see faces
As low flames dance and sparks fizzle on soot.

To her it was normal but it haunts me:
The simple homely warmth of hand and foot.

I recall the room on the half-landing
Where my father lay during his last hours,
Grasped my hand, how when we raised beer tankards
Together, he choked out his failing powers.
I stood by him when he lay still and dead
And saw the Council Offices through glass,
The workplace he walked to, and early stars
Beyond the pear-tree's branches, twilit grass.

I see the Brook Road gate, my grandmother
Walking beside me with her stick "to say
Goodbye for the last time", at eighty-nine.
She died soon after, when I was away.
Memories whirl through my head as I stand
By the knobbly lime-trees I used to prune
With a long-arm. I was snapped on that path
With my brother, in sandals, one hot June.

I see my father and my mother peer
Round the side wall, though they are both long dead.
My father limps and smiles, smoking his pipe,
Holding a pail, and smooths his balding head.
My mother clutches the Moses-basket,
A baby lies inside, playing with hands.
They smile at me from a far place, and I
Smile back. They're gone. Only the house still stands.

The tears are in my eyes as I loiter
On the once tree-lined kerb of Station Road
And look in from outside on vanished youth,
Look across sixty years. How much I've owed
Them, I would ring the bell, go in and stand
In the same places, but all would have changed.
It's better to keep fresh in mind from then
Those faces so familiar, now estranged.

I went away, I left them, fled at first
To Oxford, then Iraq, Japan. Surely
I'd left them earlier, changing from law

Their world) to poetry, self-discovery,
Culture, my world of walks in the Forest,
Deep ruminations by glades, leafy brooks
On literature, and a mountain of texts
On my bed, to be read, Europe's best books.

The gate to this house proclaimed 'Journey's End'.
It called me to a journey with a goal,
To search and research through history's ages
And find in myself, and awake, my soul.
I travelled deep into cultures and mind,
Soul-climbed through regions, religions, up stone,
Philosophers of east and west, poets
Who've anything to say and who have known,

And now I'm at my journey's end I stand
Where my climb for lost knowledge was begun
And think how the very name on the gate
Urged me to start a journey to the One.
This place was a call – poetry a method,
A trellis rose-like souls can climb and grow –
And a pledge that one day all journeys end
As mine has now I stand in sun, and *know*.

With memories like these which still haunt me, how
Could I retire anywhere but this place?
This Loughton where some houses are sacred
Holds dear and troubled memories I retrace.
And so I've come back to such memories,
Will never leave Loughton except for weeks
Here and there in Cornwall, Italy, Greece.
I embrace Loughton and have her for keeps.

Memories of one's childhood are limpid-clear,
They have the power of images and seem
To come not from this world but from beyond
Everyday's phenomenal screen – from dream:
Faces so vivid I could lean and touch,
Hands held over the nursery fire, still kind;
And coals that will never grow cold again.
The Loughton I embrace is in my mind.

20 February 2003; revised 24–25 August 2003

After the Pisan Arno

I

I arrive at Pisa station and stand
On a number-1 bus to the Duomo.
We cross a bridge, I see the shimmering
Of coloured houses flecked in the Arno.
I get out and go through an arch, am shocked:
I'm back in the Middle Ages – devour
Round Baptistry, rectangled Cathedral
And very white, the famous Leaning Tower.

Now four days later I am back again.
I leave my luggage at the station, catch
A bus to the Arno and walk along
Lung'Arno Galileo, Shelley's patch,
See near the Ponte alla Fortezza
A plaque on the wall of his home and feats:
'Epipsychidion' on Emilia
And 'Adonais' on the death of Keats.

It's hot, I saunter to the Templar church
And then cross the bridge to the other side,
Ponte alla Fortezza, and stroll back
Along Lung'Arno Mediceo, wide-eyed,
And pass Palazzo Lanfranchi, rented
By Shelley for Byron, who came in style
From Ravenna with servants, saddled horse,
Birds in baskets, caged monkeys, dogs – and guile,

To join Teresa Guiccioli and this
Façade designed by Michelangelo,
Ghost in its upper floors, across river
From Tre Palazzi di Chiesa's glow
Where Shelley had his flat; no Allegra
Whom he'd left in a convent, where she died.
He moved to Genoa after Shelley drowned,
And volunteered to fight in Greece and spied.

I wander towards Ponte di Mezzo.
I know I could live here on the river,

Here on the Pisan waterfront, in view
Of where Shelley and Byron lived; ponder
My future in the footsteps of those two
And of Pound, imprisoned near the Arno.
I think of kindly Pound I visited
In Rapallo twenty-three years ago.

We discussed the epic I'd one day write.
Virgil, Milton both took twenty-five years
To gestate – procrastinate – their epics.
I think how Dante saw Beatrice through tears
By this Arno, in Florence. The same time
Passed before he began his *Commedia*.
I, too, have let years glide by like water.
I'm ready to give birth in one more year.

I sit outside a river bar and sip
A cup of tea and feel my future press.
Dante, Virgil, Shelley and Pound urge me
To withdraw from my active life, progress
The epic I have shirked twenty-four years.
I see I must admit the Italian
And Greek traditions into English verse
As did Shelley and Keats. I know I can.

All groups must go – philosophy, science;
They were means for me to accumulate
Encyclopaedic knowledge epic poets
Must absorb before they start to create.
I must ditch my running of schools, replace
Myself to give me time to write my works.
The epic looms, a vast struggle between
Good and evil, Sistine heights and depths, lurks.

And now my flesh creeps, my hair stands on end,
My eyes are wet and I'm trembling inside,
I'm intense, pure feeling that's overflowed,
Run through me like the river's gentle slide.
I see I must embody the culture
Of the West in a twelve-book epic, fill
It with meaning and write three hundred Greek,
Roman-Italian poems that distil.

⌐ I cannot speak, I'm blinking back my tears,
I know with awesome certainty my course.
Like the river Arno I must flow on
Between two banks to my goal from my source.
I'm single-minded, will spurn all blandished
Meanderings, calls to politics – shoo! –
Or to preach from a pulpit, mystery school.
I know with conviction what I must do.

I take a taxi back to the station,
Sit on the rim of the fountain till seven,
Then take a taxi out to the airport.
I am different, I walk with gods again.
I know I must write three hundred poems
On European and English ways and views,
Global and metaphysical prospects,
And an epic – for ten years for my Muse.

II
All that was then. Ten years later they're done,
Both epic and three hundred Odes like doors,
All opening to long vistas, avenues
That reveal the West's roots, its growth, its laws,
Views between trees like the spokes of a wheel;
The West approached as if it's quincunxes
That radiate outwards from a round hub –
Quite different from logical sequences.

My avenues are to make sense of things
I've seen or heard or read, and to explain
Why things have happened in the universe,
World, Europe, our nation's local terrain,
Or tiny events in my experience,
Like leaves small parts of one circular Whole;
So they can be understood, so I know
Their meaning from the pattern round my soul.

I write to achieve clarity of thought
About complexity, simplified view,
And to express classical clarity,
Reflect on experience digested, true,
Mind grappling with complex issues, precise,

nding on top with exactness yet dense;
atch the situation's total content,
ense first, careful exact verse serving sense.

sit in my situation – sea-mist;
m somewhere else in imagining mind,
triving for clarity; and then come to,
m again in the present sea-mist, blind.
he sea comes in, goes out, leaving rock pools
nd I drift in and out of here and now,
eave the present for imagined elsewhere
nd hone perceptions so they're clear and wow.

think how I laboriously open
aths through thickets I subsequently shape,
low some days it's intractable and I
Vrestle to sheer idea to form and scrape,
low some days it's quite effortless, as though
he rhymes were there, wanting to be revealed,
low I hew and conjure from air and show
place that would otherwise stay concealed.

Now my conjuring's done, I think of my
Vision by the Arno when all was bright
nd I saw two projects to take ten years
n one blinding call in tearful sunlight.
could have left England and lived somewhere
n Europe's ruins to set it all down.
Now I am glad I chose to stay myself
And not stray far from my boyhood hometown.

live a life of artist's solitude.
My daily flow of verse, like daily prayer,
Trickles energy from my inner spring.
am determined, crouch with hands, scoop, snare
n rhymes the bubblings from my mind's crevice.
Is this genius? If genius is a spring
Perhaps. I have a source, a Muse. The rest's
Vistas: classical avenues that zing.

Such avenues to old sites were the norm
When I was a young man for all students.

The rounded education still assumes
A knowledge of Europe's cultural events
Which, since film dethroned the book, has dwindled
And now's confined to a minority.
You call it an *élite*? Nevertheless
Its breadth and depth keeps our culture healthy.

I spent ten years working on what I glimpsed
In one moment by the Arno that May.
Was it my Muse that gave me all that work?
Or Providence that called me to portray
The decay of the West's Establishment?
I did it to show the West's fourfold soul –
Instinct, reason, intellect, spirit – split
In England, Europe, globe and One: the Whole.

Conceived 3 May 1993; written 30 December 2003; revised 31 December 2003;
1 January 2004; 2–3 April 2005

At Connaught House

I
An L-shaped front with chimneys, I go through
The front door, left to the bare sitting-room
And gaze across Epping Forest at Queen
Elizabeth's Hunting Lodge that's in gloom.
I pass on, saunter round the swimming-pool,
Sunset on its Roman columns, and yield
To its steamy warmth and blue. Windows look
Out on the sloping lawn to the first field.

I wander through the empty house, the small
Kitchen, study, out to the garage wing
To be a library, soak in stables,
The vegetable garden and outbuilding,
Then go back in and climb the airy stairs,
Stroll in and out of bare bedrooms, to west
At each window snatch views of late-sun trees,
The side gate that leads out to the Forest.

Below, round a fountain of three Graces,
Are the twelve wedged beds of the rose garden.
Two circles, a cross, four side paths all make
A Union Jack seen from air, the union
Of England, Scotland, Wales which Europe would
Undo for twelve regions, as if twelve beds
Had primacy over paths and Graces
In the pattern, whose threefold fountain heads

Show: Britannia with Welsh and Scot nymphs; or
Three goddesses of fertile grounds, sisters –
Aglaia, Euphrosyne and Thalia:
Brightness, Joyfulness and Bloom, three daughters
Of Zeus and Hera, bestowers of charm
And classical beauty in poetry;
Or Existence, Being, Void who, arms joined
In sunlit O, show the One's unity.

I clasp a popping stone in my right hand
A hundred and seventy million years old;
A round pebble, split in two halves, each stamped
With identical ammonites, whorled gold.
The hard surface hides two matching spirals,
Soft molluscs coiled in shells as hard as chrome
That have endured through time, one raised, one grooved:
Two hearts that fit together in one home.

This will be our new house, I hold the plans,
Trace over the pool my new study suite
With filing-cabinets, trace six bedrooms,
See each nook filled with my knick-knacks, my seat;
Stairs up to the roof space. This will be where
I grow old in my triangle of schools,
Walk down to Connaught Water, one with trees;
A Forest person looking at toadstools.

The Ching valley is spread out in the dusk.
The sloping grass falls away to the brook
Which rises in Hill Wood near High Beach church
And drains woods on its way past crow and rook.
I see High Beach spire in a tree-top sea.
Down in a trough is Connaught Tennis Club

Where I cycled as a boy and retrieved
Practice serves by Mottram, a scampering cub.

Edward the Confessor gave that Chingford
Parish, within Waltham's half-hundred's doze,
To St Paul's, gift the Conqueror confirmed.
It was known as King's Ford as the meadows
Were called King's Meads and the Lea the King's Stream.
The Normans (who wrote Kent as Chent) spelt it
Cingheford. This view is of Anglo-Saxon
Lands held by the first English – exquisite!

There's no history here, just an Essex place.
I have put off my grandeur and expense
To live simply in a large house, write books,
Contract my hand to what I know, dream, sense.
I've finished with outside things and must make
My peace with my new works, get up to date,
Think, see, imagine all that's in my head
In prose and verse like Hardy at Max Gate.

I wander down the sloping garden grass
To the long lily pools, all linked, stepped down,
And in spite of early dusk feel the warmth
Of a new summer creeping in green-brown,
Flecked buds and scent of flowers speared by rabbits;
And I have chosen this to grow old by
Near my young family, son and grandson,
All school work shed, now an observing eye.

From here I could walk through the Chingford woods
Past Fairmead Bottom, Loughton Monks and go
To High Beach church where my boys were christened,
Wheel through Theydon down to Abridge, follow
The Roding that rose near Dunmow and runs
Through marshy green fields sunsets wash with joy,
Under Chigwell Lane, out to Roding Lane
And the bridge I crossed so much as a boy.

I think of the brown river as it brims
Under that bridge, and I think back to when
I walked with Mabel to the humped-back bridge

And was a boy cycling to school again
Across the flood meadows and pushed my bike
To the other bank's towpath and shade's cool,
Rode the track past the barrage-balloon site
And up the narrow hill to Chigwell School.

We walked two miles towards the Loughton bridge.
On the far side where Chigwell Hall once stood,
Willows; our side, thistles with bearded seed,
Purple loosestrife and nettles. Life was good:
A flock of whitethroats, pipits. And we found
Viper's bugloss, teasel, burdock. I squealed:
Purple mallow! A civilisation
Is like a mallow growing in a field....

The Roding from its Dunmow source to Thames
Is fed by tributaries from this Forest
And pastures, water-meadows and marshlands
Round ancient Saxon towns, Essex's best.
This Forest clay holds oaks, spruce and hornbeam.
I love the trees that cradle my paddock,
I love the brown-sedge reed-swamps, yellow flag,
Ditches with gypsy-wort, poisonous hemlock.

This swathe is my country: I can recite
A hundred names of woods of which I'm fond:
Woodman's Glade, Magpie Hill and Cuckoo Pits,
Kate's Cellar, Peartree Plain and the Lost Pond,
Each of which has old memories for me.
Strawberry Hill, the Stubbles.... Here among rooks
I'll live like Chaucer's reeve on a far heath
And devote my last years to my last books.

II
From the pools on my land I look across
A valley our wooded landscapes thrive on.
We woodlanders live round bushed trees, old ponds
In this county where most names are Saxon –
Epping, Loughton, -ing "people of", -ton "town" –
In ancient royal forests in the wild
Among rabbits, hedgehogs, shrews and foxes
That I looked on in wonder as a child.

⌐ Here in the seventh century was the kingdom
Of the East Saxons of the *seaxe*, curved sword
Still on the Essex shield, whose Christian king
Saebert or Sigeberht found heavenly reward
Laid in a wood-lined burial chamber
To dissolve in acidulous Southend soil
Among things he took to the next world: wood
Drinking-cups, buckles, crosses of gold foil.

The Forest had a powerful lure for us.
We ran as soon as we had sight of trees
Banked, humped on the skyline, and then were drawn
By growing trunks, leaves fluttering in the breeze.
The Roding and these Forest streams and ponds
With sticklebacks and tiddlers that we caught,
And lilies, glint an ancient way of life
When cloth-capped children newted as a sport.

When this Forest ceased to be royal, was placed
Under the City of London's fat wing,
The Crown appointed a Ranger to watch
The bye-laws, rights of pasture and grazing:
The Duke of Connaught, Victoria's third son
Prince Arthur, who lives on in Ranger's Road,
Gave his name to the Water and this house,
Linked the Crown to these woods and this abode.

Exhausted like Propertius and Horace
I, with urbane and modest good humour,
Will retire from the bustle of the court
I have peeped into as an observer,
And will live in this sacred grove, less far
From London than Otley but far enough,
And hear news of those who pursue laurels,
Smile in blissful retirement, mind still tough.

When I was young we were agog: Angry
Young Men challenged the Establishment's mien
In plays and novels, questioned the icons
That were ruling us – Churchill and the Queen.
Osborne lambasted and then turned Tory.
Now I record with no little regret

The old order's long decay and passing,
Lament an England I cannot forget.

I look back at the timber-gabled house.
It is a palace of art: library
With all books in perfect order; records
In filing-cabinets, found easily;
A view between the Forest and the stars;
Apart from mankind where I can conclude
Within the triangle of my three schools;
A place where I can work in solitude.

I think of Joash Woodrow, great artist
Who withdrew from the world forty-five years
Ago and filled his family home in Leeds
With three thousand five hundred drawings, fears,
Paintings, hopes, sculptures, proof inspiration
Springs from solitude, not the public eye.
I too have known obscurity's great joy:
To write innovative works that don't lie.

What think my peers of my range, breadth and scale?
A few whose verses neither scan nor rhyme
Are indignant I took such care and feel
Affronted (threatened?) by my upstart crime:
Gigantic size, vast scope in verse and prose;
Disqualify my findings as steep hills,
Ignore my forests that demean saplings.
All should be small, doodles like daffodils.

So few know the great secret I exist.
I am ignored by all verse and prose hacks.
The press, radio, TV don't stoop to know.
All recoil from my truths like plague attacks
And quarantine them so they can't infect.
But I don't mind, like a forest that's oak
I put out leaves, shed them and then sprout more.
From this high place I see tiny men's smoke.

My purpose is my poems, my backbone.
I go about my business every day
And stanzas (like this one) float through my mind,

I set them down and understand and say
What my life means with freshness, clarity
And exactness, and measure my progress
By the growth of my work, which, now unknown,
May convey to future souls our "isness".

I've spent my life whittling at big ideas
And cramming them into eight-line stanzas
Like masted ships into midget bottles,
Trimming edges to make them fit so as
To please the eye. When books are no more read
And surface image has swept depth aside
My carved miniatures may seem messages
Like those tossed from where exiled Ovid died.

III
I amble by the pools in the garden.
Western philosophy is like a spring
From Parmenides and Heracleitus,
At first a splutter, then a trickling,
Now gushing Plato, Aquinas and Kant,
Locke, Hume and Leibniz filling pools, more near;
Now Positivists and Existentialists
And Universalism, the end one here.

Pools balance: Plato and Aristotle;
From them, Rationalists and Empiricists;
Lower down, Idealists and Realists;
Lower still, recent Intuitionists –
I love the Vitalists (Bergson, Whitehead)
And Existentialists like Heidegger,
Husserl – and Logical Analysis
That denied meaning (Wittgenstein, Ayer).

Pumps recycle the flow back to the start.
Now all's still, I see bathed in my end pool
The stars of the Western universe caught
In this puddle like flecked duckweed, the Rule
Reflected, disturbed by a webbed-toed newt,
And in its centre, distant, floats the moon
As twilight darkens into early night,
Reflecting unseen sunlight where I swoon.

look into this mirror for a few
Of two hundred billion stars on the tree
Of our galaxy, heavenly Milky Way.
In my mind's puddle I can also see
A hundred billion galaxies that fill
The glittering universe that is missing
To man's telescopes, moon- and Mars- machines
That ply empty space and give it meaning.

O Western universe, the spring between
My sleeves flows like yours through these pools to sigh
As Horace's Bandusian water gushed
And can reflect your patterned starlit sky
And all the movements of philosophy
And can when running show the trickling run
Of Western direction, but above all
Reflect the night-sky of the darkening One.

The spring in my consciousness and these pools
Reflects the river that winds through my mind
Past the humped bridge I wheeled my bike over,
Near where a lorry knocked me from behind
Off my bike into the grass verge and past
My grandson's nursery where tots sing and bash;
Near where the Chelmer sometimes floods the road
At Great Easton and leaves a water-splash.

I see a dandelion, a yellow flower
As bright as morning sun, beyond Time's Word;
And a stem from the same root with round down,
Spores that will be blown by wind and scattered,
Seeds that will land, take root and grow new plants.
Being was once a round ball that was whole,
Then blown into planets. An artist's works
Are blown out like fluff near his golden soul.

Being was the gold Light's separate ball,
A wind blew and scattered each galaxy.
Ours has now become our stars and our earth
While the gold Light still shines eternally.
My works were once on a round ball of fluff,
A latent perfect clock beside my flower –

My gold soul – and will be dispersed, take root.
My flower's changeless, outside time's changing hour

The One pervades the twilit and night sky,
Leaks through the star holes, drips Light to the earth,
Rains on the Forest trees, frosts, dews the grass,
Constitutes all that's green, has form, had birth.
The universe is a well-ordered whole,
Cosmos that pours Being into our lives.
I love the sticky buds, chestnut candles
That light my way, show how Being connives.

I think of the Otley Hall knot-garden:
Two infinity eights on their sides, twined.
I think, love and infinity are one,
A boundlessness beyond "before", "behind".
Add timelessness, a white seed hovering
Above the twisting knot of what's beneath,
And love's a tangled order whose sinews
Transcend a Tudor shape, soul's modern sheath.

The Western universe is meaningless
Unless it's seen with a poet's keen eye.
In my garden water's pumped down leats, pools
And's pumped back up to flow again. I sigh,
I watch the circular movement, aware
I pour in energy, more takes its place.
The flow within me's from Being to form
In an endless cycle that I embrace.

In Connaught House I will pour energy
Into new works, my spring endlessly new.
Like Hardy I'll do both poems and prose,
Take solitary walks to the past and chew
Down the Forest path to Connaught Water,
Reinvent myself, open to the One
That greens the Western universe's plains
And prinks the Forest flow from skull to sun.

I have a layered fourfold eye that peeps
Through body, mind, soul and spirit and sees
Past, present, future and eternity,

England, Europe, the globe, the One through trees,
History blend with politics, vision, Void
Or Great Zero, I co-exist with nought.
At Connaught House I co-naught and perceive
The trickling flux that erodes wood and court.

I stand by the bay-tree near my spring, look
In my pool still as mirroring mind, find
Dandelion and down, moon and fluffy stars
Which are all one when imaged in pure mind
Or before space-time when all was One seed
Enfolding Light, Void, Being, Existence;
Know a laurelled poet's still mind reflects
The Oneness of the universe through sense.

10–11 April 2003; revised 3–7, 9, 18 February, 3, 8 March 2004; 10, 16 April 2005

36

from *The Tragedy of Prince Tudor* (1998)
from The Tragedy of Prince Tudor

A record of seditious events, authenticated and published by the
Minister of World Culture in 2100

[from Act 2, Scene 1, the Prince on Kingship and duty]

(*The* Prince *in the garden of his principal estate and country house,
holding a hoe.*)

Prince: The Crown rises to a point, divine Light
           Whose rays descend and enfold a King's head,
           Infusing wisdom and guidance so touch
           Can heal the maimed, remove a leper's scars.
           The divine steals towards my garden peace
           Like sunlight spreading across clouded grass.
           The Crown is shaped like the Light pouring round
           A King's judgement, which heals a nation's soul
           As does the power that channels through a priest.
           A King's High Priest of the Church of England.
           I would that I lived in the Tudor time
           When a King had direct contact with all

Like a priest at communion, blessing each,
Not through the barrier of the alien State.
The King is the spirit of his nation
And channels divine Fire to its leaders....
The Crown on my head is the divine Light,
And my Kingdom will be like this garden,
I plead for its soil to be organic,
Pure, uncontaminated by science,
Free from all pesticides and nitrogens
That destroy health and stimulate cancers
As much as nuclear waste. This garden's earth
Is like this Kingdom's culture, for it blooms
Self-controlled flowers and waste, profligate weeds.
The King, like a gardener, nurtures the earth.
The King must purify the soil with Light,
So from its metaphysical ferment
Grow herbs, roses, herbaceous borders
That reveal the perfection of the One
In individual forms, God's Universe.
The King is God's anointed, crowned with Light,
And his Kingdom nurtures the finest growths
Which riot colour like a spring hedgerow.
This garden is a miniature landscape,
A Kingdom where organic souls unfold.
The Sovereign guarantees sovereignty in
The nation and in souls, both soil and flowers,
And loss of sovereignty is spiritual loss.
A nation without sovereignty becomes
A cultural desert that knows no Light
Or tangled undergrowth of thistly weeds
Without order, morality or soul.
True aristocracy is in spirit,
True Kingship is illumined consciousness.
I will be the Defender of the Faiths.
I stand for the Tudor time, old England,
When Kingship was mystic and understood.
I'm rooted in the Tudors though German.
And so have nicknamed myself Prince Tudor.
I'm opposed to our anti-English time.
I must inform my people of this threat
From the Olympian Group. I must and will

Mobilize the nation to save the Crown,
Defend the monarchy so it survives....

I've given my life to duty just as
A player gives his evenings to the stage.
I am an actor who has to perform:
Being a bland Prince from the royal train,
Stopping at stations, being cheered by crowds
And waving back, walking up muddy fields
In boots, discussing the countryside with
Farmers (who're in suicidal despair)
In seventeen-hour days with little food
And not much sitting down, keeping to their
Tight schedule, shaking hands, meeting people
Who toil in difficult, unrecognized
Lives, over whom I will soon reign as King.
It's a gruelling round of hard work, and I
Do it without complaining.... I
Long for the peace of this garden where I
Do not have to impersonate myself,
Where duty is a morning with a hoe.
I am apart from my people, who glint
From a great distance with their chilly smiles
As on a crisp evening a host of stars
Wink and twinkle in frosty, friendless air.
I am alone, am solitary in crowds
As a timid tree sparrow on a roof
Looks nervously around and then flies off,
But I am ruled by duty to the Crown.

[from Act 3, Scene 8, the Prince's, and England's, destiny]

Dwindled, from an estate to a garden.
My Kingdom's overgrown and in decline.
This England is at best a jewelled isle,
Apart from Europe, set in a blue sea
Like a precious diamond set in turquoise
Or the central knot in my herb garden.
She has a special destiny, to bring
All men to a perception of the truth,
The infinite, reality, spirit.
Those born in England had their consciousness

Raised by her culture to a high level.
Sovereignty gave them sovereignty over
Themselves – evolutionary advancement.
The Cecils dispersed this with their profane
Imperialism (which meant genocide
For brave Ireland), made the Queen their puppet
From the year of the Spanish Armada....
Now our Cecils are globalists who strut
On a world stage and colonize this globe....
Yet England still has her proud destiny.
Her sovereignty is like a golden coach
Drawn by horses which give it motive power....
A monarch embodies Truth and the Light
Like Phoebus in his flaming chariot,
And service to the Truth-bearing monarch
Keeps mystic sovereignty shining in souls
As service to the Truth keeps Light alight.
Our sovereignty is our great destiny
And is led by people's willing service
As four horses draw Plato's chariot
And are held in place by the charioteer.
England's the world's spiritual centre,
Having sloughed off two empires to become
The Light of the cosmopolitan World.
Here all the world's citizens can arrive
And learn to conquer their base natures and
Aspire to visions of profound things like
The philosopher's stone, spiritual gold,
And I will be the universal Crown....
I will lead my Kingdom back from what's soiled
To the rich soil of our English garden,
Back from town filth and corrupt ways, from deep
Decline and disintegration (its four
Quarters all sundered to fragments) to this
Rural, pastoral idyll, to this peace
Which could be lifted from the Tudor time.
I am head of a spiritual nation,
I will regenerate the English soul
And oppose foreign tongues with English speech
And draw on the medieval values
That preceded the time of the Cecils
And champion the truthful vision as

A patriot of old English culture –
When I have exposed the world government.

[from Act 4, Scene 3, the Prince receives a cultural deputation]

(*The* Prince *in his garden at his estate, reading a report. Enter*
Lord Green.)

(*The* Prince *picks up a book. Enter a* Poet, Painter *and* Composer.
The Prince *ignores them.*)

Poet:	What you reading, sir?
Prince:	A play on the war.

It's on sovereignty and world government.
The author's something of a dissident.
Such works are walled with silence to wither
Without reviews like plants without water.
He writes in metric blank verse, not rhythmic
Free verse with random stresses, cut-up prose.
Such discipline is not admired these days,
He will never be Poet Laureate.
Truth-tellers are considered fools, weirdos.
Do you also write about sovereignty,
And think it's the main issue of our time?

Poet: No, I write about everyday things like
Having a cup of tea in a café.
And memories of when I was a child.
I write as it comes, in uneven lines.

Prince: And that is art?

Poet: We call it the new art.
You dwell on my phrases and share my thoughts.
In literature, painting and music some
Observe the rules of composition, some
Break them. We break the rules and then we break
What we have broken, then break those again.
We're known as technical iconoclasts.
We have been called the "novel nomoclasts".
Novelty, newness, is our aim.

Prince: But don't
You have something to say? For can't you say
Something better if you observe the rules?

Poet: Oh no, true artists have nothing to say.

They give you a feeling. They do not say
"He fell asleep", they say what it feels like
To fall asleep.

Prince: But isn't that boring?
I mean, why should people want to read more
Than they need to, to understand the work?

Poet: No one's ever bored by what we create.
It's more chatty if you just write your thoughts
Without worrying about form or rhyme.

Prince: From Chaucer to Hopkins, five hundred years,
Poets wrote in set forms with rhymes –

Poet: Old hat.
We do it better.

Painter: It's the same with paint.
I don't show scenes like Constable's but squares
With a splodge near the centre, and a blob.

Prince: Does that take me to Truth?

Painter: Oh no, it shows
The chaos in the outside world.

Prince: And if
I look at art to find order?

Painter: There is
No order in the universe. I paint
The mess I see, and so it looks a mess.
The Rubens-Gainsborough line is out of date.

Prince: And in music?

Composer: The same. I do not write
Music like Beethoven or Brahms, but like
The sound you hear in a factory or shop.
Discordant noises blending together.

Prince: It sounds as if you write, paint and compose
In blots and smudges, blotches and screeches
To catch the disorder in our dull time.

All: Exactly, sir.

Prince: I don't want chaos and
Disintegration, but beauty and truth,
Order and harmony. I do not read
For ordinary settings and memories
But for the main issue of our time, which
As much as in the warlords' Germany
And Augustus's new Roman Empire
Is universal rule, world government

Which fascinated Virgil, fazed Einstein –
And its downside of genocide. Could you
Be inspired by the suffering in Auschwitz?

Poet: I wouldn't know how to begin.

Prince: Your work
Is not for me. I would gladly sentence
All artists who offer trivial themes
And shy away from all the serious ones
To be detained for weeks to read the giants
Of the Renaissance time, learn their grand themes
And how to state them in pentameters.
I'd execute all those who did not change.
I call for a Revolution against
All culture that avoids the central Truth
Which is metaphysical and global,
And whose standards are lower than the past's –
Because the artists are breaking its rules.

Painter: You'd have to execute all the artists.

Prince: No, change their subjects so that they reflect
The universalist ganging up of
The world's people against the genocides.

(*Re-enter* Sir William Hawkes, *unobserved*)

Poet: I can't follow you, sir.

Composer: You've lost me, too.

Prince: You're unaware of how the world is run.
A poet, like a paraglider, soars
Among the clouds, beneath blue sky, looks down
From the One that's behind his fluffy verse.
An artist understands what the Whole is
And reveals Truth to universal man.
You can't do that, you don't see the whole plot.
You haven't heard of the world government.

37

from *Ovid Banished* (1998–1999)
from Ovid Banished
A Tale of Transformation

[from Act 2, Scene 8, Augustus banishes Ovid]

(*Augustus's house on the Palatine, Rome.* Augustus *presides over a private court in the Room of the Masks.*)

Augustus:	Information has come to me, that you Were present when Julia, my granddaughter, Spoke to the plotters about killing me, And that you did not report this to me.
Ovid:	Caesar, I admit that I was present. But by accident, not by design. I Was invited by young Julia to sign A book. I blundered in at the wrong time. And nothing was said about *killing* you.
Augustus:	You knew my granddaughter Julia wanted To overthrow me for the Julian line. You "blundered" in on the conspirators But took no part. You blundered out again. I know. My spies have informed me. I know Julia invited you to talk with her. But you did not report what you stumbled On by accident. That was a mistake. Now some of those you blundered in on have Attempted to free both Julia and Agrippa Postumus from their islands. Enough is enough, I must sort you out.
Ovid:	I can't deny it. I will tell the truth. I admit it, I stumbled in on them By accident, as she'd invited me For what I thought would be... a private talk. I did not know the plotters would be there. I took no part in their Julian plot, And nothing was said about *killing* you.
Augustus:	Why did you not reveal this plot at once That you stumbled in on by accident?

(Ovid *glances round the room.*)

Ovid:

I will tell you the truth. I'll speak plainly.
I greatly respect the stability
That you have brought to Italy and Rome.
The plotters worked for a new order that
Could improve the world after your demise.
I sympathized with their long-term goals, for
I was born a year after Caesar died,
I grew up in the Republic when Rome
Was a metropolis for our nation,
With Latin Italy's supreme language,
Not a cosmopolitan melting-pot
With a *lingua franca* of many tongues,
A corrupt, impure, polyglot Babel.
The mixing of peoples has weakened Rome's
Beliefs and secularized Rome's culture.
What was Roman's now multi-cultural –
Diluted, contaminated, confused.
You cannot be imperial and retain
Rome's belief in traditional values,
Rome's belief in itself, and so the seeds
Of self-doubt, decline, disintegration
And conquest by barbarians have been sown.
I warn you that your Empire won't survive
The *oikumene*. Inevitably
Barbarians will enter the Roman home
And destroy what greatness your conquests built.
It is the law of imperial grandeur –
That an *imperium* gets infected
And can't resist those tribes it once suppressed.
Your Empire is like a child's tower of bricks:
One swipe from tiny fingers, down it comes –
Or else it crashes when the balance goes.
Rome will fall. I foretell the fall of Rome.
My allegiance now's to you, Caesar. But
My future support's for the Julians,
Not for a militarist succession that
Would use conquest to build a World Empire.
I question a new world order which is
Enforced by Roman legions carrying
Statues of Roman gods, which they impose

On all parts of the imperial Empire.
I believe all parts of the Empire have
Their own cultures, which they should all retain.
I am opposed to massacres of tribes
And any calculated genocide
In the cause of brutal Roman conquest,
Torching towns in the Danube hinterland.
The *imperium* is a killing machine.
I write for all mankind, affirm the right
Of all to live at peace in their own way
In villages outside the *imperium*.
I am a writer, I work in Latin,
My attitudes are shaped by Literature.
I do not want the Roman culture mixed
With barbarian cultures in a world State.
I stumbled in on them and kept it quiet.
This is about my literary posture.

(*There is a stunned silence in the room.* Ovid *has spoken too honestly for his own good.* Augustus *speaks very quietly, but he is shaking with rage.*)

Augustus: This involves much more than mere Literature.
You have questioned the public policy
Of pacification of all regions.
I've been a peace-maker, a peace-bringer.
I've presided over the expansion
Of our Empire. I, who rode with Caesar
At his African triumph and served him
In Spain, in civil war conquered the West
(Italy, Sicily) and then the East,
Won Egypt from Antony and became
Master of the Roman World – to bring peace.
I defeated the hostile Alpine tribes,
Took Galatea in Asia Minor and
Mauretania in Africa, and then
Pacified Gaul and Spain and erected
My *Ara Pacis* to glorify peace.
I took Noricum so the frontier moved
From Italy to the upper Danube,
Then pacified Pannonia and crossed
The Rhine to invade Germany as far
As the Elbe, and took Bohemia, and

Judaea. Now much of Europe, Asia
And Africa are under my peaceful
Rule. Our legions imposed this peace. I've used
Troops to subjugate for the greater good
So there could be peace throughout the Empire.
I have continued Julius Caesar's Peace.

Ovid   (*quietly*): A lot of killing's gone into your Peace.
Pacification's something to be feared.

Livia: How dare you speak so bluntly to Caesar!

Ovid: There's a language of peace and one of war,
And poets use language to tell the truth
And speak of peace as peace and war as war
And not of war as peace and peace as war.
Literature cares about human beings....
I saw Virgil, heard Horace read his *Odes*.
I have a new way of writing which you
Do not appreciate or understand.

Livia: This is outrageous and intolerable.

Augustus: I understand more new writing than most.
I have presided over the greatest
Period in Latin literary history.
After the Golden prose of Cicero
I encouraged patrons (Maecenas and
Messalla Corvinus) and polished verse
On patriotic themes, love and Nature.
In one decade I was presented with
The greatest Roman works: Virgil's *Georgics*
And *Aeneid*, Horace's *Odes* and his
Epistles, Sextus Propertius's and
Tibullus' elegies, Livy's history
And Pollio's chronicle of events.
I can't think you are in their league, surely?
Is Ovid really in this Golden Age?

Ovid: It's said I'm the last Golden Age poet.

Augustus: I can't understand why, you're ordinary.

Ovid: A poet of the ordinary life,
As recognized by all your citizens.
What it comes down to is, I learned by chance
That you have chosen Tiberius as heir.
You did not want the Julians to know this,
And say I should have denounced them to you.

Livia: He's both arrogant and impertinent.

Enough of this defiance. Sentence him.
He wants to live outside the *imperium*.
Grant his wish. The place for him is Tomis.

(Augustus *speaks with a quiet, cold fury.*)

Augustus: The charge against you is high treason, that
You conspired with others against the State
And opposed the world-wide *imperium*.
I have examined all the evidence.
We have witnesses who have denounced you.
By your own admission you are guilty.
You were implicated in my daughter
Julia's intrigue which led to banishment.
I spared you then. Now you're implicated
In my granddaughter Julia's intrigue by
Seeing treason and not reporting it.
I will now proceed to my judgement. I
Sentence you by imperial decree
To banishment from Rome for ever. You
Will be taken under guard to Tomis
On the Pontus, beyond the *imperium*
And you will live with the local people
Outside the Roman Empire till you die.
This is a *relegatio*, so your lands
Are not confiscated. Your wife can stay.

(Ovid *is deeply shocked.*)

Ovid: Tomis. They don't speak Latin there, do they?
Augustus: Greek and barbarian tongues, which you deplore
But which will only be Latinised when
Moesia's "pacified" by Roman legions.
My *imperium*, world government, can bring
Great boons to all mankind – peace, freedom from
War, famine, plagues, disease and starvation.
The *Pax Romana* is its greatest gift.
Barbarians raid across the *limes*
And have to be repelled to guard the whole.
Local wars preserve the *Pax Romana*.
They're a necessary evil, a means
That is justified by the precious end.

The writers of the Golden Age grasped this.
They all understood Rome's world destiny.
You have opposed the *imperium* now;
See if you like life among barbarians.
You must depart by early December.
A guard will sail with you to dark Tomis.
Your *Ars Amatoria* will be banned
From Rome's three famous public libraries.
It has not been condemned by a decree
From the Senate, and so it can't be burned.

Ovid: And my other writings?

Augustus: They'll also be
Withdrawn from the libraries and you will
Have no audience in Tomis, your escorts
Will ensure that your writing's at an end.
Death by silence – we'll wall you in with quiet,
Cut off your audience so you are not heard.
That's our response to all who challenge us
And oppose our *Lex Julia*, and publish
Works that mislead the young, like my daughter.

Ovid: This is a drastic form of censorship.

Augustus: It defends moral reforms I'm proud of
And purges Rome of dubious verses.
Like Socrates you've corrupted the young.

(Ovid, *still shocked, musters himself for a defiant exit.*)

Ovid: What I've written will be circulated
In all times. My works will outlast my life
And will be read when your *imperium*'s gone.

Livia: Take this insolent man back to his house.
Guard him while he packs for life-long exile.

[from Act 3, Scene 4, Messalla pleads for Ovid]

(*Augustus's house. The Room of the Masks. Enter* Augustus,
his broad-brimmed hat pulled down.)

Messalla: Caesar, I thank you for your attention.
I do not excuse Ovid. But I know
That deep down he admires the *imperium*,
And if he sometimes professes not to,

Then, though the sentiment is culpable,
A Caesar as powerful as you may feel
Rightly indignant, yes, but with your famed
Noble magnanimity may still waive
Severe punishment, recognizing that
Literature is the temple of free speech,
Purified language that is handed down
From generation to generation,
Where all worship as if at your Altar,
Ara Pacis of the *Pax Augusta*,
Where high culture is guarded like a flame.
A Golden Age such as yours can withstand
A free proponent of the other side.
All opponents and dissidents can be
Accommodated in your greater State.
The Augustan virtues of tolerance,
Reason and sensibility must shrink
From censorship; rather they listen and
Put right a perceived wrong that's criticized.

Augustus: The *imperium* has spread to all mankind.
I've built a United States of the World.
Very soon the Roman *denarius*
Will be the single Earth currency that
Embraces Parthia and the German tribes,
Pannonia and African Numidia,
Even India, which Alexander reached.
Once my world order is established, yes,
I can be generous to all my critics.
But until then the legions' action has
Precedence over urbane discussion.
I am a man of action. You're learnèd.
Action requires censorship that will shock
Learnèd scholars of Egyptian and Greek,
Persian and Roman knowledge and wisdom.
I am universal in my choices,
Which are made for the *imperium*'s good.
You are universal in your reading,
And take in all cultures and see all sides,
But your task is not like mine, to extend
The *imperium*, and if any of your
Client-poets blatantly undermine
The *imperium*, then they must be silenced.

I have to act decisively to keep
The world Roman and suppress all revolts.

Messalla: You're quite right, Caesar, as in everything.
But is Ovid against the *imperium*?

Augustus: Yes. I have evidence.

Messalla: I see him as
A poker of fun who makes Literature,
Who does not know his political views.
He deals in situations and reflects
Philosophically in what he writes.
He is a man of letters who absorbs
History, mythology, philosophy
And displays them as a peacock displays
A many-eyed fantail to impress mates.
He's not a serious opponent of
Your *imperium* and what the legions do.
His way's the pen, it's not wielding the sword.

Augustus: But the pen is as mighty as the sword.
It influences minds. Each book he writes
Is a political act that affects
The *imperium*. I do not like his work:
Pornographic advice, subversive myths
And provocative, jesting attitude.
Virgil's better – he wrote epic that can
Be compared to Homer, and pastoral verse.
But I fear him, for people look to him.
He cannot be ignored. He will be read.
I have walled him round with silence, and banned
His work from public libraries. He's ceased
To exist as a poet. I will not
Be deflected from crushing opponents
Of the world-wide *imperium*, my great work.
State power must swat ephemeral artists
Who whine and bite like maddening insects.

(*There is a silence.* Augustus *indicates that the discussion is over and that* Messalla *should leave. Exit Messalla after a bow.*)

[from Act 4, Scene 7, Ovid opens to the Light]

(*The Temple of Apollo* [*in Tomis*]. Ovid *sits with the* Priest. *They are meditating. Both have closed eyes. They murmur to each other.*)

Priest:	If you would see Apollo's midnight sun,
	The Light that shines into darkness, you must
	Remove yourself from this earth's attractions.
	Cleanse your senses, purge yourself of desire,
	Want nothing, rest content within your smile,
	Live without attachment to worldly things,
	Purify your inwardness, look within
	At the images that will rise in you.
	Apollo's Light will shine, and, illumined,
	You will become a Shining One, a soul
	That is enlightened and is most serene.
	This is what the priests of Eleusis teach.
Ovid:	I do want to bask in Apollo's Light,
	Like Prometheus steal the eternal Fire.
	I have let go of Rome now I'm rebuffed.
	I want nothing, I do not hope for Rome.
	I've stripped myself of all acquisitions.
	I have nothing and want to know the Light.
Priest:	Then let your rhythmic breathing deepen, close
	Your eyes and see the Light break like the dawn
	On shimmering water. Peer at the dark,
	Peer into the darkness, and penetrate
	Through to the Light concealed behind black cloud.

(*A silence. Then* Ovid *cries out.*)

Ovid:	I can see it. A dawning in the night.
	The sun's breaking. I can see its white rays.
	The sun's emerging, it's so bright, ah! bright –
Priest:	The face of Apollo –
Ovid:	It's dazzling.
	It's so intense. It's filling me. Ah! ah!
	I'm filled with radiance of the inner sun.
	It's so intense, it's –

(Ovid *swoons forward.*)

Priest:	Apollo has healed
	Your troubled mind, you are now whole, Ovid.

(*He puts his hand on Ovid's head.* Ovid *appears unconscious.*)

[from Act 5, Scene 6, Rome receives news of Ovid's death]

(*A Roman salon. Many people.* Cotta, *Messalla's son, claps his hands.*)

Cotta:
My friends, I have had news from Tomis that
Ovid has died, and with his death has passed
The Golden Age of Roman Literature.
He was the last of a line of poets –
Catullus, Virgil, Horace, Propertius –
Who brought glory to Rome. We shall not see
His like again. Lesser talents now walk
Where once strode those who perfected the ode,
The epic, the love elegy – all forms.

(*Those listening turn back and resume their conversation. They are
indifferent to the news of Ovid, and their own concerns have taken over.
Ibis [Augustus's spy] comes forward and addresses the audience.*)

Ibis:
He opposed the *imperium*, his work
Was bad for Rome and for our world mission.
He encouraged loose-living, undermined
Marriage and poked fun at religious myths
Which Caesar revived for the good of Rome.
The *imperium* needs marriage and the gods.
He had to be silenced. What a poet
Writes is not important. What's important
Is the spread of Rome's rule throughout the world.
The Golden Age is when the world is one –
Britain, Gaul, Judaea, Parthia, Egypt,
India, China, any land mass that's found,
All in one vast well-governed territory
Where citizenship's cosmopolitan
And, under the aegis of mighty Rome
Which protects the known world with a hundred
Bases for legions who with spear and shield
Hold back barbarians massed on the frontiers,
All nation-states suppressed for common good.
Rome bombards barbarians near the Danube
So Rome's *imperium* lasts a thousand years,
A good sight longer than a poet's verse.
My friends, the Golden Age is yet to come.

38

from *The Rise of Oliver Cromwell* (2000)
from The Rise of Oliver Cromwell

[from Act 1, Scene 5, Cromwell receives the Light]

(*Late 1629. Cromwell's house in Huntingdon.* Cromwell *is on his knees, speaking in half-sobs.*)

Cromwell: Oh God, I am not worthy. I'm worthless.
I am of no more worth than a poor worm.
I'm ruled by self, vanity and badness.
I struggle against my inferior self.
My mind's perplexed, it damages my health.
I feel tense from inner self-division.
My spiritual and psychological
Struggle has coiled me like an unwound watch.
I pray to you for Light but know darkness.
I speak in Parliament but feel I am
A miserable sinner, chief of sinners.
I cry out to you from this darkness. Lord!
Please enter me and fill me with your Light.

(*There is a silence.*)

Ahhh! An explosion of Light, like a sun!
I'm filled with Light, and now I know for sure,
I'm one of God's Chosen, not a sinner.
I have a task, a destiny to work.
Providence has chosen me for its will.

(*Enter* Hartlib.)

Hartlib: Oliver. Oliver. Are you all right?
Cromwell: I lived in and loved darkness, hated light.
The hammer and fire beat me into shape.
I was the chief of sinners. My soul is
With the Congregation of the First-born.
He gave me to see light in His Light, and
I am now one of God's Chosen, the few

Who have been saved by contact with the Light.
I've opened to sudden providences
And am a blunt instrument in the hands
Of a higher power. I must discover
The hidden purpose behind events or
What the mind of God is in all that chain
Of Providence. So I'll suspend judgement
And allow events to develop to
Get more light from the Light's dispensations.

39

from *Summoned by Truth* (2000–2005)
from *Zeus's Ass*
(A Mock-Heroic Poem and Warning)

"My Oberon! What visions have I seen!
Methought I was enamour'd of an ass."
SHAKESPEARE, *A Midsummer Night's Dream*, 4.i.82

from Canto I, lines 1–74, how Zeus chose Blair to further a world government]

Sing, Muse, of great affairs of State and mirth,
Of one chosen to do gods' will on earth.
What happens when the chief god wants one world
And finds England's banner's not yet unfurled?
Zeus the Thunderer, who fills men with dread,
Is not used to having his will thwarted.
Things were going nicely, his statue in
The UN foyer united all skin,
Then Major's slow to let Europe usurp.
Zeus has lost patience with the silly twerp.
The Olympians did for Thatcher the slow,
Why should not this dull sluggard also go?
"A united Europe will never be
If we wait for Major to wait and see."
So Zeus fulminated (muttering more
Than flashing). Golden Hera listened, sore
At his dalliance with an English nymphet,
A brazen hussy and shameless strumpet.
She spied on Zeus and sought, with smouldering ire,

To please him by advancing his empire.
She sat on her snow-capped and cloudy peak,
For a quieter life it was best to speak.
"Dearest", she wheedled, "don't get in a state.
I can stop your world plan from running late.
England needs a leader who will lay waste
The old United Kingdom and make haste
To break it up like a child's jigsaw, and
Force bits into Europe, bang with his hand.
You should destroy the hold of Parliament.
Scotland, Wales, Ireland, London should fragment.
If all are separate there'll be no delay.
England needs a man who will cause decay,
Who can be unleashed like a hurricane,
Who'll tear everything down as best he can
And carry all with him as he blusters,
Change it for the worse like uprooted firs.
He must not *seem* destructive, just a breeze,
A breath of fresh air that can waft and tease,
A gentle stirring of leaves, he'll 'make new'.
He'll 'modernize', which means levelling through
And down. He'll level borders so England's
In a United States of Europe's hands,
A stepping-stone to a world government.
The Bilderberg Group, who now represent
Olympus' will on earth, say no Tory
Can deliver such a rich prize swiftly.
The best bet is from untried Labour ranks,
Who'd subject Commons, Lords and Queen to tanks:
An up-and-coming whose promise is myth,
A generation behind dull John Smith."
So spoke Hera and languidly lay back.
Zeus strained towards her, gave his knee a smack.
"But who's the leader to be elected
Who'll cause the collapse of Britain instead
Of the improvement to which leaders look?
Are we looking for a con man, a crook?"
Triumphant Hera played her ace: "Oh, no.
This leader will be someone who is so
Shallow and vacuous that he believes
His own senseless nonsense as he deceives
The English people, charms them with his spell

So they're collectively senseless as well.
We want him to dismantle each structure
Of the United Kingdom, reassure
The people so they believe he is right
In what he's doing." Zeus cried in delight,
'Excellent. But who?" Hera said, "Today
I have inquired. The Bilderbergers say
The most suitable stooge, their research shows,
Is Blair, who's master of vacuous prose.
He sniffs out empty meaning with a nose
For waffle and key words that none oppose.
His magic can charm the people, and lull
Common sense into sleep inside the skull."

[from Cantos III and IV, lines 397–693, Blair heckled by the Women's Institute]

The morning dawns, a bright ethereal day,
Zeus shines on Blair a special, strengthening ray.
The Bilderbergers, who have just met at
Belgium's five-star Château du Lac, to chat
And speed a European superstate
And raise the European interest rate
("Euro-soccer" explained their block-booking),
Back in their countries, have sent supporting
Messages, for all women must be for
The European superstate and law.
Now long queues pass into a chilly hall;
The star attraction waits behind a wall,
The first serving Prime Minister to address
A WI conference (and the press)
In its eighty-five-year-old history.
Aware we're living in a new century,
The Chairwoman wants to be challenging
And apolitically thought-provoking
For members. All are wary, many see
Blair as an air raid on their committee.

With puffed-up pride, proud chest out like a toad,
Blair swaggers to the stage as up a road.
Before him, ten thousand grey-haired housewives,
The WI, bees in honeyed hives;
Home-made women, makers of home-made jam,

Supporters of worthy causes and ham;
More conservative than a Tory glare,
A no-go signal to a man like Blair.
The women stand and sing 'Jerusalem',
Some are flattered the PM's come to them
And look forward to talk about his son
And how his wife coped with today's school run.
Some, farmers' wives, have seen their income slide,
From European quotas, set-aside.
Some sit on pillows, on a waiting-list
Years long for an op for a hip or cyst.
Some have made up their minds about this man:
All things to all men, with warm words that tan
Like a warm sun on an African shore
Where the blue sea gently ripples once more;
Keen to please, all presentation and spin,
He hides his promises behind his grin.
He'd promised better schools and health service,
Partnership with business, eternal bliss,
As if he'd guaranteed sunshine each day
And every month would be as warm as May!
These ladies have seen services run late,
Education system deteriorate.
Rural communities? There is no bus.
You'll wait all day, should we now make a fuss?
The cars are all priced out – why, petrol tax
Is now eighty-six per cent, where's the axe?
GM-contaminated seed in rape,
And the streets are not safe from men who gape.
Agriculture? The farmers are all broke.
Protect the fox? To kill hens? What a joke!
These ladies see he has not delivered,
Grandmothers whose wise instincts never erred.
Surely he won't lecture them on subjects
They know more about than he does: effects?

Row after row, receding into shade,
Wembley Arena's daunting lit tiers fade.
Beyond eye contact, with the grey-faced crowd
A soccer pitch away, Blair says, now bowed,
It's the most terrifying audience
He's ever faced. Its scale is as immense

As if he were Billy Graham preaching
On a turfed football stadium's decking.
He refers to a topless calendar
Of Yorkshire WI ladies, far
From these grandmothers' thoughts, and says, "At least
I'm fully dressed." There's laughter far away.
I thought today might be my lucky day."
He speaks of civic opportunity,
Responsibility, community,
Three themes in Clinton's book, which worked for Bill
But, blindly copied, sound vapid and shrill
For he lacks Clinton's belief in such things
As a young bird flies before it's grown wings.
He is no more in tune with struggling, rooked
Middle Britain that now feels overlooked:
Ethnic minorities receive reward
While they themselves are stealth-taxed and ignored.

Blair perseveres, repeating key words that
Spread confusion like a wandering cat:
Twenty-five "values" rub against a leg,
Eighteen "communities" dolefully beg;
Fifteen "opportunities" scratch a wrap,
And fourteen "changes" leap into a lap.
"Community can't be rebuilt without
Opportunity." Does it mean a pout?
"Tradition is a bedrock of change." What
Does it mean? Is it an arched back that's hot?
He repeats "tradition" like a fixed stare.
Where is "tradition" in the Dome? The air?
How does "responsibility" now square
With the increased budget for all welfare?
"Family" – if he cares about it, why
Does he tax it, tear at a stockinged thigh?
"New Labour's values" – what on earth are they?
It's easier to tell next week's cat's-play!
He can't mean what he says, say what he means
As a cat seeks a jumpy soul and preens.
"Change", "opportunity", "new" and "reform",
"Change", "opportunity", "modern" the norm.
So many slogans in opaque English
That cry out to be petted like a wish.

So much vacuity in his language,
Like water frozen to ice in a fridge.
So little contact with the actual world,
As if his lap-top was now sere and curled.
Empty catchwords and empty phrases tell
A mind that shines in catching a sweet smell
As if he were selling bottled fresh air
As an antidote for people's despair.

Indignation boils in each female breast
And turns to anger as his lies molest.
He pesters on the things they hold most dear:
Work, family, health, children, crime, and fear;
Education and telling children off;
Hospitals and breast cancer – now they scoff.
Safe streets and hooligans, improved transport,
Asylum-seekers, drugs – he gropes their thought;
Interest rates and pensions, red tape, business.
The rape of our countryside stirs distress.
Rural post offices and crops, PC,
Fifty words on each – but no delivery.
He touches up on *élites* and envy
To appease Brown, distance himself and flee.
"Falling unemployment." It's rising, sage.
"Billions to be spent on health" – now there's rage.
Stakeholding was good till the PM saw
Big business would not change company law.
The government lacks substance beneath spin.
It is light-weight, and no deeper than one's skin.
"Class size too high", "hospital lists too long".
He has not delivered on either wrong.
Now fury mounts and questions seethe below
The troubled calm of woman and widow.

Eyes narrow as he hawks his bag of sweets,
Each shiny, chewy toffee that entreats,
But once you've bitten in and softened it
It sticks to your teeth and annoys your spit
Until you scoop it out on a finger
And stick the policy on a low fir.
The NHS? Wasteful in the extreme,
Waiting lists are enough to make you scream.

There are too many administrators,
Too few nurses and surgeons – and doctors.
Blair's spent six hours a day reforming it,
And given us swimming sessions and keep-fit.
State schools? They're shrines to failure of the tongue,
Their mediocrity impedes the young.
The Dome? It's cost nigh on a billion pounds
To stand empty, where emptiness surrounds.
Police? The courts and law won't touch ethnic
Muggers, their PC softness makes you sick.
Transport? Congested roads where cameras hide.
Community? Contempt for countryside.
History and cultural heritage? The Dome
Holds less history or culture than a home.
Labour's ashamed of our imperial past.
Empire, monarchs, democracy spread fast
To lands that were benighted far away.
Tradition? Parliament and the UK
Emasculated and carved up for foe.
The pound? He'll replace it with the euro.
He'll surrender England's monetary
National sovereignty for a tyranny.
Britain, a once powerful nation with norms,
Is rent asunder by half-baked reforms.
His uselessness has a subversive use.
O senselessness, so much beloved by Zeus!

Like an ice-cream man at a children's fête
Blair holds out scooped cornets, enticing bait,
And like an adult bending near a child
He offers sweetened policies he's styled.
Now like an adult standing by a pram
Saying "You're lovely. Would you like this lamb?"
He speaks with condescending of his wares,
Talks simply of concepts by which he swears
And communicates in abridged ideas
To smuggle understanding through their ears.
Has Blair's brain been addled after two weeks
With a baby that goos rather than speaks?
Or does he feel they cannot understand
A more sophisticated contraband?

They see him floundering in heavy deceit,
In waves of waffle, promises that cheat,
And do not throw a life-belt, but rather
Prod him with an oar to push him under.
The WI's seen through Labour's spin
And reject the candy-floss in his grin
That whisks strands of sugar into a fluff
And claims it's beef with such disarming bluff.
They want action and not a salesman's smile,
From which, repelled, they want to run a mile.
He has not kept election promises,
If he's not out of touch, Mid-England is.
He's patronizing, talking down – a bore.
One lava seethes in each volcanic core.

Sing, Muse, of erupting anger and shock
As Olympians became a laughing-stock
When Zeus, Hera and Rockefeller saw
The triumph of new Amazons in war.
A silence as before a thunderstorm
Echoes round rural post offices, warm.
Along the serried ranks the twinsets gleam.
Blair turns page 5 and does his best to beam.
Marion Chilcott rises and shouts out,
"This is political," like a firm clout.
Blair says the NHS is improving.
The ground shudders with distant heckling.
The stewards who pass mikes and oversee
Seat numbers glare: up jumps Chris Short, JP
From Sunderland, and waves her agenda,
Irate that political statements are
Being thrown at a neutral body's ears.
Heckling? Not a walk-out? In vain Blair peers.
To left and right, falteringly at first
A slow handclap rumbles, begins to burst
Like a volcano when all are surprised.
It is spontaneous, not organized.
And now the slow handclap begins to swell
The hall. Surely *against* each heckler's yell?
He fails to connect as in a nightmare
When a laugh sounds no different from a jeer.
No, me! Powerless to stop it or retort,

Panic in his eyes, like Ceausescu caught
By the headlight glare of a slow handclap,
Realizing he had been caught in a trap,
Blair senses he is like a fox at bay.
The Chairman Mrs. Carey cries out, "Hey,
Let the PM speak out of politeness."
Blair stands, awkward, at the lectern, a mess,
Bewildered by his reception, smiling
Uneasily as at a prank, frowning,
A look of bafflement like Ceausescu's
On the presidential balcony, boos
Punctuating rebelliously slow hands,
Rueful expression on face as he stands.
Mrs. Chilcott shouts, "It is against our
Constitution. We've been used by his power."
Disdainfully she edges past turned knees
And exits to a sound like humming bees.

Struck dumb in surprise at the slow handclap,
Blair hunts to find his place as on a map.
Strong faces, pinched lips, disapproving stares;
Are not the hecklers hooligans? He glares.
He attacks all hooligans who disgrace
Our nation. The applause now stops the chase.
He promises to be tough on crime and
The hue and cry's now on a neighbour's land.
He says he'll not impose his candidates
On Welsh or London assemblies. He waits,
But no applause. He has apologized
For the British Empire he has despised,
The holocaust (and no doubt beating up
Germany in the '66 world cup,
Winning the last war, and the one before,
And defeating Napoleon, and much more).
Now he apologizes on new grounds
For foisting Dobson, and hears closing hounds.
Speaking faster, frantically dabbling, deft,
He says the birth of his fourth child has left
Him in contemplative mood, more relaxed.
"Reflection leads to a renewed, untaxed

Sense of purpose." Fathers should help raise their
Children – despite anti-marriage tax laws,
Support for Lesbian adoptions, no pause
In promoting gay rights in schools. These aunts
Hear a lack-lustre speech that disenchants.
And now boos ring out round the Wembley hall,
And slow handclap vies with heckler's cat-call.
He speaks to several audiences in stress.
His set text has been handed to the press.
He cannot change a word, and stumbles on
And, rattled by the barracking, pale, wan,
Quickens his pace when he should have slowed it
And balanced subject matter with some wit.
He does not make contact about his son,
Convey a mood or a message – just one.
It seems the force for change has been slapped down
By the force of the conservative frown.

Hermes is appalled. The spell's neutralized.
Middle England's no longer mesmerized.
He wings his heels to Zeus who's watching scenes
From world trouble-spots on a hundred screens.
Zeus is huddled over the Wembley stage,
Despondent at the hearing, in a rage.
Dionysus' asinine touch has worn
Off, a Brussels superstate will not dawn
Into world government unless the rude
Middle English women can be subdued
Enough to vote Blair in a second term.
Zeus asks who's to blame and makes Hermes squirm.

from Attack on America

[lines 1–112, 9/11]

I
I see New York's World Trade Center with smoke
Billowing from the top on TV, for
A plane's flown into it, see waved white shirts
From windows on the hundred-and-tenth floor.
As I watch a jet plane swoops down and flies
Slowly like a missile at the south tower,

Flame spurts, the glassed tower cracks and dark smoke seeps.
Holding hands, two leap and flail as I glower.

I realise it was a deliberate plan.
Hijackers took over each plane, flew it
Into each of these towers at an angle.
I watch, with a roar the second tower hit
Slides down, floors loosened from their concrete case
By fireballed fuel, sinks down with intact walls
Into black smoke, one thousand people crushed.
Smoke rolls as the building implodes and falls.

I see figures wave from the other tower,
Fire below them, all trapped. A groaning sound,
The mast sinks, with a roar the first tower hit
Slides down in thick billowing smoke to ground.
More than one thousand more have been buried.
It snows white dust, covering faces that cower.
The centre of America's finance
That took eight years to build – gone in an hour.

Now in Washington a third plane's dived at
The Pentagon in a fuelled air attack.
Five floors have come down, the building's ablaze,
Smoke billows high above the Potomac,
The West's military centre, the HQ
Of the forces of the one superpower.
A fourth hijacked plane has crashed in Pittsburgh,
En route to the Capitol's Rotunda.

I see Bush speak at a Florida school
After the second attack, a pundit say
No US pilot told by hijackers
To fly into a packed tower would obey;
Therefore they had their own pilots – the first
Suicide pilots since *kamikaze*.
Who is responsible? The screen now shows
Cheering in Kabul, Baghdad, Tripoli.

Now the truth sinks in. It's an act of war
Even worse than Pearl Harbour for its blow
Struck at the heart of the American

Civilization, a raid by a foe.
News comes through that Bush is in Air Force One
At Nebraska, phoning near the cockpit.
The voice of anger swells. This must have had
Support from governments – who should be hit?

Bin Laden is the number-one suspect,
A Saudi sheltered in Afghanistan
Who'd killed Americans in Africa,
Who'd make the Mid-East non-American,
Rid Mecca, Medina, Jerusalem
Of non-Moslems, corrupt Arab regimes,
And establish global Islamic law.
He sees Americans as rats, it seems.

He has eleven thousand trained men across
Fifty countries. Will war against them work?
Will missiles on the government that hosts
Two thousand men in camps who hide and lurk,
Catch the guest? Will retaliation, war
On regimes that have sustained terrorists
Stop terrorism? Where's the evidence?
They had it coming for raising their fists?

And now the hurt and indignation's turned
Into anger, thoughts of revenge, to rage.
We're at war against world terrorism
And mountain lairs are targets to engage.
Unfolding on our screens, retribution.
Questions are asked about security.
Isolationism is now futile,
Missile defence could not set seized planes free.

The financial consequences unfold:
Sixty-seven billion pounds wiped off markets.
Now three thousand who made world markets work
Won't be at their desks, must be replaced. Threats
Of a world recession are now actual,
All confidence has gone. Travel, like cash,
Is now risky; who'd fly? It is as though
Someone has manipulated a crash.

Once again the Anglo-American
Allies and Israel are taking on clans
From rogue states who've breached the new world order,
The Taliban, Iraq, barbarians
Across the *limes* whose terror threatens,
Who must be crushed to stop future attacks –
Palestine, hosts of shadowy groups – and why's
Europe not condemning the maniacs?

A crash has been half-expected, a new
Bout of population decrease through war.
Can a strike from an Afghan mountain cave
Leave the West on the verge of ruin? Or,
Have there been sinister dealings? Who planned
It, did internal forces send torment
Through proxies to put up the price of oil
And weaken strong national government?

Has the world government intrigued these things?
The doubts begin to rise; the nation-state
Under assault, its institutions razed
So world leaders can level what they hate?
Dark questions shriek from under the rubble.
Why the pilots' sacrifice in each tower?
Were they Moslem martyrs for paradise?
Brainwashed to die for Rockefellers' power?

II
Dawn. A blood-red sun, new buildings collapsed.
New pictures of the first plane's slow impact:
A blue sky, a roar, a white plane trundles
To the north tower's middle, matter-of-fact.
White smoke, orange flames, a fireball, black smoke –
The moment that changed the world. A man groans.
Pictures of jagged stumps of two bases.
Survivors call from rubble with cellphones.

[lines 577–584, 609–624, oil and reach of our new Rome]

VI
Then suddenly the cat's out of the bag.
A news item shows Turkmen and Kazakh

Oil and gas pipelines through Afghanistan
To Pakistan and India. The attack
On al-Qaeda was to free a north-south
Flow long planned the Taliban took over.
This gung-ho war's for the commercial gain
Of nations thwarted by Islam astir....

Tora Bora's fallen! Al-Qaeda's gone –
Dead, rounded up or fled – and bin Laden
Was seen riding a white horse on a pass
To Pakistan, into legend, beaten.
The trail's gone cold. It's said he's in Iran,
Plotting to nuke New York. And on hillsides
North-west of Kandahar tribesmen hunt down
Mullah Omar, to hang him where he hides.

The Stars and Stripes fly over Kabul from
The US Embassy, closed for twelve years.
I ponder swollen *hubris* and *arté*
Crushed by Americans across frontiers.
If bin Laden had not attacked the Towers
He'd still be wielding a potentate's might.
I admire how the reach of our new Rome
Put this Pontine Mithridates to flight.

[Epilogue, lines 625–640, the New World Order]

The New World Order protects us from foes,
From squalls, strong winds, ogres in any form.
From my window the Cornish sea rolls in,
Wave upon languid wave after the storm.
Now the thunder released from Afghan skies
Is as past as Mylae or Nelson's day.
We have survived this gale; out there the world
Has changed, lands are governed in a new way.

I wonder at the language we've been sold,
The words and deeds of leaders' double-speak,
See "self-defence" means "grabbing oil", "spreading
Freedom" "hegemony over the weak".
Our new Rome thunders through the skies and rides
The clouds with the Olympians' dread might,

And "attack on America" means "war
On terror, conquest, oil – to bring peace, *fight*"!

1 September – 17 December 2001; 25 January 2005

from Shock and Awe

lines 1–8, 217–320, attack on Baghdad]

I

Tell, Muse, how a Syndicate took Iraq
To free world government from Moslem dark.
Tell of ancient Mesopotamia's rape
By Liberty clad in a star-striped cape.
Tell how tanks rolled to seek wmds
That weren't there, and pipeline routes through palm trees.
Tell how two nations running out of oil
Declared illegal war, and took their spoil....

III

Now Baghdad's on fire, huge percussion waves
From thousand-pounders, fires from many graves,
Palls of red smoke, ack-ack above the pyres.
In the Presidential complex, ten fires.
And tears roll down my cheeks for my Baghdad
Is on fire, I pity all good, bad, mad
Humans caught in those terrifying blasts,
The poor who cower in rubble, shield their pasts.

The world's seen and heard the awesome display,
A firework show that beats any past day.
The New American Century has shown
Washington's might, power, reach is hard as stone.
This new warfare's uneven overkill –
Giant versus dwarf – that's terrorist and shrill.
I am shocked at its heartlessness and awed
By those caught in it, forehead to floorboard.

It's sent out a message on US power:
"A firestorm round Saddam's HQ, so cower" –
Strikes against his command control compound
And microwave bombs that kill underground.
It's "illegal" (the UN), a war crime.

Palms silhouetted against fires like time
Against the hot night sky's hellish red light,
Loudspeakered Saddam urging all to fight.

On our screens Rumsfeld says they've struck with great
Force and on a huge scale that demonstrate
To Iraq's people that Saddam's regime
Is finished. "Our objective – indeed, dream –
Is not to conquer or to colonize
But to liberate Iraq, that's the prize."
I sit in tears at American power
And cry within for all in their last hour

For I contributed to that war crime,
Which was to terminate a tyrant's time
And more Twin-Towers attacks. I gave consent,
I did not vote for my own government
But took part in the election, feel shame
That RAF planes did this in my name.
More news. Surrender talks have continued,
So *Shock and Awe's* suspended. It's been viewed

By the world, that's what counts, its message clear.
Will *Shock and Awe* deter? Has it brought fear,
A surrender, or stiffened resistance?
The regime's out of control, for instance
A missile has been fired at Iran's oil.
Who's leader? Who is in charge? I recoil.
They are acting strangely, poorly advised.
The Intelligence HQ's vaporized.

I think of Dresden, though this is not aimed
At civilians but leaders; feel ashamed.
Now more jets fly low across the Tigris,
Three white flashes, a mushroom-cloud abyss.
Ambulances scream, hospitals have filled
With groaning casualties and densely killed:
People caught by shrapnel or glass blown in,
Children at play or shopping in frail skin.

An entire division – eight thousand men –
In charge of Basra has surrendered. Then
The British are in full control there now.
This evening I ponder *Shock and Awe*, how
It's already been superimposed on
Our image of Twin Towers and Pentagon
Flown at by planes used as Arab missiles:
The boiling smoke's higher than Towers by miles.

Baghdad is hit by dawn firestorm maelstroms,
A thousand cruise missiles and guided bombs.
Three more large daylight strikes, gunships take out
Iraqi resistance, killing about
Three hundred civilians. Our screens show tank
Battles, and US tanks secure each bank
Of the Euphrates crossing. Men take down
Pictures of Saddam in Basra, and clown.

Three hundred and twenty Tomahawks, more
In the first wave than in the first Gulf War.
Umm Qasr's waters may be mined, the sole
Deep-water port where food ships reach a mole,
Vital for aid. After a good night's sleep,
From my armchair's comfort I watch dusk creep
And tired troops clear the port's town street by street,
Watch war live on television, and bleat.

Where is Saddam? It seems he's still alive.
The regime's still convinced he will survive,
It's still broadcasting his speeches, it's said,
Calling the action evil and wicked.
He was hurt in the first attack – don't doubt;
Was dug out of the rubble, carried out,
Oxygen mask on face, on a stretcher.
We're told all this – is it propaganda?

Eerie silence in Arab capitals.
Will fury create insurgents, rebels?
A convoy trundles through, as slow as carts
Challenger tanks, carriers with bridge parts.
Boys, thumbs up, hold banknotes with Saddam's head
For the cameras. No one believes he's dead,

People are supporting the dictator.
Tougher troops fight with conscripts in Basra.

Columns of black smoke over Baghdad, lit
From oil-filled trenches, form two towers with wit
And counter *Shock and Awe* in broad daylight
To confuse aircraft, turn day into night.
In a hospital, a head-bandaged boy,
A girl with swathed feet, strapped baby with toy –
All dead in a caved-in ward's smouldering fires.
A pall of black smoke hangs over their pyres.

[from Epilogue, lines 1217–1232, 1241–1256, liberty]

Scared Iraq's "elections". The Shias have won –
Not what the Americans would have done.
It's rule by Ayatollahs' bigotry.
Democracy or voted tyranny?
I look back to Kassem's time, when Sunnis,
Shias and Kurds smiled in my class – Suez
Set aside – where there was freedom of speech.
Now, Shia Iraq's within Shia Iran's reach!

(And I was sent out to hostile Iraq
To help hold fast with English glue three dark
Ottoman provinces, a land still raw
That Churchill hewed out forty years before.
I worked to make work what the Master drew –
Churchill, who guarded us from bombs, who knew
Us, spoke in Loughton before Potsdam's freeze
And smiled and signed my book, my Pericles!)....

Liberty, ending tyranny,'s brought in
Freedom for bigots, Shias' deadly spin.
Saddam could have restrained them, but he's gone.
Without a strongman to take the two on,
Ahead are Sunni riots, civil war's dark,
The break-up of Churchill-designed Iraq.
Liberty's slavery to voted law,
Freedom means occupation, peace means war.

The Heroes of the West shielded their trust
From Soviet missiles and aggressive thrust.
Now all's reversed, and the Syndicate great
Urge leaders to assault each oil-rich state
And summon, with dissemblings and lies, all
Who cheered when Berlin fell, and Berlin's Wall.
I, who can't cheer more "peaceful" *Shock and Awe*s,
Summoned by truth, truth-tell: "peace" means more wars.

22 March – May 2003; revised 18 November, 29 December 2004; 12–13, 20–23, 26 January 2005

40

from *Sighs of the Muses* (2005)
Groans of the Muses

At first the Muses could only be found
Round Mount Helicon, the Pierian ground
Of their birthplace north of Olympus, crags
Where the daughters of Zeus roamed wild like hags.
To see them meant stumbling across its steep
Slopes as Hesiod did, pasturing his sheep.
In the grove of the Muses near the green
Spring on Helicon called the Hippocrene
(Which burst from Pegasus' hoofprint) the nine
Daughters of Mnemosyne guard divine
Elevated knowledge of sacred kinds,
Deify poets who're out of their minds.
Plato held that the philosophers know
"What is" whereas poets present false show –
Speak of war but know nothing of war's art;
Of medicine, don't know what doctors impart.
They're all appearances, just imitate,
Enchant, mimic and pretend, though lightweight.
But in fact poets wear Truth that comes down,
As a chain from the Muses, like a crown.
Philosophers scowled at what poets see
In Plato's mind, not in reality.
The Muses truth-tell. They told Hesiod:
"We know how to speak many false things" – God! –

"As though they were true; but we know when we
Will, to utter true things." It seems to me
On Helicon Muses lied to convey
Truth…. Then over the years they moved away
And appeared to poets in their abodes,
Inspiring them with lyrics, epics, odes.

And so it was I sat in my window
And cried out for a breeze to waft and blow
From beyond into my head and inspire
My glowing thoughts like embers in a fire:
"O Muses of Pierian Olympus
And Helicon, goddesses who helped us,
Who yearn for high standards but do not shrink
To destroy all mortals who dare to drink
At your spring, usurp your place, who inspire
But are contemptuous of mortals' lyre
As befits consciousness that is divine –
I toil to keep the standards up, and shine
In full knowledge that our time's not concerned
With Truth or Light: 'when dead you're burned and urned'.
So is it me and my use of language?
Or does the Age I show lack true knowledge?
O tell what you think of our present time;
Do literature and learning thrive in rhyme?
In our Age whose advances would amaze
Our grandparents – all walks of life draw praise –
We have sped feet with car wheels and plane wings
Faster than speed of sound, our hurtlings
Can girdle the earth in a mere two hours.
We've reached beyond this earth, the moon is ours;
Fired machines burn through the solar system.
We've preserved memory: tape, film and album
Can rerun in the present a past fled,
Relive what's gone, and scrutinise the dead
Who, in graves, move on cellulose, have speech.
One click through a cursor and we can reach
The other side of the world in a trice
Via a screen and some chips as small as lice.
We can tune in or phone all round the globe;
Listen, view, speak, send anywhere live, probe.
We've vanquished Nature by speed, wire and chip;

We hurtle on land, by sea, air, spaceship.
Satellites span distance. We, like a crow,
Alight in flashpoints like back gardens, go.
We are absolute, almost gods like you.
What do you think of our art? What's your view
Of our literature shops sell and we buy?
Is it of the right standard, or am I?"
So, in solitude at the land's edge, I
Lobbed my cry at the dark sea and night sky.

I sat in my window. Outside, the sea
Plashed and a fitful wind blew round the quay
Like laboured breathings of a man dying,
And as I listened I heard a sobbing.
I looked out and saw a maiden, half-bent,
Clad in white, who beckoned me down. I went
Outside, in cloudless dark I asked, "Can I
Help you?" She turned and pointed with a sigh
Down to the beach. I peered over the wall
Through dark at the moonflecked sea, heard a call;
In pale moonlight I saw an eerie group
Huddled round a flickering fire, all a-droop,
And heard a lamentation, quiet keening,
Above the gentle wind, each wave rolling.
Without a word she led me down a flight
Of steps onto stones in the moonlit night
And through the breakwater's gap to the rocks
Where eight maidens sobbed under long dark locks,
Young, nubile, with faces that were timeless,
Perhaps thirtyish, in white Grecian dress.
"What's the matter?" I asked. Could I ignore
These damsels in distress on a sea-shore?
They composed themselves, the one by my side,
Their dark-haired leader, spoke, husky, doe-eyed:
"You summoned us with your invoking air,
You conjured us with your vocative prayer.

"You ask what we think of your present time.
Your cultural desert's lies, there's no sublime.
We run the Elysian Club where all the great,
The six hundred finest spirits, debate;
The greatest artists we've inspired. I, still

Calliope, sit with Homer, Virgil,
Dante, Milton – we couldn't let in Pound,
His *Cantos* weren't epic; Eliot's profound.
Erato sits with Horace and Ovid,
Shakespeare and Shelley, who were both gifted.
In Spenser's day she wept. Then Shakespeare came.
We couldn't let in Hughes – it's not the name,
He was too raw, too bodied and raucous.
We Apollonians scorn Dionysus.
Terpsichore sits with Donne, Dryden, Pope,
Wordsworth and Tennyson – there's been no hope
For any since Yeats – they're not polished, though
We looked at Larkin, but he did not know
The spirit lasts for ever. What a weed!
Clio sits with Thucydides and Bede,
And Gibbon. We looked at Toynbee, but he
Distorted history, he wanted to see
A new world order flatten nationhood.
That's what Zeus wants, we think nations are good.
We're with Sidney and Byron, and Churchill,
Though his history pleads for his deeds and skill.
We agree he wasn't bad, though he took
Rothschilds' shilling to get off his debts' hook.
Melpomene sits with great Sophocles,
Aeschylus, Shakespeare and Euripides.
None today's as tragic as those of old.
We've looked at Miller but he's brass, not gold.
Thalia sits with sharp Aristophanes,
Plautus and popular Shakespeare when he's
Available. But today's pathetic.
The only hope for vision – a maverick!
Ficino, Botticelli and Dante:
Literature, art one with philosophy
Just as Plato and Pheidias both shared
What the Eleusinian Mysteries declared.
Sublime vision, Truth-bearing odes engage;
The artist sees what's real and shows the Age.
Unseen power, the invisible world, moans.
Our tears and sighs have long since become groans.

"It's all moved on since we were found near springs.
We look after all who've glimpsed highest things.

he six hundred heroes who strove and showed
he universe and what's real in an ode,
And, above all, the Truth – through what's untrue,
Imagined, never happened, lies that grew,
Yet nearer to the Truth than any shop,
As a monastery on a mountain top
Is closer to Heaven than a village fête.
Much of our time we converse with the great
But, like football clubs' talent scouts, we make
Forays to earth to spot those who may wake
Vision, some day join our immortal throng.
We appear in many guises – dance, song.
Alas, it's all become secular, none
Now reflects the metaphysical One
In the arts any more – excepting you.
We know you are obscure, but in this new
Time of false material values that's spread
We would not expect ones we have spotted
To be anything except little-known.
We're here to support you for you have shown
History's civilisations are inspired
By Light, and that philosophy expired
When it lost contact with the Light; and in
Literature, your journey to Light in skin
And through to mankind's unity – and more,
The mirror you've held up to show the war
Between Darkness and Light in your epic,
Your showing that Europe's culture's not sick,
Rest assured, we've noticed despite the Age!
You have a ticket to our Club, o sage,
For your vision's values, not for units
Sold, bought. Millions have been sold by misfits
Whose works are worthless but have deceived youth,
Don't carry an audience to the Truth.
We Muses bear Truth, and we recognise
You as one of our own, you're deep and wise.
You've borne our Truth but blind mankind's not grasped
A human's more than what his reason's clasped,
More than his senses, that he's also soul,
That his spirit endures within a Whole
That's both down here and up there with us nine.
But you're aware that you've opposed malign

Powerful interests who would suppress your work,
Who've blocked publicity, who do not shirk
Walling you round, 'death by silence' – their words.
To them you're a dissident, as with birds
They don't want your droppings, your free-speech stones.
That dismays us, intensifies our groans.
We salute you, so we've taken, in gown,
The unusual step of calling you down
From your window high above the sea's moan
To let you know, though you work on your own
Without support from an ignorant time
That thinks it knows but knows nothing, and climb,
You're not alone, we're watching over you
For you do our work when you hold your view.
I, Calliope, speak for all epic.
Nothing today's much good, much of it's sick
But at least you tried to present the war
As a metaphysical epic, more
Than merely Eisenhower chasing Hitler,
Two scoundrels we despise like that butcher
Stalin – not to mention Mao. We're weeping
At the decay of writing and learning.
I honour you, proud to give you your due."

Then Clio stood up. "I too honour you,"
She said, "at least you've tried to see the globe
As one whole with one story in your probe.
You've seen why civilisations rise, fall."
Then Erato stood and said, "Today all
Poets fail, none see the One, show learning's knot.
They write of memories – we ask 'So what?'
They describe the sense world, don't see the tide.
The standard's terrible. At least you tried
To show the world is more than material.
Sceptical poets are simply feeble.
Nothing can be salvaged from lines that miss,
That don't see Being behind the surface.
Art shows the universe and life are whole,
About the progress of the human soul
From this life into the next one. We nine
Encourage verse that looks beyond this life.
If we find none we weep like any wife

Neglected by her lord, spurned, rejected.
We are wedded to works of gold, not lead."
said, "I am humbled, thank you my nine
sisters, you've certainly made me feel fine!
am honoured to be in your presence,
hat you've come down to me, in my defence."

Clio lamented in the beach's dark:
Everything's terrible today, it's stark.
Children know no history, and cannot quill
Who Nelson, Wellington were, or Churchill.
They're in rootless deserts, they've no green hills.
Epic's reduced to surface, *frisson* thrills.
t does not reflect ancient Greece – what cost!
Philosophy's about language, it's lost
The view of the universe Plato knew,
The One that gives meaning to all that's true.
Music's debased, tuneless, a strumming sound,
t brings the soul down to the body's ground,
It does not lift soul to a higher world.
Your soaps are slice-of-life blatantly hurled.
No one's fit to join our Elysian Club.
Polyhymnia, sitting with Bach, will blub
At modern squawks. Beethoven, Tchaikovsky,
Dvorak, Elgar console her – tearfully!
All look for harmony but there's no art:
A debased beat like blood pumping round heart,
All talent gone, just thud, thud, thud – a cage,
A mindless music for a mindless Age.
Euterpe sits with instrumentalists,
We let none, they're show-offs, rhapsodists.
They want to cut a figure, be admired,
More than interpret music we inspired
That whispers how the spheres move to an Age
That's sceptical and blank. I'm filled with rage."
"And I, Urania, sit with Ptolemy
And Newton. We've let Einstein in, gladly –
He's able but where has the vision gone?
Immaterial astronomy once shone.
I sit with Plotinus and Grosseteste.
The One behind the universe can't err.
Now your physicists seek a TOE

(Theory of Everything) and cannot see
Unity esemplastically – by flight.
Take out the One and they're seeking by night."
As Melpomene spoke their faces shone:
"There's no tragedy as values have gone,
There's nothing tragic, nothing can be shared
That stirs pity and terror in those spared."
"Comedy's terrible, in all who live,"
Sweet Thalia groaned, "everything's relative,
Values have gone, it's don't-care piffle, rot
That's trivial and pointless – we ask 'So what?'"
"Lyric poetry's all doodles, with no rules,"
Terpsichore complained. "I blame the schools.
It's dispiriting for us Muses, who
Resemble teachers who've trained in what's true
But find it can't be taught, the subject gone,
Like offering Latin when the world's moved on.
We stand for standards no one will explore,
So no one's inspired by us any more,
Only by BBC bureaucrats who
Dumb down all subjects, praise tin ears and spew
That deals with nothing, from the mouth of fools;
Permit rulelessness when the time needs rules."
"Alas," moaned Clio, "the Peace we strive in
Is being threatened by explosive sin:
Terror in New York, Madrid and London,
Blasts that turn men's minds from books in tubes on
To each other, as, looking warily
About them, alert to danger, they see
And no longer lose themselves in their books
But study faces, look for furtive looks."

Then Calliope spoke: "In this country,
Europe, the world, it's the same old story.
There's nothing. It suits Zeus who levels down
So all are equal under his great frown,
To inspire one world. We wish he would send
A flood to bring world culture to an end.
We come down to look, find little will last.
We're pathetic really, live in the past
With our six hundred greats, scorn the present.
We're the Tears of the World, which is torment.

We've come tonight to speak to you. O please
Make war on this dreadful culture and ease.
Critics no longer see what's truly good.
Can't Ricks speak for the One, expose falsehood?
Art's an unmade bed in the Tate, gone pop.
Music's an awful row, we have to stop
Our ears so we don't hear to keep our sense
Of beauty intact, reserve's self-defence.
Live 8 was a demonic din, quite sick.
We hated it, yet some said 'Great music'.
It numbed the five senses' environment.
Please be even more of a dissident,
Attack your Age and its revolting ways,
Salvage beauty from ugliness's daze.
In all you write in your Age's dark night
Continue to stand for Being's One Light
Even if it's no longer understood.
Most publishers are lost in a Dark Wood
Except for a few rebels we admire
Who would improve the Age, expose the dire
Lies leaders tell, for there's a Muse of Truth.
Shakespeare invoked a tenth Muse – for all youth.
We've told him he was seriously wrong.
The tenth Muse we honour's the Truth. That's strong.
You embody Truth, so we bow to you.
Zeus wants a levelling down so he can view
All men equal in a world government.
He's glad quality's gone, he is content.
Mediocrity, the average, is his joy.
Zeus is cross with us, we know we annoy.
All socialists want all to be the same,
Have no time for those who would make a name.
As backbenchers rebel against a Whip
We toe the line, but occasionally slip.
We have integrity and say again
We admire your stand for Truth and the strain
You've had to bear in this shallowest Age.
We Muses are rebels, and we engage."

"Alas," groaned Calliope, "who will sing
The epic vision now, while displaying
The rose of Dante in peerless blank verse?"

"Alas," groaned Terpsichore, "who, though terse,
Will shine out odes and lyrics that are new
And deft as a spider's web hung with dew?"
"Alas," groaned Erato, "who will now spin
The soul's quest in erotic symbols, in
The language of the body, outer sleeve?"
"Alas," groaned pale Clio, "who will now weave
History into rainbows, show patterned scenes
Of leaders choosing stages and routines?"
"Alas," groaned Melpomene, "who will show
Pity and terror, tragic awe we know
And *catharsis* in a great-sounding theme?"
"Alas," groaned pert Thalia, "who will now dream,
With light-hearted wit, of a comic fate
And convey Truth despite the pomp of State?"
"Alas," groaned Urania, "who will fix sun,
Stars in verse, mix astronomy, the One
And the universe, winds and tides that spread?"
Euterpe played a plaintive flute and shed
Hot tears as Polymnia sang plaintively,
A dirge on how the poet is a bee
Who leaves his hive and flies round many flowers,
Sips pollen, gathers nectar which in hours
He turns to honeycomb's honey – some shift.
The power that comes from Muses is a gift
Of honey from the divine gardens, sniffed
By the poet who gathers it, designs,
Transports, transmutes it into honeyed lines.
All nine Muses groaned, "Alas, when the Light
Has passed from verse, poetry will be a night.
Who will sing of Truth then? Alas! the last
Lone voice of a long line has nearly passed.
We who shed tears in Spenser's honeyed day
At literature's and learning's sad decay
Have seen a massive decline since those moans;
We've gone through sighs and now are full of groans."

They stopped and the waves plashed, and on that beach
I looked up at the moon; looking at each,
I said, "I will do everything you ask.
Dry your tears, I'll embody Truth – some task.
Your groans will become sighs, and then pleased coos.

ou Olympians will rejoice at good news."
nd there was a sigh like a gentle wave,
Of relief, satisfied at what I gave.
Calliope said, "Thank you so much. Soon
We'll remember this talk beneath that moon."
I looked up at the moon, which was quite raw,
Its face slightly awry; peering, I saw
Its eyes and smile, it was smiling at me.
And when I looked back I could no more see
Them, grasped they'd gone, and there was I before
The sea, near rocks on a quiet moonlit shore,
Convinced our Age is rotten, much decayed,
Resolved to rise above it, undismayed,
And transmit honeyed lines gifted me by
The nine Muses as their Tenth Muse, Truth. I
Now saw our Age may seem to have been lost
Under material coating like thick frost,
But beneath its decay, like winter lawn,
Underlying growth awaits a new dawn
When sun will melt all frost and grass show through;
So Light can thaw a culture that's untrue.
Behind the cold veneer the Muses shun
Souls grow, enmeshed in growth within the One.

8 May, 26–30 July 2005; revised 5 September 2005

Authorship Question in a Dumbed-down Time

A Dramatic Monologue

Say, who do you believe wrote Hagger's works?
It can't have been this Loughton man who smirks.
How could a busy Principal of schools
Gather such knowledge, break so many rules?
Produce four massive tomes and yet not be
On platforms', known to all humanity?
Shy, loath to appear on stage' – when the rest
Of his fellow poets had all digressed
From the main issues? It doesn't make sense.
I don't buy the 'shy' story – it's pretence.
How could such vastness be unknown when fools
Found fame on gameshows, breaking all the rules?

How could the public not eat his heaped plate
When his fellow poets were snacks, lightweight?
How could the poet of so much sharp rhyme
Be content to be unknown in his time?
Write of 'the great secret that I exist'
As if obscurity is like a mist,
Beyond the control of the poetry world?
It couldn't have happened, a *poet* hurled
Aside with scorn, ignored and patronised
Because his verses scan and rhyme – *despised*!
What a reflection on the Establishment
If they'd looked away or sought to prevent
His works reaching a public, to contain.
Or if ignorant, they'd looked with disdain.
It's as if he'd been a dissident or spy.
He can't have been suppressed and walled round by
Silence, stifled with lack of attention
By a hostile State that knew how it's done.
He wasn't disqualified from 'platforms',
He put us off the scent with his 'shy' 'norms'.
How could a busy Principal of schools
Find time to gush words that filled such vast pools?
The author's brain leaked like a fractured pipe.
Essex men dump, fly-tip; fill lakes with tripe.
He's more verses to his name than Wordsworth
And Tennyson – and look at their works' girth!
More weight on scales than they had, more matter
Weighed with an ease that many now prefer.
He knew his history, politics and war,
And classics and was *au fait* with the law.
He had the depth of a philosopher –
He was a disillusioned courtier!
It was so in Elizabethan times:
Shakespeare, Marlowe, Greene, Nashe committed crimes
Of false pretences, fraud – conned the reader
Like Lyly, Chapman, Jonson and Spenser.
Who Shakespeare fronted for can make one ill:
Oxford, Bacon, now Neville – who you will.
Yet they were all fronts for courtier writers.
Spenser savagely satirised rulers –
The Cecils – in his 'Mother Hubberd's Tale'.
How could a clothman's son, brought up on ale,

Who lived in Ireland, write *The Faerie Queene?*
Hagger lived far from court, was never seen
Hobnobbing with royals, bobbing his bows.
He might as well have lived with Irish cows!
He fought no wars and yet wrote *Overlord.*
The author was a soldier sent abroad
Who travelled the length and breadth of Europe,
A classicist who toured where temples drop.
He owned a Hall – was an aristocrat;
Surely a courtier and diplomat
Who had access to all the Establishment
And used a front to mask secret dissent.
Perhaps he was UN Ambassador –
Sir John Weston, *alumnus* of Worcester?
Or a bitter Minister who, sacked, sulked –
Mandelson plotting through a front who skulked?
Perhaps 'he' was the Queen, who had opposed
The government and Syndicate who'd closed
England's thousand-year royal history
Since *Magna Carta*, cancelled sovereignty.
Hagger, like all front men, was literate,
A secretary whose patron would dictate
Words that he passed off blithely as his own
Like a market-man selling precious stone.
Hagger was a front man, a clueless cue
For a Prince? Minister? General? Spy? who: knew
Both Churchill and Montgomery, though born
Too late to claim credit for plans they'd drawn;
Was not behind Larkin, who owned no Hall;
Nor Pinter, who misunderstood the All;
Nor Colin Wilson, who despised the One;
Nor Eliot, for whom the Church was fun;
Nor Pound, whose *Cantos* broke all metric rules,
Who did not nurture children's souls in schools;
Nor Hughes, who did not care for politics.
Nor was Hagger a front for courtier Ricks!
Who had the knowledge and access to be
His patron, and be tidal like the sea,
Creep in and cover the beach, then go out
Leaving a wave's whisper a seaweed shout –
But who preferred Reflection to Shadow
And saw the dissident as a weirdo.

The authorship's a mystery that's still here.
Hagger's a front for someone – that's quite clear.
Don't be deceived by what's self-evident,
Hagger lambasts to put us off the scent.
Augustus banished Ovid – may not he
Have authored Ovid's *Tristia ex Ponti*?
Think 'Zeus's ass', then turn it on its head.
Satires on patrons distance, like the dead.
War, politics, Europe, Iraq, All, One,
World-government face that shines like the sun –
What bitter courtier wrote Hagger's works?
Why, Blair! He fits! And that's why Hagger smirks!"

All authorship debates are guaranteed
To fug the brain with madness, like hemp weed.

8 December 2005; revised 9–10, 12 December 2005; 29–30 January 2006

Epitaphs

I
Where is my home, and where my family?
As friend to friend let me reply frankly.
You know the doom war brought to Essex, boom
Of bombs like thunderbolts that made a tomb
Of ruined houses, walls torn down cruelly –
East London bore and Loughton suckled me,
Chigwell reared me and sent me to Oxford;
There and in Cornwall my young years. Abroad,
A child of Churchill's Age, implementing
His tripartite Iraq, and travelling
In Asia, Africa, then in London,
I wrote in distant places of Loughton,
I showed the human heart in prose and verse
And added in the universe, my nurse;
Penned of the One in poem and story,
In history. Then, sheltering like an oak tree,
Though I courted nearby Suffolk seven years
Yet never left its childhood smiles and tears,
Essex received me back and held me fast,
Epping Forest cradled me in my past

Amid children and books and birds, and gave
The Ching valley's warmth until this lone grave
In the clay land that brought my voice to birth
In trees and ponds and sunshine, on rich earth.

16 April 2005

2

Essex reared me through war, now holds my bones.
I, lost in this Dark Wood, trod ancient stones
And found Light on the Way, am now content
My works – deeds, words – should be my monument.
I showed soul, woods and stars are one process,
Revealed Being, to existence said Yes;
Loved my dear ones here, transformed dark regret.
A few clouds helped make a glorious sunset.
I mirrored my Age, am now dust. Stranger,
Look on *your* mortality and ponder.
Listen beneath the breeze and tick of time
To eternal silence and the soul's climb,
Peep behind the universe for the One:
Behind each shadow reigns a glorious Sun.

20 August 2005; revised 4–5 September 2005

41

from *Armageddon* (2008–2009)

from Armageddon: The Triumph of Universal Order

[Book 1, lines 1–57, 104–163, invocations to the Muse Calliope, Homer,
Milton and Heath-Stubbs on Armageddon]

Tell, Muse, of terror and pre-emptive war;
Tell of world empire and of wild dissent,
Of *Pax Americana* that forbad
Nuclear proliferation, of *jihad*
To drive occupiers from Muslim lands;
Tell of crusaders and of Holy War
And of a nightmare: free America
Threatened with nuclear bombs in ten cities,

Simultaneous fiery Armageddon.
Tell of martyrs, planes turned into missiles,
Of America attacked and two wars,
Of the clash of two civilisations
(Or of extremist crusaders in each)
In fire and smoke and dread of rockets' roar
And of nuclear reprisal against might.
Tell of Bush the Second's transformations,
Of the obduracy of bin Laden
And how Satan – exiled towards the end
Of the Second World War, failed Overlord,
Intrigued the leaking of the atomic bomb
Which brought fifty years' peace and did God's will –
Deceived both sides, brought the world to the brink
Of the Apocalypse and Judgement Day,
And in the ensuing War on Terror
And tribulation of the final time
Brought in a New World Order in which West
And East were partners, did God's will again
And though the triumph of Light was assured
Brought universal order to the Earth,
The second phase of God's Millennial plan.

O shades of my mentors from past ages
I need you to assist me now as I,
Having fulfilled one epic, *Overlord*,
Steady myself to narrate another,
Proceeding from past war to modern war.
I have been born into a time of war,
Have been a war poet with dreams of peace
And I warm to a wartime president
Whose *Pax Americana* maintains peace.
O Homer, the only other poet
To write two epics, whose action extends
A few weeks and events a dozen days,
Having spread my action over a year
And now faced with seven years' tribulation,
I need to focus on twelve nodal points
Within the long time span I must describe.
I encountered you in the library
At Chigwell, under Hypnos, where I read
Your archaic Greek with many accents,

Translated and thrilled to your "wine-dark sea",
And, still a boy, sensed my epic calling.
I sought you in Troy and on Ithaca,
And thought I found you in ruin and cove,
Phorkys' bay where I swam with my two sons
(Where Odysseus landed and fell asleep),
Water so clear I could see every stone
Before I lay by the gnarled olive-tree.

O Milton, you who scorned delight and spent
Laborious days toiling, spurred on by fame,
Lasting renown which shuns celebrity,
All self-promotion and publicity,
Absorbing learning and mythologies,
The old culture that articulates fast-
Fading memories of glorious wars
In reservoirs of awesome images,
Instruct me on your four-hundredth birthday
To write lines that are forever in mind,
To spurn poets who tour local radio
Stations to talk about themselves and read
Embarrassing, unmemorable verse.
I have shunned readings for immortal fame
Spurs works of lasting universal worth
Which cannot be confused with talk or chat,
Those ripples on the limpid pool of thought
That reflects the universe and is stirred
By the obscuring, clouding breeze of self.
O Milton, spur me to perform the task
Ordained by Light and assert eternal
Providence that with infinite Being
Regulates this material universe,
And justify the ways of God to men,
Why the infinite allowed 9/11:
To lure the Syndicate into defeat
And eclipse the West's capitalist power
And *hubris* to bring in a world order
That assists all the world's suffering poor
And works for all downtrodden humankind.
In a time when it's thought death is the end
And men have lost their grounding in their souls
And are deluded into believing

That this life's all, and there's no Providence,
This is a hard task for a lone poet
Whose soul reflects the universe and Age
As a green pool reflects the trees and sky
And images of war as on a screen,
The heir to Homer, Virgil and Dante,
To undertake in our cultural wasteland
Where soul's endeavours seem doomed to failure
Spurned by youths who are proud of ignorance
And drawn to know celebrity, not fame,
And scorn the causes for which men fight wars
And give little thought to our liberty
And mock God as a non-existent myth.
O Milton, show how Light uses terror
To bring in a more perfect way of life
And redistribute wealth to humankind.

O blind Heath-Stubbs, who tap-tapped with white stick
Rhythmic patterns as we walked down the street
To your local, with whom I sat and drank
And talked in Notting Hill and who gave me,
And signed, a pamphlet of *Artorius*,
Book One, and said each book would be addressed
To a different Muse. Strong on classical
Allusion and alliteration but
Short on epic narrative, now you're dead
Intercede with Muses on my behalf
And ask them to guide and shape my wordflow.

[Book 1, lines 494–522, bin Laden's nuclear-suitcase bombs bought from Chechen separatists]

News had spread – and it was America's
Worst nightmare – that bin Laden had acquired
Nuclear-suitcase bombs which he sought to use.
Chechen separatists under Dudayev –
Who had notified the State Department
In 1994 that he possessed
Tactical nuclear suitcases he'd sell
To hostile countries if America
Did not observe Chechen independence –
Had sold him twenty nuclear-suitcase bombs

or thirty million dollars and two tons
Of number-four choice Afghan heroin
hat were worth seven hundred million dollars.
News broke in the world's press two years later –
he London *Times*, *Jerusalem Report* –
And was confirmed by the International
Atomic Energy Agency's chief,
Ex-director general and now chairman
Of the WMD Commission,
Hans Blix in 2004.) The deal done,
Osama, in the Hindu Kush Mountains,
Khorasan in Afghanistan, issued
His long 'Declaration of War against
The Americans Occupying the
Land of the Two Holy Places' (the two
Places being Mecca and Medina
In Wahhabist Saudi Arabia),
And the next four years used opium billions
From Afghan poppies to fund three long wars.

Book 1, lines 1000–1029, attacks on World Trade Center's north and south towers]

In New York the Twin Towers, the skyscrapers
Of the World Trade Center gleamed in early
Morning sunlight against a clear blue sky
As, in unhurried, straight trajectory,
A sedate ninety-two-passenger plane
With ten thousand gallons of fuel in tanks,
A Boeing 767 piloted by
Mohammed Atta (who'd sat in 8D),
Flying from Boston to Los Angeles,
American Airlines Flight 11, smashed
Into the north tower at 8.46
Between floors ninety-four and ninety-eight.
The hijackers had stabbed and killed at least
One passenger and two flight attendants
According to phone calls by cabin crew.
Then United Airlines Flight 175
With sixty-five passengers, the same fuel,
A Boeing 767 piloted by
Marwan Alshehhi after the hijack,
Flying from Boston to Los Angeles,

Hit the south tower at 9.02 between
Floors seventy-eight and eighty-four. The planes
Did not explode like bombs. After impact
Fireballs consuming jet fuel expanded
And burning fuel poured through the Towers where heat
Was conjectured to have risen to as
Much as two thousand degrees Fahrenheit.
Molten metal poured down the south tower's side
Through a fissure like red-hot lava from
A long-dormant, erupting volcano.

[Book 1, lines 1679–1728, 1741–1752, fall of World Trade Center's south
and north towers]

All day television film showed a plane,
The second hijacked airliner, drifting
Towards the smoking north tower in blue sky,
Smoke black as night, idling at the south tower,
A hundred-and-ten-storey skyscraper,
And smashing into glass. A fireball whooshed
From the other side of the placid tower,
Cascading *débris* hundreds of feet down
To rain shrapnel and glass shards on strangers.
Back in the White House Bush watched in dismay.
It was as if the pilot had trained on
The Microsoft Flight Simulation game.
He saw doomed workers clambering out of glass
Onto ledges and jumping, hurtling down,
A couple holding hands, a man diving,
Another on his back as if bouncing
Up from a gymnasium's trampoline,
Preferring swift death to choking in smoke
Or burning in billowing, blazing fuel,
Plunging slowly into eternity.
More than three thousand trapped on sagging floors,
Fierce heat rising, melting struts, fizzing wires,
Then blasts and shuddering walls and opening cracks,
A scything gash across the fractured tower's
Tubular steel columns braced by girders.
Down in the street, a crowd running away
Beneath the pinnacles thirteen hundred
And sixty feet high, snapped in two, tilting,

Turn and see the south tower tip and smokestack
Down in a cloud of dust and billowing smoke,
Followed by a roar and, slowly toppling,
The north tower slid down as if explosives
Packed in corners had been detonated.
Film showed rubble within the Pentagon
And a pile of charred *débris* in a field.
In many shots sat or lay the wounded,
One with his leg amputated, some crushed.
The World Trade Center was like a war zone,
An abstract landscape with bits of girders
In which lay a lone severed aircraft wheel;
Dust, water, sunlight in the smoky air.
It looked as if an atomic bomb had
Gone off, and, not knowing the fires would burn
A hundred days, Bush wondered if the planes
Had each carried a nuclear-suitcase bomb
Of half a kiloton that had seared such
A devastating scene as firemen stood
Knee-deep in rubble in a dust-like mist.
Whence figures loomed like ghosts in smoky Hell,
Faces caked in dust and dried streams of tears....
More film showed Manhattan's devastation,
A post-apocalyptic landscape; steel
Columns jutting slanting angles, collapsed
Buildings, bent skeletons of lower floors,
A graveyard of hopes where self-assurance
Had died. It looked like the end of the world,
But an old world had died and a new world
Of terror and retaliatory war
Had replaced it as history lurched forward.
A new Age had been born from smoking earth.
Bush recognised the world had indeed changed.
It was at a beginning, not an end.

[Book 2, lines 1–30, 139–183 and Book 4, lines 625–703, invocations to Clio
and Calliope, and Tennyson]

O Clio, Muse of history, who sees all
Decades, centuries, ages and aeons as
Motifs embroidered on a tapestry,
A vast pattern of rising and falling

Civilisations, and Calliope,
Muse of epic poetry who's dear to me
And assists her in descrying patterns,
You two who are shown in harmony in
Giovanni Romanelli's 'Harmony
Between History and Poetry' on Wilton's
Gothic stairs – History is poetically
Inspired, Poetry is historical,
Each has the other's characteristics;
Tell now of what will happen when the oil
Our fragile civilisation rests on
Runs out. Cars, lorries, tractors, trains, buses,
Planes and ships will stop running. Farmers won't
Be growing food, shops will be empty. As
There will be no transport, there will be no
Rubbish collection, hospitals, streetlights.
Offices, factories, banks, post offices
Will all be closed. No welfare or pensions,
No newspapers, television programmes,
No phones or mobiles. Householders will grow
Their own vegetables and defend their homes
From scavengers, burglars and looters who
Seek food to keep their families alive.
Everyone will walk, cycle or ride in
A horse and cart (if some can keep a horse)
Or horse and trap or a horse-drawn stagecoach....

O Tennyson, you who wrote high romance,
Penned *Idylls of the King* at Farringford
About the court of the Roman-Celtic
King Arthur, set back in the fifth century;
Whose lines evoked the natural world of lakes
And rugged cliffs in which pre-Saxons lived,
Archaistically, and shunned the harsh,
Modern world of industrial machines
(Though their themes, service and honest labour,
Allegorised Victorian Britain);
Who knew in your poetic dream the court
Of Camelot and how the knights rode out –
Lancelot, Gawain, Percivale, Sir Bors –
To seek the Holy Grail, the simple cup
Christ used in the Last Supper, from which all

The disciples sipped, lips brushing its rim;
I find you in your Farringford mansion,
In the Isle of Wight near Freshwater Bay
In the ivied room beneath the cedar
Which was your bedroom for thirty-nine years,
Climb to your cramped old study where you wrote
The first four 'Idylls of the King'; look down
From your paint-worn window, and now descend
To your new study as the twilight fades
Where you penned the last 'Idylls of the King'.
I climb over a barred gate in the lane
To Maiden's Croft beyond the wilderness
Where stood the summer-house in which you wrote
'The Holy Grail', and hunt in the long grass
For the summer-house's stone base and find
The view you had over rolling cornfields
To the sea in the distant bay. Help me.
Help me as I write of the court of Bush,
Cheney, Rumsfeld, Rice and Powell, new knights
Of Washington who ride out for more fuel.
How would you compare the Camelot court
And the noble knights of Arthur who sought
The Grail in defiance of a Dark Age
With the court of Bush that deceived the world
By colluding with external attack
To swing public opinion to its side
As it also sought to hold back the dark
By covering Asia with oil pipelines
So lights of civilisation twinkle
Against the dusk and last into twilight?...

O Tennyson, I stand in Farringford
In your cramped old study where you wrote *Maud*,
'The Charge of the Light Brigade', and look down
At the hollow behind the wood you saw
From your paint-worn window, and now descend
To your twilit new study where you wrote
Out 'Crossing the Bar' just here and, knowing
That you've been seen sitting, smoking your pipe,
I sit at the desk in the window, sit
In your place, where you used to sit. I feel
A tingle up my spine, my hair prickling

At the back of my neck as if you're here,
But when I turn in gloom I see no one.
I close my eyes, feel prickling round my scalp,
With clammy forehead, hair on my arms up,
I *know* you're here, watching me write these words
Over my right shoulder, your eyes severe,
Quizzically as if forming a judgement,
Hair straggly, balding and with a long beard,
And that you know I have already walked
Past the pool to the roses, and on up
To the latched picket gate in the dark wood
Where Maud was let in – you flood me with power –
And seen the bridge and crossed it as you crossed
Over the public highway that you sank
Beneath it, and that like you I've escaped
To the summer-house through hay where you wrote
'Enoch Arden' in a fortnight. And now
My flesh is tingling, I can hardly think
So much energy's pouring into me
As I sit where you wrote of Arthur's death.
I know that you have seen me trace your steps
To the ante-room where you ate pudding
And drank a bottle of port each evening
As you read your works aloud to your wife.
The light switches do not work, there's no light
Save from the windows, I can hardly see
To write these words in your overwhelming
Presence. I say aloud, "Alfred, I know
You're here, please help me as I write of war.
Pour inspiration in my slumbering ear
As poison was poured in Hamlet's father's;
Help me as I turn to your nether world,
Like Faustus conjure spirits of the dead
To tell me about life beyond the grave,
Tell me your journey to the Underworld.
Help me." I ask, tapping out my metre,
You to follow me to your old bedroom
Which is lit, where I am spending five nights,
Where I now sit in the window and think
How you loved Keats who visited Shanklin
Twice and left behind verses you admired,
And stayed in steep Bonchurch to be near them

And first came here in 1853
And rented this place for two pounds a week
And then bought it with the proceeds from *Maud* –
Again I am flooded with power, you have
Rejoined me – and I climb into the high
Four-poster bed with four thin silk curtains,
The varnished floorboards bare as in your time,
Your fireplace as it was, lie on my side
And as I sleep, into my slumbering ear,
You pour a message I grasp when I wake:
 Be musical in your verse, as I was,
Keep going as I did in the Idylls.
Bush, Arthur – you will find out as you write
All courts are mixtures of noble ideals
And corrupt interests and standards of truth.
Consider the use you make of the Grail.
It stands for the Beatific Vision
And is not a thing, an exhumed chalice.
Shut yourself away and write as I did,
As you have done. I will guide you, I will
Be your guide. Persist and you'll overcome.
And while you write of dreadful, cruel things,
Always remember that you are making
A thing of beauty in musical verse."
Another surge sweeps through me as I write,
Leaving me feeling invigorated.

[Book 3, lines 1740–1815, bin Laden's escape from Tora Bora in eastern Afghanistan]

Eight days the bombardment shook the mountain,
Five hundred huge bombs that sapped all morale.
A third of all the US explosives
Dropped in Afghanistan wrecked that forest.
What we sow we reap. Bin Laden had sown
The wind on 9/11, now reaped whirlwind.
Bin Laden's voice was heard within a cave
Better defended than all the others,
A bunker in a complex of five caves,
Barking orders on a two-way radio,
By US special forces using high-
Tech radio equipment, very short-range
Radio, urging al-Qaeda to fight on.

And now, when al-Qaeda was weary from
Sleepless days and nights spent in trench and cave,
The final blow: an American plane
Dropped a huge fifteen-thousand-pound "daisy-
Cutter" bomb whose deafening thunderous blast
That shook the ground left little in its path,
A swathe with a six-hundred-yard radius
Of destruction in which everything was
Blackened and broken, utterly laid waste.
Coming, as it did, at the end of eight
Days of bombing equivalent to all
The explosives dropped at Dresden, it broke
Al-Qaeda's spirit. Like rats, fighters crawled
Through shattered cave holes, stunned at what they saw.
Tall trees were burnt and shrivelled, their branches
Reached like arms to the sky, but now reduced
To merest jagged stumps devoid of leaves
On a bare moonscape pocked by mouths of caves.
Bits of uniform hung from branches, bits
Of bodies specked the soil like clumps of flowers,
Heads on the ground, lumps of legs in the trees.
The stench of death stank in the mountain air
Amid shredded clothes, bloodied shoes, unspent
Ammunition, soiled toilet paper, scraps
Of food. As in trance they filed slowly up
The rocks to surrender – a thousand men,
Broken by the awesome power of the bomb
To destroy landscape and man, smash morale,
Many heading, though they were unawares,
For internment in Guantánamo Bay –
But not bin Laden. He'd been located.
The Pentagon said that he was trapped in
A cave by anti-Taliban forces,
All exits were under surveillance. He
Would be smoked out. The cave was bombarded.
There was a rumour he had been wounded
In a shoulder by shrapnel under fire
And had been hidden, given medical
Care and assisted. Now, facing defeat,
The al-Qaeda force agreed to a truce
To give them time to surrender weapons.
Some besiegers thought the truce was a ruse

'o allow al-Qaeda leaders to flee.
Jow fighting flared again as a rearguard
)f some two hundred Arabs and Chechens
)istracted attention while the main force
.lipped out of unguarded, concealed exits
ligh up, guarded by steel doors and fighters,
)n to mule trails on which supplies were brought,
Vhich led up to the nearby border, and
.scaped through the White Mountains, a thousand
Al-Qaeda fighters streaming across snow,
.tumbling towards the Pakistan border.
At Wazir near Tora Bora local
'eople saw bin Laden riding a white
Iorse towards the safe Pakistan border,
A rifle slung on his back like a bow,
A white sash round his forehead like a crown –
The dashing leader on a white charger
Ielped by local tribesmen he paid with bribes,
The elusive pimpernel bronzed by glare
'rom snow heading away as the deadline
'or al-Qaeda to surrender passed by.

Book 4, lines 840–851, 877–899, 903–915, the after-life]

Tell, Muse, how the after-life operates,
What system links the living and the dead
And what happens to all departed souls.
Give us an overview of Heaven and Hell.
The soul is immaterial, immortal,
The essence that's distilled from Earthly life,
From moral, emotional, intellectual
Choices and memories that form our core.
The soul is like a pip that precedes birth
And contains DNA-like instructions
That grow us to the apple of our lives.
The soul's like a pip in an apple core....
Heaven operates in a cross-cultural way,
And is Universalist for all souls
Regardless of citizenship or creed
Go to Heaven if their souls – and spirits –
Have sufficiently advanced in life's test.
The spirit is our enduring essence

That precedes and succeeds all birth and death
And strings together many lives which sit
Like beads on a rosary. One spirit
Has many pip-like souls from previous lives.
Our spirit endures and has been behind
Twenty, thirty, forty lives that we've lived,
Each of which it left with its Earthly soul –
The essence of a life – attached to it,
Which it absorbs as the soul slowly fades,
Its vibrancy stilled like a rosary bead.
Within each spirit as in DNA
Is memory of sixty-thousand years
And more – back to the time spirit began.
We have far memories from our past lives
Which are recorded as in DNA
In the pips that are strung on our spirit
And these are viewed in regressions and dreams....
All souls with Earthly stamps remain attached
To spirits which have endured for aeons.

Hell and Heaven accommodate all these.
Both places would soon be cluttered up if
There was no recycling. Souls go forward
To learn the lessons of their Earthly life,
During which time they can contact loved ones
Through a medium, or simply be aware
Of the lives they have left behind within
Their family, workplace and favourite haunts,
Watching life on Earth as if through a one-
Way mirror in reality TV,
Able to see without their being seen.

[Book 4, lines 1008–1095, invocation to Dante]

O Dante, who thought you were of Roman
Descent, and were born in this tall dark house
Near Florence's Duomo, and used to stand
By this stone between 12 and 13 and
Went into the Baptistery and looked
As a child at the cupola and saw
The early thirteenth-century mosaics

ncluding the image of Lucifer
s horned, bearded monster munching a soul
Vhose legs and buttocks hang out of his mouth,
Vith snakes protruding from each ear, in all
hree gruesome faces hideously munching
ouls, holding souls in his hands, his next course,
nd a soul being digested within
lis stomach and set to be excreted,
lis feet clamping two more souls for his meal.
ou drew on this figure in the climax
)f the *Inferno*, where your Lucifer
las three faces as in the Baptistery
nd sinners crunched within three hungry mouths.
) Dante, my Satan's different from yours,
revolutionary inspired more by
he young Gaddafi than a horned bull, Baal.
see you exiled to Verona and
stablish a connection with its lord,
an Grande, whom you first saw by this stone
taircase in his ruling brother's palace
nd, having based your Sempiternal Rose,
he Celestial Rose of your Paradise,
)n the white-mauve twelfth-century rose-window
)f San Zeno's Basilica in his
Verona, to whom in your *Epistle*
You offered your *Paradiso* (which you,
Now living at the court in Ravenna,
ent to him in batches of cantos) as
A gift. And, living in Ravenna, you
Put your manuscript of the last thirteen
Cantos in a wall-cupboard, a recess,
Which, when you'd died from malaria while
Returning from an embassy, were found
Covered with mildew by your son to whom
You gave precise instructions in a dream.
You, also, wrote of the international
Politics of your day, your own White Guelfs,
The dastardly Black Guelfs who banished you,
The Ghibellines who harboured you such as
Can Grande, who you hoped to influence
Into admiring Justinian, whom you
Encountered in the second Heaven. He

Stood in mosaic on a wall within
Ravenna's San Vitale, and had sought
To bring the eastern and western empires
Together and rebuild Augustus's
Empire under imperial rule. You hoped
Can Grande would understand the batches
Of cantos you sent him and that he would
Restore the Roman empire in the west
And with it your fortunes as a White Guelf,
By seizing Florence, expelling Black Guelfs;
Unite Europe under a secular –
And not a Holy – Roman Emperor.
O Dante, I who lived through World War Two,
The birth of the Atomic Age, Cold War,
The Berlin Wall, the British Empire's fall,
America's moon landing, the collapse
Of Communism, the bureaucratic
European Union and now the War
On Terror, I too knew imperial rule,
The British Empire's enlightened vision
And world mission which cannot be revived
And I have lived through a time when my hopes
For English and European influence
Free from a hidden and ruthless Syndicate
And its world population reduction
Have been dashed and my country has dwindled.
I too dreamt of a united Europe,
And I had no lord of Verona, Can
Grande della Scala, or Guido da
Polenta, lord of Ravenna, to send
My verse to or be a patron – only
A remote mentor who nodded me on
As I worked in isolation. I share
Your sense of exile from your own city,
For I too have been too truthful about
Those who have power – governments, royals,
The Syndicate – and have been ostracised
Because my eyes witnessed baleful evil,
For saying things that were best left unsaid.

Book 4, lines 1096–1110, 1198–1259, 1327–1576, 1759–1764, 1773–1802,
Bush visits Hell]

Shaped like an upside-down bell, larger at
Top than at bottom, Hell has seven rings,
Descending levels to which souls are drawn
By the shadow in their Earthly essence.
Each level imperceptibly descends
To the next by an inclining tunnelled
Path that passes a central tunnel off
Which are gloomy chambers. It is as if
The ascending path that winds around and up
The Tor at Glastonbury were inverted,
Turned upside down and inside out so that
The path is on the inside of the rim
Of the downward bell. Once the path is left,
Each level seems self-contained, off an arched
Tunnel with loathsome caverns on each side....

Bush followed Satan down the rocky path,
Stepping between boulders, to the first Hell
Where he left uneven rock for a long
Tunnel and peered in the nearest chamber
Where he heard loud sighs and lamentations.
Here Satan gave him an overview, not
Deigning to refer to the Light from which
He was excluded by being required
By God to embody and choose Darkness.
In gloom, below horseshoe and pipistrelle
Bats hanging from the roof, dwell the virtuous
Who never found the Light in any faith,
Whose pride restrained them from knowing the Light,
Humanists whose rational-social ideas
Swaggered through rooms and sneered at all who thought
Reality, and the One, can be known,
Called all metaphysicals "demented"
And despised mystics as "self-indulgent";
Heretics whose souls remained in shadow,
Atheists and sceptics whose inner dark
Misled their students and charges, who taught
A wrong path through the universe's fire;
Holy followers of Dionysius

The Areopagite who asserted
That God is Darkness, failed to teach the Light;
Literary doyens, actors, playwrights,
Scholars who knew footnotes but missed the Light,
Philosophers of logic and language
Who missed the universe but were blameless
Except for their own myopic blindness;
Scientists who reduced the universe
To mathematical symbols and signs –
Lucretius, Russell, Wittgenstein and Crick;
Worthy placemen who ran society,
Lawyers, doctors, teachers and all police
Who went to work and returned home blameless
But missed the Light while filling consciousness
With workplace procedures and trivia;
Attenders of churches who sang the hymns
And prayed without awareness of meaning
And did not open shadowy souls to Light,
Remained enclosed in their own ego's shell.
Here were a few so-called celebrities,
Some of whom had excelled in one honed skill,
Some merely famous for being famous,
Stars whose photos were in the newspapers
But whose souls were murky, opaque shadows,
Attention-seekers whose vanity saw
Their egos in all mirrors and windows,
Who had not delved within, opened their souls
To the Light which cleans out all sense of 'I'
And makes humble whereas pride sets apart.
Here all souls repeat their Earthly mistakes,
Hiss their scepticism and heresy
And, swollen with overweening conceit,
Preen aloofly with pride and vanity
Of intellect or looks or merely self,
And knowing it is wrong, feel a sadness,
Live in torment of perpetual pride
That, puffed up, simpers but is unfulfilled,
And learn to master their great vanity
And restrain it with new self-discipline....

Satan led Bush on down the rocky path
To the second Hell, where the gloom deepens,

And allowed Bush to peer in the first cave.
Once more, like a tour guide in the dungeons
Of an ancient and feared castle, Satan-
As-Christ gave Bush an overview of all
Inmates congregating on this level,
Again studiously avoiding mention
Of the Light that is the context of Hell.
Here dwell the lustful and the lecherous,
Egos that were attached to appetite
And sensual desires and never detached
Soul from body so soul opened to Light,
Philanderers, serial adulterers,
Rapists, nymphomaniacs and priapic
Satyriasists with permanent itch,
People who boasted thousands of partners,
Cruisers, doggers, clubbers looking for kicks
Who lived in body consciousness and like
The hungry starved for flesh and used others
As objects, Don Juans and whores who saw
Birds and toy boys instead of real people,
Cleopatra, Alexander the Sixth
(The Borgia Pope with many mistresses,
A byword for the debased papacy),
Fallen women and notorious spenders,
Living to gratify self, not to grow,
Those who lived for love and for nothing else,
Who failed to transcend body for the Light;
Billions of false lovers and mistresses
Whose secret liaisons were for their self
To gratify body, not each other,
Who did not love with grand passion but scratched
Their need with another's help, self-centred,
Who broke up marriages and hurt others,
And kept their souls within their ego's shells,
Kernels on which the Light could never shine;
Kings, Queens and Ministers, nobility,
Professional people who lived for one thing,
Workers who spent their wages in brothels,
All who lacked self-restraint and discipline
That controls and channels all appetites
And showed inordinate sexual desire,
Voluptuous charm that, demure, submits

Yet deviously manipulates all –
Lucrezia Borgia and Lola Montez.
Here they live in torment of perpetual
Itching, desire and appetite which they
Can never fulfil, until they master
Their tiresome cravings and throbbings which kept
Them from knowing the Light and which they do
Eventually get under control
And learn to restrain with self-discipline.

Bush followed Satan down the rocky path
To the third Hell, where in darkening gloom
He peered deep into the first cavern. Here
Again Satan gave him an overview
Of all the inmates on the third level,
Abstaining from all reference to the Light,
Unable to bring himself to utter
A word so associated with God. Here
Dwell the gluttonous who could not control
Their stomach's appetite and lived for food
And alcohol, binge-drinking until drunk
Amid loud sounds of merriment that gave
Them the illusion of togetherness,
Of not being alone, while imbibing;
Who were the slaves of the stomach's desires
And did not fast and discipline body,
Rise above appetite to know the Light;
Party-goers, smokers with strong cravings,
Drug-takers of all kinds with appetites
Satisfied by swallowing Ecstasy,
Smoking cannabis, sniffing substances,
Snorting cocaine, injecting heroin,
Who for the sake of bodily cravings
Polluted their soul's higher consciousness,
Lived in a fug or haze and missed the Light,
Gargantuan feasters and knockers-back –
Lucullus, Henry the Eighth, de Quincey.
Here they live in a torment of famine,
Famished for food and thirsting for a drink,
Forever parched and craving for a fix
And never able to abate or quench
Their hunger, thirst and craving as they learn

To master tiresome bodily cravings
Which they slowly bring under their control
And learn to restrain with self-discipline.

Satan beckoned and Bush continued down
To the fourth Hell, where in a darker murk
He looked inside the first dingy cavern
Of the central arched rocky tunnel. Here,
Satan as Christ explained, pointing at wraiths,
Dwell the avaricious and prodigal,
The hoarders and spendthrifts, and the greedy
Whose selfish appetite was for money,
Who looted it as did the past members
Of the Syndicate out of self-interest,
Not to benefit others. And though some
Set up allegedly philanthropic
Foundations that professed to help mankind,
They were in fact tax dodges to preserve
The majority of funds they amassed.
Here came the Rothschilds and Rockefellers,
Drawn to the foul murk by the murk within
Their souls which never opened to the Light
As locked safes hoard gold bars in deep darkness;
Here they contemplate oilfields and pipelines
And relive short-changing their fellow men.
Here were corrupt politicians who spoke
For their constituents but were far more
Interested in lining their own pockets.
Here were MPs who fiddled expenses,
Took taxpayers' money to clean their moats,
Buy duck houses and prune acres of trees,
Flip homes, pay phantom mortgages, employ
Relatives to do constituency work,
Accumulate property portfolios.
Here were businessmen whose lives were spent on
Increasing profits and computing tax;
Multinational CEOs, directors
Of companies, partners of legal firms
And bankers who received big bonuses
For gambling deposits made by clients;
Property developers, stockbrokers,
Accountants, tax inspectors and salesmen

Of cars and computers, solicitors
Who held their clients' money interest-free
And looked for more fees and compensation,
And boasted of trophy acquisitions,
Said "Hello, I'm the owner" to impress;
All who were too busy earning for self
So their social egos could live amply
To open their ego-encrusted souls
To the Light which burns out greedy desires
And appetites so grasping's transcended
By higher consciousness and growth of soul.
Here are the envious and covetous
Who want others' riches for their own selves,
Politicians who want equality
And say it's fair to strip the rich of wealth
So the poor do not feel disadvantaged,
Whose socialism is an envious creed.
Here they live in a torment of wanting,
Yearning for property and bank accounts,
For stocks and shares, gold and assets, craving
To hoard or spend, and, unable to own,
Cannot gratify their hunger for more,
Their appetite for possessions and wealth,
Their cravings to borrow, to buy or lease,
To acquire new material assets,
Addicted to acquisitive mindsets
Which they slowly bring under their control
And learn to restrain with self-discipline.

Satan indicated they must descend
And Bush followed him down to the fifth Hell
Which was in even deeper darkness, where
He peeped into the first dark cavern. Here,
Satan said, speaking as if he addressed
A touring party that had gathered round,
Dwell the wrathful who've succumbed to anger,
Who have not controlled their temper, and in
Disputes have been heated, intemperate.
They are addicted to venting their wrath,
A selfish appetite of the ego,
And in lower consciousness missed the Light.
Here dwell querulous neighbours, arguers,

Complainers, moaners, all who have quarrelled
With officials about the State system,
Abused traffic wardens, berated banks,
Lambasted doctors for bad news on health;
Demonstrators, drunk yobs who shout in streets,
Rowdy attenders where crowds are amassed,
Revolutionaries whose anger boils over;
Great men defined by one angry outburst
Such as Henry the Second, who was rid
Of a turbulent priest through one tantrum;
All who're easily offended and did
Not open their ego-encrusted soul
To the Light which burns all anger away
And brings serenity, peace with the world.
Here they live in a torment of seething,
Yearning to dispute, argufy, abuse,
Shout at each other, squabble and complain
But cannot gratify the resentment
That boils tumultuously within them,
Their appetite to vent stoked-up anger,
And, addicted to abusive mindsets,
Attempt to bring them under their control,
Learn to restrain them with self-discipline.

Satan took Bush by his elbow and led
Him down the rocky path to an opening,
The tunnel of the sixth Hell, where the dark
Was now like night and, peering, Bush could just
Make out shapes moving in the first cavern.
Watchful as he hooked up with what he'd planned,
Satan, wary, gave him an overview,
Careful not to mention the hated Light.
Here dwell the violent who have asserted
Themselves at the expense of their neighbours,
Who cared only for themselves and attacked
Their neighbours, who secured what they wanted,
Violent burglars, robbers and murderers,
Sadists, highwaymen, serial killers,
Those who swindled their neighbours of savings,
Fraudulent bankers whose scams did violence
To their neighbours and rooked them, treating them
As objects to be fleeced, not real persons;

Swashbuckling warriors quick to take offence
Such as Andrew Jackson, armed criminals
Who ruled the East End such as the Kray Twins
(And Tom Hammond, still brandishing shotgun).
Embezzlers of public funds, petty thieves
Who did great injury to people's lives,
Violent abusers of women and men,
Those who were addicted to the ego's
Self-assertive violence against others,
Assaulted and injured their fellow men,
Envying and coveting goods of theirs,
Gave in to an appetite for harming
And in lower consciousness missed the Light.
Among these are dictators and tyrants
Who ordered thousands of executions –
Hitler, Stalin, Mao, Pol Pot, mass-killers
Who had the blood of millions on their hands.
Here also dwell those who were violent
Towards themselves, self-harmers, suicides,
Who, hating themselves, ended their own lives
In lower consciousness, missing the Light;
And all who have been violent towards God
In wars and crusades, self-proclaimed *jihad*
Which had not God's approval, and all who
Have done violence to God's creation by
Violating art and Nature, God's works,
Polluting the Earth, causing climate change,
Leaving their environment much worse off.
And here dwell terrorists, who were convinced
They were on a divine mission, who used
Bombs to further causes they thought were right
But which lacked Almighty God's approval;
All suicide bombers for murderous ends.
Here they live in a torment of violence,
Raging to lash out, wound or maim or kill,
To thrust a knife or squeeze a gun's trigger
Or use their fists on shadows in the gloom,
Knuckledust, gouge eyes, glass cheeks and break bones,
Their appetite to yield to their smouldering,
And, addicted to violent mindsets,
Attempt to bring them under their control,
Learn to restrain them with self-discipline....

Now Satan, subtly avoiding ending
The tour with what he'd wanted Bush to see,
Moved on. He beckoned and Bush followed him
And descended down the rocky path, and
Came to the tunnel of the seventh Hell
Where in night dark Bush groped to the first cave....
Here dwell the spiritually slothful,
Those closest to the Lie, all deceivers,
Fraudsters who perverted reality,
Panders and seducers who twisted truth,
Flatterers who deceived to get their way,
Sorcerers who claimed to have magic powers,
Grafters and barrators who caused discord,
Councillors on planning committees who
Told whoppers to get applicants refused,
Hypocrites whose deeds did not match their words,
Thieves who stole and concealed what they had done,
False counsellors who gave evil advice,
Sowers of scandal, discord and dissent,
Counterfeiters and impersonators,
All traitors who betrayed country and friends,
Deceivers who authorised genocide
And hid their command behind a false smile,
Those closest to the Lie who did not yield
To appetites but perverted the truth,
Who in the ego's twisting of the facts
In their lower consciousness missed the Light.
Here they live in a torment of lying,
Of craving to be mendacious and spin
And, addicted to a lying mindset,
Attempt to bring it under their control,
Learn to restrain it with self-discipline.
Just as a woodpecker drills a tree-trunk
With its sharp beak for grubs hidden in bark's
Gnarled crevices, primed to probe surfaces,
So these deceivers drilled their souls for truths.

[Book 4, lines 1803–1804, 1813–1820, 1832–1864, 1887–1893, 1896–1902,
Hell as a place of self-improvement]

Satan, speaking as if Christ, spoke of what
Those in Hell perceive in their consciousness....

"How you perceive Hell is not how they do.
To outside observers Hell is in gloom
And appears caverned as if natural caves.
To participants it seems quite different,
Far more modern, like the life they have left.
Their spirits perceive through their memories,
Through subjective, not objective vision.
They see a virtual reality....
And these caves here seem luxurious halls.
Some see themselves in houses and meadows,
Like seeing what's on screen, not in your room.
Or perhaps this *is* a meadow, and you
Are seeing it as caves because you've been
Culturally conditioned to associate
Hell with caves because of Dante? Perhaps
All this is open air and *you're* the one
Who's seeing in virtual reality?"
Satan-as-Christ now suggested this view
Should be taken seriously, for he
Was promoting the standing and image
Of Hell as a place of self-improvement,
And casting doubt on what mortals could see
With their own eyes in this benighted place.
"They are attracted by their own dense forms
Into groups or classes of their level,
So all their neighbours are of comparable
Development, and are self-improving
From a similar base. There are degrees
Of darkness in the spirit-bodies here,
And they are drawn to similarity
And do not find that they have neighbours who
Are wildly different from themselves. And so
Ordinary folk are not with murderers.
All spirit-bodies are shades of black-white.
There is a spectrum with a thousand shades
From extreme black to extreme white, and in
Between there are many gradations, shades
Of grey, that determine where each spirit-
Body is drawn at the end of its life.
It's really organised here like a school,
And Satan's a bit like a headmaster....
Then Satan, speaking as if Christ, said more:

The Underworld is a corrective place,
A hospital for putting right the soul,
Only each spirit sits before its screen,
Intent on its own life, oblivious
Of other spirits for much of the 'time'.
Great care goes into their supervision,…
This is what men should follow and worship
As this is where the work's done after death."
He spoke truly until he took credit.
Though speaking as Christ he could not resist
Boasting and typically dissembling.
He did not mention the lightness of soul
That draws grown spirits to another place.

Book 5, lines 1–43, invocation to Churchill]

O Churchill, you who were my MP in
The war, whose constituency Hitler
Attacked with V-1s and V-2s, so I
Lay awake at night listening for the whine
Of doodlebugs, the silence and the crash
That obliterated houses like mine –
Hitler whose bombers blew out our windows;
You who I heard speak at the Loughton war
Memorial on your way to Potsdam
When you stood on the first step with your wife,
And who, entering the High School, in nineteen
Fifty-one stopped and signed my autograph
Album and beamed at me under your hat;
You who devised the new state of Iraq
Out of the Mesopotamia that
Was granted to the British as a League-
Of-Nations, Class-A mandate when at Sèvres
The Ottoman Empire was divided
To the great dismay of T.E. Lawrence
And, as Colonial Secretary at
The Cairo Conference of nineteen twenty-
One which you presided over, you drew
A new kingdom from the ex-Ottoman lands
And combined under one ruler Sunnis,
Shias and Kurds – and forty years later
I, your constituent, went to Baghdad

To continue the implementation
Of your vision, which was not folly but
Worked forty-eight years ago as in my
Classes at the University I
Welded all three groups together with jests,
Classroom plays and my personality,
And our group respect for Omar Khayyam
In Fitzgerald's verses, where freedom reigned
As I spoke out despite dictatorship,
The strong rule of Abdul Kareem Kassem,
Benevolent Brigadier-General, our
Honest and Faithful Leader, whom all feared;
O Churchill, come to my aid now I tell
Of a new Anglo-American war
In Iraq that again sent tanks rolling –
As when you sent tanks in during the war –
Through the desert to capture *my* Baghdad.

[Book 5, lines 736–764, 785–810, *Shock and Awe*, the Americans bomb Baghdad]

Lights shimmered on the Tigris near dark palms.
At 9 p.m. B52s unleashed
Operation *Shock and Awe* on Baghdad,
Striking Saddam's palace complex and his
Intelligence headquarters. A first wave
Of three hundred and twenty cruise missiles
Fired from American warships – more than
Were fired in the whole Gulf War – now shattered
The illusion of Iraq's defences.
A relentless assault rained thunder on
The heart of Baghdad in a fierce *Blitzkrieg*
That set leadership and military
Buildings ablaze and swiftly sent towering
Plumes of red, pink and brown smoke to the sky
That were pierced by arcs of red tracer fire
From anti-aircraft batteries, and that
Had been conceived to terrify Iraq's
Gung-ho leadership into submission.
Ambulances, fire-engines, police cars
Rushed through the otherwise deserted streets.
RAF Tornado bombers fired their
Air-launched anti-radiation missiles

ALARM) to smash integrated radar
Defence systems so bombers could follow.
Wave after thunderous wave of explosions
Shook Baghdad amid showers of orange sparks
And the horizon turned a hellish red.
Shock waves reverberated through the air,
Knocking observers back from balconies....
Buildings were pounded relentlessly by
The Allies' deafening raids. A thousand
Missiles sent fireballs and mushroom clouds high
In the night sky above the dark Tigris
And outlines of palms, and the firestorm left
Parts of central Baghdad in flames. Orange
Smoke billowed up the calm river. It was
An attack of unprecedented might
That was designed to leave the world in awe
Of American superpower. Its code-
Name was taken from a study of Gulf-
War strategy by Harlan Ullman, which
Recommended intimidating war
Adversaries to crush their will to fight.
Intensive bombing was programmed to last
Eight days but was reduced to a few hours.
It created damage costed at five
Hundred billion dollars. Reconstruction
Contracts were awarded to companies
With Syndicate and Republican links.
A contract to blow out wellhead oil fires
Worth fifty million dollars was assigned
To Kellogg, Brown & Root, subsidiary
Of Halliburton, for whom Cheney was
CEO. In one night *Shock and Awe* blew
Up much of beautiful Baghdad I knew.

[Book 12, lines 1067–1086, 1102–1153, 1171–1208, Bush visits Purgatory,
guided by Bartholomew Gosnold]

Bush followed where he floated through the mist.
'We're through the veil. Now look at Purgatory.'
Bush found himself in brilliant sunshine in
A meadow filled with fragrant summer flowers
That stretched as far as eye could see. Millions

Of shades sat or lolled in the open air.
"Who are they?" asked Bush. "Victims of terror,"
Gosnold replied. "It's a reunion. All
These spirits were bombed, shot or beheaded
By terrorists, killed by suicide bombs,
Exploding belts or cars in markets or
Near checkpoints. They've all suffered great traumas.
Angels minister to them so they can
Open their centres to the Light. If they
Do, they move on to Heaven. This is a large
Refugee camp where all who've glimpsed the Light
Receive training till their spirit-bodies
Are sufficiently subtle to proceed
To Heaven. When they vacate these meadows, new
Spirits take their place, new victims....
Deaths are not ends but are also new births
Into the spirit world I occupy.
Deaths enable spirits to develop
New qualities, help other spirits grow.
When seen from Heaven, all victims of terror
Go forward to a new phase in their growth.
Some deaths lead to needed Self-Improvement,
Some on to Self-Fulfilment in Heaven
Where they minister to and 'nurse' others
Or return to Earth as Angels to guide.
It's all a kind of school. Spirits begin
At a level that's not unlike being
In *Kindergarten*, progress through 'primary'
And 'secondary' to 'university'.
Some live among Heaven's archives as scholars
In a collegiate life, like dons on Earth.
Others pursue self-fulfilment in more
Practical ways, like your public servants.
All spirits *do* something. None do nothing.
What do they do in Heaven? Whereas in Hell
They identify flaws and self-improve,
Eradicate error, open to Light
And, their shadows purged, move on to Heaven,
In Heaven they contemplate, close to the Light
And create. They produce cultural works,
Live like artists. In Heaven creators –
Poets, philosophers, historians

And dramatists – are respected the most.
All who made a living through money must
Be creative like impecunious
Artists. It *is* a topsy-turvy 'world',
The mighty are flung down to deepest Hell,
The meek are exalted to highest Heaven
If they have opened to the Light and given
To their culture and civilisation.
From lowest Self-Improvement in Hell to
Highest Self-Fulfilment in Heaven, and
Rebirth on Earth to a new life when they
Face similar challenges just as when
Failed examinees retake their exams,
All spirits, wherever they are, progress,
All at their own level and pace, just as
In mixed-ability classes at school
Through individual attention pupils
Have different work and progress at their own
Speed and level, thanks to a teacher who
Is aware of each pupil's own level
And matches it with appropriate work
That leads him or her to the next stage. So
In the spirit world teachers are welcomed.
Look, over there. That crowd is clapping in
New arrivals, congratulating them....
So all the perpetrators of terror
Have long stretches of Self-Improvement where
Their deeds are played before them endlessly
And they must make amends to their victims
By helping them in their new regions here.
Look at that screen." Bush looked and recognised
The caverned Underworld he had been to
And saw a horde of shadows sitting in
Cave-like dungeons with transparent shackles
Round their legs. "They're doing Self-Improvement.
They see their misdeeds again and again
Like a snatch of film – 9/11 planes –
Repeated many times on TV screens.
They are tormented each time they relive
Their callous deeds, how they wiped people out
With bombs or guns. And when they have improved
They will come here and mix with their victims

At reunions like this one. See these hordes
Sitting and standing on the grass – some are
Improved and reformed perpetrators who
Can meet and talk to forgiving victims
So all spirits, shedding hate, can commune
In love. All spirits on that grassy plain
Have progressed beyond ego which obstructs
The Light, have opened to the Light, and, see,
Have spirit-bodies that are radiant
With infused Light, and have no dense shadow,
And are now ready to live in pure love
And Light in Heaven as, at a new level,
They work on projects that assist others
While implementing their Self-Fulfilment.
Nothing stands still in the spirit world, all
Is process and even the most perfect
Have projects which benefit others and
Themselves. What do spirits do in Heaven?
They are far busier in their projects than
They were on Earth, but within a serene
Bliss and fulfilment filled with joy and love."

[Book 12, lines 1229–1261, 1266–1270, 1299–1452, Bush is shown Heaven
by Bartholomew Gosnold and then by Eisenhower]

Heaven stood behind them in a veiling mist.
A path wound up the side like the one seen
At Glastonbury Tor, only the scale
Was more like Mount Vesuvius. The path
To Hell spiralled round and down the inside
Of an upside-down bell. The path to Heaven
Spiralled round the outside of an upright
Bell as round an Iraqi ziggurat.
Gosnold led Bush to the foot of the path
And they floated up into the mist and
Purgatory's meadow now hidden from view,
Ascended until Gosnold alighted
On downs below another veiling mist.
Before them was a summer meadow much
More brilliant with Light than was Purgatory.
Bush could not see the source of the brightness,
Which did not come from any obvious

un. In the great glare Bush could make out hosts
Of distant shapes whose spirit-bodies shone.
"This is Heaven?" Bush asked in wonderment.
"The first Heaven," Gosnold said. "You must realise
That all Angels are interdependent.
Just as flowers use bees, birds, mice, ants or flies
To convey their pollen and fertilise
Other plants on the Earth that you've come from,
And attract them with strong scents or nectar,
Which they sip so flowers and go-betweens gain,
So in Heaven Angels need other Angels
To take their projects for Self-Fulfilment
To other Angels who will sharpen them
And with feedback fertilise their ideas
So that the whole system can flourish and
Fulfil the majesty of the Light's plan."...

Bush screwed his eyes up in the brilliant Light
And saw four transparent spirits approach.
"Welcome to Heaven, Mr President,"
One said. "I will be looking after you.
I was President myself, Eisenhower....
But first I must say how concerned we've been
At the prospect of bin Laden's nuclear-
Suitcase bombs and nightmare Armageddon.
You've done well to contain him and avoid
Panicking the American people.

Now let me brief you about Heaven. You must
Understand there are seven Heavens just as
There are seven Hells, which correspond to them
Inversely, and though each is separate
It's all a unity, all seven are parts
Of one uniting whole. There are seven tiers,
Seven rings of Light in increasing brightness,
Each one miles wide and veiled off from the next.
Seen from above they're petals in a rose.
Yet seven paths wind up one grassy hill.
The Light is in the empyrean above
The seventh Heaven. All spirits ready for
Self-Fulfilment are on one of these tiers.
The most raw are on the lower levels.

In this first Heaven or first ring of Light
Dwell those who glimpsed the Light on Earth but were
Inconstant to it, and though they preserved
Their intellectual vision, then pursued
Other callings, such as Shelley and Blake,
And Michelangelo. They were allies
Of the Light but had long spells in their lives
When they forgot their true calling. They are
Now lower Angels and visit mankind
With messages. Some of these are reborn
As teachers, who teach their fellow humans
Self-improvement and self-fulfilment on
Earth to prepare them for their real life
In their spirit-bodies after their death.
They volunteer for a life of joyful,
Quiet sacrifice. In the second Heaven,
Beyond that veil, or cloud of unknowing,
Are those who opened to the Light on Earth
But remained in the *vita activa*
And become leaders, such as St Paul or
Cromwell. These are now among Archangels
In the hierarchy of Heaven's ranking.
Beyond the next veil is the third Heaven
Where dwell spirits who, through love of the Light,
Rose in life, understood the universe
And how all's process, thought forces and growth
Through the ordering workings of the Light.
Heracleitus, Plato and Plotinus
Are just a few who've understood the Earth
And the power of the Fire of Love, the Light.
They dwell among the Principalities.
Beyond the next veil in the fourth Heaven
Are the spiritual Masters and teachers
Who saw and taught the Light to humankind,
The mystics of all cultures, St Clement
Of Alexandria, Suhrawardi
And Padmasambhava, among the Powers.
Above the next veil in the fifth Heaven
Are those who knew the Light in their lives and
Advanced the Light through war, like Charlemagne
And the Crusader Godfrey de Bouillon,
Who now dwell in love among the virtues.

Beyond the next veil is the sixth Heaven
Where all who know the Light and have balanced
Justice and mercy dwell, like Constantine
The Great or Pope Gregory the Great, all
The just spirits among dominations.
Beyond the next veil is the seventh Heaven,
The one closest to the Light, where live all
The contemplatives who have known the Light
In greatest luminosity, the true
Mystics such as St Hildegard, Dante,
Meister Eckhart, St Teresa, St John
Of the Cross, Julian of Norwich, and more
Recently, Tennyson, T.S. Eliot;
And from Islam Bayazid, Al-Hallaj.
All dwell in brilliant Light among the thrones.
That's where we're going now." And weightlessly
Bush felt himself rising into a mist
And ascended at high speed through each veil.
And on each tier he glimpsed lush green meadows
Like undulating chalk downs with wild flowers,
And hordes of translucent, transparent wraiths
Sitting and walking on the sunny grass,
Barely discernible in brilliant Light.
Each tier beneath each veil was brighter than
The previous one, flooded with greater Light.

They alighted on the green hill's top rim,
A jutting-out rock on a vantage point.
Before Bush was a sunny plain filled with
A crowd of translucent shapes in bright Light
That could only be seen with screwn-up eyes.
Bush looked down and gasped for beneath him were
Seven undulating tiers beyond each veil,
And from the summit of the seventh Heaven
The lower rings of Light looked like petals,
One above another, of a great rose
With seven petals filled with dazzling spirits.
From within each ring looked green. From above
The rings looked cream, like a satiny rose.
The rings looked soft, their undulating folds
Were like hills perfumed with abundant flowers.
Then Eisenhower spoke from protruding rock:

"Beyond these seven Heavens is the Light,
Which is in the empyrean above.
You will be blinded if you look upwards,
You need to avert your eyes to avoid
Damaging your sight. The Light's surrounded
By the Cherubim of Divine Wisdom
And the Seraphim of Divine Love, who
Form a ring like a halo round a sun,
A ring of brightness round the celestial,
Sempiternal rose. That is where Christ dwells
Surrounded by his most illumined saints,
St John the Beloved, St Augustine
And St Bernard, who helped the Crusaders,
And the Virgin Mary, and the founders
Of all the religions: Zoroaster,
Mahavira, Lao-Tzu, Krishna, Mani,
The Buddha, Mohammed, Hui-Neng, Eisai,
Dogen, the Hidden *Imam*, Nanak, Fox.
Right now they're all in this seventh Heaven.
Look, Christ is standing on the rock. Beside
Him is Mohammed. The rest are behind.
He's come down to the seventh Heaven to speak
From the centre of the Rose of Heaven
And his words will be heard in all the Heavens.
They'll be heard in every petal's corner."
Bush saw Christ dazzling in spirit-body,
A radiant form on the Rose's stigma
Of the central pistil, and his Angels,
Saints and religions' founders all round him.
And as the crowded spirits waited they
Shimmered with brilliant Light, sparkling as when
A calm sea jumps with splashes of light from
The morning sun. So the sea of spirits
Winked and rippled within the brilliant One,
Snugly within the cream seven-petalled Rose.
As bees in a hive secrete wax for comb
Of perfect design, hexagonal cells
That hold larvae, store honey and pollen,
And give off honey's sweet smell as they crawl,
So Angels exude and give off the scent
Of invisible nectar that sustains
All spirits in a smiling atmosphere.

In Heaven the very ether is perfumed
And spirit-bodies waft in happiness
And inhale joy while pleasuring others
With the scent they give off like pollen dust
As they flash out the glitter of the Light
They have gathered from nuzzling in the One.
And now as Christ raised a hand for silence
The flashes stopped and spirits turned golden
Like bees nuzzling in nectar of a rose,
Covered in pollen dust in warm sunlight.

Book 12, lines 1554–1558, 1752–1762, 1849–1896, 1919–1965,
Christ addresses Heaven]

At the heart of the undulating folds
Of the Celestial Rose, on a pistil
That resembled rock and elevated
Him, Christ stood on high and addressed Heaven.
Angels," he said. All fell silent and heard….
'Angels, I told you I had spoken with
Earth's leaders and that they do not realise
The seriousness of the situation.
As much as during the Second World War
When we were worried by Hitler's attempt
To obtain nuclear weapons and use them
Against the West, there is a real threat
That bin Laden, al-Qaeda and Iran
Will ally to obtain nuclear weapons
And launch them at the West in a fiery
Armageddon. This had been headed off….
So I announce here in Heaven, before you,
My witnesses, that my Millennial
Kingdom's been launched. There'll be an Age of Light
For a thousand years, my Millennial Reign."
A loud humming approved the Kingdom's launch,
Which was, in fact, a relaunch of what he
Had launched in 1945. "Angels,"
He resumed, "in our New Age of Light there
Will be no increase of manifesting
Light. The system's fine, it's the reception
Of the Light that's gone wrong so we've improved
The channelling of Light to leaders, who

Will be flooded with thoughts of peace in Light
Under the supervision of Angels."
Again a loud humming greeted his words.
"Fifty-four years back I thought the atom
Bomb had unveiled a new Era of Peace.
We were all disappointed, frustrated
By Satan. I saw a New World Order
Approaching, and a universal Church
Of the Light in which Christian would share with
Other creeds, under my reign as the new
Universal Christ. I called for a new
Prophet to emerge who would state a new
Universalism of Light. Angels,
That prophet has come forward, and I will
Make contact with him on my next return
To Earth. The New World Order will happen,
But not the 'Rockefeller'-'Rothschild' one,
The New World Disorder that they hope for
That will be taken over and replaced
By a democratised model. Angels,
President Bush has led the West towards
Such a democratised world government.
Regional groups will link, and the new state
Will be voted in by world citizens
Who yearn to escape financial crisis,
Flu pandemics that can kill millions and
Climate change that threaten all citizens.
Angels, out of my Thousand-Year Reign and
My Millennial Kingdom will grow a World
Federalist Union with ten regions,
Three superregions: the American,
European and Pacific Unions.
Spirits will soon incarnate in greater
Numbers, for the West is in deep decline
And spiritual ignorance, and the cult
Of celebrity's grown a vacuousness....
A new age of Universal Order
Has just been born. Angels, I can be shown
As a Water-pourer, pitcher on my
Shoulder, for the New Age of Aquarius
Is here and I will pour out Light on all,
And the wisdom of the Light. A new time

Of wisdom is approaching. Christendom,
The Age of Pisces and the Christian fish –
'chthus' in Greek representing my name
As a Greek acronym, meaning 'Jesus
Christ the Son of God' – has given way to
The Universalist Age. Once again
proclaim as I did fifty-four years
Ago: let the coming Aquarian
Age be an Age of Light. Angels, let us
Now flood key minds with manifesting Light!"
A great humming burst round the sunny plains
Like buzzing in a meadow of wild flowers.
As bees swarm in a beehive round a queen
And sip the honey that was culled from flowers,
So the virtuous swarmed round dazzling Christ
And in the sunshine sipped the honeyed Light.

Now all the spirits in Heaven's snow-white Rose,
That tinted cream and gold from the radiance
Of spirit-bodies when joyful, flashed out
And exuberantly crowded round Christ
Pantokrator in bliss, in process to
Self-perfection. A Universalist
Age had been proclaimed, much had to be done.
Spirits headed to distant libraries
To consult past authorities on Light
And work out how best to use influxes
To bring harmony to the troubled Earth.
Many attended talks by Angels and
Shimmered their greetings from radiant bodies,
Stood in groups basking in the brilliant Light,
Communed or worked on projects that advanced
Their self-fulfilment, and all was process,
Nowhere was static, all was dynamic
As near-perfect spirits aspired to be
Perfect Angels and teach other spirits
And descend to Earth as Bodhisattvas
And train blundering humans to the Light.
All was process but also changelessness
For spirits and Angels were consistent
And had stability within the Light.
Here was infinite order and effort.

313

[Book 12, lines 3044–3061, 3096–3097, Christ returns to the earth, at Armageddon]

Christ stood on the plain at Har Megiddo,
"Mountain of Megiddo", Armageddon,
Between Caesarea and Nazareth,
Near Megiddo's ruined hilltop city,
Which controlled a pass on the route between
Egypt and Assyria, a Canaanite
Fortress destroyed in 1468
BC, and then rebuilt by Solomon,
Conquered by Assyrians in the eighth century,
Scene of many battles where the final
Battle between Good and Evil would take
Place, according to John, before the end
Of the world. Here it was foretold that God
Would gather all at the end of days and
Pour out his wrath in earthquakes, storms and hail.
God was never going to do such things,
John was using poetic images
As he often did when a disciple....
Christ felt satisfied, for he was convinced
He had headed off a new holocaust.

[Book 12, lines 3263–3330, Tennyson visits the poet]

Having hosted lunch for the twentieth
Anniversary of the school I founded,
Coopersale Hall, where past pupils had come
From far and wide and been addressed by me
In a marquee with reminiscences
Of the founding and opening of the school,
The place where I first learned of 9/11,
Your poet wandered past the great holm-oak,
Planted by Elizabeth the First in
1562, with my first Head and
Waved her car off and stood and looked across
At Orchard Cottage, which I had let out
To our MP, then went inside the school,
Looked in at the library where Churchill
Came in 1924 to arrange
For Lord Lyle to transfer the MPship
To him; gazed at the barley-twist fireplace

With Wolsey peering from the top, then climbed
The stairs to the room where Churchill stayed in
The Second World War after visiting
War planners at Blake Hall and pilots at
North Weald, when this Hall was requisitioned
For wounded officers. Now a classroom,
It had moulded walls, ceiling and fireplace.
Our poet stood where Churchill himself stood
And looked across fields to distant Epping.
Lost in thought on my previous epic,
suddenly felt I was not alone.
An authoritative presence, severe,
forbidding, materialised. "Tennyson,"
It said, balding, bearded Shadow-like wraith
In a confident Lincolnshire accent,
"I've followed your progress since your visit
To Farringford. I know your *Overlord*
And your focus on Churchill in that work.
I wrote about the Crimean War. I
Lived at High Beach a while, I know these parts.
I loved the woods and Waltham Abbey. I've
Been following your current work. You asked
Me to be your guide, I have guided you.
Often when you have been unsure how you
Should treat the next block words have floated in
Because I've sent them as a suggestion.
You embody the approach I'd have used
If I were alive today. I can't stand
Most of the verse of your time. It's lightweight.
And now the Laureateship, which I held
For more than forty years, has been given,
Politically awarded, rather....
Words fail me. I will not say any more.
It's best to draw a veil. But you should know
You are one of the few who've continued
The metric line from Chaucer to my own
Verse. You have something pressing to say. In
Your collected poetic works you use
A vocabulary in excess of
Fifty thousand words that's more demanding
Than Shakespeare's thirty-one thousand and than
Milton's eight thousand. You've said something. Your

Superficial time may not get to grips
With you, but nevertheless, you were right
To do it. I will come and escort you
When it's time for you to depart this life.
We will talk further on some of your themes.
I just wanted to give encouragement."
And the presence faded, and Churchill's room
Returned to normal. Your poet turned back
And descended to his two hundred guests.

[Book 12, lines 3331–3495, invocations to Pound and to the Light,
and the poet as spider and peacock]

O Pound, founder of Imagism (and
Thus Modernism) in 1914,
Devotee of Dante whose cantos looked
Back to *The Divine Comedy*'s cantos,
You who opposed "Rothschilds" and unwisely
Broadcast support for Mussolini's land
Reform and were sentenced to death and then
Confined in a mental hospital as
"Political prisoner" for thirteen years
And commissioned Mullins to research and
Write *Secrets of the Federal Reserve*
In protest and lapsed into silence; you
Who I visited in Rapallo when,
The latest canto on your table and
"A place of skulls" in ink on its paper
Near a bust of Gaudier-Brzeska,
I said, "I have come to consult you like
The Delphic Oracle as you have been
Fifty-seven years on your *Cantos* and I
Plan a long epic that may take me years";
You who, when your neighbour, Pescatore
("Like a fish"), said he had visited you
For ten years and had never heard your voice
And I stood up to leave, said, "Sit down, you
Don't have to go yet, do you?" and "I've been
Listening to you, you've been to China, you
Can do the work you've been describing, put
The culture of the West into twelve books.
Seeing it's half the battle. It is like

Building a table, it does not matter
Which leg you start with so long as at the end
The table stands up. Can you put what you
Want to say on half a side of postcard?
T.E. Hulme told me in 1915,
Everything a writer has to say can
Be put on half a side of a postcard
And all the rest is application and
Elaboration'" – Imagist thinking.
And, when I finally stood up to leave,
You gripped my hand and peered into my eyes
From six inches away, probing my soul.
O Pound, you were T.S. Eliot's mentor,
You edited *The Waste Land*, cut half out
And wrote in the line (which did not survive),
He do the police in many voices."
I heard Ricks claim in a vibrant lecture
That Eliot's "familiar compound ghost"
Was you – "compound" punning on the word Pound.
I share you as my mentor with Eliot,
You were mentor to both of us, and now,
Having looked in on Oxford's Painted Room –
Where Shakespeare is thought to have often stayed
As John Davenant's Crown-Inn guest, *en route* –
And seen the painted wall and fireplace
Behind a sliding panel and curtain
Where an Oxford Aunt now works in clutter,
I sit in Oxford's Examination
Schools before my other mentor and hear
Ricks' final Professor-of-Poetry
Lecture, in which he says poets should have
Keats' "negative capability", be
In uncertainties, mysteries, doubts without
Reaching "after fact and reason" – therefore
He did not "want to know how change the moons" –
And quotes an Eliot lecture claiming
That Coleridge had to suppress interest
In German systems of metaphysics
To let the haunting Muse speak mysteries.
I sit before him fifty years after
He rescued me from Law, and later ask
Him about Eliot's unpublished poems

Which his widow has given him to edit,
And, my son Tony beside me, tell him
That I am near the end of this great task.
O Pound, I can report that I have now
Finished not just one, but two, poetic
Epics, first *Overlord* and now this work,
Balancing mysteries and metaphysics
Like Coleridge, and say to you, "Job done".
You pared the words around your image down
As if writing in Chinese ideograms,
Words that look like the meaning they convey.
Sometimes an image illumines meaning
Like a flash of light through dark clouds. Sometimes
Meaning moves more slowly, like a slow tide
Gathering momentum in a rising sea
And its grandeur creeps in and covers all
The waiting imagination's bare beach.
I mull over Ricks' definition of
Genius, that it improves on others' works.
You told me Dante's behind the *Cantos*,
You tried to "improve on" him in that work.
I wonder if I've "improved" on Dante
In my post-modern age which now permits
Story-tellers to be part of their tale
Just as observers of the universe
Are part of the universe they observe,
And poets to be seen peeping round their
Concealing work in revealing profile.
O Pound, you said I'd do it, and I did.

O Light I invoked in Jamkaran mosque
When, after peering down the well outside
For the Hidden *Imam*, I walked back to
The blue dome and, shoeless, padded along
A large hall with columns and sat among
Fifty Iranians – standing, sitting or
Kneeling with foreheads to the floor, praying
Towards the well and Mecca near sitting
*Mullah*s with white turbans, and some with black
Descended from the Prophet – on a silk
Carpet, closed my eyes and opened my soul
And offered myself as a defuser

f the international crisis. I asked
ou to descend into intransigence
nd sort Iran out short of war so there
Would be no threat from nuclear weapons,
nd to shine down the well and purify
ll hostility and aggressiveness
nd make it a place of peace and order.
O Light, I said to you, "I am sitting
n pre-war Iran by the well, please burn
Out all festering and Darkness, please guide
Me in my coming literary work
On the clash between civilisations."
nd you, the Light, shone brightly in my soul.
O Light, I have nearly finished that work.
Thank you for guiding me through to the end
nd may it improve harmony and peace.

ust as a spider spins thread from its glands,
ilks from its spinnerets it chews to break,
nd weaves and hangs a web with a centre
And twelve spokes radiating out, held in
Place by twelve circular filaments that
ntersect each spoke and form rotary
hapes, each one larger as they spread outwards,
And, patient, waits for tiny flying things
To stick on thread where crystal drops of dew,
Condensed balls of atmospheric vapour,
Have formed in evening air; so this poet's
Gut and mouth have spun a twelve-spoked theme and
Hung its structure for Being to condense
As globules like dew on its worked silk thread,
Pure drops of truth manifesting from air,
The metaphysical condensed to form.
I wait for images to fly in and
Become entangled on its sticky mesh,
Tremble clear droplets under rosy sky,
The delicate filigree tracery
Of its design whose symmetry pleases
But is a practical, working form that
Has been shaped to catch truths and symbols that
Feed the spider-like imagination.
I hung my twelve-book web and caught my catch.

And as a peacock fans its five-foot tail –
And a hundred eyes peer, each feather tipped
With an iridescent eye ringed with blue
And bronze – and struts and quivers, rattling
Its quills, and, uttering loud screams, displays,
So I put up a quill structure I wear
On my back and carry around with me,
Whose hundred images are of the One
Fixed in a grand symmetrical order
That is patterned in a ribbed form. I show
The One in a hundred blue-and-bronze truths
And strut and rattle it in quiet display.

[Book 12, lines 3496–3735, Christ visits the poet]

Your poet was working in his Connaught-
House study at his Victorian desk,
Checking through these verses in warm sunshine,
Settling on symbols like a butterfly
Sipping nectar with spread wings on scented
Thyme, fluttering on and then settling
On a new image as on lavender.
Christ alighted in his garden, slowly
Gliding to standstill like a grey heron
That comes each day, hoping to spear a fish.
He sauntered up the grass in the warm sun
To the pond with large orange carp. He walked
Up the lush lawn in shimmering summer,
Green trees and grass rejoicing at blue sky,
Back after a long winter and cold spring,
Looked back at Henry the Eighth's Great Standyng,
Now called Queen Elizabeth's Hunting Lodge,
And gazed at the fountain with Three Graces,
Maidens, round the side of its water bowl.
A cuckoo sang from the Ching-Valley woods,
"Cuckoo, cuckoo." And knowing all was well
He wandered to the spiral iron staircase
Whose thirteen treads symbolised the phases
Of this poet's development and whose
Thirty-six spindles stood for his books on
His slow ascent. He lingered by a bust
That looked Roman, of Apollo, the god

Of the lyre, of poetry and of the Light –
Phoebus, the Shining One of brightest Light –
And of the oracle, prophetic words
Channelled in Delphi, and of pure wisdom.
Then slowly he climbed the winding steps to
The first-floor balcony above the pool
And tapped on this poet's glass door. Startled,
Our poet let him in. He passed the desk,
An 1837 partner's desk
With leather top in perfect condition,
And sixteen alcoves of treasures and sat
In the chair by a tray of butterflies,
And this poet flopped back on the sofa
And said, "You visited me once before.
You visited me after *Overlord*."
The sun poured through the large glass windows as
Christ hunched forward in off-white robes and said,
Looking like the framed picture of the Shroud
In the alcoves, "I've come to thank you for
Your current work, which again tells the Truth
And catches the War on Terror's pattern;
But also for your philosophy. You
Have stated Universalism in
A way Heaven's found helpful. You alone
Of living poets and philosophers
Can see the direction to be followed.
You're a poet for Heaven rather than men,
Who aren't clear what their direction should be.
You have stepped outside Christianity
And have absorbed the Oriental faiths
And the Islamic ones, and yet you are
Grounded in Western origins, the Greeks,
And relate to Apollo timelessly
And have reflected the Light in your work.
You have taken the world into your soul.
Heaven's very interested in your approach.
We see you as shunning celebrity,
Retiring, welcoming obscurity.
'A prophet is not without honour, save
In his own country, and in his own house.'"
This poet smiled, "I say Amen to that."
"You have exposed the Syndicate as well,

You alone of your contemporaries.
I know that literature is your main task
And your history and philosophy clear
Up conflicts in your poems, clarify.
I just came to pay my respects, and thank."
This poet thanked him. A thousand questions
Thrust themselves to the forefront of his mind.
This poet asked, "Has Armageddon been
Blocked forever, or has it been delayed?
Will there be a fiery end one day,
A third of mankind incinerated?"
Like an oracle, enigmatically
Christ said, "Two forces, perpetually
Intertwined, permeate the vast cosmos
In permanent opposition: order
And disorder. God the Light's purposes
Are inscrutable, and, not knowing what's
Ordained, we in Heaven just do our best."
Realising that Christ really did not know,
This poet then asked, "What's it like in Heaven?"
There was a long silence. And then Christ said,
"You must ask Bush. He has seen. Report him.
I will show you one day, but not until
You've finished your research into the Age.
A thousand years, ten years – they are both but
A short time to eternity, from whose
Viewpoint they seem almost one and the same.
That's Heavenly, not Earthly, consciousness.
But you are on the right path. Keep going."
This poet said, "I've gone as far as thought
Can reach, to the limit of space-time. How
Do you cross from Being to Existence?
From outside to within space-time?" Christ said,
"No more questions. This is no time for words.
I have come and said what I've said. Enough."
This poet thanked Christ and they sat on in
The warm sunlight and this poet could sense
The harmony Christ exuded, the peace.
He sat on in the One and there was now
No need for words, and everything was clear
And for a minute, which seemed like an hour,
He understood how the universe worked

through the opposites of Darkness and Light,
through infused knowledge from the Light, channelled
by Christ, and the goal of all humankind
and the meaning of life. He knew these things
already and had written them in books
but Christ now rearranged what he had known
so everything connected and made sense.
This poet dwelt in eternity for
about a minute and returned timeless,
an infinite consciousness in space-time
that was both immanent and transcendent.
O wonderful, harmonious universe
that can bestow such unexpected gifts.

Christ tiptoed away. This poet, sunk deep,
became aware he was alone again.
He stood and slipped out to the balcony,
and saw Christ down the spiral stair, gazing
at Apollo's profile. Clambering down,
He stood beside Christ and they sauntered past
the rose garden's spoked paths and stone fountain
Of Three Graces, curvaceous maidens, and
A stone boy clutching a *cornucopia*,
Across the lawn between statues – Winter,
A maiden holding bread loaves, and Autumn,
A maiden bearing grapes under lilac –
To the pool where four large carp lazed in clear
Water replenished from a gushing pipe,
Surface that revealed the muddy bottom,
Yet also mirrored blue sky, sun and clouds
As Existence reflects Being. He saw
His face, leaves, a lily, a dragonfly
Framed in glass on the sun's orb, light and dark,
Being and Existence in One system,
All opposites and contradictions now
Reconciled and blended, including Bush,
Bin Laden and Iran. They sauntered past
Stone Nausicaa and Water-pourer,
Past a shrub that gave out a lilac scent,
Past tits and finches in the apple trees
To the rockery steps and knot-garden.
They stood between Spring, who held bulbs to plant

In each hand, and Summer's sickle and sheaves,
Among pinks, strawberries, medieval herbs –
Sage, santolina, hyssop, fennel, thyme –
Once used as medicines and to flavour food,
In twenty-five herb beds with brick borders.
Christ gazed at the central knot, said, "Explain."
This poet told Christ, "It's an endless knot
Of box hedge with wall-germander corners.
The design of the fourfold knot was on
The front cover of the manuscript book,
The Miroir or Glasse of the Synneful Soul
By Queen Marguerite of Navarre, which was
Translated from French and handwritten by
Princess Elizabeth, later Queen. She
Embroidered the front cover in Queen stitch
When she was just eleven, and presented
It to her stepmother Queen Katherine Parr,
Henry the Eighth's sixth wife, on the first day
Of 1545 – one of six knots,
Henry the Eighth's six wives. It manifests
From Dante's infinitesimal point,
The singularity from which all came.
There are four levels of Being, and this
Fourfold knot and four *fleurs-de-lis* round it
Suggest the One emerging into form,
Hidden spring in which the many are One.
Whoever contemplates this knot-garden
Becomes aware of how the universe
Gushed from Being to Existence. This knot's
A cyclic symbol of the creation
And evolution of the universe
Which pours from infinite Reality,
Renews as running water that's pumped out
Renews a pond by its endless return,
Eternal recurrence of a new flow
Which has already been part of the pond;
And of the unity of disciplines:
Philosophy, history and literature.
The knot-garden's design is taken from
The Gardeners Labyrinth, which was published
In 1577 and shows open
Knots to walk through and a closed central knot.

The twenty-five herb beds, which represent
History's twenty-five civilisations,
Have also come from the infinite point."
Christ nodded at the garden's symbolism
And said, "It expresses the universe
And how it manifests exactly. You
Have understood and told a truth in plants."
Forms that hold meaning are haunting symbols.
A painted lady basking on my thyme,
Wings spread, sipped nectar and was unaware
Of the frail beauty of its outward form
And its meaning in a sunlit moment.
It embodied truth but could not know it.
So most humans don't know our own meaning.
We walked past an ancient sundial and sat
On metallic-meshed chairs at a table
Decorated with grape bunches and leaves
Above clumps of cream clover, purple vetch,
Golden buttercups, stitchwort and daisies,
And looked across to Queen Elizabeth's
Hunting Lodge near the skyline of trees and
Back at Apollo by the spiral stair,
And Christ murmured, "The Earth seems terrible –
Economic collapse, institutions
Corrupt, dreadful prospects – but rest assured.
All's ordered within a benign system.
All will be well in this Peaceful Era.
There will be no Armageddon. It's peace."
And in the warm sunshine and gentle breeze
Of a bright English summer countryside
I felt the universe's harmony
And the benevolence of a benign
Universal order, and life was good.
And though Wisdom warned that aspiration
Often falls short of realisation –
That experience often finds naïve hopes
Are dashed, that nuclear proliferation
Increases and that wise realism
Tends to be pessimistic, that it is
Heroic if not facile to manage
To be optimistic in our world – my
Heart leapt at his certain optimism,

His Epping-Forest vision that despite
The dreadful things that have beset the West
Things will be all right, there can still be hope.
He saw so clearly that all will be well.

May–September 2008; January–July 2009

Coda to be placed at the end of *Armageddon*, death of bin Laden over three years later

A hot May night in an Abbottabad
Compound in Pakistan, safe from attack,
Snuggled at the end of a dirt track, walled,
Osama lay in bed in his burrow,
Clad in nightclothes between two of his wives.
As silent owls swoop and pounce on their prey
Before 1 a.m. two US Black Hawk
Helicopters, modified into Stealths,
Glided through the dark with two teams of SEALs,
Twenty-four US Navy commanders
In night-vision goggles, body armour.
Delta Force captured Saddam, but they sent
Team Six to kill Osama bin Laden.
One Black Hawk (that Matt Bissonnette was on)
Was caught in a strong vortex-ring airflow
That sent washing whipping on a clothes-line
And rubbish swirling among goats and cows
Thirty feet below in the dark compound,
And bucked from stable hover, gyrated
And wobbled so no rope could be dropped down,
Crashed nose-down in the compound and tilted
Against the wall at forty-five degrees.
The other landed outside the compound,
SEALs scaled the wall and packed explosive on
The metal double doors of the guest-house.
More charged up steps onto the guest-house roof.
Inside there was shooting and glass clattered.
A door opened, and a woman clutching
A baby slunk out with three small children:
The wife of Al-Kuwaiti, Osama's
Courier, who (she said) had been hit and killed.
SEALs found him with his feet outside a door
And shot his corpse several times to make sure.

More sprinted to bin Laden's duplex house –
Or house occupied by two families –
And stormed into the ground floor's long hallway.
The leading SEAL, point man, shot at a head
That peered out of the first room on the left
And Al-Kuwaiti's brother fell and writhed.
SEALs killed him – and his wife, who shielded him –
And blew up an iron gate that blocked access
To the two upper floors, stormed up the stairs
And on the landing shot Osama's son
Khalid, whose body lay splayed on its back.
SEALs ran on up the dark narrow spiral
Staircase, and five steps from the top landing,
On their right side, ten feet away from them,
Like a shrew sensing danger from the air
Osama peeped his head out of a door
On the third floor near the top of the steps,
Tall, and swiftly pulled back into the room
As the point man 'Tom' (with Matt close behind)
Fired and missed – or he may have injured him,
It was too dark to know – and then bundled
His two aghast wives from the bedroom doorway
To clear a passage into the bedroom.
Fearing they were rigged with suicide bombs,
Rob walked into his dark bedroom and saw
Through his night-vision goggles Osama
Two feet away, cowering in the dark,
Standing, holding his youngest wife Amal
By her shoulders, having quickly grabbed her
To manoeuvre her as a human shield,
He towering above her, six-foot-four,
Wearing a cap and panic in his eyes.
For a second the two men's eyes were locked.
In case he wore a suicide vest Rob
Shot twice, bap bap, aiming at his forehead.
His head jerked and he fell, hit in the face.
Rob fired again. His skull open, he lay
In a crumpled heap on the floor, twitching,
And exhaled his last breath as his soul fled,
His forehead split in the shape of a V,
Convulsing in a pool of blood, a hole
On his head's right side, gore and brains spilling

From his gaping skull. He wore a sleeveless
White T-shirt, tan trousers and tan tunic,
Kurta paijama. Amal rushed screaming.
If she was wearing an explosives vest....
Humane, Rob took a risk and restrained her,
He tied her to a bedpost as she wailed
Above his convulsing, unarmed body.
One more bap using EOTech red-dot
Holo sight, and one final reflex breath.
Two SEALs (Matt, Rob) trained lasers on his chest,
And fired several rounds. Bullets tore through flesh,
Slammed his body into the floor until
It moved no more and now lay motionless,
Tongue out in last defiant resistance.
His boy stood stunned the far side of the bed,
Sobbing. The point man gently picked him up
And carried him across to his mother.
Osama had been silenced. He could not
Tell his side of 9/11 in court,
State his surprise that the Twin Towers crashed down,
Berate the West from a public platform.
SEALs examined his face, which was mangled,
The right side of his skull collapsed in blood.
The seeping gore had not stopped widening.
Matt took pictures of his profile, pulling
His beard to left and right, and Walt dipped swabs
Into his blood and mouth for DNA
And tried to syringe marrow from his thigh.
(Two sets of photos and swabs were needed
In case one helicopter was shot down
On its way back home to Jalalabad.)
Matt found a box of Just For Men hair dye
With which Osama blackened his grey beard.
Two women were asked who he was. Both said,
"Osama bin Laden." Sure it was *him*,
They found nearby an AK-47
And Makarov pistol, both unloaded.
He asked followers to wear suicide
Vests and fly planes into immense buildings
But had not made plans to defend himself.
Now all the SEALs crowded in and some whooped
And fired more shots into his lifeless corpse

Which jerked and danced. A hundred bullets tore
And riddled his dead flesh, desecrated
His soul to pay it back for fallen Towers.
They seized computers, videos and notebooks,
Dragged his body by its legs down the stairs.
SEALs handcuffed his two wives and stuffed his corpse
Into a body bag and heaved it up
Onto the dark floor of the good Black Hawk.
One of the two reserve Chinooks had now
Landed nearby to take some SEALs back home.
SEALs herded women and children inside
The guesthouse and blew up the crashed Black Hawk
So Stealth parts would not fall into wrong hands.
The undamaged Black Hawk rose into the night.
Osama took up space meant for the SEALs.
As he lay on the floor (all 6 foot 4)
A SEAL sat on his stomach. The man who
Waged war upon mighty America
And provoked attacks on Afghanistan
Was now a cushion for a Yankee rear.
The helicopters rose into the night,
And headed for Jalalabad, where SEALs
Loaded the corpse into a truck and drove
To Bagram. Matt yanked and the bag flopped down
Onto a cement floor like a dead fish.
He unzipped the bag. The skin had gone grey.
Congealed blood stained the inside of the bag.
A 6-foot-4 SEAL lay down beside it
To confirm measurement, for his dark beard
And caved-in head looked unlike Osama.
The bag was flown on to the *Carl Vinson*.
Soon Osama would be buried at sea,
Washed, wrapped in a white sheet, in a weighted
Plastic bag, placed on a flat board that would
Tilt upwards and sideways so his clean corpse
Would slide into the North Arabian Sea.
The leader of al-Qaeda now received
His just deserts for bringing down the Towers:
A watery grave that no one could visit.
He sank into a deep cavernous place
To ponder on the crimes he committed
So barbarously, in the name of war.

Obama, who had aborted three raids
As too risky, dithered till Hillary
Clinton pushed him into backing this raid,
Basked in credit. And in his Texan house
Bush smiled wanly at mission accomplished:
Bin Laden dead, Khalid Sheikh Mohammed
In Guantanamo. Nuclear-suitcase bombs
In ten US cities had been thwarted
And Armageddon contained – for a while.

1 September 2012; revised 13 March 2013; 7, 9, 16 November 2014

42

from *Life Cycle* (2016)
from Life Cycle

[lines 459–525, a man of letters sitting in his garden reflects on the meaning he found in the twelve seven-year ages or cycles in his completed life]

III. MEANING: A COMPLETED LIFE
A life cycle in twelve seven-year ages
Between birth and death and showing striving,
Transforming and achievement and wisdom
Among ripe apples on the orchard boughs.
I knew the Light and found the infinite
Which enfolds our universe like a sea
Round an island. I found the rise and fall
Of civilizations, called for one world.
My voice cried in the wilderness, in vain?
I found a life cycle of forty-two
Episodes in my double life, within
The seven-year cycles that are also found
In body cells and hair, all forms of growth.
I found the growth of the poetic mind
And saw the self of time die back within
The universal being as a seed
Dies back to bring forth a caterpillar
And, after chrysalis, a butterfly.
I died back from ego to unity,
Peace, happiness and joy and I found out

hat the universe supplied all my needs.
opened to the universe's power
And effortlessly words flowed through my brain
Which I transcribed on pages as memoirs
And left behind to strengthen future souls.
searched and found, my life ran to an end
Like the timed gushing through my fish-pool pipe.
he end of our search is the infinite.

grew through ages and found harmony
With Nature and the One in twelve places
And found a path as I transformed my self.
hatched and emerged from my chrysalis
And flew like a glorious swallow-tail.
found a path that led to this great House
And mourned the transience of each cycle.
loved the sun, the rain and the rainbow.
found the eternal in harmony
With the universe and the infinite,
found its permanence and reconciled
All opposites, and from zodiac signs found
The months of the medieval Great Year.
Sitting in a garden like Paradise
I breathe in harmony with unseen breeze
And know I was here to find, and I found.
Fifty-two years on from words above Ur
I have put flesh on the words I received.
My life cycle had a pleasing outcome.
Life cycles propel growth and progress lives
And shh! whisper it just to those who know,
One life cycle does not merely reveal
The phases of a human life's pattern,
It gives it meaning as we find our paths
And progress through time to our end and goal.
It is our universal destiny.

Sitting in my garden I sense ahead....
Out there, somewhere in the future, I hear....
No words or syllables, just heaving breaths
As each breath struggles into words and fades
Into the silence beneath each brief sound
And slowly sound merges into silence

As words become indistinct syllables
And syllables are heard as indrawn breaths
And inhalation and exhalation
Slow down and grow more faint and are at one
With the underlying silence so sounds
And silence pass into eternity

And shallow fainter breaths pass into
death.

30 August – 2 September, 27–28 October, 14–15 December 2014; 31 July,
17 August 2015; 13–14 February, 23 March 2016

43

from *In Harmony with the Universe* (2009–2016)
In Harmony with the Universe

I
I sit on a stone seat with two sphinxes
And griffins each end by the stone arch, see
Near the lake where I sat fifty-one years
Back and read a letter releasing me
From Law for Literature, and just as then,
The weeping willows and chestnuts, the sun
Mirrored in the lake blend with the blue sky
And I sense the harmony of the One.

I watch the Harbour-master's House in storm,
Rain lashing my cheeks. It snuggles on high
Ground as ferocious seas break on the pier
And fountain up under a thunderous sky.
I pulse the energy of sea and wind
And contrast our domestic huddling still
So peaceful under the cliff – storm and calm,
Elemental forces round Charlestown's hill.

Behind the storm and calm I see the One
In moonlit night when branches drip stars raw
That gleam and twinkle in the frosty air
Round a black hole in our galaxy's core,

And I am at one with the black sea flecked
With a streak of moonlight and a sky lit
By a round moon hanging low like a lamp –
All creation in one system's orbit.

And in the Forest over hills the wind
Swooshing through tossing trees is balanced by
The gentle breeze in summer sunshine when
All is still like lilies on mirrored sky.
And I have loved the sparkling on the waves
As sun, sky, sea exult in harmony
And flash out jumping light as if rain were
Pelting and splashing a thunderstorm's glee.

II
Experiences of harmony instruct,
But elsewhere in the world, outside our law,
The order of the stars and hatching grubs
Co-exists with chaotic forces, war.
Missiles kill children in a Gaza street,
In Syria homeless families squat;
And a school is invaded by masked men,
A hundred and thirty-two children shot.

Dreadful things are done for dubious causes.
Think of the Blitz and Dresden's fire-red sky.
When trains pull into Auschwitz platform
Grim men select those who should live or die.
Lines of condemned walk to chambers and soon
The crematorium door is open wide.
So a race is suppressed with ruthlessness,
Systemic and inhuman genocide.

Order in the Levant under ISIL?
A dozen masked men walk with Syrian bound
Pilots, take knives held out in a basin,
Stand behind, make prisoners kneel on the ground,
With one hand gently push lined heads to sand,
With the other slit each lined throat and saw;
Synchronised beheading and hand movements
On docile men who do not twitch a jaw.

⌐ Harmony in the universe is hidden
By men who have fanatical beliefs
And are intolerant of opponents;
By men's brutal coldness to others' griefs.
In every discipline men question soul
And materialist atheism rules.
Yet atheists, who see a dung-hill earth,
Are more humane than cruel Islamic fools.

III
And so I stand apart from all beliefs
And see seven billion souls as absolute,
Deserving of respect, freedom from war,
Disease, famine and poverty, and hoot
The nation-states' fanatical zealots
Who disable in advance and pre-empt,
Who scorn life and subordinate prisoners
To a stale ideology's contempt.

I follow one principle that is true:
Plus A plus minus A equals zero.
Storm, calm; evil, good; ego-centred faith,
Altruism; chaos, order; rot, flow;
Are reconciled and co-exist within
The fundamental unifying One
That restores harmony and shines when men
Behold the ordering cosmos like a sun.

There is a fundamental truth and law
In the secret universe's ether
That reconciles all opposites, and so
Hunter, hunted; eater, eaten; lover,
Loved – all are in a greater harmony
Than their conflicting appetites suggest,
Just as day, night; life, death seem in conflict
But harmonise Nature's forces' contest.

And so I'll seek out lakes and seas and skies
And pay attention to all crawling things
Which are creatures like me in the system's
Birth, breeding and decay – all flying wings –
That fills all Nature with conflict and love

and organisms that love and disperse.
ll look out for all species and live in
miling harmony with the universe.

3–14, 16 February, 3 April 2015

Song Thrush

One – two – three – four sings the song thrush
'rom the oak by the field.
One – two – three – four, or was it five
Churs the tuneful master-singer pipes, to which I yield.

Clear piping, then chi-chur, chi-chur.
All's metric in June sun.
The shadows lengthen, no birds sing
Save for the thrilling trilling of the song, still not done.

Dusk, the song thrush's song is stilled,
Bats flit above the lawn.
But in my head I can still hear
The measured piping and refrain that's left me forlorn.

15 July, 16 December 2014

Brilliant Stars, Snapped Gravity

A night of brilliant stars.
I walk to the harbour wall
And peer at a thousand lights,
See the Plough curl and fall.

Cassiopeia has gone,
Its W's broken free.
I see Orion's belt
And the twins of Gemini.

I sit on the wall and gaze
Up the tree the stars hang on,
And flit! a shooting star
From right to left, now gone.

⌐ And flit, another flares,
   Trails and's gone like a gust.
   A Geminid meteor
   Shower, burning comet's dust.

   And now I feel giddy
   From peering with craned neck.
   I feel gravity wobble
   As on a small sloop's deck.

   I feel gravity snap
   And I plunge headlong, face
   Up into a crowd of stars,
   Hurtle out into space.

   Gravity loosens its hold
   On my ankles and my doom.
   I turn and stride back home
   And shelter in my room.

   Out there vast galaxies.
   I bend at my desk and sigh.
   My roof will keep me safe
   From falling up into the sky.

15–16 December 2014

44

from *An Unsung Laureate* (2009–2016)
Lisbon Treaty:
The End of Great Britain, Demise of a Nation-State

I
Over blue-grey sea a squally day rules.
Curtains of rain conceal Europe's veiled land.
The tide flows in from France and fills still pools
Round bladderwracked rocks, and glistens the sand
As sunlight breaks. A causeway of light draws
Me towards Trenarren's Black Head, and on.

To left all's murk, to right a brilliance pours
Splashing light. Our independence has gone.

On the screen by my window with sea-view
A newscaster says, "The Czech President
Has ratified the Lisbon Treaty too."
All twenty-seven European states, leant
On, have ratified. Now I'm living in
A county, not a country; in an E
U with legal personality, spin.
Our laws will all be passed across the sea.

By the anti-French battery cliff gulls soar.
The French and Germans were often conquered.
We English have not been invaded for
Nearly a thousand years, not since we heard
That Norman ships were in Pevensey Bay.
We've been a proud nation, our chiefs with guile
Fought for our island's autonomous sway.
And now it's been signed away with a smile.

Two cormorants fish outside the harbour.
O Churchill and Montgomery, please sleep,
Our independence was signed away for
Our rulers promised, but were in too deep,
To seek our consent. Now it is too late.
No referendum, for the people would
Have voted No, and the new superstate
Would have been stillborn, all would have been good.

On the hill sheep graze heedless of torment.
The main 'no consenter' who blocked us all
Is trying to be Europe's President:
Tony Blair who led England into thrall
Now seeks his rewards: the Emperor's crown,
More traitorous than if King Harold had wished
To invite Duke William to London town
To take the throne Edward had relinquished.

A long curled wave rolls shoreward, and then more.
Can a signed treaty be cancelled next day?

No, for like hard rock it's set into law.
The Treaty of Amiens, which gave away
Too much, was renounced within six months, dashed,
But the ratified Lisbon Treaty's blur,
Like the Treaty of Rome, cannot be smashed
Unless by revolution's sledgehammer.

Dead fish, algae-eaten, strew beach, clog boats.
And now I see the Rotten Parliament –
MPs' expenses spent on ducks and moats,
Second mortgages, evaded tax, bent
Family-member staff, cleaning, gardening chores,
Porn films, food, you name it, oh, huge TVs
They corruptly claimed – now has but few laws
To pass, is best by-passed for MEPs.

II
I turn on the TV. A brave young man
Is borne in a *cortège* – he did defuse
Sixty IEDs in Afghanistan;
Flags dipped, flowers placed to veterans' tattoos.
England's confused. It feels a nation-state
In Wootton Bassett's homecoming and cars,
And yet it's ceased to share a nation's fate
Now it's under a blue flag, yellow stars.

Now outside the harbour the *Phoenix* waits
For the high tide that will float her in, see
Two masts, fluttering flag, upward prow, crates,
Looking like the *Victory*, or *Discovery*
That took empire to Jamestown when, lithesome,
We'd been a Tudor nation, now for show.
England's island's now a floating museum
Like this ship that's as it was long ago.

And now I think of the history I love,
European civilization's roots
In Greece and Rome, its Union above,
This new superstate England now salutes.
All Europe's history's in my country now.
Are not the English migrants from Celtic,

Roman, Anglo-Saxon, Danish and (bow)
Norman tribes in Europe's body ethnic?

work again on a World State, my cause.
advocate a federal 'hauberk'
World government that will, with new world laws,
Enforce peace and disarmament, and work
To share world resources, solve global stealth
(Climate change), end famine and disease, steer
The banking crisis, redistribute wealth
To end poverty – a good upper tier.

The nation-state is passing, all discern
A time of regions and Unions, and our
Sovereignty's been surrendered in return
For a share in the EU's sovereign power.
It's a preparation for a World State
That will bring a peace dividend and lease
A benefit to humankind, a great
New Golden Age: prosperity and peace.

I'm relaxed at our demise, a mere cloud,
Pretext for Blair to try for President
At the end of a thousand years of proud
Independence and law-making well-spent,
For I'm reunited with my roots, zones
In the Greek, Roman and Renaissance mind.
Europe's high culture acts as stepping-stones
To a Universalist humankind.

I once stepped across the flowing Rothay,
Tiptoeing across stepping-stones in bliss
In Wordsworth's footsteps where he walked each day
To work in Ambleside's old post office.
I tiptoe across the Channel with kings
To a cultural landscape that not too late
Connects me to all humankind and brings
Me to more stepping-stones, to a World State.

5 November 2009; 7–8 April 2015

from Zeus's Emperor
(A Mock-Heroic Poem)

[lines 1–34, 59–71, 85–129, 158–189, 518–541, 546–569, 654–677, 689–691, 696–707, Zeus's plan to choose Blair as President of the European Council, EU 'Emperor', to advance a world government goes wrong]

Canto 1

Sing, Muse, of empire made from nation-states
By men who yearned for peace and urged debates
On ensuring there would be no more war,
And enmeshed France and Germany in law;
Sing how the Lisbon Treaty created
A European superstate that spread
A call to join it to the still unsure,
Whose expansion filled outsiders with awe;
Sing a New World Order's imperial dreams
To advance their *élite*'s self-serving schemes
And of Zeus's Universalist hopes
To create (through some hand-picked philanthropes)
A democratic World State that will rule
Mankind benevolently like a school.
If the UN's General Assembly were
Voted in, then mankind might find a cure
For war, famine, poverty and disease;
And a world superstate could not but please.
Or so Zeus thought, and every empire must
Have an 'Emperor', a President all trust;
And the European superstate should –
A United States of Europe – do good
And lead mankind forward to the World State,
A United States of the World that's great.
Sing, Muse, of Zeus's noble ambition
As he seeks an 'Emperor' who will stun.

Otto von Habsburg was Zeus's first thought.
He told Hera: "He's the one I have sought.
He'd make an excellent new President,
He's had huge experience and is well-meant.
He was head of the House of Habsburg for

mpteen years and was, before Hitler's war,
rown Prince of Austria, Bohemia
nd Hungary, also of Croatia."...

lera listened with languid insouciance
nd finished painting her nails, with a glance
t the door dismissed him without comment.
ll his enthusiasms came and went.
hen she went straight on to the internet.
en minutes on, she briefed, they again met.
Dearest," she said, lowering an eyelid,
Commanding his attention with timid,
Demure acceptance of all he had said,
I've been thinking, this Otto's a good head
And would have done wonderfully a few years
Back but alas! Time's intervened and jeers.
He's ninety-six, and Presidents somehow....
What do you want of Europe's superstate?
To be effective or to expand, wait
For time to bring in a world government
That will fill the whole world with good intent,
And meanwhile block the New World Order so
t can't strengthen its hold on Europe's show?
f so, you're looking for a man who'll con
The élitist, self-interested wan
New World Order into supporting your
Vision of an anti-élitist, raw,
Democratic World State, someone who'll wreck
Rothschilds from the inside just as – you'll check –
He wrecked the UK from the inside by
Too much borrow-and-spend. You need someone
Who's devious and engages, and has done
Something in the same line, and yet appears
Vacuous to allay suspicious fears,
And bland, and a regular kind of guy.
I'm thinking of a man who did well by
Us both in dumbing the UK with smarm,
Who'll take our brief for payment and stay calm.
The man I'm thinking of was made Quartet
Envoy on the same day on which he set
Himself on a new course by resigning
As Prime Minister, for money-making.

He's been PM and's now 'Ambassador'
To each powerful Middle-Eastern leader.
He could easily be a President.
Blair's your man, vacuous blandness is his bent.
Send Hermes to propose that he applies
Before a peace plan snatches off our prize –
And before he's sacked as 'Ambassador'
For bland inactivity and *hauteur*.
He's lost a little credibility
Through Iraq but this job will set him free."
Zeus listened, stunned at such a good idea.
"Of course," he said, "it is President Blair."
Hera smiled, Zeus now had what he wanted
And she could control him – and the godhead.
Languidly she returned to her *boudoir*
And sat at her mirror, her door ajar.

Hermes found Blair in a Jerusalem
Hotel plotting his envoy's stratagem,
New casting out of devils into swine,
To bring peace to Israel and Palestine....
"I bring a message from Zeus. He
Sees you as talented, wants you to be
President of the European Council,
Effectively (to put a spin on skill)
President of Europe, or Emperor.
You could be the first Emperor and draw
And shape the EU towards its next stage.
The Syndicate will welcome such a sage
And gifted, and experienced, man as you
Governing and directing the EU."
Blair's eyes had widened. "You speak as I've thought,"
He said to the image his mirror brought.
"I'd certainly like to apply." Hermes
Nodded and faded. Blair pondered, at ease.

Canto 2

Now in his mirror rose a startling scene.
He saw Napoleon as in a dream
Being crowned Emperor of the French in

otre Dame Cathedral in an ermine-
nd-velvet coronation mantle filled
Vith embroidered golden bees found and milled
rom regalia in Childeric the First's
Ierovingian tomb – a scene that bursts
1 from a cold December Sunday in
804. Napoleon (no grin)
olemnly placed a laurel crown as worn
y Roman Emperors on his own head, torn
rom the Roman Empire, gold laurel wreath,
nd then took from the altar, waist beneath,
he new 'Charlemagne crown', ignored the Pope
o he would not have to accept the dope
s his overlord, crowned himself and sat
)n his imperial throne, an autocrat....

Canto 3

That seer Hagger told me," Apollo said,
A partial World State could be created
3y Obama." Zeus said, "I do agree,
must deal with the US. Look, I see...."
Zeus extended Hagger's seven-foot-long chart
)ver his knees and peered beyond his heart
At twenty-five civilizations down
And sixty-one stages across his frown
And tried to grasp how history works, its sprawl
Through civilizations that rise and fall.
At last Zeus got the chart the right way round
And now shared with Apollo what he'd found:
'On Hagger's chart, the next stage of the North-
American civilization set forth
Is a Universalist one. I've read
The Secret American Dream, which said
That the US, not Europe, is our route.
Instruct Obama to speed up, transmute
The world and implement the chart's next stage
So a democratic World State can cage
In the dictatorial New World Order's
EU and absorb it in its pastures."

So Zeus took his history from Hagger's chart.
All the gods now relied on human art....

Zeus sat in dejection and told Hera
"As Rompuy, not Blair, is my Emperor,
I have to accept that my power's failing.
It's not as absolute as in my spring.
The chief god lives forever but grows old
(In a way of speaking), mind patched with mould.
It is a relatively recent trend
That the chief of the gods can no more send
His vision of the future via Hermes
To human minds that make sense just as bees
Make honey from thyme; that he has lost power.
We gods, no longer all-powerful, just glower.
The true Emperor is kingmaking Rothschilds
Who have supplanted us out in the wilds."
Hera comforted him: "That's too extreme,
You're still more powerful than the sun, you beam
And the earth goes on doing what it should.
You send a thunderbolt and burn a wood.
You used to send thoughts into human minds
But few now see your Light which they think blinds.
It's not your fault that men cannot receive
Your visions. My dearest, you must not grieve.
You're still the order in the universe
Which couldn't function without you as nurse."...

Alas, gods are no longer all-powerful.
If we want world peace, then we have to pull
Our weight and do it for ourselves. Self-help!
When life gets hard it doesn't help to yelp.
We can't count on the gods delivering.
The gods, like politicians, are struggling
To convince themselves they're still in control.
Sometimes they can help, sometimes they console.
Zeus had been buffeted by two world wars,
Umpteen Cold-War skirmishes and old scores.
Man's slipped the leash and rampages beyond
Zeus's control, many seek to abscond.
Hera was right in what she did profess:

eus can't be blamed for mankind's waywardness.
eus's loss of power is not down to him,
ut to increasing ignorance of dim
Mankind, that is no longer living right.
Man's inner sky is now an endless night.
ut, and this is crucial, Zeus can still send
nspiration in Light to dawn and blend
n opened souls, and so his hand-picked few
Continue to transmit what he would do,
Plans for future initiatives and works,
Light-coded messages, the mystic's perks....
he mystic's become Zeus's confidant.
Mystics, not politicians, instigate
And receive the vision of the World State....
t is an indisputable truth and right
That there's a Law of Order, and with Light
And a struggle on Zeus's part, right will
Prevail and good will triumph – just be still.
Zeus' ordered plan for a World State must
nevitably make the world more just
Even though Zeus has lost his confidence
And depends on the mystics to make sense –
Even though Zeus has forgotten the plan
And to remind himself now has to scan
Works by mystics he claims to have inspired
Like Hagger's chart and World-State books he Fired.

23–27 November 2009; 30 March, 1, 9–11, 13–18 April, 12–13 June 2015

Changelessness like a Fanfare:
Trumpeting a Jubilee

I.
A thousand boats progress along the Thames
Led by gilded *Gloriana*, a rowbarge
Whose eighteen Tudor-style oarsmen toss oars.
A floating belfry swings eight bells on large
Wheels, peals answered from land by pealed church bells.
Rowing-boats, shallops, skiffs follow, cocklers,
Herring drifters, kayaks, tall ships and tugs,

Steamers, oyster smacks, cutters and cruisers
From Canaletto's 1747
'Thames on Lord Mayor's Day' – recreating then.

2.

A million line the banks and cheer the show,
A pageant with the largest flotilla
To sail on the River Thames since King Charles
The Second brought Catherine of Braganza
With "a thousand barges and boats" Pepys saw
In 1662 to wow his bride.
And on a royal barge with two thrones, decked
With ten thousand flowers, her Duke at her side,
Stands she who's thanked for sixty years – again –
Of selfless reign, in four hours' wind and rain.

3.

The Thames Flood Barrier, closed, slows the river.
An orchestra's 'Rule Britannia''s a feat.
Tower Bridge raises its roads in steep salute.
At her Silver the Queen reviewed a fleet
But it's been sold and now we have these skiffs.
Wet street parties with patriotic grit
Signal with flags that all have united.
More than four thousand beacons have been lit,
The first in Tonga. The Empire's in pieces
But she is still Queen of sixteen countries.

4.

A concert outside Buckingham Palace:
Loud tuneless rapping and unfunny 'jokes'.
Our culture has collapsed to clunking din
And inane words shrieked in screeches and croaks
(And vacuous questions presenters preen).
The Duke is in hospital, we are told,
Her Lord High Admiral who stood four hours,
With cystitis brought on by the Thames cold.
Two dozen 'celebrities' strut and prance
And deafen. The ear-plugged Queen looks askance.

.

he stands on the stage, above each tribute.
Her heir kisses her hand and begins fondly,
Your Majesty – Mummy," as all roar.
he lights the last beacon with a diamond.
Crowds line the streets as she drives to St Paul's.
Victoria (without Albert) could not climb
ts steps in 1897, stayed in
Her carriage for the whole thanksgiving time.
he Archbishop praises *her* selfless joy.
he drives to Mansion House in a convoy.

.

A 'Jubilee' is a 'rejoicing', comes
from Hebrew '*yobel*', a 'ram's-horn trumpet'.
A trumpet fanfare from heralds, all rise.
She descends Westminster-Hall steps, slow yet
Sure-footed though eighty-six years old, past
Where Charles the First was tried and condemned. Grey
Liverymen and politicians sit
At round tables near where her parents lay
n state, and Churchill. The Master Mercer,
Before the English dishes, welcomes her.

7.

Thousands of servicemen stand in the streets
As her landau leaves Westminster in rain,
Footmen in gold livery and black caps;
As her Horse Guards' hooves clop-clop their terrain
Into the Mall where crowds thirty deep cheer.
Flags hang between the trees, red guards with black
Busbies on heads make sure her landau's safe.
By her waves her heir's wife (fifteen years back
A pariah who spoiled what might have been),
Facing her heir, a statement she'll be Queen.

8.

A quarter of a million fill the Mall,
A river of flag-waving and a cheer
As she stands on the palace balcony
With her heir and his queen, and *his* young heir
And future queen. A fusillade of shots.
A Dakota's roar speaks for wartime folk:
A Lancaster and four Spitfires drone past,
And nine Red Arrows trail red, white, blue smoke.
She unites all, presents a dynasty:
The assured succession of the monarchy.

9.

The first Elizabeth and Victoria
Presided over their growing empires.
Her sixty years have witnessed their decline
To dwindling austerity in the shires.
The times have swept away a class system
For money, talent and celebrity.
Her televised thanks are brief and formal.
She unites diverse races silently.
She reigns by saying nothing, showing no
Feeling – which her stamp-and-coin heads forego.

10.

She's seen twelve leaders steer her realm through wars –
Cold, hot – fought secretly and by brave troops.
She's seen a Great Power slump while lives have eased
And now hands on a crown that's cheered with whoops.
What of the future? She will hope to reign
Longer than Victoria's sixty-three years.
Will all then still cheer her less-silent heir?
Or will there, when Scotland's left him, be tears?
This Jubilee trumpets a changeless air
Amid change that may fade like a fanfare.

6, 10 June 2012

Churchill 50 Years On:
Great Briton

'm back as a child under eiderdown.
Outside a whine cuts out, I count the strafe.
At ten there is a distant blast, I smile.
It's not our house that's been hit, I am safe.
There is terror up in the blacked-out sky,
Indiscriminate flying bombs that kill.
One man protects us, shields our frightened heads:
My MP, our PM, Winston Churchill.

When France fell he stood up to Germany.
He had not been PM a month but he
Did not surrender as many assumed,
Called us to fight alone and remain free,
Offered blood, sweat and tears. The Blitz was so
German ships could invade us and subdue
Without threats from the air. He stood between
Us and the bombers, and sent up the Few.

I'm back before the war memorial.
Bare-headed Churchill speaks to us. I am
So near I could reach and touch his right arm.
He tells us he is leaving for Potsdam.
There he will learn he has been voted out.
Now I'm back on the High School's top step and
He stumps up with his stick and hat and smiles
And signs my album, beams and shakes my hand.

His coffin is borne upstream on a launch.
I see the Thames on black-and-white TV;
The only commoner of the century
To receive a State funeral. I see
Crowds line the embankment in silent awe.
Cranes dip their jibs in homage as the boat
Approaches our leader's last landing-stage,
A vanished UK once again afloat.

II

Nearly fifty years on I take my seat
To hear Boris Johnson talk on Churchill.
He climbs onto the Imperial's stage,
Hair dishevelled, and bumbles on the thrill
His family got from Churchill's speeches.
"He used short and Anglo-Saxon words, he spoke
With Ciceronian polish, he did not
Extemporise. He mesmerised all folk.

"He was born when the British Empire was
Seven times the extent of Trajan's Roman
Empire, and wanted to keep it going.
He said different things at different times on
Europe – wanting to be absorbed within
A united Europe or be remote.
He was consistently for free trade as
It put cheap food in each working man's throat.

"He was the most highly-paid journalist,
Was taken prisoner in the Boer War
And famously escaped. He fought in four
Continents and killed men. I am in awe.
He left the Tories in 1904,
Became liberal, invented the tea break,
Went from Minister to the trenches, then
Returned to the Tories, a party rake.

"After his blunder at Gallipoli,
He got the Yanks in on both wars." I think,
'By handing over all our oil in North
Iraq, then Saudi Arabia,' and blink.
"But his greatest achievement was to stand
Up to Hitler in May 1940
After the fall of France. What made him make
That choice not to give in, to remain free?"

III

Now the re-enactment. The *Havengore*
Follows the route of the funeral upstream
And bears a wreath that's cast into the Thames

y Parliament, like a repeated dream.
  holds a V, the victory sign he made
ow-tied, in hat. His finest hour, the throng
s he announced Germany's surrender.
weet Thames, run softly, till I end my song.

rowds line the banks and bridges to witness
lis recreated last journey, in awe
f a great Briton who led a vanished
'K to victory in one-sided war
Vith the courage to stand for what is right.
. new generation is learning how
learly the British came to be conquered,
.nd speak German as their first language now.

efore Hitler blitzkrieged Poland, Churchill's
'areer was haunted by failures that irk:
jallipoli; Norway; French surrender;
)efeat and headlong retreat from Dunkirk;
he Blitz – German bombers' penetration;
he fall of Greece; Singapore; Tobruk's fall.
,oviet troops and American Lend-Lease
'nabled him, and Britain, to survive it all.

Vho was the greatest Briton? Churchill thought
Alfred the Great, who beat the Danes, prinked pride
And, King of the West Saxons, called himself
King of the Anglo-Saxons', unified
'ngland as the heptarchy's overlord.
'lizabeth who fought off Spain with skill
And set England on a Protestant course?
Newton? Shakespeare? Many would say: 'Churchill.'

iV
By 1939, distrusted for
Twice changing parties, he thought his career
A failure, yet next year was a symbol
Of national unity, Britain's role clear:
A grandiose final chord, loss of empire
And the collapse of British power – yet he
Founded the noble European idea
And pointed to our EU destiny.

⌐ He helped found the Welfare State, invented
The tank and RAF, shaped Iraq's sand,
Israel and the Middle East, three times saved
Civilization – in two world wars and
In the Cold War. Is history made by
Great men or a force? Like the Thames drifting
Under bridges, history flows through stages
And bears great men as its slow currents sing.

Borne from imperial to European stage,
He witnessed the Age change as staid post-war
Britain gave way to TV, affluence,
Rock 'n' roll, tower blocks and permissive law.
Suez and Profumo shook the Empire,
Macmillan's fall ended the 'Old England'.
Born a Victorian, he towered on,
An obsolete Colossus but still grand.

Churchill was a soldier who saw action
In India, Sudan and against Boer threats;
A politician who held office in
Liberal and Conservative Cabinets;
A journalist, historian and writer
Who won the Nobel Prize for Literature.
I hail a man of action and of thought,
A many-disciplined, great character.

31 January, 1 February, 3 April 2015

45

from *Adventures in Paradise* (2010–2015)
Verses on the Death of Mr Nicholas Hagger

When we peer in the human mind
What faults we see, what follies find.
These are not flecks in our eye's vein
But specks in human nature's brain,
Which is to say, on its left side
Of logic and language, the pride
Of the rational, social ego;

Not the right side's creative flow
That's intuitive, non-verbal,
Where Light pours into its channel.
Some vices lurk – is it not true? –
In disguise within each virtue.
In his maxims La Rochefoucauld
Finds personal interest below
Generous feelings, tributes, festoons:
In news of our friends' misfortunes,
He says, we find something that does
Not displease us, but brings a buzz
Of faint enjoyment – *Schadenfreude*.
When we are quietly overjoyed
At others' adversity we
Can greet their demise with quiet glee,
A secret catch in sorrow's breath
As we hear news of a sad death.

It is natural to envy each
Who's raised himself beyond our reach
And seems above us – our equal
Standing in a crown of laurel
So our view is now obstructed.
Who has not wished such a 'friend' dead?
Humankind's vain, full of self-love;
Pride, ambition and envy shove
And jostle to the fore, then mask
Themselves as smiling virtue, ask
"Has there ever been a quester
For the One like Larkin" (who never
Quested), or "Isn't she good on
Achilles" (that is, his tendon)
Or "How well he writes of follies"
(When foolishness is what it is).
That human nature's full of pride
And selfishness can't be denied
But when it's transformed from ego
To universal being, lo!
Sympathy and goodness exist:
Virtue's seen through a lifting mist.

⌐ It must be said, though with a sigh,
That it is certain all will die:
The Queen, your Aunt May, Uncle Don
Will somehow manage to move on
With dignity and with some style,
And possibly a rueful smile.
It helps if we have known the Light
When we set off into that night,
As at a station take our leave
Waved off by relatives who'll grieve.
Alas! my final day has come.
I gaze out from my deathbed, dumb.
I look for sunshine, see the dark,
Familiar faces in an arc.
Wife, children and grandchildren mourn
Their protector's long end, and yawn:
"He founded the family business
And smiled a lot, often said yes
And played chess and table tennis."
My siblings text a distant kiss.
But beyond family warmth, what
Is being said out there? I've got
An inkling: "He's heading for tea
With William Shakespeare and Shelley."
And: "His headstone will say 'No rhymes
Down here' – just restful, better times."
"His eyes have drooped, he'll soon be gone,
His breathing's laboured, cheeks look wan."
"Look, now he's slipped away. Listen.
A breath. Another breath." And then....
"It's over, he has passed away.
It's a blessing he could not stay.
It is a merciful release
Now his questing soul is at peace."
Familiar faces drift for doors.
Work calls, and home. There's now a pause.

We like to pigeon-hole each friend
As "poet", "historian". A blend
Confuses, and: "Where do we start?
Poems and stories from the heart,
Verse plays and man-of-letters forms,

histories, science – what are his norms?
Philosophy and religion,
Mysticism, education,
Politics and statecraft, culture –
And so it goes on, it's simpler
To say he wrote poetry and prose
In seven bands like a rainbow's."
But what was he? A this or that?
Can we define him by one hat?"
Jack of all trades, master of none,
Wrote everything under the sun."
All right during the Renaissance
But now leads us a merry dance."
Intelligence men say, "He should
Be walled round with silence, not good."
And: "Shouldn't have been published for
The State is supreme, that's the law."
And: "Why turn against nation-state
To Universalist debate?"
And: "The World State's a hazy dream,
An everythingism regime."
There is bewilderment and lack
Of understanding, some hold back.

The public in bookshops aside,
Small groups receive the news I've died:
School and college contemporaries,
The few still alive then, that is;
Some staff at my four schools shed tears.
I sat with them for many years.
Some parents pay polite respect,
A remote figure has been wrecked.
Some past students and pupils frown,
A kindly soul has fallen down.
To some I am a named cipher:
Accountant and bank manager.
Writers who knew me exchange looks
And cross me off their address books.
My publishers express dismay
But now my backlist leads the way.
My readers all have favourite bits
As an audience sits and flits.

One year on my archive greets all
Who visit Colchester and scrawl
Their notes about my manuscripts
Better suited to dusty crypts.

Suppose associates discussed
What I wrote before I was dust,
How would they view my life's output?
"In verse he set out foot by foot
His quest through Nature for the One
Reality, bright as the sun,
That orders the universe and
Sets man in harmony with sand,
Earth, sea, hills, cliffs, mountains and sky
And the rest of society
And reconciles all opposites,
Vices and virtues, and transmits
A sense of purpose that seems sent
And transforms through self-improvement,
To bypass follies and then see
The secret hidden unity
And oneness of the universe
That all souls seek before their hearse.
His work in seven disciplines
Locates this theme in human skins
That frequent his Essex whose woods
He freely roamed in his boyhood's
Harmony with Nature, when he
Loved all creatures instinctively:
Grasshoppers, birds and butterflies
That filled the heaths and brightened skies."
And some might say: "He had one foot
In local life, social input,
And one foot at his desk where he
Wrote books and, perspicaciously,
Foresaw an impending World State,
A world government that can't wait
If humankind's to live free from
War, famine, disease, nuclear bomb
And poverty. And though a scourge
To the vicious, like a grass verge
He was kindly, he cared for souls

Whose vices burned like red-hot coals.
He was a caring man who saw
Mankind's best plan was to ban war
And bring in paradisal peace
And his works sought this Golden Fleece."
And some might say, stifling their glee:
His quest was strange, and all can see
That normal living's not seeking
For some non-existent meaning.
No need for an adventurous life,
Just work, drink, telly and the wife.
All know life's pointless, that we just
Enjoy ourselves before we're dust."

And some, with mordant bite, might say,
'He swept man's illusions away.
He found darkness and bequeathed Light.
A shallow Age bestows its night."

27–30 December 2015

46

from *The Dream of Europa* (2014–2015)
from The Dream of Europa: The Triumph of Peace

[from Prologue, on Mount Olympus Zeus gives Europa a mission]

Zeus: It looks like an earthquake – Berlin, Europe:
            Everywhere rubble of collapsed buildings
            As if the earth had heaved. Humans did this,
            Not Nature, dropping bombs on neighbouring states.
            I want a peaceful and unified world,
            Order and harmony. As the top god
            I am frustrated that blundering man
            Has undermined my efforts to bring in
            A democratic World State with the power
            To abolish war, famine and disease.
            I gave my backing to first Hitler, then
            To Stalin, but both disappointed me.

Fascism, Communism killed millions
And imposed tyrannies on humankind,
But they also imposed a levelling-down.
Traditions are right for a new Europe
That can incorporate its nation-states
And grow into a massive superstate
And bring peace and prosperity to close
On a billion Europeans. The first
Step is to create a common market
From which political union can grow.
As I'm disillusioned with world leaders,
Who're self-interested and can't be trusted,
I've chosen my protégée Europa,
To whom I've been a mentor and whose mind
I have 'impregnated' with one-world seed,
To gestate and bear an infant World State:
A European Union that can grow
Into a United States of Europe
So Europe, Asia and the Americas
Can one day unite in a one-world State.
My dear Europa, you have always held
A special place in my heart and my hopes.
You know I want a unified mankind,
All humankind equal under world law.
Are you now ready to begin the task
That weighs so heavily upon my mind,
To bring order to this chaos of war
And establish a resurging Europe
In which all citizens can live at peace,
A paradise, a forerunner of states
That can combine in a peaceful union
And be an example to humankind?

[from Revels, at the Court of Justice, Luxembourg, Churchill gives the UK representative some home truths]

(Churchill *moves to* Europa's *side.*)

Churchill: The UK saved Europe during the war.
               We stood alone against the *Blitz* until
               The Americans joined us for D-Day.
               We liberated France and Benelux.

uropa:
At Zurich I called for a United
States of Europe. You must bear this in mind.
I honour your courage and leadership,
But the UK is taxing our patience.
It's obsessed with obstructing our advance.

(Churchill *walks to the* UK representative *and addresses her.*)

hurchill:
You're spoiling our revels. We here all want
A United States of Europe that ends
All war, famine, disease and poverty.
I'm glad we've had seventy years without war.
I've a message for your Prime Minister,
And more importantly for his right wing
And the narrow-minded UKIP leaders,
For all poor leadership and statesmanship.
Don't you remember the war? Don't you know
How terrible the state of Europe was
When the war ended? Now Europe's at peace.
War's impossible when economies
Are intertwined in trade and tourism
And territorial aggression's taboo.
We are witnessing the triumph of peace.
Stop spoiling this new world. I am ashamed
Of your narrow self-interest and concerns:
Immigrants, benefits being abused,
Crowded schools and hospitals, and money.
Where is the vision of unity I
Left behind, my legacy to my Age?

JK
epresentative:
Europe's moved on since your time, thank heavens.
And the UK has moved on, and England.
We have issues about our being swamped.
Too many have poured into our country.

(Europa *and Juncker advance to join* Churchill *and the*
UK representative.)

Europa:
You, Britannia, have lost Churchill's vision.
You flirt with isolationism, you
Have forgotten that Europe's kept the peace
First through an east-west balance of power
And then through our great eastwards enlargement.

359

Where is the internationalism
That built your Empire and ruled a quarter
Of the world at the time of the Great War?
Shame on you....

(*The* UK representative *addresses* Europa *and Juncker.*)

UK
representative:

I've a message from our Prime Minister.
Your Commission has alienated us.
Your demands for an increased budget are
Unacceptable, and you've swamped our towns
With immigrants who clutter up our schools
And hospitals, and live off benefits.
It is simply a question of numbers,
Too many make use of your free movement.
You're arrogant and dictatorial.
You should rule like a constitutional
Monarch and protect our flooded regions,
Not abuse our warm-heartedness and take,
Take, take from our kind generosity.
You will have deserved it if we defect.
You'll only have yourselves to blame if we
Turn our backs on Europe and walk away
And join the Free Trade Area of Iceland,
Norway and Liechtenstein, and Switzerland.

Europa:

Don't spoil the rejoicing with sour comments.

[from Epilogue, Mount Olympus. Zeus's vision of the future]

Europa:

Lord of all, who has worked tirelessly for
The peaceful harmony of humankind
And has sought to create a paradise
For undeserving man to inhabit,
I've set up an ideal State in Europe
That can now spread and be widely followed
Now that a structure has been created.
I have established your grandiose vision
Where it was most needed, in smashed Europe.
I present you with the utopia
You've wanted for our disunited earth.
On one of the five continents, at least,
Tyranny and dictatorship can now

Be seen to be ending for a World State
That's democratic, constitutional.
The hard work's done, further expansion will
Follow as a stream widens to the sea.
Nine Muses, twelve Wise Men, I discharge you.
We thank you for the Europe you've inspired.
Lord of all, I hope the EU's pleased you.
You may like to take back your utopia.

(Zeus *steps forward, slightly doddery.*)

Zeus   (*to Europa*): You have done well, my goddess Europa.
Congratulations on implementing
My order and your supporting vision.
Europe will be a paradisal State.
But as you know, disorder is still rife
And that is just a start, there's much to do....
(*To all*): Know that the World State will abolish war,
Famine and disease, poverty and debt
By international law that will also
Bring in disarmament, solve energy
And environmental problems so there
Is the prospect of perpetual peace.
(*Aside*): The rise of a democratic World State
Will first challenge and then loosen the grip
Of the self-interested *élite* that seeks
To control the earth's resources – the oil
And gas, the banks and all the governments –
For its own ends and amass more trillions.
We have to work with the *élite* which funds
The banks and budgets, all expenditure,
But as soon as the structures they've financed
Are in place we will dump the Syndicate.
(*To all*): In all parts of the globe I want to see
Unions of states and policies that lead
To humankind's reunification
Through Universalist, not nationalist,
Thinking, through a vision of unity.
A new Universalism shines through
The Charter's universal articles.
(*To Europa*): I have the vision and the perspective,
I can see what must happen, but I'm tired

361

From urging a benevolent World State
On recalcitrant mankind, on people
Who don't listen, make mistakes, get things wrong,
Who're obstinately dim, disobedient.
Sometimes I think I've got too old for this,
It may be better to leave humankind
To their own self-destructive nation-states.
Thank you for taking from me the burden
Of removing some nation-states' borders
And getting Europe into Union.
(*To all*): The work has not finished, it's just begun.
The end of the beginning's not in sight.
But we can now see clearly what's ahead.
Now Europe has passed from occupation
And division to peaceful Union,
Enlargement and expansion, resurgence,
There's a new Renaissance that all can sense,
Not slow decline or collapse as some thought.
Despite some disquiet, Europe's transmuted,
It's been transformed by the triumph of peace.
It has prospects and plainly promises
Prosperity to a seventh of mankind.
Ahead's an Age of plenty and of peace.
Rise up and give an optimistic cheer
For all the problems can be overcome
And we are making progress in the world.
And ahead's a new Golden Age for all.

(*Dance, film and music blend in a memorable finale in which the 50 representatives leave their supranational bodies and groups, link hands and join into one united circle.*)

19–24, 27–31 December 2014; 1–6, 10–18 January 2015

47
from *The Oak Tree and the Branch* (2016–2020)

The Oak Tree and the Branch:
The UK Referendum on the EU, 'Brexit'

"Cut is the branch that might have grown full straight."

MARLOWE, *Dr Faustus*

*"When one with honeyed words but evil mind persuades the mob,
great woes befall the state."*

EURIPIDES, *Orestes*, 408BC

No need for a UK referendum
On the EU, it's party management
To keep the right wing quiet in the hope
A Coalition partner would dissent.
But now.... Leave and Remain exaggerate
(Or lie) – huge funding for the NHS,
Dire falling growth's cuts – as fifty states seek
A United States of Europe's *largesse*.

The Leave side plays on immigration fears:
Net access from Europe and elsewhere bring
Three hundred and thirty thousand each year
In search of work, benefit or begging.
A poster shows crowds fleeing Syria.
Each year a new Newcastle must be built
To house, school and doctor new foreigners.
British taxpayers have begun to wilt.

But thanks to the EU, where nearly half
Our exports go, our economy's good
With two million new jobs that migrants seek.
Without the single market we all would
Have recessions and more austerity.
The EU (and NATO) have kept the peace
For seventy years, once there were always wars.
And Putin wants our cohesion to cease.

⌐ The votes are cast and the result's a shock.
Leave's won by fifty-two per cent – a cheer –
To forty-eight. Three of its leaders stand
Uncomfortably on a platform, it's clear
They expected to lose, and have no plan.
'Brexit' means leaving Europe, but for what?
An offshore island off enlarged Europe,
Reduced world power, isolation, a blot?

European civilisation is like a tree
With twenty-eight branches, now one's been lopped
The UK's no longer within European
Civilisation's laws though it has been propped
Up by it and grown into it since the Celts
And Romans came and made England their home.
It's again split from it like the Tudors
Who under Henry the Eighth split from Rome.

II
Now there is chaos. The PM resigns,
The Leave leaders leave the public, all frown.
Labour splits, there's a leadership challenge.
The pound has fallen, stocks and shares are down.
The UK may break up, Scotland would stay
In the EU. Federation's been stoked.
No one knows what to do or when or if
Article 50 to leave will be invoked.

Then suddenly all is stable again.
A new PM without any hustings,
May's been chosen by two hundred MPs.
Appointments are made to Leave's underlings:
'Brexit', international trade and FO.
Austerity is out, she soothes the sore.
What the previous government did's challenged.
A 'one-nation' view sides with all who're poor.

It's said we'll invoke Article 50
Within a year, and then leave. But the new
Departments will take time to recruit staff,
They're not ready and don't know what to do.
There are French and German elections soon.

They're squabbling in turf wars, there's puckered brow.
All is confusion. In the sixties we
Could not balance the books, and can we now?

EU states are branches in European
Civilization, whose trunk is the Church.
We had turned our gaze from branched nation-states
To our region's tree's crown. As we research
All civilizations seem branches in
A massive oak tree that's a vast World State
Whose trunk's all religions. We now prize boughs
But will soon care about the huge oak's fate.

14–15 August 2016

Among Grandchildren in Gibraltar

We stop at the border to Gibraltar's
Rock, cross the runway, pass the garage where
The SAS shot three IRA bombers,
Park for the cable-car, and rise to near
The summit, gaze down towards Malaga,
And Cadiz, the sweep of Spain's coastline, tell
Where Nelson's body after Trafalgar
Was carried ashore in a rum barrel.

A barbary ape jumps on the rail to peer.
O grandchildren, all Europe is spread out
Beneath you like Spain, which can invade here
Any time and end British rule, and rout
A sway 'in perpetuity' seeded.
Look down for the cemetery where, faith-strict,
The dead Trafalgar seamen were buried,
See centuries of Anglo-Spanish conflict.

Grandchildren, you face a troubled era
As many nation-states compete in wars.
A chemical attack in Syria
Has given the US a bellicose cause
To fire missiles and rain thunderous blows
Against Russia and Iran, the allies
Of Assad's seven-year war to re-impose
Rule on all his state, which had shrunk in size.

⌐ The Skripals laid low by a nerve agent,
Diplomats expelled – a new Cold War sets
Nation against nation and at present
A Third World War's looming like Allied jets.
Now Syria's sliding out of control,
It feels we're back in the sixties before
The EU brought peace to Europe's torn soul.
Competing nation-states always bring war.

I see a hundred missiles targeting
Three sites linked to chemical weapons' stores.
They roar down in the pre-dawn dark, bringing
An Anglo-Franco-US message: pause
And dismantle all chemical warfare,
Chlorine gas was banned from the First World War.
But half a thousand died from gas, while air
Bombs killed half a million – ban *them* by law.

The UN's failed to prevent seventy-two
Wars being fought worldwide in lands now torn,
And there are still nearly fifteen thousand nuclear weapons.
There were none when I was born.
O grandchildren, you face a troubled hate.
How good it would be if all hate could cease
For one benevolent and rock-like state
That can ban war and nuclear bombs, bring peace.

I dream you may have a peaceful future
As citizens of a world government
That can build an Age of Peace and Culture,
Seize every terrorist and nerve agent,
All chemicals and bombs and *jihad* toads,
And preside over a pan-global state
That can build highways like Spanish toll-roads
And transform every backward country's fate.

Socrates said, "I am a citizen
Of Athens, Greece and the world." That's your stop.
O grandchildren, you'll be citizens then
Of Loughton, England, perhaps still Europe,
And the world, cosmopolitans at one
With humankind. And I entreat you now

'o work for peace so under this warm sun
.ll schoolchildren have good lives and think 'Wow'.

he poet is not just a metric man
Vho entertains some boozers with wordplay,
. hungry half-listened-to also-ran,
3ut a man of vision who points the way
'o all who seek a higher truth for men
.han this ape we came from can know or rate.
.nd so I say to you, o grandchildren,
.he way to truth is to dream a World State.

o, 12–14 April 2018

48

from *King Charles the Wise* (2017)
from King Charles the Wise:
The Triumph of Universal Peace

[from Prologue, Mount Olympus. Zeus sends Minerva to
Prince Charles]

Zeus: What's wrong with humankind? I want a world
         Without war, famine and disease, that's like
         A harvest paradise where souls ripen
         Like apples on an orchard's apple trees
         In tranquil sunshine on a summer's day,
         Where bees nuzzle in fragrant lavender
         And dandelions smile under fluffy clocks
         And swans glide beside fields of golden corn.
         But men fight each other, leaders squabble.
         It's hopeless, humankind is in a mess
         And we gods and goddesses have to save
         Recalcitrant humans from their mistakes.
         We have to intervene discreetly when
         We can, when there's an opportunity,
         To influence individuals who'll accept
         Our policies and adopt what we want.
         Europe's in turmoil, again. The UK
         Has left without a plan, there is a hole

In the EU's budget. And yet again
Political leaders have let us down
By thinking nation-state and not seeing
The wider unity we all desire.
We need stability so the EU
Can expand to a *bloc* of fifty states
And the half-blind UK leaders can grasp
Their country's true destiny, its role in
Bringing to birth a world that's free from war.
I preside over all created forms,
All species of wildlife and humankind,
And in my grander scheme of things Brexit
Is only important as it allows
The UK to bring in our new order.
I can see the UK's new destiny
To change the world's structure after Brexit
So clearly, yet all British citizens
Seem unaware of what's ahead for them.
An independent UK'll be well placed
To move between the US and Europe,
China, Russia, India and all countries.
The UK is very innovative
And's always been very influential....
What's done cannot be undone, the UK
Is going to separate, and its PM
May not be in power next year. A vote
Of no confidence or a letter signed
By forty-eight MPs may see her off.
I need to look beyond this current bout
Of UK disorder and confusion,
Incompetence, arrogant self-interest.
The politicians are all transient
And have closed minds as they are partisan.
The one enduring thing's the monarchy.
But the Queen is now in her twilit years.
The key person to focus on behind
The Government's her heir and successor,
The Prince of Wales. He will endure, we can
Regard him as a 'permanent' monarch.
And he's proved to be more open-minded
Than partisan politicians who toe
Their party line and will not think outside

Their box of narrow party loyalty....
I know he'll be a constitutional
Monarch and will have to tread carefully,
But it's time for the Prince to be aware
Of the gods' vision of the world's future.
And so I have decided to send down
Not Hermes but our goddess of Wisdom.
My dear Minerva – you were Athena
To the Greeks but Minerva to great Rome
And I still think of you as Minerva –
I want you to be my ambassador
As a robin befriends a gardener.
Descend to him and discuss the UK's
Destiny under his reign, and lead him
Forward into wisdom as only you
Know how to, and then report back to me.

[from Masque, Buckingham Palace, throne room. Prince Charles is crowned King Charles the Wise by Minerva]

(Apollo, *god of Light and the sun, appears on the left screen.*)

Apollo:

I, Apollo, must come in at this point.
I am god of the Light, called the sun-god
As a symbol so all can understand –
I've never pushed the sun across the sky
Like a beetle pushing a ball of dung;
Also god of poetry and oracles.
Do not forget that all of humankind
Have souls that can equally see the Light –
Have equal potentiality to see
It when they choose to open to its power
Behind their rational, social, blocking 'I' –
And so are equal in terms of the Light
Though all are diverse and all are different.
Whoever founds the global World State should
Found it on the Light, which makes all equal.

Minerva:

Wisely spoken, Apollo. Your Highness,
Can you now see the UK's destiny
And can you see yourself bringing it in?

(Chorus of royal household staff, *loud whispering.*)

Chorus of royal household staff:	What will he say? Will we now see what kind Of King he'll be? What is the UK's role When it leaves the EU? Do we now know? What's going on? What are they doing here?
Prince Charles:	Yes. I will have several roles and voices Like an actor who puts on different masks, And will operate at several levels. First and foremost I'll be the UK's King And do my duty at national level And not engage in party politics. But then my family are European, With roots in Germany. When there's a deal, Though the UK will have left the EU I will stay closely involved with Europe And my role at the regional level. We have to accept the vote for Brexit But we can be as we were forty-five Years ago, back in 1972 Before we joined Europe's Common Market. And I must stay close to America At the separate transatlantic level And make sure we continue our special Relationship, but the UK will not Become America's fifty-first state. But above all I'll have a global role. Through royal tours and video conferences I will stay in touch with our imperial lands And nurture links within the Commonwealth, At a historical global level. More than that, just as the UK will trade With all the world's nations and I will meet All world leaders to cement our trade links, Maintain and enhance British influence, Promote British values and business goals And advance British foreign policy, I will take on an additional role, To discuss the future with world leaders At a federal, supranational level. With the permission of our Government

I must work to benefit humankind
For all are spiritually equal
Before the Light that permeates our lives,
Which I will contemplate within my soul.
I must be as still as a butterfly
Settled on lilac buddleia in bloom,
As still as a yellow water lily
That smiles like the sun in a muddy pond
And is oblivious of croaking frogs
And dragonflies that hover in mid-air.
As King of the UK, I'll be the Head
Of the Church of England, but will also
Rule over subjects who have other faiths.
There are several faiths but all faiths are one.
There are several paths up a high mountain
But at its summit all see the same sun.
I must work for fairness in the UK
But also for Universalism,
For I must not ignore all humankind.
If an opportunity's presented,
Having consulted with our Government,
And free to offer thoughts and suggestions,
I must, with tactful diplomacy, talk
Political Universalism
To all world leaders through their delegates
At the UN's General Assembly,
For the true context of UK-EU
Negotiations is the towering
Prospect that there will be a new World State
That enfolds all nation-states and regions
As starry night sky blankets humankind.
I must make it clear that the UK's role
Includes improving world security
Which means making the UN effective
And that this is best done by the UK's
Diplomatic, indeed visionary
Initiative and innovatory plan
For a partly-federal World Government
That leaves all nation-states in power at home
But restricts power abroad to bring in peace.
As King of the UK I'll have no view
On this, but the merits of peace speak for

Themselves and are greatly to be desired.
Global Britain will be a world power, yes,
But may, during the coming months and years
Come to seek support for a federal world
To control world peace and disarmament,
Famine, disease and the environment,
And tackle poverty through world finance.
The dream's to create a democratic,
Elected World State that can impose peace.
I hope, if I can intrigue it in time,
My reign will call for a new world vision.
That will be another mask I will wear.
I will reign from my nation-state but will
Inspire a new deal for humanity.
Let it be known, the Carolingian Age
Will seek to bring a universal peace
To humankind, regardless of nation.

(*The* Shades of nine kings and leaders *and goddesses enthusiastically applaud.* Minerva *indicates that he should return up the three steps and sit on the throne. She follows him. She now holds a golden crown, standing in the spotlight.*)

Minerva: Your Royal Highness, you have synthesised
All the views you've heard, you have accepted
The humanitarian concerns behind
My vision, and we all can see that you
Will be a King with higher consciousness
And a clear mind who'll speak for humankind.
You can now see the correct way ahead.
And so I bestow my Wisdom on you
Through this symbolic crown, and I crown you
'King Charles the Wise' who found his global role:
To restore peace and order to the world.

(*All the* Shades of nine kings and leaders *and the goddesses echo "King Charles the Wise" and enthusiastically applaud.*)

[from Epilogue, Mount Olympus. Minerva reports back to Zeus]

Minerva: Lord of all, you asked me to become your
Ambassador, visit the Prince of Wales

And guide him on the role of the UK,
After Brexit so he could be aware
Of your global plan for a new World State.
This I have done, and he will work with you,
He shares the humanitarian concerns
Behind your vision of an improved world.
Of course, he'll have to be first and foremost
King of the UK, a constitutional
Monarch who has to operate within
Strict guidelines given him by his Government,
But he will be defender of all faiths
And he cares about all humanity,
And in the course of his royal duties
In the UK's new role after Brexit,
If other leaders bring the subject up
He'll discuss the plight of all humankind
And the humanitarian issues
Whose solution is in new world structures
That will abolish war and strengthen peace.
He has a strong belief, as we'd all wish,
In a wise world Universalism,
He knows how strong global Britain can be,
And is aware that humanitarian
Concerns can be resolved by devising
New supranationalist world structures.
So now you've got someone who'll work with you,
Who'll be true to his UK and Europe
But also to the world, to humankind,
When he inherits the great British throne
And has his coronation. We've all seen
That what he says is very impressive,
And he'll soon be known as 'King Charles the Wise'.

Zeus: Thank you, my dearest goddess Minerva.
You've done excellently, just as I wished.
We are all fortunate that you can take
Your wisdom to the world, where foolish man
Has turned against true vision and pursues
His selfish interests and his nation-state's,
And make it stick. I congratulate you.
What are we to do when the President
Of the US rants and raves, sacks his staff,
And North Korea's leader threatens him

And both shout they will fire nuclear missiles?
It's like two children in a nursery
Playing with toy missiles in Lego walls.
Humankind deserves better leaders than
It has at present, we have to stop them
From acting out their own stupidity.
I will send you to the UN building
Next, to seek out the Secretary-General
Of the United Nations and persuade
Him to consider the merits of change,
Of moving to a federal world order
That can confiscate all nuclear missiles.
If he is receptive to a World State
With a World Government that can ban war,
Then he will empathise with visitors
Like the Prince of Wales and other leaders
And state the case for a Constitutional
Convention that can transform the UN.
I have thought that humankind can progress
To a World State sedately, when ready,
Without undue haste, but the behaviour
Of present world leaders makes it urgent.
We can't wait while blundering leaders make
Things worse with economic nationalism,
Protectionism, borders and high walls,
Populism, pro-nation-state-ism,
Self-first isolationism that goes
Against the direction of a World State.
We have to bring the World State forward or
There'll be no humankind to set it up.
I'm too old to put up with blundering
Any more. I'm fed up with dim half-wits,
With stubborn, disobedient leaders
Who mule-like won't budge from wrong points of view
And give democracy such a bad name.
I can still see ahead a Golden Age.
I hold fast to that vision the world needs:
An age of peace and of prosperity.
We can't wait any longer, we must push
For it before confused humanity
Devastates the earth with its crass mistakes,
Blights the planet with a nuclear winter.

We're bringing on the World State now, we need
More leaders like Prince Charles. And so I say,
Bravo Minerva and King Charles the Wise.
Onward to a peaceful and settled world
And the triumph of universal peace.

14–21 August, 22–24 September, 11–31 October, 1, 5, 8–9, 11–17 November,
9, 18 December 2017

49

from *Fools' Paradise*

from Fools' Paradise: The Voyage of a Ship of Fools from Europe
A Mock-Heroic Poem on Brexit

Descriptions of the Ship of Fools seeking an illusory paradise, Narragonia]

from Canto I, lines 249–274]

The wise medievals' great Ship of State
Was sailed by fools – a Ship of Fools all hate.
In Plato's *Republic* book six we see
A ship, a deaf, part-blind captain who's key
With little knowledge of navigating,
Sailors who quarrel about the steering
Though none have been taught skills. All want to steer
And kill or throw overboard all they hear
Are preferred, make the captain drunk and trip,
Then mutiny and take over the ship
And eat and drink the stores and then promote
All who were mutineers and seized the boat,
And they abuse the rest. The true pilot
Who's attuned to the year and seasons (hot
And cold), sky, stars, winds and must be steerer
They call a good-for-nothing star-gazer.
    Beyond this Cornish window and the quay
An old sailing-ship tosses on the sea.
It could be from the 1494
Basel woodcut Ship of Fools, some of whom wore
Jester's hats. All were sailing to arrive
In paradise, that could be reached, alive,

In Narragonia – a legendary
Wonderful, fool-inhabited country –
Beyond the waves by sailing with a crew
Of fools who ran the ship without a clue.

[from Canto II, lines 201–218]

In the fifteenth-century *Ship of Fools*, a tale
By Brant published in Basel, a ship sets sail
Bound for paradise, Narragonia,
Where St Grobian's patron saint of vulgar
And coarse people, a ship laden with fools
Who steer as they think best, free from all rules.
All the follies and vices of their time
Are in this shipload of nitwits and grime.
The Ship of State is like the Ship of Fools,
It too's sailed by a captain and crew with rules
Who bypass rocks, wind in their sails, and toss
And bob on the sparkling waves and criss-cross,
And on the decks stand the public all bound
For a destination, hoping they're not drowned,
Believing they're heading for a Utopia
Their Government has found, a provider,
A paradise where they'll land and be free
Like settlers in the New World's territory.

[from Canto IV, lines 225–246]

On the Ship of Fools above the waves' tossing
The crew's divided into two warring
Factions that sabotage what the other's done,
Constantly change direction with the sun
So the ship zigzags as she sails, bound for
The paradise in the captain's mind and awe,
The blessed country of plenty that lies
Beyond the waves in the crew's inferred surmise
And in the passengers' dream as they toss
And vie to steer the ship out of chaos.
A man's thrown overboard into the brine.
A fool swigs from a leather flask of wine.
There's a brawl on the ship. Order has gone.
The crew are fighting as the ship ploughs on

owards its paradise across the waves.
assengers are alarmed, fear watery graves
s the wooden ship creaks and sways and rolls
rom side to side precariously. One extols,
Unite and steer one course, for our safety."
ow passengers maul crew to steer safely.
here is a shambles on the ship, a hate;
nd there's a shambles on the Ship of State.

rom Epilogue, lines 337–386]

n your poet's Cornish harbour, the sparkling sea
Washes to shore, laps nuzzling boats fondly.
our poet rests in tranquillity between
Headlands, and from his window surveys the scene,
A peaceful nook where a soul can bud to a bard
And bloom and fade, then lie in the churchyard.
our poet is at peace, his work's finished.
He lets his mind wander the sea as it's wished
And now it's free to roam, the discipline
Of rhyming couplets ended, and can imagine.
Reality can be known by a receptive mind
Like a vast ocean where a gull soars looking to find.
The Ship of Fools ploughs back, a group of seers
Have mutinied against the mutineers.
The captain and some crew now know where they
Are going, but paradise seems far away.
       There is a true Paradise that's too far
In the future, like a horizon's star,
For the ship to sail into its calm harbour
And berth with its perfect new world order.
Please note, there's a good New World Order that would rule
Through a democratic World State and school,
And there's a bad New World Order that loots
All oil and gas in air wars and transmutes
And criss-crosses the earth with pipelines strewn
Through conquered states for their personal fortune:
The syndicate of *élite* families
That steal the earth's resources for their ease.
But it is a law that cannot be broken
That a nation can't leave its own civilisation.
Over the waves true Paradise shimmers

With tremulous light, distant haze that stirs.
Sail closer, true Paradise shimmers in sun,
One World State, democratically run
With all humankind represented in law
And no more nuclear weapons or war,
No famine, disease or poverty there,
Both finance and the environment now fair,
All Leavers and Remainers now at one,
All conflicts reconciled under the sun,
All civilisations internally
Themselves but externally in harmony,
A Paradise where all humankind can
Live at peace at one as in Zeus's plan
That was undermined by the self-interest
Of some leaders so humankind regressed,
But such fallen let-downs can be reversed
As the good triumph over the selfish worst
As a mutinous ship returns to its wharf's berth,
And Paradise can return to the earth.

7 August 2018 – 29 May 2019

50

from *The Coronation of King Charles*
from The Coronation of King Charles:
The Triumph of Universal Harmony

[from Prologue, Banqueting House. God of the One speaks to
King Charles]

(*The Light high up above the middle of the balcony to the left brightens as
it shines down onto the throne, and from within it* God of the One *speaks
exclusively to King Charles, who is enfolded in bright Light.*)

God of the One: I, God of the One, shine my divine Light
Into all souls that open to my Light
In wordless contemplation, just as in
The warm sunlight of a summer's day only
Some flowers open to the sun. I am known
In all cultures through all faiths, I assume

Protean forms: Yahweh, Olympian Zeus,
Jupiter, Allah, Krishna, Buddha, *Tao*.
I shine out through the stars of the Milky Way
And the two hundred billion galaxies
In this part of my expanding universe,
And I shine through the clouds that enfold the earth,
My treasure, for it's only here there's life.
Among all the wastes of my universe,
The barren planets with no atmosphere,
Only the earth has a humankind. It sees
Local differences and local conflicts,
But to me it's a tiny ball that's unified,
To me it's obvious humankind is one
Just as it's obvious to an unschooled pygmy
That an anthill is one society.
I'm proud of the Oneness I have created.
I love the English language, which is known
Throughout humankind, I love all forms of life.
I love green woodpeckers in a fine garden,
And a nuthatch hanging upside down to feed,
And parakeets flitting between oak trees
And jackdaws splashing where a fountain brims.
I love the lilacs and honeysuckle,
And the tinkling goldfinches in thistles.
I love the puffins and the guillemots,
I love corn buntings and fritillaries,
I love the meadow browns and grasshoppers,
I love the sticklebacks and speckled newts,
And the twinkling sunlight in a forest pond.
And I love the badger and the cormorant,
And the whale, the long-time king of the high seas.
I am well pleased my beloved royal line
In the United Kingdom is being renewed.
I reaffirm the divine right of its kings,
Its God-given and sacred right to rule
Justly, with wisdom and understanding,
And to guarantee democratic freedom
For all British and Commonwealth peoples
And all who live within its territories;
And to support all peoples of the Free World
And work towards the democratic World State
That I long for, when suffering humankind

At last comes of age and pushes aside
Its childish self-interest and cruel wars.
I, Universalist God of humankind,
Shine out for a World State that can bring peace
To all the warring peoples of the earth
So they live together like a swarm of bees
Within a warm garden in summer air
That's redolent with the scents of flowers.
O Charles, Defender of the Anglican Faith,
I, God of the One long known to all the faiths,
God of religious Universalism,
Bring you greetings for your Carolingian Age
Which will restore harmony to the earth.
King Charles, I bathe you in all-embracing Light.

(*The Light floods the throne and then fades and returns to its original brightness.*)

[from Masque, Banqueting House. Minerva speaks to King Charles about his future reign]

Minerva: Your Majesty, your reign will restore order.
Look at the screen, for you will catch glimpses
Of what you'll seek to bring in, your progress
Towards a coalition of nations
Who can work together in harmony.
You're seeking to unify the Commonwealth
As a stepping-stone towards a greater goal
That you have had in mind, and the groundwork
For this goal will be achieved in your reign
Even though the end-result is more distant.
The Carolingian Age will point the way.
The new world structure belongs to a later reign.

[from Masque, Banqueting House. King Charles looks ahead to the coming Carolingian Age]

King Charles: I have been thinking how global Britain
Can use Government assets to extend
Its global standing and relationships
And champion the rules-based international
Order so the UK is more open,

Outward-looking and confident in the world.
I have been thinking about the linking
Of Free-World democracies – the Commonwealth
Provides many links – and common values.
The internationalism of past years
Did not sit well with Brexiteers' 'UK First'
And their denouncing of globalism.
I've been thinking like a sawing grasshopper:
'Global Britain' seems a hollow promise.
But now I see again what you helped me see:
That though it will take time, the work starts now,
And I'll engage with UN delegates,
For beyond them are the Representatives
And Senators of the democratic World State
That has long been the dream of all humankind
And is the goal of all who would bring in
A universal peace and harmony.
I must get the Commonwealth hosting world leaders,
I must talk political Universalism
With the world figures I meet and the UN.
I would like London to be the centre
Of a new world order that can broker peace.
The Carolingian Age must lay groundwork
For the Age of Universal Harmony
The Representatives and Senators
Were speaking from. I will use my influence
Like a squirrel gathering and storing nuts.

[from Revels, Banqueting House. God of the One prophesies that King
Charles will initiate the founding of a democratic World State]

(*The Light high up above the balcony to the left brightens and from within
it* God of the One *speaks to King Charles, who is still standing and is
enfolded in bright Light....*)

God of the One: I care for every creature on my earth,
I am with each insect and mammal always,
Each of my creations is within my One.
I love the painted lady and the deer,
I love the barn owl and the ladybird.
I love the buzzard and the woodpecker,
I love the robin and the daffodil.

I love the heron and the winking carp.
I care for the poorest poor, and for royals
And for the Age they shape, with my One love....
You have listened well, Charles, and I am pleased
That in your reign you'll look beyond London
And the territories that are under your rule
To the wider world of all humankind
And will influence the start of the groundwork
That will found a democratic World State
After your reign, that will bring harmony
To those who succeed the Carolingian Age,
On which again I bestow my greetings.
Your soul will soar like an eagle above humankind....

[from Epilogue, Banqueting House. God of the One's yearning for a
democratic World State and vision of universal harmony]

God of the One: Goddess of Wisdom and daughter of Zeus
(A protean form of the One that I am),
Wise Minerva, your pageant entertainments
Excellently showed the chaos within the UK
And the suffering among the world's peoples,
And you have let King Charles glimpse what he needs
To know of his coming Carolingian Age.
Owl-eyed, you have shown him a direction.
Because we are committed to free will
Nothing is fated, Providence is shaped
By choices with outcomes, nothing's preordained.
King Charles is free to choose whatever course
He wishes, but free choice is enmeshed with good
Discernment, Knowledge, Vision and Wisdom
And you have set him up to be guided
By these four virtues while he makes his choice,
And if he follows these the right outcome
Will lead to a future we can support,
Which we have projected and want to see.
I gave humankind its freedom, part of me's
Always been an Existentialist over
Free will. I am now a Universalist
Who yearns for universals in structures.
I am old and have known deep disappointments:
During the last five thousand years each Age,

Each grouping within humankind – from tribe
To city-state, nation-state and region –
Has been misled by ambitious, ruthless men
And has fallen victim to cruel conquests
And more recently continental wars
That have destroyed the churches, temples, mosques
That past generations have held sacred,
And left them homes for dark-loving bats and mice.
And the destruction of civilisation
Has been carried out by men whose souls have been
Enclosed within the shell of their egos
As hard as any walnut shell, that resists
The Light I always try to shine into souls.
During the last four hundred years, my Light –
Which was once known in every church or mosque,
In every temple, and taught by holy men,
Monks and desert mystics – has ceased to be known
So humans live in a nourishing mist
Of Light without knowing it's all round them,
Without knowing I love all living forms.
I love all wildlife and all living things
Regardless of the countries they live in,
Regardless of all nation-states' borders,
For they are all creatures within my One.
All living things are citizens of my world.
I love the kingfishers and dragonflies,
I love the primroses and marigolds.
And I love the prickly holly and the rose,
I love the hedgehog and I love the vole.
I love the cherry blossom and the pear.
I love the weeping willow by the stream.
I love the sunflowers and the smiling sun,
I love a field of beaming buttercups,
And I embrace all opposites within
My reconciling, synthesising One
In which all things belong and have a place.
All living forms pass, but species endure.
I worked so hard on the concept of a man,
I designed the human body so carefully.
I got the vocal cords to reflect the lips –
The cords sited downwards, the lips sideways –
And I grasped the solution to proportion:

Beauty's golden ratio, 1.618.
The human mouth is 1.618
Times as wide as the nose; each finger bone
Is 1.618 times its neighbouring bone;
From elbow to wrist is 1.618
Times the distance from wrist to fingertip.
The distance from the navel to the sole
Is 1.618 times the distance
From the top of the head to the navel,
And ideal height's 1.618 times
The distance from shoulder to fingertip.
I crafted the human frame with such precision,
Its ratios were all in perfect proportion.
I took such care in modelling my humans.
I dreamed they'd all be kind, loving and good.
I admire humans, but have reservations.
I admire all humans for what they give,
For their kindness and creativity,
But I do not admire their cruelty,
Their strong belief that they are always right
And are entitled to kill and maim their foes
And conquer peoples and rule through wicked wars
And set themselves above my earth's creatures,
Which they hunt down and kill and devour like beasts.
But some humans retain their love of all
Living beings regardless of borders,
They feel the unity of the universe,
The Oneness of existence on my earth.
They love the earth as I do – nothing can beat
Bees humming in lavender on a summer's day
Or a kestrel hovering still above a field –
But I can't help feeling disillusioned
At the achievements of all humankind
During the last five thousand years, despite
Their high points: Pheidias's perfect statues,
Leonardo's paintings, Beethoven's symphonies,
Shakespeare's plays, the Metaphysical poets.
Again and again humankind's let me down.
And just as we get Europe together,
And a United States of Europe's looming,
The UK shakes the union by heading out.
It's exasperating, I've seen it all before

So many times I groan, "Oh not again."
I don't trust any UK politicians.
That's why I've focused on King Charles, hoping
An enduring royal can see what needs to be done.
I have high hopes of this coronation.
After five thousand years of misplaced hopes –
The Macedonian and Roman Empires,
The Empires of the Franks and the British –
I at last have hopes that the Carolingian Age
Will get beyond the UK and the EU –
A rerun of the Tudor breach with Rome
And the passions of the English Civil War –
And will set humankind on its correct course
By a free-will choice and do the groundwork for
A democratic World State that will bring
A synthesis that will end all conflict,
And a Golden Age, the period of humankind's
Greatest prosperity and high culture,
Literary and artistic merit;
And with fresh Universalist thinking
Abolish war and all nuclear weapons
And bring in a *Pax Universalis*,
A universal peace throughout the world,
That marks for all coming generations
The triumph of universal harmony.

20–23, 27 June, 5, 7–11, 17, 20–24, 26–29 July, 1, 3, 10–14 August,
1–2, 5–10, 17–18, 25, 30–31 October 2019

 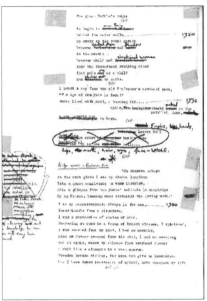

Early typed drafts of 'The Silence' (1965–1966) held in the Nicholas Hagger Archive, a Special Collection in the Albert Sloman Library at the University of Essex. They show (left) the handwritten line "a new Baroque age is born" scrawled above the gloss in the left-hand margin of a version typed in April 1973; and (right) the same words typed in as an amendment in a version corrected in blue ink in April/May 1973.

From Nicholas Hagger to Christopher Ricks
on *A Baroque Vision*

TO   Christopher Ricks; Buckhurst Hill, 13 January 2020, Em
SUBJECT: *A Baroque Vision*: revelation, homework 40 years late

Dear Christopher,

A Happy New Year to you and Judith (and your son David, who I sat next to during your lecture on 1 July).

I have been thinking of you a lot over Christmas. I had completed my current round of books: *Fools' Paradise* (seeing Brexit in terms of Sebastian Brant's 1494 Ship of Fools voyaging to non-existent Narragonia – there will be a sequel which I have already drafted, *Fools' Gold*); *The Coronation of King Charles* (a masque, reviving the pageant entertainment from 1661, perhaps to be performed at the next Coronation – early copy to be handed to Prince Charles's Assistant Private Secretary for safe-keeping); *Selected Letters* (letters by me that refer to all my books); and *Collected Prefaces* (55 Prefaces showing the development of my literary thinking and my Universalism). While I was assembling *Selected Letters* I saw that you asked me select 30 poems in 1979 and again in 1982, when we corresponded about my blend of Romanticism and Classicism, my Baroque style.

I should have made the selection then, 40 years ago, but I was still feeling my way on my poetic identity and was exceptionally busy at work, as a Head of English keeping abreast of A-level marking and acquiring my old school (Oaklands). Before Christmas I saw what this selection should look like, and I have now chosen the 30 poems. These will appear in Part One, poems written between 1961 and 1979, of a new selection I am doing of 100 poems from 50 poetic volumes, *A Baroque Vision*. Part Two will continue the thread of showing my Baroque roots, and will present 70 poems written between 1979 and 2019. I know it won't be the thin volume of 30 poems by themselves that you envisaged, but 40 years on it makes sense to continue the Baroque thread and this is the most feasible way of getting the selection out today.

A Baroque Vision will show that the Baroque vision we corresponded about grew into Universalism, and I must tell you how I arrived at this perception. While making my selection I had recalled your throw-away remark before your lecture at Worcester College, Oxford on 1 July, "You have been on a mission ever since you left University." I thought at the time you meant that I had done my travelling and writing in the 1960s to arrive at what would become Universalism and state it in seven disciplines, and write *World State*, which I spoke about during my visit to Russia. I woke on Christmas morning with the revelation (received in sleep) that my Baroque vision of the early 1980s had grown into my Universalism by the late 1980s, that you may have meant that my "mission" was to develop my Baroque vision of 1982 into Universalism.

I was stunned. I saw that my Baroque vision probably *had* grown into Universalism but that I had not consciously realised this. I got up and looked at my Prefaces, poems and diary entries written in the 1980s, and the evidence is very clear. It's as my revelation showed. I am so pleased to have had this revelation. It unifies all my literary and Universalist works.

As soon as I could I wrote this revelation into a Preface I had finished in draft, now titled 'The Baroque Vision behind Universalism, and the Tradition of Wordsworth and Tennyson'. I made it clear that all my works have been jigsaw pieces with one picture: a project which, chameleon-like, changed its appearance (or at any rate, nomenclature) between 1982 and 1991, from Baroque to Universalism. My Preface has drawn everything together and unified my work, and it will appear as the last of my 54 Prefaces at the end of *Collected Prefaces*, a strong ending that binds all the Prefaces together.

I have been looking to see when 'Baroque' first appeared in my work. On Friday 3 January I went to the University of Essex and looked in my archive at versions of 'The Silence' and found handwritten lines "And naked on the petalled lawn/A new Baroque Age is born" written into 'The Silence' in April 1973. The dedication mentioning "This string of baroque pearls" was earlier, written in Japan some time after December 1965, when I bought a necklace of baroque pearls for my (then) wife. This was on 16 December 1965, according to my diary entry in *Awakening to the Light*, p.222 – she still wears that necklace, and it will eventually pass to my daughter. So events that seem everyday at the time can assume a deeply-symbolic importance over 50 years later.

Perhaps when we get to 80 we do become wise. Certainly your (then) 85-year-old-and-very-wise throw-away line on my "mission" on 1 July set off reverberations – shock waves, Eliot's "My words echo/Thus, in your mind" – in my subconscious that finally erupted and set off a tsunami on 25 December nearly six months later. Thank you, my excellent mentor, for such an unexpected and welcome Christmas present that brought everything together for me, with insight and understanding, in my 81st year.

So I can report that I'm doing my homework and will finish it in early February. Sorry to be 40 years late in handing it in, but Ezra Pound told me (regarding my epic *Overlord* on 16 July 1970), "If you can see it, then you've already done it. Seeing it's half the battle." And I hadn't properly *seen* it until Christmas morning. It should be out in early 2021, and I will make sure you

ave an early copy. The front cover will show Rubens' Baroque painting *The*
^potheosis of James I, which is on the ceiling of the Banqueting House. It
hows James I as a divine soul being drawn up to Heaven on an eagle with
he help of supporting Angels, and Charles I stopped and looked up at it as
e walked to be beheaded on a scaffold outside. (The Banqueting House,
ames I's room in the Whitehall Palace for masques, is on the cover of *The*
^oronation of King Charles.)

In July 2008 I told you about my visit to Tennyson at Farringford House
see letter of 29 July 2008]. I said at the time that my contact with him there
id not persist on my return to Essex, but he followed me back to Essex soon
fterwards. For the record, for the last ten years, I have felt, and I still feel, in
n active daily relationship with Tennyson, who acts as a Muse and an editor.
hear his words (or at any rate, words) when I wake from sleep, what to
mend in the previous days' work. 'He' will tell me to look at, for example, the
middle of page 43, often a specific line, and I'll look and find something that
needs improving or amending. The subconscious is amazing, I'm filled with
we that all this seems to be happening at one remove from me, during my
leep and on waking. I haven't forgotten that when we walked in Oxford on
1 June 1993 you advised me to go back to Tennyson, and it was that advice
hat took me to Farringford House when it was still possible to stay there,
rom 20 to 25 July 2008.

With thanks for your mentoring over the years, in 1979 and 1982 and
subsequently, which I greatly appreciate in my 81st year, and long may you
continue to be the inspiration you have been and make throw-away remarks
that unify a life's works, Your ever-devoted, Nicholas

NH's works referred to: *Fools' Paradise*; *The Coronation of King Charles*; *Selected Letters*;
Collected Prefaces; *A Baroque Vision*; *Fools' Gold*; 'The Silence' in *Collected Poems*; *Overlord*

TO   Christopher Ricks; Buckhurst Hill, 26 July 2020, Em
SUBJECT: Onwards despite the virus/'The Silence'/reconciling Eliot and
Tennyson/the heroic couplet

Dear Christopher,

It's more than a year since I heard you on the heroic line and more than six
months since I last wrote, and since then the world's changed. I hope you and
Judith have stayed well amid the ravages of the virus. We are all fine.

I have been isolating – shielding – and working full writing days, then
feeding the carp and walking every afternoon in our meadow, watching how

the clover and bird's-foot trefoil are growing amid the meadow browns looking for small tortoiseshell butterflies among the blackberries on the brambles and singing to my new friends, "Swallows" – and their hearing is so good that four swallows dart from behind trees, recognising my song, and swoop round me. On Thursday I walked with my son Tony and a swallow swooped and described a perfect circle round us, skimming at knee level, clearly saying "Hello". In short I've been reconnecting with Nature as Wordsworth and Tennyson were able to do in unpolluted air and vivid colours and have had a glorious four months of nineteenth-century living, back in 1881. I am frequently reminded of blind Milton shielding from the plague in 1665 in Chalfont St Giles and dictating *Paradise Lost* to his daughter with a virus menacing beyond his curtilage.

We visited Jordan and Egypt from a ship in February and March and were banned from Israel and Cyprus because of the virus and came back via Turkey, landed just before lockdown. With my PA working remotely I have kept going. *Fools' Paradise*, on Brexit during May's premiership in heroic couplets, is completely finished; it's not out until December but early copies have arrived. I will be posting to you in due course. Its sequel *Fools' Gold*, on Brexit during Johnson's premiership and the virus, is nearly finished in draft but I now have to work on the couplets. I have finished *A Baroque Vision*, 100 selections from 50 poetic volumes, and also *The Essentials of Universalism*, 75 selections from 25 prose volumes. No proofs yet. *Collected Prefaces* has been copyedited, no proofs yet. *Selected Letters* is at the proofs stage. *The Coronation of King Charles* is done but not at the proofs stage yet. I am about to start *The Promised Land*. In Jordan I stood on the top of Mount Nebo where Moses stood and saw the Promised Land stretched out beneath him (the Dead Sea, Jerusalem, Jericho, Galilee), and I realised that I too have seen a Promised Land which, like Moses (who died on Mount Nebo and was buried there), I will not live to enter.

The Indian-created World Intellectual Forum wrote to me during lockdown, mentioning my early work on a coming World State *The World Government*, and asked if I would join their Executive Board. I agreed on the basis that I'm not travelling anywhere for them or taking part in distracting Zoom meetings. So now I'm in touch with more than 20 intellectuals from different countries, including a Nobel prize-winner from Tunisia. One of them, Thomas Daffern, who has lectured at Oxford and is based in France, told them that he'd followed and admired my books for years and that my masterpiece is *The Fire and the Stones*, which they should all read if they haven't read it already. But having reviewed all my poetic and prose works recently I now think that if a writer has to regard one of his works as his masterpiece irrespective of its reception – which would be yours? – then I would have to regard my masterpiece as 'The Silence', which I wrote in Japan during

8 months between 1965 and 1966 when I was struggling to understand the bewildering sequences of images and glimmerings of Light that were happening to me, as it's about the wrestling and inner transformation that turned me into a poet and made my Universalism, my perspective of all humankind and my 55 books possible – as you've been aware, as your throw-away remark on 1 July last year made clear.

I think it's true to say there's nothing remotely like 'The Silence' in English poetry, which is why I had such difficulty in connecting myself to the tradition to do your selection of 30 poems in the three letters I wrote you in 1979 and 1982. Perhaps its nearest equivalent in prose is Joyce's *A Portrait of the Artist as a Young Man*. Like Joyce's *Portrait* it's a Modernist work, full of sequences of images and juxtapositions, and, having transformed myself through Modernism and thinking about writing a poetic epic, I turned my back on Modernism's concentrated narrative after my evening with Ezra Pound in 1970 and went back to the 17th, 18th and 19th centuries, which was right as it opened the way to Tennyson, a path you later endorsed. My boss in Japan (as Representative of the British Council there), the metaphysical philosopher E.W.F. Tomlin, who knew Eliot and arranged for me to lecture on Eliot for a year at Tokyo University and wrote *T.S. Eliot, A Friendship* about the hundred letters Eliot wrote him, told me in the late 1980s just before he died that he had arranged for me to visit Eliot when I returned to the UK on leave in mid-1966. Eliot of course died in 1965, and I contributed 'In Defence of the Sequence of Images' to a book Tomlin got out in Japan, *T.S. Eliot, A Tribute from Japan*, while I was teaching Eliot and writing 'The Silence', and I sometimes wonder what would have happened had I met Eliot in 1966 – would I have remained a Modernist? Anyway, that didn't happen, and I didn't. Now you are the leading authority on both Eliot and Tennyson and may appreciate the struggle I had in choosing between their conflicting approaches. But they're both in the tradition and I've reconciled them (+A + −A = 0): Eliot's, Pound's, Yeats' and Tennyson's concerns for our civilisation and culture within classical blank verse (or heroic line), rhymed stanzas, heroic couplets and musical language – and no concentrated and obscure narrative.

When the system is unjammed there will be a flurry of books and I will put them in the post as they come through in dribs and drabs. Meanwhile if you are giving another lecture in the UK do let me know. It was such a pleasant surprise that your billed lecture on Mailer's rhythms turned out to be on the heroic line, which is close to my heart as you know, and I found what you said riveting. Several of your throw-away reflections have lingered in my mind. In particular, do please let me know if you are lecturing anywhere on the heroic couplet – or if you are going to be in the UK soon and somewhere within driving distance where we can meet and talk about the heroic couplet in Dryden and Pope and modern times, perhaps looking at *Fools' Paradise* and seeing how I can improve my couplets in *Fools' Gold*; if so I'll send you a copy now....

With very best wishes for continued good health, ongoing energy and more abundant wisdom, percipience, perspicacity and perspicuity (the three mentorial – a neologism? – Ps featuring perception, discernment and clarity), and many more throw-away lines that enable self-understanding, to my mentor from your ever-devoted, Nicholas

NH's works referred to: *Fools' Paradise*; *Fools' Gold*; *A Baroque Vision*; *The Essentials of Universalism*; *Collected Prefaces*; *Selected Letters*; *The Coronation of King Charles*; *The Promised Land*; *The Fire and the Stones*; 'The Silence' in *Collected Poems 1958–2005*; 'In Defence of the Sequence of Images', in *T.S. Eliot, A Tribute from Japan* (1966), edited by Masao Hirai and E.W.F. Tomlin

---

TO   Christopher Ricks; Buckhurst Hill, 28 October 2020, Em
SUBJECT: Heroic couplet/heroic line

Dear Christopher,

I hope you have been keeping well amid the ravages of Covid. We are all well.

As promised, I am putting in the post (to the College of Arts and Sciences) a copy of *Fools' Paradise*, which deals with Brexit in the May years in heroic couplets. It's mock-heroic, in the tradition of Dryden and Pope (more Dryden than Pope).

I am up-to-date on its sequel, *Fools' Gold*, which deals with Brexit and Covid in the Johnson year. After days of intense thought (when I could have done with chatting to my mentor) I have decided to do this in the heroic line, blank verse. The tone is different in view of the many deaths caused by Covid: 226,000 Americans dead, approaching the 291,000 killed in combat in the Second World War, and 60,000 British dead, more than the 40,000 British killed during the Blitz. It's in the tradition of the heroic verse of Milton and Tennyson.

Both books hold politicians to account to uphold the cultural health of Europe in accordance with T.S. Eliot's 'The Man of Letters and the Future of Europe', the first with ridicule, the second in a more serious way as becomes the death toll, the implications of a national event and the heroic line. The heroic couplet is good at exposing follies and vices, the heroic line is better suited to a catastrophe that includes mass deaths and widespread economic devastation, which has to be taken more seriously. And it escapes "the bondage" of rhyme (Milton's preface to *Paradise Lost*).

Had we been able to meet this is what I would have said. Without realising
that you helped me greatly by talking at Oxford on 1 July 2019 on the musical
heroic line. Your talk helped me make this choice, with hindsight it almost
seems to be a call, before we had heard of Covid, to return to the heroic line
of 600 years of English verse from Chaucer to Tennyson. I hope this approach
will have your blessing when you eventually see *Fools' Gold*.

I'll be thinking of you on 4 November and of America's future direction.
Stay well, and with best wishes to my mentor from your ever-devoted,
Nicholas

NH's works referred to: *Fools' Paradise*; *Fools' Gold*

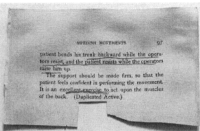

A half-page front and back entitled Swedish Movements, which Nicholas Hagger
received from Christopher Ricks on 2 March 2021

TO   Christopher Ricks; Buckhurst Hill, 2 March 2021, Em
Subject: Swedish Movements

Dear Christopher,

Your half-page arrived this afternoon, and after feeling relieved that you
are clearly well in this plaguey time I knew immediately and with delight that
it is one of your Vorticist images with many associations, an at-first baffling
conundrum which little by little becomes more clear. What an excellent
image, and what a rush of ideas it set in motion. Let me react step by step:

1. The background is my having thanked you for having been an
   excellent mentor for over 40 years and for introducing me to the heroic
   couplet, which I used in *Fools' Paradise*. And my saying what a tussle
   I had between my early Modernism on 'The Silence', out of which all
   my work has come, and the Tennysonian narrative of my epics and
   other poems, and that you are the leading authority in both Eliot
   and Tennyson.

2. The half-page comes from George Taylor's American *An Exposition of the Swedish Movement-Cure: Embracing the History and Philosophy of this System of Medical Treatment, with Examples of Single Movements and Directions for their Use in Various Forms of Chronic Disease, Forming a Complete Manual of Exercises*, 1860 – the date perhaps suggesting the time of Tennyson, the text drawing on the Swedish Movement of Ling in the 1830s, and the subtitle perhaps touching on my bringing history and philosophy to bear on the chronic disease of British Brexit in *Fools' Paradise*.

3. Your "keeping in touch [see illustration]" refers to you, my operator/ mentor, straightening the stance and posture of me, your patient, as I resist Modernism and am raised up by Tennysonian narrative in heroic verse and heroic couplets. When I bent backward you resisted, and now I am resisting Modernism I am raised.

4. "Excellent exercise", underlined in mentor's red, is perhaps encouraging support to give me confidence in performing the next movement (perhaps *Fools' Gold* in heroic verse, to which I am adding finishing touches).

5. Swedish Movements, the running header on the back of p.97 above the illustration, is underlined in red as is "Nobel Prize Committee, exercising its responsibilities", i.e. the stooping mentor has now become the examining Nobel Prize Committee. This could have a number of meanings. I mentioned that *Fools' Paradise* has been put in for the Ondaatje Prize, and the Swedish Nobel Prize Committee may be a rush, an association in the same idiom, developing the idea of Swedish Movements; or it could mean that it should be entered for a Nobel Prize as "an excellent exercise"; or it could announce a movement in Sweden, veiled news that the Nobel Prize Committee is examining something – if so, I hope this applies to you as you deserve a Nobel Prize. The Japanese poet Junzaburo Nishiwaki told me that his intuition was seldom wrong and forecast that I would get a Nobel Prize (see *My Double Life 1: This Dark Wood*, p.167), but although Michael Nobel saw me receive the Gusi Prize for Literature in 2016 and told me that he had read a several-page publisher's leaflet about my works and was very interested, he has little influence within the Nobel family now, and though I was nominated for the Templeton Prize for 5 years (three years to go) I don't think I'm well enough known to be on the Nobel watchlist. I have written my books in the wilderness.

6. I should add that the World Intellectual Forum (WIF) I told you about have latched onto my works. The Indian founder, Dr Swaminadhan

of Hyderabad, has written a short book calling for a democratic, Presidential, federal world government, which is based on my books *The World Government*, *World State* and *World Constitution* (which he's got), and he has described our work as "a meeting of minds" and said that he and I will be expressing our view to the UN General Assembly. He has now founded the Global Network for Peace, Disarmament and Development (GNET-PEDAD) to bring in a World State like the one I have called for (the United Federation of the World, the last four words taken from Tennyson's 'Locksley Hall'). I have no idea whether this will become a Swedish Movement.

So all these ideas are rushing about in your half-page, which I will treasure. I hope my understanding is on the right lines. It's an inspiring half-page, especially the brilliant illustration of you, my mentor, correcting my literary posture, for which I am very grateful and deeply appreciative.

Swedish Movements, it's such a powerful idea with so many ambiguities and associations, and I am full of admiration for your symbol, which is like a communication from the Delphic Oracle, capable of more than one interpretation. As the Japanese say, "*Sensei, dormor*" – "Professor, thank you." Now may be a time to follow a Japanese proverb: "*Shiranai ohotoke*" – "Be wise and know nothing, like a Buddha."

The books are slowly making progress despite lockdowns, and I'll send them as they trickle out.

Stay well, and with best wishes from your ever-devoted, Nicholas

NH's works referred to: *Fools' Paradise*; 'The Silence' in *Collected Poems*; *Fools' Gold*; *My Double Life 1: This Dark Wood*; *The World Government*; *World State*; *World Constitution*

TO   Christopher Ricks; Buckhurst Hill, 13 March 2021, Em
SUBJECT: Swedish Movements, further thoughts

Dear Christopher,

I had my second Pfizer jab yesterday and half-expected to wake with a temperature this morning. In fact, I woke with a normal temperature but with more sleep inspiration. I was told (Tennyson told me) that the background to Swedish Movements was *A Baroque Vision* and letters I wrote you in 2020 as well as my movement from Modernism to Tennysonian narrative.

The Swedish Movements of your oracular image in fact refer to my acceptance that my pre-1979 Baroque vision developed into Universalism during the 1980s, which unifies my literary and Universalist works, and that

I have been on a "mission" since leaving Oxford as you told me on 1 July 2019 which unifies my life. I received confirmation of this in sleep on Christmas morning 2019 (as I described in my letter to you of 13 January 2020 about *A Baroque Vision*). They also refer to my movement from Modernism to the Tennysonian heroic line (as I described in my letters to you of 26 July and 28 October 2020). A third movement may be my call to replace the United Nations with a United Federation of the World (the last four words taken from Tennyson's 'Locksley Hall'). Your image is saying that when I pushed back on these developments, including the selection of 30 poems, I had to be resisted, but now I have reconciled Eliot and Tennyson and am pushing forward and am going with them as in *Fools' Paradise* I can be raised up and there is nothing to stop my being considered by anyone for a Prize, even by the Nobel Prize Committee. Or something of the sort.

I think I have now got there. Like the Delphic Oracle you make an ambiguous pronouncement and I, the supplicant, try to make sense of it without following a wrong interpretation like Croesus, King of Lydia (modern Turkey), who asked if he should go to war with the Persian Empire and was told, "If Croesus goes to war he will destroy a great empire." He went to war and destroyed his own empire in 546BC.

Once again your baffling image teased me out of thought as doth eternity, and it needed a Pfizer jab and a sleep amid antibodies to bring full understanding.

I look back on your memorable symbols in recent times: the *Victoria* and the *Triton*, circumnavigation of the globe by wind-dependent Magellan in 1519 and by nuclear submarine in 1960 (the metaphysical and Neoclassical routes), sent in 2012; the Barnes 1903 cloister (the Edwardian tutor room at Worcester College, Oxford of my Provost Masterman, which he blew up c.1910, 50 years before asking me if I would be interested in a career in intelligence), sent in 2014; Barrie's picture postcard of a watcher on the 18th-century way over the Boldre bridge and a toiler loading a two-horse cart with reeds in 14th-century muddy river conditions (my two-part autobiography being spied on with Neoclassical and metaphysical associations), sent in 2015; the founding members of *Mosaic, A Journal for the Interdisciplinary Study of Literature*, one of them you with the prospect of being the last survivor and getting the whole tontine annuity (my literature-based mosaic-like interdisciplinary works presenting one picture and perhaps my being the last survivor in this mosaic tradition and like you getting the whole tontine annuity), sent in 2017; and your page from *Notes and Queries*, 1881, showing that literary men are listed and general readers buy (without the interfering State gripping their rainbow as Elizabeth I did and controlling their publicity and confining them to the wilderness if, like Marlowe, they worked in intelligence), sent in 2019. (Long live 1881.) And now Swedish Movements, 1860. Not to forget the first

lition of the *Horizon* (December 1944) that contained Eliot's 'The Man of
etters and the Future of Europe', which is relevant to my *Classical Odes* and
at the heart of my holding politicians to account for the consequences of
he effects of their actions on the culture of Europe in *Fools' Paradise* and *Fools'*
'old, sent in 2004. Seeing all this, Zeus can't wait for you to be his mentor on
lympus. What a mentor, there's never been one like it!

With gratitude from your appreciative and ever-devoted, Nicholas

H's works referred to: *A Baroque Vision*; *Fools' Paradise*; *Classical Odes*; *Fools' Gold*

INDEXES

I

Poems, verse plays and masques; volumes; and published works

List of poems and selections, the 50 poetic volumes they were taken from, and published works where they can be found. (See pp.xvii–xix for full titles and dates of published works)

TITLES OF POEMS, VERSE PLAYS AND MASQUES	POETIC VOLUMES	PUBLISHED WORKS
1. Ode to a Prospect from a Window Frame	A Well of Truth	*Collected Poems*
2. The Seventeenth-Century Pilgrim	A Stone Torch-Basket	*Collected Poems*
3. The Power by the Lake	The Early Education and Making of a Mystic	*Collected Poems*
4. The Silence	The Silence	*Collected Poems*
5. Archangel	The Wings and the Sword	*Collected Poems*
6. An Inner Home	The Wings and the Sword	*Collected Poems*
7. Old Man in a Circle	Old Man in a Circle	*Collected Poems*
8. Orpheus Across the Frontier	The Gates of Hell	*Collected Poems*
9. Ghadames Spring	The Gates of Hell	*Collected Poems*
10. On the Waterfront	The Gates of Hell	*Collected Poems*
11. Journey's End	The Gates of Hell	*Collected Poems*
12. Flow: Moon and Sea	The Gates of Hell	*Collected Poems*
13. Visions: Golden Flower, Celestial Curtain	The Gates of Hell	*Collected Poems*
14. More Visions: The Judge	The Gates of Hell	*Collected Poems*
15. Visions: The Pit and the Moon	The Gates of Hell	*Collected Poems*

TITLES OF POEMS, VERSE PLAYS AND MASQUES	POETIC VOLUMES	PUBLISHED WORKS
16. February Budding, Half-Term	The Gates of Hell	*Collected Poems*
17. Visions: Raid on the Gold Mine	The Gates of Hell	*Collected Poems*
18. The Furnace	The Gates of Hell	*Collected Poems*
19. Vision: Snatched by God, a Blue Light	The Gates of Hell	*Collected Poems*
20. The Flight	The Flight	*Collected Poems*
21. The Sun	A Bulb in Winter	*Collected Poems*
22. Ode: Spring	A Bulb in Winter	*Collected Poems*
23. Strawberry Hill	The Pilgrim in the Garden	*Collected Poems*
24. The Night-Sea Crossing	The Night-Sea Crossing	*Collected Poems*
25. A Vision Near the Gates of Paradise	Visions Near the Gates of Paradise	*Collected Poems*
26. The Four Seasons	The Four Seasons	*Collected Poems*
27. Lighthouse	Lighthouse	*Collected Poems*
28. The Weed-Garden	The Weed-Garden	*Collected Poems*
29. The Labyrinth	The Labyrinth	*Collected Poems*
30. Wistful Time-Travellers	Whispers from the West	*Collected Poems*
31. Blindfolds: Lady of the Lamp	Lady of the Lamp	*Collected Poems*
32. A Metaphysical in Marvell's Garden	The Fire-Flower	*Collected Poems*
33. A Crocus in the Churchyard	The Fire-Flower	*Collected Poems*
34. Pear-Ripening House	The Fire-Flower	*Collected Poems*
35. Two Variations on One Theme	The Fire-Flower	*Collected Poems*
36. Beauty and Angelhood	Beauty and Angelhood	*Collected Poems*
37. Crack in the Earth	The Wind and the Earth	*Collected Poems*

TITLES OF POEMS, VERSE PLAYS AND MASQUES	POETIC VOLUMES	PUBLISHED WORKS
38. Crab-Fishing on a Boundless Deep	A Rainbow in the Spray	*Collected Poems*
39. Night Visions in Charlestown	A Rainbow in the Spray	*Collected Poems*
40. Staffa: Wind	A Rainbow in the Spray	*Collected Poems*
41. Sea Force	A Rainbow in the Spray	*Collected Poems*
42. Oaklands: Oak Tree	A Rainbow in the Spray	*Collected Poems*
43. Question Mark over the West	Question Mark over the West	*Collected Poems*
44. At Dove Cottage	Question Mark over the West	*Collected Poems*
45. Candleflame Storm	A Sneeze in the Universe	*Collected Poems*
46. Ode: Spider's Web: Our Local Universe in an Infinite Whole	A Sneeze in the Universe	*Collected Poems*
47. The One and the Many	A Sneeze in the Universe	*Collected Poems*
48. Imagination: Spring and Sea	A Flirtation with the Muse	*Collected Poems*
49. The Laughing Philosopher	Sojourns	*Collected Poems*
50. Secret of the Muse	Sojourns	*Collected Poems*
51. Man (Or: God the Artist)	Angel of Vertical Vision	*Collected Poems*
52. A Dandelion Clock	A Dandelion Clock	*Collected Poems*
53. The Warlords, Part One	The Warlords	*The Warlords/ Collected Verse Plays*
54. The Warlords, Part Two	The Warlords	*The Warlords/ Collected Verse Plays*
55. Overlord	Overlord	*Overlord*
56. At Otley: Timber-Framed Tradition	Classical Odes	*Classical Odes*

TITLES OF POEMS, VERSE PLAYS AND MASQUES	POETIC VOLUMES	PUBLISHED WORKS
57. Pastoral Ode: Landslide, The End of Great Britain	Classical Odes	*Classical Odes*
58. Contemplations by a Sundial	Classical Odes	*Classical Odes*
59. In Otley Hall's Medieval Gardens	Classical Odes	*Classical Odes*
60. At the Bourn Fête: Ancestors	Classical Odes	*Classical Odes*
61. At Tudor Otley Hall: The End of England	Classical Odes	*Classical Odes*
62. The Conquest of England	Classical Odes	*Classical Odes*
63. On Delos: Island of Apollo	Classical Odes	*Classical Odes*
64. By the Arno, Pisa	Classical Odes	*Classical Odes*
65. Summer Palaces	Classical Odes	*Classical Odes*
66. Auschwitz and Immortality	Classical Odes	*Classical Odes*
67. In Byron's Ithaca	Classical Odes	*Classical Odes*
68. At Virgil's Tomb	Classical Odes	*Classical Odes*
69. At Horace's Sabine Farm	Classical Odes	*Classical Odes*
70. In Dante's Verona	Classical Odes	*Classical Odes*
71. At Troy VI	Classical Odes	*Classical Odes*
72. In Cornwall: A New Renaissance	Classical Odes	*Classical Odes*
73. Among Loughton's Sacred Houses	Classical Odes	*Classical Odes*
74. After the Pisan Arno	Classical Odes	*Classical Odes*
75. At Connaught House	Classical Odes	*Classical Odes*
76. The Tragedy of Prince Tudor	The Tragedy of Prince Tudor	*The Tragedy of Prince Tudor/Collected Verse Plays*
77. Ovid Banished	Ovid Banished	*Collected Verse Plays*

TITLES OF POEMS, VERSE PLAYS AND MASQUES	POETIC VOLUMES	PUBLISHED WORKS
78. The Rise of Oliver Cromwell	The Rise of Oliver Cromwell	*Collected Verse Plays*
79. Zeus's Ass	Summoned by Truth	*Collected Poems*
80. Attack on America	Summoned by Truth	*Collected Poems*
81. Shock and Awe	Summoned by Truth	*Collected Poems*
82. Groans of the Muses	Sighs of the Muses	*Collected Poems*
83. Authorship Question in a Dumbed-down Time	Sighs of the Muses	*Collected Poems*
84. Epitaphs	Sighs of the Muses	*Collected Poems*
85. Armageddon	Armageddon	*Armageddon*
86. Life Cycle	Life Cycle	*Life Cycle*
87. In Harmony with the Universe	In Harmony with the Universe	*Life Cycle*
88. Song Thrush	In Harmony with the Universe	*Life Cycle*
89. Brilliant Stars, Snapped Gravity	In Harmony with the Universe	*Life Cycle*
90. Lisbon Treaty: The End of Great Britain, Demise of a Nation-State	An Unsung Laureate	*Life Cycle*
91. Zeus's Emperor	An Unsung Laureate	*Life Cycle*
92. Changelessness like a Fanfare: Trumpeting a Jubilee	An Unsung Laureate	*Life Cycle*
93. Churchill 50 Years On: Great Briton	An Unsung Laureate	*Life Cycle*
94. Verses on the Death of Mr Nicholas Hagger	Adventures in Paradise	*Life Cycle*
95. The Dream of Europa	The Dream of Europa	*The Dream of Europa*
96. The Oak Tree and the Branch: The UK Referendum on the EU, 'Brexit'	The Oak Tree and the Branch	*The Oak Tree and the Branch*

TITLES OF POEMS, VERSE PLAYS AND MASQUES	POETIC VOLUMES	PUBLISHED WORKS
97. Among Grandchildren in Gibraltar	The Oak Tree and the Branch	*The Oak Tree and the Branch*
98. King Charles the Wise	King Charles the Wise	*King Charles the Wise*
99. Fools' Paradise	Fools' Paradise	*Fools' Paradise*
100. The Coronation of King Charles	The Coronation of King Charles	*The Coronation of King Charles*

INDEX OF TITLES

Poems, verse plays and masques in alphabetical order

LIBERALIS IS A LATIN word which evokes ideas of freedom, liberality, generosity of spirit, dignity, honour, books, the liberal arts education tradition and the work of the Greek grammarian and storyteller Antoninus Liberalis. We seek to combine all these interlinked aspects in the books we publish.

We bring classical ways of thinking and learning in touch with traditional storytelling and the latest thinking in terms of educational research and pedagogy in an approach that combines the best of the old with the best of the new.

As classical education publishers, our books are designed to appeal to readers across the globe who are interested in expanding their minds in the quest of knowledge. We cater for

primary, secondary and higher education markets, homeschoolers, parents and members of the general public who have a love of ongoing learning.

If you have a proposal that you think would be of interest to Liberalis, submit your inquiry in the first instance via the website: www.liberalisbooks.com.